McGraw Hill Education

Bothell, WA • Chicago, IL • Columbus, OH • New York, NY

Cover and Title Pages: **Nathan Love**

www.mheonline.com/readingwonders C

The McGraw·Hill Companies

Education

Send all inquiries to:
McGraw-Hill Education
Two Penn Plaza
New York, New York 10121

Printed in the United States of America.

8 9 RMN 17 16 15 14

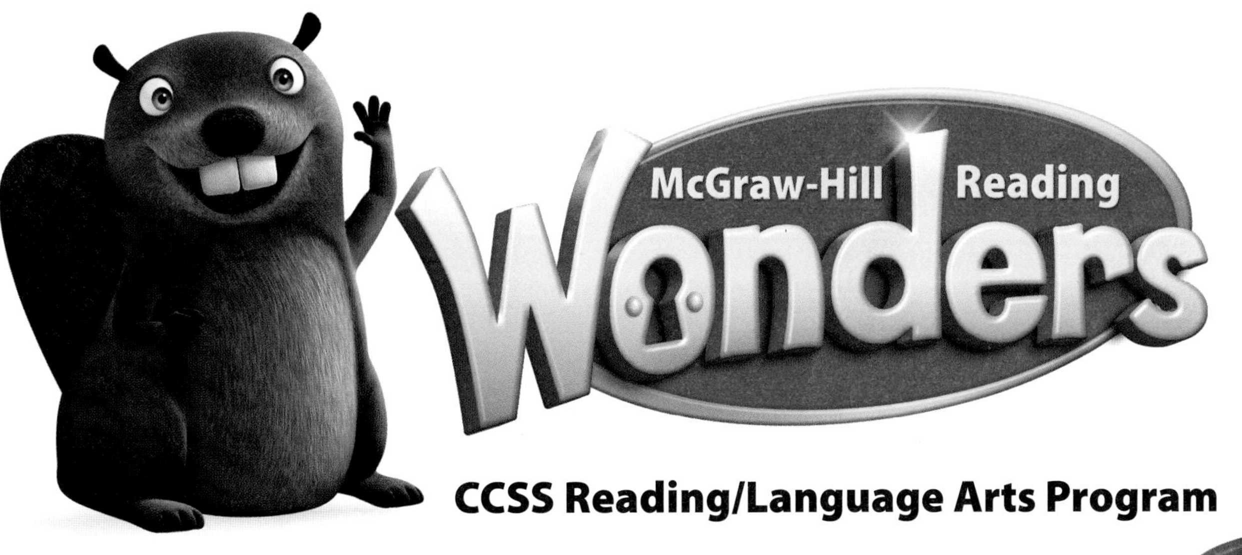

CCSS Reading/Language Arts Program

Program Authors

Dr. Diane August
Managing Director,
American Institutes
for Research
Washington, D.C.

Dr. Donald Bear
Iowa State University
Ames, Iowa

Dr. Janice A. Dole
University of Utah
Salt Lake City, Utah

Dr. Jana Echevarria
California State University, Long Beach
Long Beach, California

Dr. Douglas Fisher
San Diego State University
San Diego, California

Dr. David J. Francis
University of Houston
Houston, Texas

Dr. Vicki Gibson
Educational Consultant
Gibson Hasbrouck and Associates
Wellesley, Massachusetts

Dr. Jan Hasbrouck
Educational Consultant
and Researcher
J.H. Consulting
Vancouver, Washington
Gibson Hasbrouck and Associates
Wellesley, Massachusetts

Margaret Kilgo
Educational Consultant
Kilgo Consulting, Inc.
Austin, Texas

Dr. Jay McTighe
Educational Consultant
Jay McTighe and Associates
Columbia, Maryland

Dr. Scott G. Paris
Vice President, Research
Educational Testing Service
Princeton, New Jersey

Dr. Timothy Shanahan
University of Illinois at Chicago
Chicago, Illinois

Dr. Josefina V. Tinajero
University of Texas at El Paso
El Paso, Texas

Bothell, WA • Chicago, IL • Columbus, OH • New York, NY

PROGRAM AUTHORS

Dr. Diane August

American Institutes for Research, Washington, D.C.

Managing Director focused on literacy and science for ELLs for the Education, Human Development and the Workforce Division

Dr. Donald R. Bear

Iowa State University

Professor, Iowa State University

Author of *Words Their Way, Words Their Way with English Learners, Vocabulary Their Way,* and *Words Their Way with Struggling Readers, 4–12*

Dr. Janice A. Dole

University of Utah

Professor, University of Utah

Director, Utah Center for Reading and Literacy

Content Facilitator, National Assessment of Educational Progress (NAEP)

CCSS Consultant to Literacy Coaches, Salt Lake City School District, Utah

Dr. Jana Echevarria

California State University, Long Beach

Professor Emerita of Education, California State University

Author of *Making Content Comprehensible for English Learners: The SIOP Model*

Dr. Douglas Fisher

San Diego State University

Co-Director, Center for the Advancement of Reading, California State University

Author of *Language Arts Workshop: Purposeful Reading and Writing Instruction* and *Reading for Information in Elementary School*

Dr. David J. Francis

University of Houston

Director of the Center for Research on Educational Achievement and Teaching of English Language Learners (CREATE)

Dr. Vicki Gibson

Educational Consultant
Gibson Hasbrouck and Associates

Author of *Differentiated Instruction: Grouping for Success, Differentiated Instruction: Guidelines for Implementation,* and *Managing Behaviors to Support Differentiated Instruction*

Dr. Jan Hasbrouck

J.H. Consulting
Gibson Hasbrouck and Associates

Developed Oral Reading Fluency Norms for Grades 1–8

Author of *The Reading Coach: A How-to Manual for Success* and *Educators as Physicians: Using RTI Assessments for Effective Decision-Making*

Margaret Kilgo

Educational Consultant
Kilgo Consulting, Inc., Austin, TX

Developed Data-Driven Decisions process for evaluating student performance by standard

Member of Common Core State Standards Anchor Standards Committee for Reading and Writing

(Dole) Patrick Brennan; (Echevarria) Victoria Sanchez, CSULB; (Fisher) Courtesy of Douglas Fisher; (Gibson, Hasbrouck) Roger Pelissier; (Kilgo) Courtesy of Margaret Kilgo; (Paris) Courtesy of Scott G. Paris; (Shanahan) Courtesy of Timothy Shanahan; (Tinajero) Courtesy of Josefina V. Tinajero; (Bumgardner) Ccurtesy of sixcentsphotography; (Walker-Dalhouse) Dan Johnson, Marquette University; (others) McGraw-Hill Companies, Inc.

Dr. Scott G. Paris

Educational Testing Service, Vice President, Research

Professor, Nanyang Technological University, Singapore, 2008–2011

Professor of Education and Psychology, University of Michigan, 1978–2008

Dr. Timothy Shanahan

University of Illinois at Chicago

Distinguished Professor, Urban Education

Director, UIC Center for Literacy

Chair, Department of Curriculum & Instruction

Member, English Language Arts Work Team and Writer of the Common Core State Standards

President, International Reading Association, 2006

Dr. Josefina V. Tinajero

University of Texas at El Paso

Dean of College of Education

President of TABE

Board of Directors for the American Association of Colleges for Teacher Education (AACTE)

Governing Board of the National Network for Educational Renewal (NNER)

Consulting Authors

Kathy R. Bumgardner

National Literacy Consultant

Strategies Unlimited, Inc.
Gastonia, NC

Jay McTighe

Jay McTighe and Associates

Author of *The Understanding by Design Guide to Creating High Quality Units* with G. Wiggins; *Schooling by Design: Mission, Action, Achievement* with G. Wiggins; and *Differentiated Instruction and Understanding By Design* with C. Tomlinson

Dr. Doris Walker-Dalhouse

Marquette University

Associate Professor, Department of Educational Policy & Leadership

Author of articles on multicultural literature, struggling readers, and reading instruction in urban schools

Dinah Zike

Educational Consultant

Dinah-Might Activities, Inc.
San Antonio, TX

Program Reviewers

Kelly Aeppli-Campbell
Escambia County School District
Pensacola, FL

Marjorie J. Archer
Broward County Public Schools
Davie, FL

Whitney Augustine
Brevard Public Schools
Melbourne, FL

Antonio C. Campbell
Washington County School District
Saint George, UT

Helen Dunne
Gilbert Public School District
Gilbert, AZ

David P. Frydman
Clark County School District
Las Vegas, NV

Fran Gregory
Metropolitan Nashville Public Schools
Nashville, TN

Veronica Allen Hunt
Clark County School District
Las Vegas, NV

Michele Jacobs
Dee-Mack CUSD #701
Mackinaw, IL

LaVita Johnson Spears
Broward County Public Schools
Pembroke Pines, FL

Randall B. Kincaid
Sevier County Schools
Sevierville, TN

Matt Melamed
Community Consolidated School District 46
Grayslake, IL

Angela L. Reese,
Bay District Schools
Panama City, FL

Eddie Thompson
Fairfield City School District
Fairfield Township, OH

Patricia Vasseur Sosa
Miami-Dade County Public Schools
Miami, FL

Dr. Elizabeth Watson
Hazelwood School District
Hazelwood, MO

TEACHING WITH McGraw-Hill Reading Wonders

INTRODUCE

Weekly Concept
Grade Appropriate Topics, including Science and Social Studies

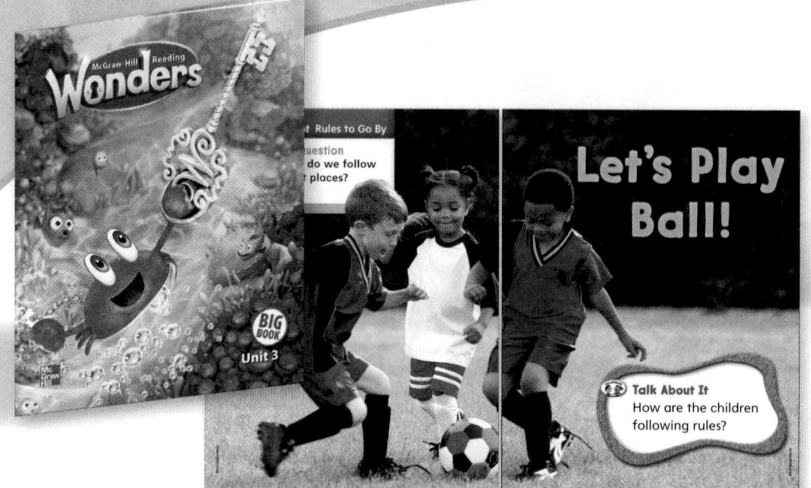

Reading/Writing Workshop Big Book

- Videos
- Photographs

TEACH AND APPLY

Listening Comprehension
Complex Text

Shared Reading
Minilessons
Comprehension Skills and Strategies, Genre, Phonics, High-Frequency Words, Writing, Grammar

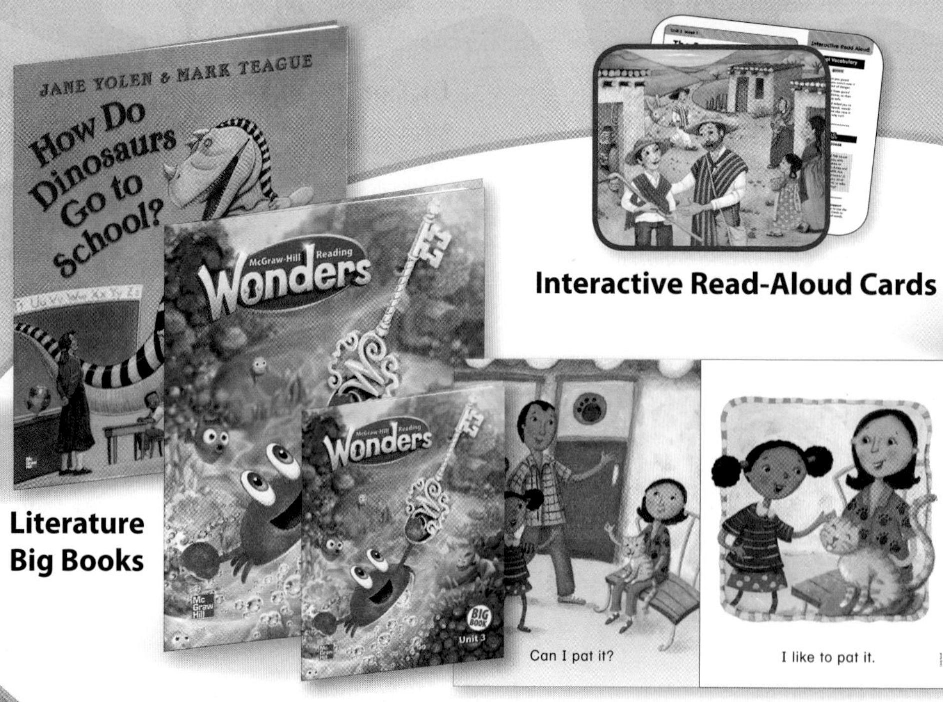

Literature Big Books

Interactive Read-Aloud Cards

Reading/Writing Workshop Big Book and Little Book

- Visual Glossary
- eBooks
- Interactive Texts
- Listening Library
- English/Spanish Summaries

Master the Common Core State Standards!

- eBooks
- Interactive Texts
- Level Reader Search
- Listening Library
- Interactive Activities

Leveled Readers

DIFFERENTIATE

Leveled Readers
Small Group Instruction with Differentiated Texts

- Online Research
- Interactive Group Projects

Collection of Texts

INTEGRATE

Research and Inquiry
Research Projects

Text Connections
Reading Across Texts

Talk About Reading
Analytical Discussion

Unit Assessment

Benchmark Assessment

- Online Assessment
- Test Generator
- Reports

ASSESS

Unit Assessment

Benchmark Assessment

PROGRAM COMPONENTS

Big Book and Little Book of Reading/ Writing Workshop

Literature Big Books

Interactive Read-Aloud Cards

Teacher Editions

Teaching Posters

Puppet

Leveled Readers

Your Turn Practice Book

Visual Vocabulary Cards

Leveled Workstation Activity Cards

Assessing the Common Core State Standards

Retelling Cards

Photo Cards

High-Frequency Word Cards

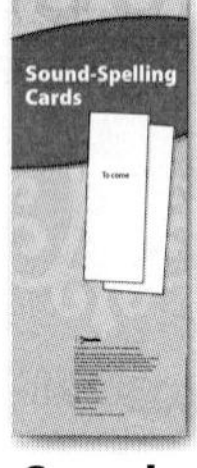
Sound-Spelling Cards

Response Board

Unit Assessment

Benchmark Assessment

Go Digital

For the Teacher

Plan
Customizable Lesson Plans

Assess
Online Assessments Reports and Scoring

Professional Development
Lesson and CCSS Videos

Teach
Classroom Presentation Tools Instructional Lessons

Collaborate
Online Class Conversations Interactive Group Projects

Additional Online Resources
ELL Activities
Tier 2 Intervention
Interactive Games and Activities
Word-Building Cards
Sound-Spelling Songs
Sound Pronunciation Audio

Manage and Assign
Student Grouping and Assignments

School to Home
Digital Open House Activities and Messages

For the Students

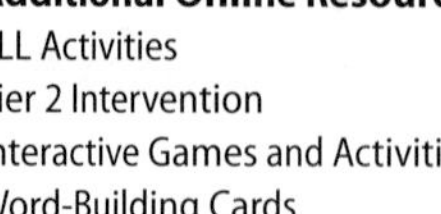

My To Do List
Assignments
Assessment

Words to Know
Build Vocabulary

Read
eBooks
Interactive Texts

Play
Interactive Games

Write
Interactive Writing

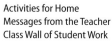

School to Home
Activities for Home
Messages from the Teacher
Class Wall of Student Work

www.connected.mcgraw-hill.com

UNIT 7 CONTENTS

Unit Planning

Weekly Lessons

Program Information

Nathan Love

UNIT 7 OVERVIEW

Week 1

BABY ANIMALS

READING

Oral Language
ESSENTIAL QUESTION
How are some animals alike and how are they different?

Build Background

CCSS L.K.5c **Oral Vocabulary Words**
appearance, behavior, wander, plenty, exercise

CCSS L.K.1b Category Words: Animal Parts

Comprehension

Genre: Informational Text

Strategy: Reread

CCSS RL.K.3 **Skill**
Connections Within Text: Compare and Contrast

Word Work

CCSS RF.K.2d **Phonemic Awareness**
Phoneme Isolation
Phoneme Blending
Phoneme Deletion

CCSS RF.K.3b **Phonics** /u/u ♪
Handwriting: Uu

CCSS RF.K.3c **High-Frequency Words:** *for, have*

Fluency
Letter and Word Automaticity
Model Fluency

LANGUAGE ARTS

Writing
Trait: Word Choice
Use Action Words

CCSS W.K.2 Shared Writing
Write an Animal Card

Interactive Writing
Write an Animal Card

Independent Writing
Write an Animal Card

Grammar
Verbs

Week 2

PET PALS

READING

Oral Language
ESSENTIAL QUESTION
How do you take care of different kinds of pets?

Build Background

CCSS L.K.5c **Oral Vocabulary Words**
responsibility, train, compared, social, depend

CCSS L.K.1b Category Words: Pet Words

Comprehension

Genre: Fiction

Strategy: Make, Confirm, and Revise Predictions

CCSS RL.K.3 **Skill**
Plot: Problem and Solution

Word Work

CCSS RF.K.2d, RF.K.2e **Phonemic Awareness**
Phoneme Isolation
Phoneme Blending
Phoneme Substitution

CCSS RF.K.3a **Phonics** /g/g, /w/w ♪
Handwriting: Gg, Ww

CCSS RF.K.3c **High-Frequency Words:** *of, they*

Fluency
Letter and Word Automaticity
Model Fluency

LANGUAGE ARTS

Writing
Trait: Word Choice
Use Action Words

CCSS W.K.2 Shared Writing
Write an Explanatory Text

Interactive Writing
Write an Explanatory Text

Independent Writing
Write an Explanatory Text

Grammar
Verbs

UNIT 7

Week 3

ANIMAL HABITATS

Oral Language
ESSENTIAL QUESTION
Where do animals live?

Build Background

CCSS L.K.5c **Oral Vocabulary Words**
habitat, wild, complain, stubborn, join

CCSS L.K.1b Category Words: Animal Homes

Comprehension
Genre: Fantasy

Strategy: Make, Confirm, and Revise Predictions

CCSS RL.K.1 **Skill**
Plot: Cause and Effect

Word Work

CCSS RF.K.2d, RF.K.2e **Phonemic Awareness**
Phoneme Isolation
Phoneme Blending
Phoneme Substitution

CCSS RF.K.3a **Phonics** Review ♪
Handwriting: Vv, Xx

CCSS RF.K.3c **High-Frequency Words:**
Review

Fluency
Letter and Word Automaticity
Model Fluency

Reading Digitally, T248

Unit 7 Assessment
Unit Assessment Book
pages 85–98

Writing
Trait: Ideas
Ask *How* and *Why* Questions About a Topic

CCSS SL.K.3 Shared Writing
Write Questions and Answers

Interactive Writing
Write Questions and Answers

Independent Writing
Write Questions and Answers

Grammar
Verbs

Half Day Kindergarten

Use the chart below to help you plan your kindergarten schedule to focus on key instructional objectives for the week. Choose Small Group and Workstation Activities as your time allows during the day.

Oral Language

- **Essential Questions**
- **Build Background**
- **Oral Vocabulary**
- **Category Words**

Word Work

- **Phonemic Awareness**
- **Phonics** /u/u, /g/g, /w/w, /v/v, /ks/x ♪
- **High-Frequency Words:** *for, have, of, they, said, want*
- **Letter and Word Automaticity**

Reading/Comprehension

- **Reading/Writing Workshop**
  A Pup and a Cub; I Hug Gus!; A Vet in a Van
- **Big Books:**
  ZooBorns!; The Birthday Pet; Bear Snores On
- **Interactive Read-Aloud Cards**
  "Baby Animals;" "The Family Pet;" "Anansi: An African Tale"

Language Arts

- **Shared Writing**
- **Interactive Writing**
- **Independent Writing**

Independent Practice

- **Practice Book pages**
- **Workstation Activity Cards**

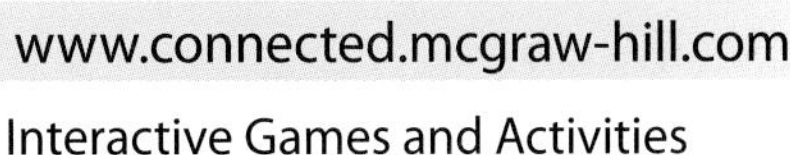

www.connected.mcgraw-hill.com
Interactive Games and Activities

OPENER

Reading/Writing Workshop Big Book

Unit 7

The Big Idea
What are different kinds of animals?

The Animal Kingdom

Bow, Wow, Wow
"Bow, wow, wow!"
"Whose dog art thou?"
"Little Tommy Tucker's dog.
Bow, wow, wow!"

Wild animals this way!

4 5

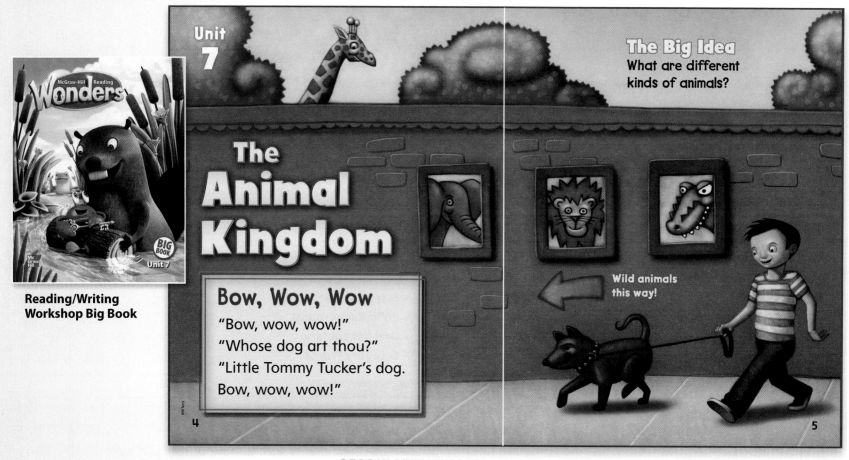

READING/WRITING WORKSHOP BIG BOOK, pp. 4–5

The Big Idea *What are different kinds of animals?*

Talk About It

Have children name some animals, including household pets, other domestic animals and livestock, and wild animals. Ask children to think about how these types of animals are alike and how they are different. What do all of the animals need in order to survive, and how do they get what they need from their surroundings? As children engage in the discussion, encourage them to give details to describe the animals and their environments. Acknowledge their responses, and ask additional questions to help children elaborate on their ideas, observations, and descriptions.

Sing the Song

Introduce the unit song: "Bow, Wow, Wow." Read the lyrics of the song. Ask children:

→ *What kinds of pets do you or your friends or family members have?*

→ *What are some kinds of animals that make good pets? What are some animals that do not make good pets?*

→ *What kinds of things do pets need to stay healthy and happy in people's homes?*

Play the song "Bow, Wow, Wow." After listening to the song a few times, ask children to join in. Audio files of the song can be found in the Teacher Resources on www.connected.mcgraw-hill.com.

UNIT 7

Research and Inquiry

Weekly Projects Each week students will be asked to find out more about the topic they are reading about. Children will be asked to work in pairs or small groups to complete their work. Children use what they learn from their reading and discussions as well as other sources to find additional information.

Shared Research Board You may wish to set up a Shared Research Board in the classroom. You can post illustrations and other information that children gather as they do their research.

WEEKLY PROJECTS

Students work in pairs or small groups.

Week 1 Animal Features Report

Week 2 Pet-Care Poster

Week 3 Habitat Diorama

Writing

Write about Reading Throughout the unit children will write in a variety of ways. Each week, writing is focused on a specific writing trait. Scaffolded instruction is provided through Shared Writing and Interactive Writing. Children review a student writing sample together and then write independently, practicing the trait.

WEEKLY WRITING

Week 1 Write an Animal Card

Week 2 Write an Explanatory Text

Week 3 Write Questions and Answers

Music Links

www.connected.mcgraw-hill.com Integrate music into your classroom using the downloadable audio files in the Teacher's Resources online. Songs for this unit include:

WEEKLY SONGS

- → Old MacDonald Had a Farm
- → My Umbrella
- → Get a Guitar
- → What Can You See Out Your Window?
- → It's a Volcano
- → Freddy the Fox Was Carrying a Box

HOLIDAY SONGS

- → There Came to My Window
- → This World Is Ours
- → Se, Se, Se

Celebration Posters

Celebrate Display the Spring Celebrations poster. Use it to remind students of important holidays during the season. Commemorate the holidays by selecting from the activity suggestions provided in the Teacher Resources found at www.connected.mcgraw-hill.com.
Teaching Posters are available for Fall, Winter, Spring, and Summer.

Teaching Posters, pp. 1–4

WEEKLY OVERVIEW

Literature Big Book

Listening Comprehension

ZooBorns!, 4–33
Genre Informational Text

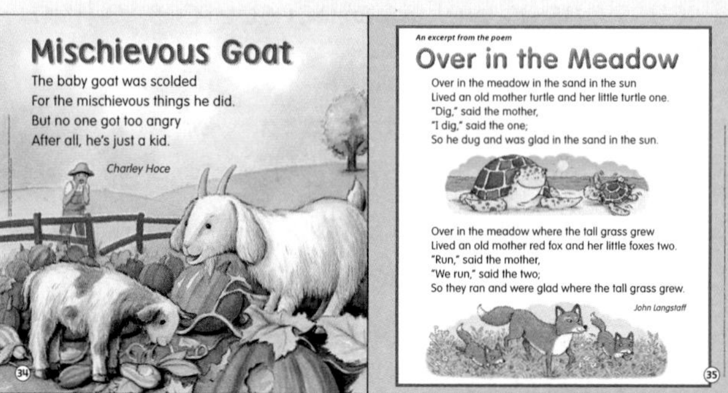

Mischievous Goat
The baby goat was scolded
For the mischievous things he did.
But no one got too angry
After all, he's just a kid.
Charley Hoce

An excerpt from the poem
Over in the Meadow
Over in the meadow in the sand in the sun
Lived an old mother turtle and her little turtle one.
"Dig," said the mother,
"I dig," said the one,
So he dug and was glad in the sand in the sun.

Over in the meadow where the tall grass grew
Lived an old mother red fox and her little foxes two.
"Run," said the mother,
"We run," said the two;
So they ran and were glad where the tall grass grew.
John Langstaff

Poetry, 34–36
Genre Poetry

Interactive Read-Aloud Cards

"Baby Farm Animals"
Genre Informational Text

Oral Vocabulary

appearance	plenty
behavior	wander
exercise	

Minilessons

✓ **Comprehension Strategy** .... Reread, T13

✓ **Comprehension Skill** .... Connections Within Text: Compare and Contrast, T22

Go Digital

www.connected.mcgraw-hill.com

BABY ANIMALS

Essential Question
How are some animals alike and how are they different?

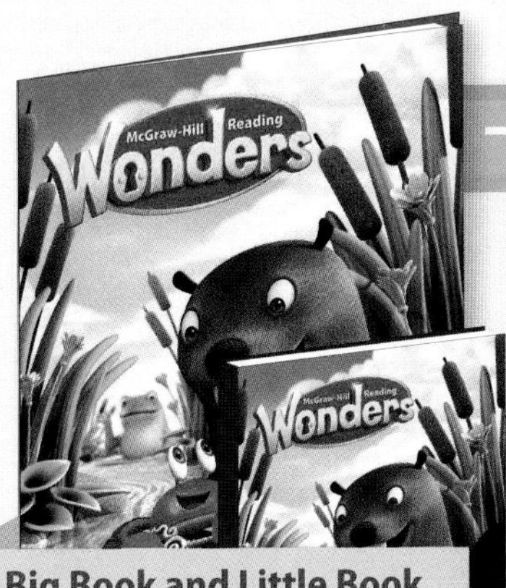

Big Book and Little Book Reading/Writing Workshop

Shared Reading

"A Pup and a Cub," 8–15

Genre Nonfiction

High-Frequency Words for, have, T17

Minilessons ✓TESTED SKILLS CCSS

✓ **Phonics** .... /u/*u*, T15

Writing Trait........................ Word Choice, T18

Grammar .... Verbs, T19

Differentiated Text

Approaching

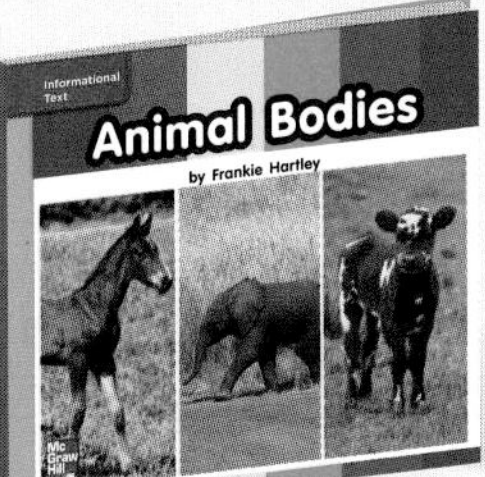

On Level

Beyond

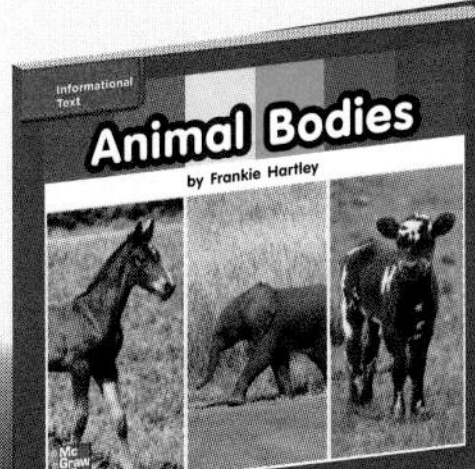

ELL

TEACH AND MANAGE

What You Do

INTRODUCE

Weekly Concept

Baby Animals

Reading/Writing Workshop Big Book, 6–7

TEACH AND APPLY

Listening Comprehension

Big Book
ZooBorns!
Genre Informational Text
Paired Read Poetry
Genre Poetry

Minilessons
Strategy: Reread
Skill: Compare and Contrast

Shared Reading

Reading/Writing Workshop
"A Pup and a Cub"

Minilessons
/u/*u*, High-Frequency Words: for, have,
Writing, Grammar

Interactive Whiteboard

Interactive Whiteboard

Mobile

What Your Students Do

WEEKLY CONTRACT

PDF Online

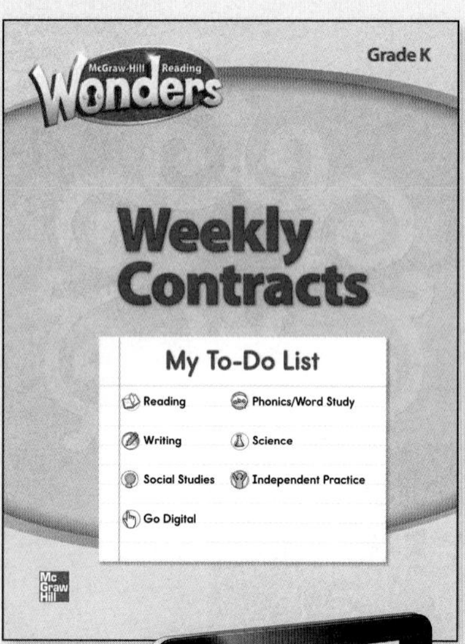

PRACTICE AND ONLINE ACTIVITIES

Your Turn Practice Book, pp. 185–192

Leveled Readers

Online To-Do List

Online Activities

Mobile

WEEK 1

DIFFERENTIATE

Small Group Instruction

Leveled Readers

Mobile

INTEGRATE

Research and Inquiry

Animal Features Report, pp. T52–T53

Text Connections

Compare Animals, p. T54

Talk About Reading

Becoming Readers, p. T55

Online Research

WORKSTATION CARDS

19 **Animal Sort** — SCIENCE

Animals move in different ways.

1. Dr... animals. 2. Talk about animals.

23 **Write a Report** — WRITING

A report gives information.

It rains in spring.

1. Draw yo... favorite season. 2. Write one fact about it.

19 **Word Bingo** — PHONICS/WORD STUDY

Play a word game using words with *Uu*.

1. Find the word. 2. Set your marker on it.

bus	run	cut
duck	pup	cub
us	sun	nut

3. Three words in a row wins the game!

Go Digital! www.connected.mcgraw-hill.com • Interactive Games and Activities • Grade K 19

8 **Compare and Contrast** — READING

Friends can be alike or different.

1. Read about friends. 2. Talk about the friends.

3. Draw friends doing something they both like.

Go Digital! www.connected.mcgraw-hill.com • Interactive Games and Activities • Grade K 8

More Activities on back of cards

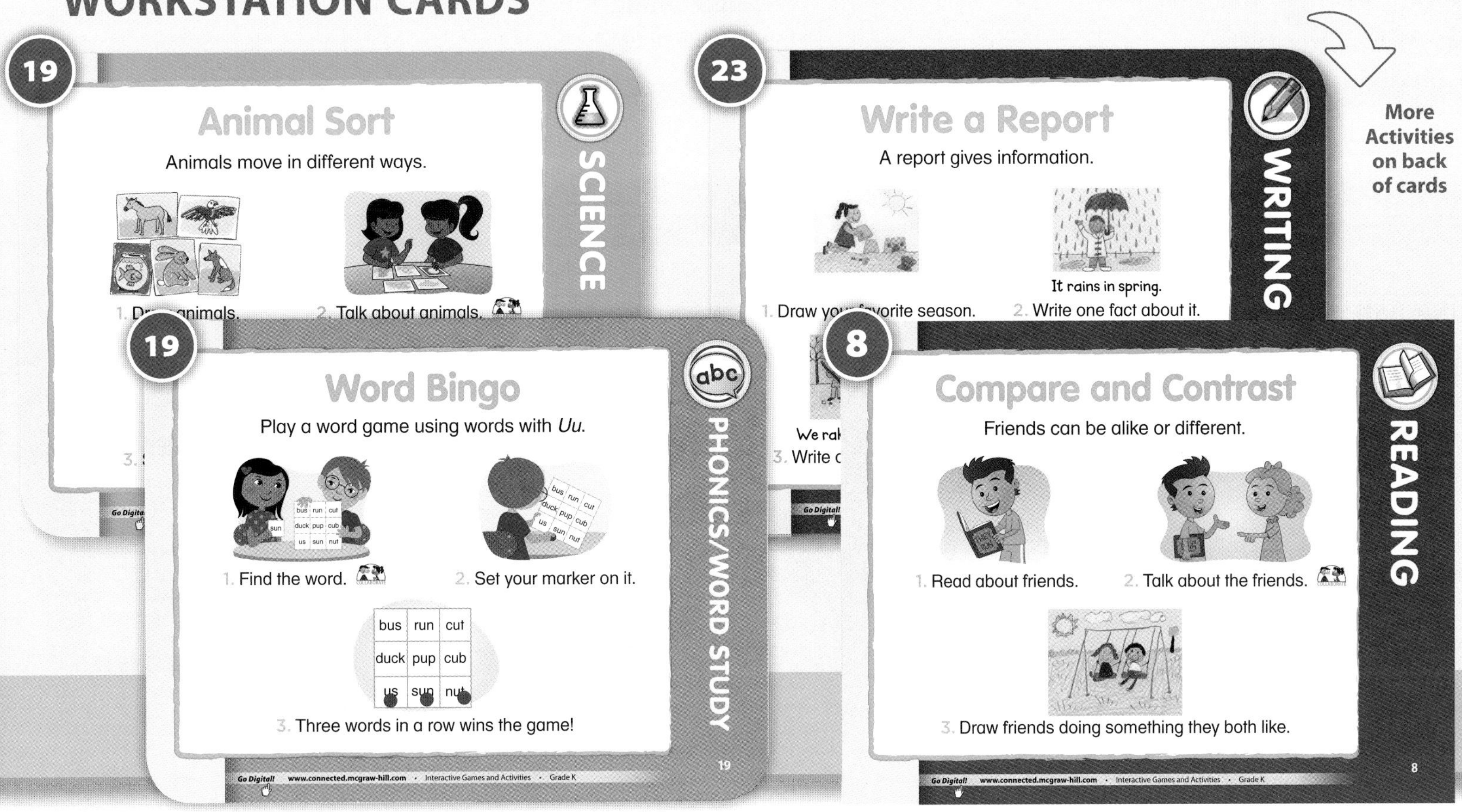

Nathan Love

DEVELOPING READERS AND WRITERS

Write About Reading • Analytical Writing

Write to Sources and Research

Respond to Reading, T13, T61, T69, T75, T79

Connect to Essential Question, T13, T45

Compare and Contrast, T27

Research and Inquiry, T52

Teacher's Edition

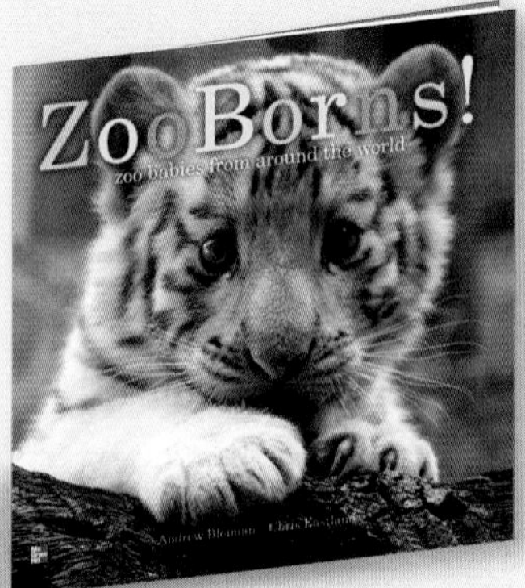

Literature Big Book

ZooBorns!

Paired Read: *Poetry*

Interactive Whiteboard

Leveled Readers

Responding to Texts

Writing Process • Independent Writing

Informational Text

Sentences That Inform, T40–T41, T50, T58

Conferencing Routines

Peer Conferences, T50

Interactive Whiteboard

Teacher's Edition

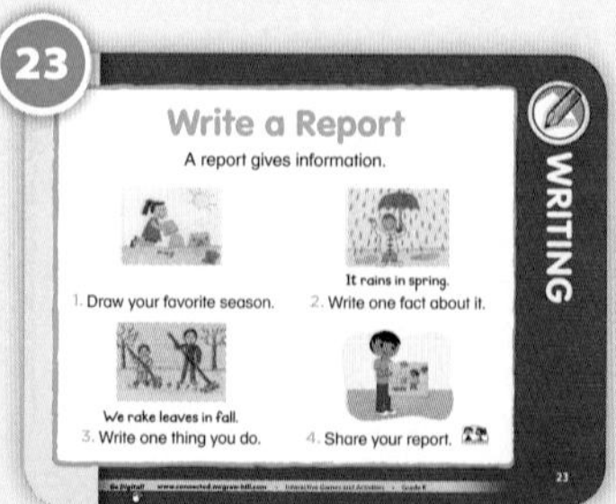

Leveled Workstation Card

Write a Report, Card 23

WEEK 1

Writing Traits • Shared and Interactive Writing

Writing Trait:
Word Choice
Sentences That Inform, T18, T32

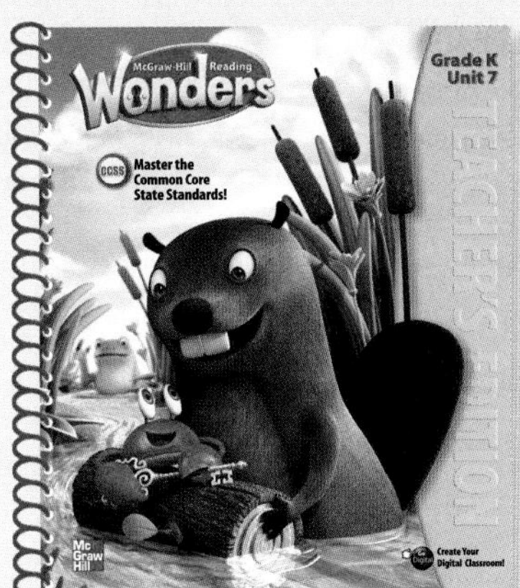
Teacher's Edition

Word Choice, p. 18
Verbs, p. 19

Reading/Writing Workshop

Interactive Whiteboard

23
Write a Report
A report gives information.
1. Draw your favorite season.
2. Write one fact about it.
3. Write one thing you do.
4. Share your report.
WRITING
A Worker Report
1. Think of a worker who helps you.
2. Write a sentence.
3. Draw a picture.
A Famous Person Fact
1. Listen to a story about a famous person.
2. Draw a picture of something that person is famous for.
3. Label your picture.

Leveled Workstation Card
Write a Report, Card 23

Grammar and Spelling/Dictation

Grammar
Action Words (Verbs), T19

Spelling/Dictation
Words with Short *u, a, i,* and *f, b, r, c, t,* T47, T57

Interactive Whiteboard

Teacher's Edition

make
Online Grammar Games

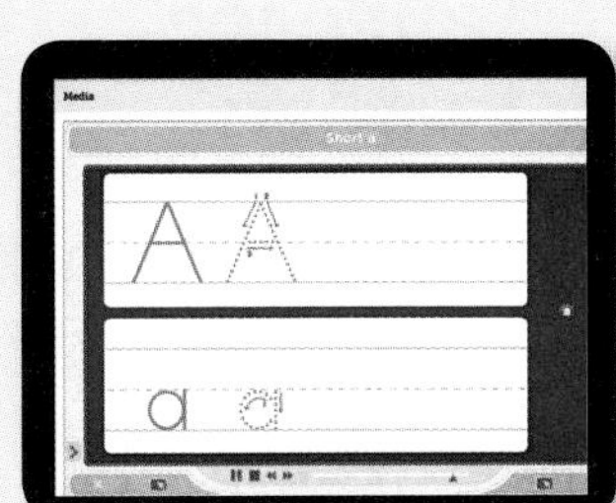
Handwriting

SUGGESTED LESSON PLAN

	DAY 1	DAY 2
READING		
Whole Group — **Teach and Model**  Literature Big Book Reading/Writing Workshop	**Build Background** Baby Animals, T10 **Oral Vocabulary Words** appearance, behavior, T10 ✓**Listening Comprehension** • Genre: Informational Text • Strategy: Reread, T13 **Big Book** *ZooBorns!* ✓**Word Work** **Phonemic Awareness** • Phoneme Isolation, T14 **Phonics** • Introduce /u/u, T15 **Handwriting** Uu, T16 **High-Frequency Words** for, have, T17 **Practice** *Your Turn* 185–186	**Oral Language** Baby Animals, T20 ✓**Category Words** Animal Parts, T21 ✓**Listening Comprehension** • Genre: Informational Text • Strategy: Reread, T22 • Skill: Connections Within Text: Compare and Contrast • Guided Retelling, T27 • Model Fluency, T27 **Big Book** *ZooBorns!* ✓**Word Work** **Phonemic Awareness** • Phoneme Isolation, T28 **Phonics** • Review Short *u*, T28 **High-Frequency Words** for, have, T29 **Shared Reading** "A Pup and a Cub," T30–T31 **Practice** *Your Turn* 187
DIFFERENTIATED INSTRUCTION Choose across the week to meet your student's needs.		
Small Group — **Approaching Level** 	**Leveled Reader** *Two Cubs,* T60–T61 **Phonological Awareness** Onset/Rime Blending, T62 (TIER 2) **Phonics** Sound-Spelling Review, T64 (TIER 2) **High-Frequency Words** Reteach Words, T66 (TIER 2)	**Leveled Reader** *Two Cubs,* T60–T61 **Phonemic Awareness** Phoneme Isolation, T62 (TIER 2) **Phonics** Connect *u* to /u/, T64 (TIER 2) **High-Frequency Words** Cumulative Review, T66
On Level 	**Leveled Reader** *Animal Bodies,* T68–T69 **Phonemic Awareness** Phoneme Isolation, T70 **Phonics** Review Phonics, T71	**Leveled Reader** *Animal Bodies,* T68–T69 **Phonemic Awareness** Phoneme Blending, T70 **Phonics** Picture Sort, T71 **High-Frequency Words** Review Words, T73
Beyond Level 	**Leveled Reader** *Two Kinds of Bears,* T74–T75 **Phonics** Review, T76	**Leveled Reader** *Two Kinds of Bears,* T74–T75 **High-Frequency Words** Review, T76
English Language Learners 	**Leveled Reader** *Animal Bodies,* T78–T79 **Phonological Awareness** Onset/Rime Blending, T62 (TIER 2) **Phonics** Sound-Spelling Review, T64 (TIER 2) **Vocabulary** Preteach Oral Vocabulary, T80 **Writing** Shared Writing, T82	**Leveled Reader** *Animal Bodies,* T78–T79 **Phonemic Awareness** Phoneme Isolation, T62 (TIER 2) **Phonics** Connect *u* to /u/, T64 (TIER 2) **High-Frequency Words** Cumulative Review, T66 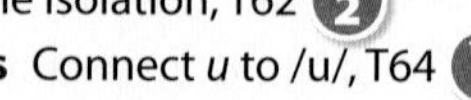 **Vocabulary** Preteach ELL Vocabulary, T80
LANGUAGE ARTS		
Whole Group — **Writing and Grammar**	**Shared Writing** Writing Trait: Word Choice, T18 Write an Animal Card, T18 **Grammar** Action Words (Verbs), T19	**Interactive Writing** Writing Trait: Word Choice, T32 Write an Animal Card, T32 **Grammar** Action Words (Verbs), T33

Nathan Love

Go Digital

CUSTOMIZE YOUR OWN LESSON PLAN

www.connected.mcgraw-hill.com

WEEK 1

DAY 3	DAY 4	DAY 5 Review and Assess
		READING
Oral Language Baby Animals, T34 **Oral Vocabulary** exercise, wander, plenty, T34 ✓ **Listening Comprehension** • Genre: Informational Text • Strategy: Reread, T35 • Make Connections, T35 **Interactive Read Aloud** "Baby Farm Animals," T35 ✓ **Word Work** **Phonemic Awareness** • Phoneme Blending, T36 **Phonics** • Blend Words with Short *u* and *b, f, r, d, s, n, f, t, r, c*, T37 • Picture Sort, T38 **High-Frequency Words** for, have, T39 **Practice** *Your Turn* 188–190	**Oral Language** Baby Animals, T42 ✓ **Category Words** Animals Parts, T43 ✓ **Listening Comprehension** • Genre: Poetry • Strategy: Reread, T44 • Literary Element: Alliteration T44 • Make Connections, T45 **Big Book** Paired Read: Poetry, T44 ✓ **Word Work** **Phonemic Awareness** • Phoneme Deletion, T46 **Phonics** • Blend Words with Short *u, a, i* and *t, b*, T46 **High-Frequency Words** for, have, T47 **Shared Reading** "A Pup and a Cub," T48–T49 **Integrate Ideas** Research and Inquiry, T52–T53 **Practice** *Your Turn* 191	**Integrate Ideas** • Text Connections, T54 • Talk About Reading, T55 • Research and Inquiry, T55 ✓ **Word Work** **Phonemic Awareness** Phoneme Deletion, T56 **Phonics** • Read Words with Short *u* and *f, b, r, c*, T56 **High-Frequency Words** for, have, T57  **Practice** *Your Turn* 192
		DIFFERENTIATED INSTRUCTION
Leveled Reader *Two Cubs*, T60–T61 **Phonemic Awareness** Phoneme Blending, T63 **Phonics** Reteach, T64 **High-Frequency Words** Reteach Words, T66	**Leveled Reader** *Two Cubs*, T60–T61 **Phonemic Awareness** Phoneme Deletion, T63 **Phonics** Blend Words with /u/*u*, T65 **Oral Vocabulary** Review Words, T67	**Leveled Reader** Literacy Activities, T61 **Phonemic Awareness** Phoneme Deletion, T63 **Phonics** Reread for Fluency, T65 Build Fluency with Phonics, T65 **Comprehension** Self-Selected Reading, T67
Leveled Reader *Animal Bodies*, T68–T69 **Phonemic Awareness** Phoneme Deletion, T70 **Phonics** Blend Words with Short *u*, T72	**Leveled Reader** *Animal Bodies*, T68–T69 **Phonics** Blend Words with Short *u*, T72 **Phonics** Reread for Fluency, T72	**Leveled Reader** Literacy Activities, T69 **Comprehension** Self-Selected Reading, T73
Leveled Reader *Two Kinds of Bears*, T74–T75 **Vocabulary** Oral Vocabulary: Synonyms, T77 	**Leveled Reader** *Two Kinds of Bears*, T74–T75 **Phonics** Innovate, T76	**Leveled Reader** Literacy Activities, T75 **Comprehension** Self-Selected Reading, T77 
Leveled Reader *Animal Bodies*, T78–T79 **Phonemic Awareness** Phoneme Blending, T63 **Phonics** Reteach, T64 **High-Frequency Words** Review Words, T81 **Writing** Writing Trait: Word Choice, T82	**Leveled Reader** *Animal Bodies*, T78–T79 **Phonemic Awareness** Phoneme Deletion, T63 **Phonics** Blend Words with /u/*u*, T65 **Vocabulary** Review Category Words, T81 **Grammar** Verbs, T83	**Leveled Reader** Literacy Activities, T79 **Phonemic Awareness** Phoneme Deletion, T63 **Phonics** Reread for Fluency, T65 Build Fluency with Phonics, T65
		LANGUAGE ARTS
Independent Writing Writing Trait: Word Choice, T40 Write an Animal Card Prewrite/Draft, T41 **Grammar** Action Words (Verbs), T41	**Independent Writing** Writing Trait: Word Choice, T50 Write an Animal Card Revise/Final Draft, T50 **Grammar** Action Words (Verbs), T51	**Independent Writing** Write an Animal Card Prepare/Present/Evaluate/Publish, T58 **Grammar** Action Words (Verbs), T59

DIFFERENTIATE TO ACCELERATE

ACT Scaffold to Access Complex Text

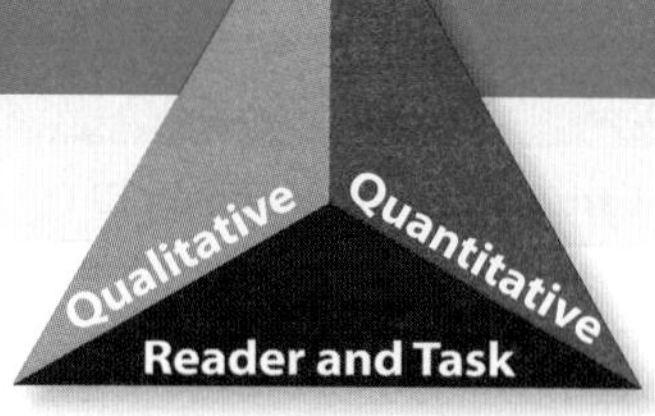

IF the text complexity of a particular section is too difficult for children

THEN see the references noted in the chart below for scaffolded instruction to help children Access Complex Text.

	Literature Big Book	Reading/Writing Workshop	Leveled Readers	

Quantitative	*ZooBorns!* **Lexile** 520 Paired Selection: Poetry **Lexile** NP	"A Pup and a Cub" **Lexile** 110	Approaching Level **Lexile** 10 Beyond Level **Lexile** 420	On Level **Lexile** 80 ELL **Lexile** 80
Qualitative	What Makes the Text Complex? • **Lack of Prior Knowledge** Unfamiliar Animal Names, T22 ACT *See Scaffolded Instruction in Teacher's Edition, T22.*	What Makes the Text Complex? **Foundational Skills** • Decoding with short *u*, T28–T29 • Identifying high-frequency words, T29	What Makes the Text Complex? **Foundational Skills** • Decoding with short *u* • Identifying high-frequency words *for, have* *See Level Up lessons online for Leveled Readers.*	
Reader and Task	The Introduce the Concept lesson on pages T10–T11 will help determine the reader's knowledge and engagement in the weekly concept. See pages T12–T13, T23–T27, T44–T45 and T52–T55 for questions and tasks for this text.	The Introduce the Concept lesson on pages T10–T11 will help determine the reader's knowledge and engagement in the weekly concept. See pages T30–T31, T48–T49 and T52–T55 for questions and tasks for this text.	The Introduce the Concept lesson on pages T10–T11 will help determine the reader's knowledge and engagement in the weekly concept. See pages T60–T61, T68–T69, T74–T75, T78–T79 and T52–T55 for questions and tasks for this text.	

Nathan Love

NP = Non-Prose

WEEK 1

Monitor and *Differentiate*

IF you need to differentiate instruction

THEN use the Quick Checks to assess children's needs and select the appropriate small group instruction focus.

Comprehension Strategy Reread, T35

Phonemic Awareness/Phonics /u/*u*, T17, T29, T39, T47, T57

High-Frequency Words *for, have*, T17, T29, T39, T47, T57

If No → Approaching **Reteach,** pp. T60–T67

ELL **Develop,** pp. T78–T83

If Yes → On Level **Review,** pp. T68–T73

Beyond Level **Extend,** pp. T74–T77

Level Up with Leveled Readers

IF children can read their leveled text fluently and answer comprehension questions

THEN work with the next level up to accelerate children's reading with more complex text.

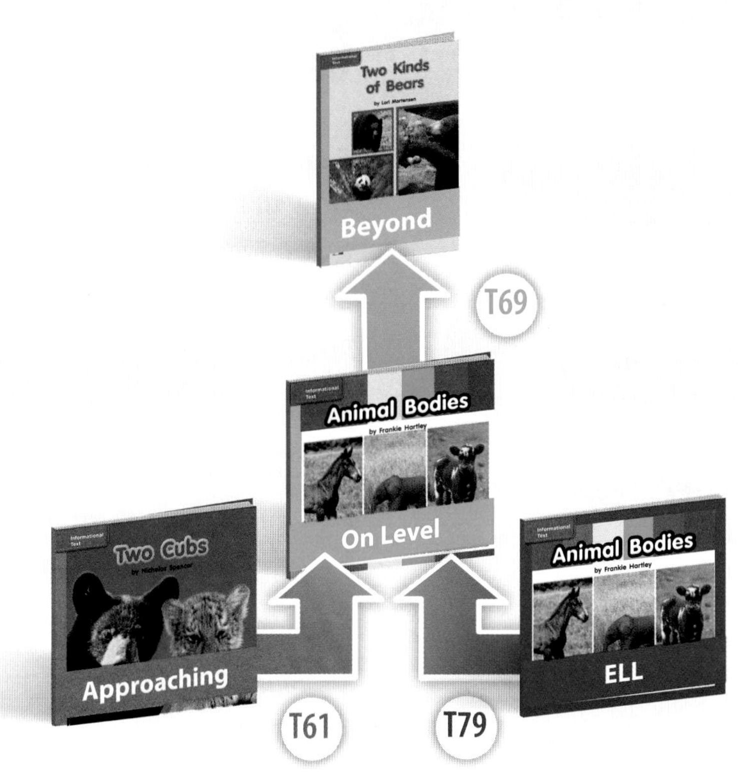

ENGLISH LANGUAGE LEARNERS SCAFFOLD

IF ELL students need additional support **THEN** scaffold instruction using the small group suggestions.

Reading-Writing Workshop T11 "Amazing Animals" Integrate Ideas T53	Leveled Reader T78–T79 *Animal Bodies*	Phonological Awareness Onset and Rime Blending, T62 Phoneme Isolation, T62 Phoneme Blending, T63 Phoneme Deletion, T63	Phonics, /u/*u*, T64–T65	Oral Vocabulary, T80 appearance, behavior, wander, plenty, exercise High-Frequency Words, T81 *for, have*	Writing Shared Writing, T82 Writing Trait: Word Choice, T82	Grammar T83 Verbs

Note: Include ELL Students in all small groups based on their needs.

WHOLE GROUP
DAY 1

Materials

Reading/Writing Workshop Big Book
UNIT 7

Literature Big Book
ZooBorns!

Visual Vocabulary Cards
appearance
behavior

Photo Cards
dolphin
rabbit
umbrella
umpire
undershirt
up

Sound-Spelling Card
Umbrella

Response Board

High-Frequency Word Cards
for
have

Think Aloud Cloud

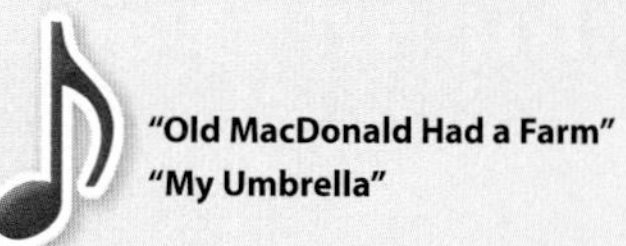
"Old MacDonald Had a Farm"
"My Umbrella"

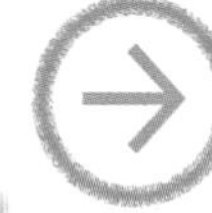

Introduce the Concept

Build Background

Reading/Writing Workshop Big Book

OBJECTIVES

CCSS Confirm understanding of a text read aloud or information presented orally or through other media by asking and answering questions about key details and requesting clarification if something is not understood. **SL.K.2**

CCSS Identify real-life connections between words and their use. **L.K.5c**

ESSENTIAL QUESTION

How are some animals alike and how are they different?

Read aloud the Essential Question. Tell children you are going to sing a song about animals and the sounds they make.

Old MacDonald Had a Farm

Old MacDonald had a farm. E-I-E-I-O
And on that farm he had some chicks. E-I-E-I-O
With a chick, chick here, and a chick, chick there.
Here a chick, there a chick, everywhere a chick, chick.
Repeat with (ducks/quack, pigs/oink, cows/moo)

Sing "Old MacDonald Had a Farm" with children. *What sound does the duck make?* (quack) Point out that animals make all kinds of sounds. Tell children that this week they will read about ways baby animals are the same and ways they are different.

Oral Vocabulary Words

Use the **Define/Example/Ask** routine to introduce the oral vocabulary words **appearance** and **behavior**. To introduce the theme of "Baby Animals," explain that different animals have different appearances and different behaviors. *Tell about two animals that have different behaviors.* (Possible answer: Fish swim and birds fly.)

Go Digital

Baby Animals

Video

Visual Glossary

Oral Vocabulary Routine

Vocab
Define
Examp
Ask:

Visual Vocabulary Cards

Define: The way something looks is its **appearance**.

Example: I could tell from its appearance that the lion was hungry.

Ask: What do you like about the appearance of a dog?

Define: **Behavior** is the way a person or an animal acts.

Example: One behavior of a dog is to bark.

Ask: What animal behavior have you seen or heard?

Talk About It: Baby Animals

COLLABORATE

Guide children to describe how some animals look alike and some look very different. Make a list of their responses. Display pages 6–7 of the **Reading/Writing Workshop Big Book** and have children do the **Talk About It** activity with a partner.

Weekly Concept Baby Animals
Essential Question
How are some animals alike and how are they different?
Go Digital!
Amazing Animals
Talk About It
How is a kitten like a duckling?
How is it different?
4
5

READING/WRITING WORKSHOP BIG BOOK, pp. 6–7

Collaborative Conversations

Take Turns Talking As children engage in partner, small group, and whole group discussions, encourage them to:

- → Take turns talking.
- → Listen carefully to the speaker.
- → Ask others to share their ideas and opinions.

ELL

ENGLISH LANGUAGE LEARNERS SCAFFOLD

Beginning

Comprehend Explain the differences between the animals in the picture. Point out the characteristics of the animals and then review them with children. Ask: *Is this animal big?* (no) *Are these animals the same?* (no) Allow children ample time to respond.

Intermediate

Describe Ask children to describe how the animals in the picture are alike. Then have them explain how they are different. Elicit more details to support children's answers.

Advanced/Advanced High

Expand Have children use complete sentences to describe the similarities and differences between the animals shown in the picture. Ask them to give two details about each animal, using one of the following prompts:

- *The animals are alike because they both ____.*
- *The animals are different because ____.*

Listening Comprehension

Literature Big Book

OBJECTIVES

CCSS Name the author and illustrator of a text and define the role of each in presenting the ideas or information in a text. **RI.K.6**

CCSS Actively engage in group reading activities with purpose and understanding. **RI.K.10**

- Recognize characteristics of information text
- Strategy: Reread

ACADEMIC LANGUAGE

- *informational text, facts*
- Cognates: *texto informativo*

Read the Literature Big Book

Connect to Concept: Baby Animals

Tell children that they will now find out ways animals are the same and ways they are different. *What different kinds of baby animals have you seen before?*

Concepts of Print

Sentences and Print Style Remind children that sentences begin with a capital letter and end with an end mark. Display page 9 of the **Big Book**. Read aloud the second sentence: *Check out my bright orange mop top. Let's count the number of words in this sentence.* Point to each word as you count aloud. *Now let's count the number of sentences on this page.* (three)

Genre: Informational Text

Model *ZooBorns!* is an informational text. Remind children of these characteristics of informational texts:

→ They give facts about real people, animals, or events.

→ They often have photographs.

Selection Words Preview these words before reading:

miracle: an amazing event that seems impossible
related: things that are alike or part of a family
zookeeper: a person who cares for animals in zoos

Set a Purpose for Reading

→ Identify and read aloud the title and the author's name. Tell children that the photographs in this book were taken by many different people.

→ Ask children to listen as you read aloud the Big Book to find out how these baby animals are alike and how they are different.

Go Digital

ZooBorns!

Think Aloud Cloud

Strategy: Reread

Explain Guide children in recalling that good readers reread things when they have trouble understanding something. If something is not making sense as they are reading, reading the words again can help make the information clear. They might reread the page they are on or pages they read earlier.

Think Aloud Read aloud page 6 before sharing this Think Aloud: I just read that this animal's ears help it somehow, but I don't understand exactly how. I can reread: *My big ears help me hear yummy insects crawling across the sand.* Oh, I see. The animal hears insects that it can catch and eat. Rereading helped me understand.

Model As you read, use the **Think Aloud Cloud** to model the strategy.

Think Aloud On page 9, I read something about a mop, but I don't see a mop in the picture. I'm not sure what the author is talking about. I'll reread the page to figure this out. *There's no such thing as a bad hair day for me!* Oh, I see now. The animal's hair just looks like a mop.

Respond to Reading

After reading, prompt children to tell about ways two of the animals were different. Discuss the ways that rereading helped children understand the book. Then have children draw their favorite baby animal from the selection. Guide children to label their drawing with a sentence telling what they like about the animal. If necessary, provide the sentence frame *I like* ______.

Make Connections

Use *ZooBorns!* to revisit the concept behind the Essential Question *How are some animals alike and how are they different?* Page through the **Big Book**.

Write About It Have children write about how specific animals in the story are alike and how they are different.

ENGLISH LANGUAGE LEARNERS SCAFFOLD

Beginning

Listen Read aloud page 10. Then say: *Wait, I don't understand. Why is this animal called a frogmouth? Listen as I reread: They call me a frogmouth because of my beak. Do they call this animal a frogmouth?* (yes) *Is it because of the animal's feet?* (no) *Is it because of the animal's beak?* (yes) Make sure children understand the meaning of *beak*. Allow them ample time to respond to your questions.

Intermediate

Derive Meaning Read aloud page 10. Then say: *Wait, I'm not sure why this animal is called a frogmouth. What should I do?* (Read again to help you understand.) Reread aloud the page. Ask: *Why is this animal called a frogmouth?* (Its beak looks like a frog's mouth.) Restate children's responses, adding details in order to develop their oral language proficiency.

Advanced/Advanced High

Discuss Read aloud page 10. Ask: *How can rereading this page help me understand why this animal is called a frogmouth?* (The page tells the reason: because its beak looks like a frog's mouth.) *How can looking at the illustrations help me understand?* (You can see that the animal's beak is very wide and looks like a frog's mouth.) Model correct pronunciation as needed.

Word Work

Quick Review

Review /l/, /k/: Ask children to tell the initial sound of the *lamp* and *king* Photo Cards.

Build Fluency: Sound-Spellings: Show the following **Word-Building Cards:** *a, b, c, d, e, f, h, i, k, l, m, n, o, p, r, s, t.* Have children chorally say each sound. Repeat and vary the pace.

MINILESSON 5 Mins

Phonemic Awareness

OBJECTIVES

CCSS Isolate and pronounce the initial, medial vowel, and final sounds in three-phoneme words. **RF.K.2d**

CCSS Associate the long and short sounds with common spellings for the five major vowels. **RF.K.3b**

Phoneme Isolation

Photo Card

1 Model Display the **Photo Card** for *umbrella. Listen for the sound at the beginning of* umbrella. Umbrella *has the /u/ sound at the beginning. Say the sound with me: /u/.* Say these words and have children repeat: *under, up, until.* Stretch initial /u/.

Let's play a song. Listen for the words with /u/ at the beginning. Play "My Umbrella," and have children listen for /u/. *Let's listen to the song again and clap when we hear words that begin with /u/.* Play and/or sing the letter song again, encouraging children to join in. Have children clap when they hear a word that begins with /u/.

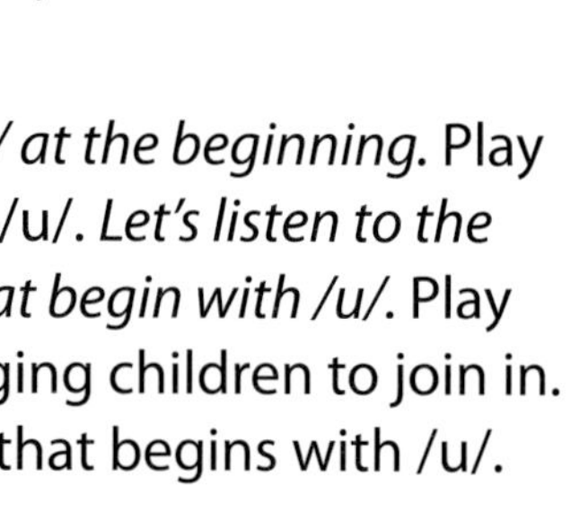

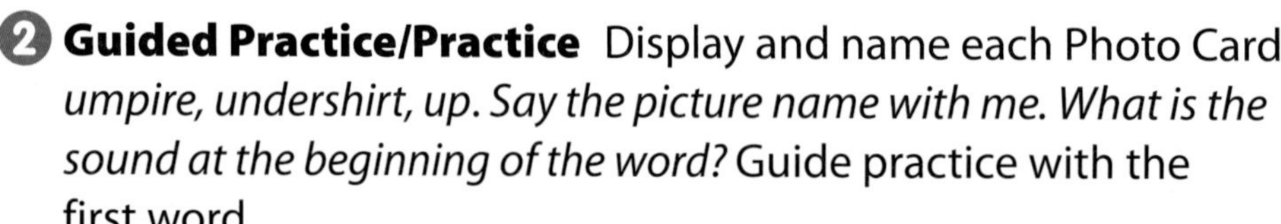

2 Guided Practice/Practice Display and name each Photo Card: *umpire, undershirt, up. Say the picture name with me. What is the sound at the beginning of the word?* Guide practice with the first word.

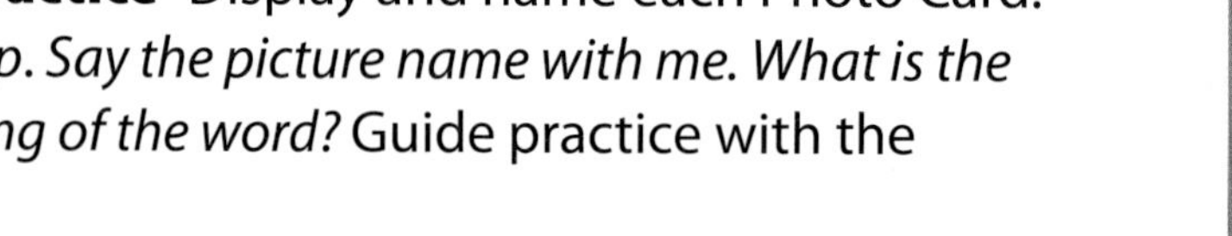

Photo Cards

Go Digital

Phonemic Awareness

Phonics

ELL

ENGLISH LANGUAGE LEARNERS

Pronunciation
Display and have children name Photo Cards from this lesson to reinforce phonemic awareness and word meanings. Point to the *undershirt* Photo Card and ask: *What do you see? What is the sound at the beginning of the word* undershirt? Repeat using the *umpire, up,* and *umbrella* Photo Cards.

ARTICULATION SUPPORT

Demonstrate the way to say /u/. Open your mouth just a little and keep it very relaxed. Keep your tongue in the middle of your mouth. Use your voice to make the /u/ sound. Place your hand on your throat. You should feel the sound. Say *us, uncle, under* and have children repeat. Stretch /u/ when you say the word.

Phonics

Introduce /u/*u*

1 Model Display the *Umbrella* **Sound-Spelling Card**. *This is the* Umbrella *card. The sound is /u/. The /u/ sound is spelled with the letter* u. *Say it with me: /u/. This is the sound at the beginning of the word* umbrella. *Listen: /uuu/,* umbrella. *What is the name of this letter?* (u) *What sound does this letter stand for?* (/u/)

Display the song "My Umbrella" (see **Teacher's Resource Book** online). Read or sing the song with children. Reread the title and point out that the word *umbrella* begins with the letter *u*. Model placing a self-stick note below the *U* in *Umbrella*.

2 Guided Practice/Practice Read each line of the song. Stop after each line and ask children to place self-stick notes below words that begin with *U* or *u* and say the letter name.

My Umbrella

I can hide underneath my umbrella.
I can hide underneath my umbrella.
My umbrella goes up when the rain comes down.
I stay dry underneath my umbrella.
When I look underneath my umbrella,
When I look underneath my umbrella,
I understand how nice an umbrella can be.
I stay dry underneath my umbrella.

Corrective Feedback

Sound Error Model the sound /u/ in the initial position, then have children repeat the sound. *My turn.* Umbrella. */u/ /u/ /u/. Now it's your turn.* Have children say the words *up* and *under* and isolate the initial sound.

ENGLISH LANGUAGE LEARNERS

Phoneme Variations in Language: Speakers of Spanish, Hmong, Cantonese, Haitian Creole, and Korean may have difficulty perceiving and pronouncing /u/. Emphasize the /u/ sound and demonstrate correct mouth position.

YOUR TURN PRACTICE BOOK pp. 185–186

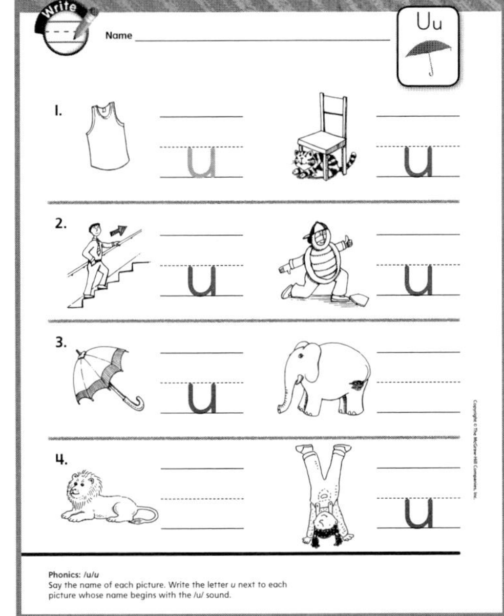

Word Work

MINILESSON 5 Mins

Handwriting: Write *Uu*

OBJECTIVES

CCSS Write a letter or letters for most consonant and short-vowel sounds (phonemes). **L.K.2c**

CCSS Read common high-frequency words by sight. **RF.K.3c**

ACADEMIC LANGUAGE
uppercase, lowercase

1 Model Say the handwriting cues below as you write and then identify the uppercase and lowercase forms of *Uu*. Then trace the letters on the board and in the air as you say /u/.

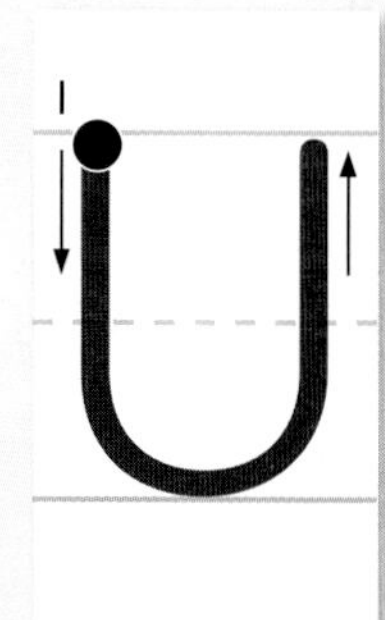

Straight down, curve around, straight up.

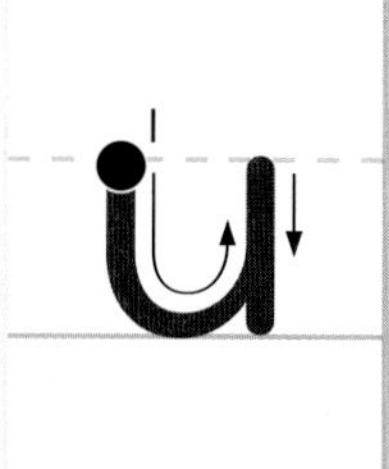

Straight down, curve around, and up. Straight down.

2 Guided Practice/Practice

- Say the cues together as children trace the letter with their index finger. Have them identify the uppercase and lowercase forms of the letter.
- Have children write *U* and *u* in the air as they say /u/ multiple times.
- Distribute **Response Boards** or paper. Observe children's pencil grip and paper position, and correct as necessary. Have children say /u/ every time they write the letter *Uu*.

Daily Handwriting

Throughout the week teach uppercase and lowercase letters *Uu* using the Handwriting models. At the end of the week, have children use **Your Turn Practice Book** page 192 to practice handwriting.

Go Digital

Handwriting

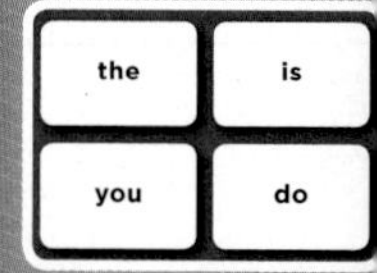

High-Frequency Word Routine

High-Frequency Words

for, have

for

High-Frequency Word Cards

1 Model Display page 24 of the **Big Book** *ZooBorns*. Read the third sentence. Point to the high-frequency word *for*. Display the **High-Frequency Word Card** *for* and use the **Read/Spell/Write** routine to teach the word.

- → **Read** Point to the word *for* and say the word. *This is the word* for. *Say it with me:* for. *The petting zoo sells food* for *the goats.*
- → **Spell** *The word* for *is spelled f-o-r. Spell it with me.*
- → **Write** *Let's write the word* for *in the air as we say each letter: f-o-r.*
- → Point out that the letter *f* in *for* has the same /f/ sound as in *fit*.
- → Have partners create sentences using the word.

Introduce *have*. Display p. 27 of *Zooborns!* Read the third sentence on the page. Point to *have*. Explain that in this sentence, *have* is used to explain something the hippo must do. *Have* can also be used as a way to say you own something as in "I *have* two cats." Display the High-Frequency Word Card *have* and use the **Read/Spell/Write** routine.

2 Guided Practice/Practice Build sentences using the High-Frequency Word Cards, **Photo Cards**, and teacher-made punctuation cards. Have children point to the high-frequency words *for* and *have*. Use these sentences.

I can go for you.
I have a kitten for you.
You have a kite for me.

Also online

High-Frequency Words Practice

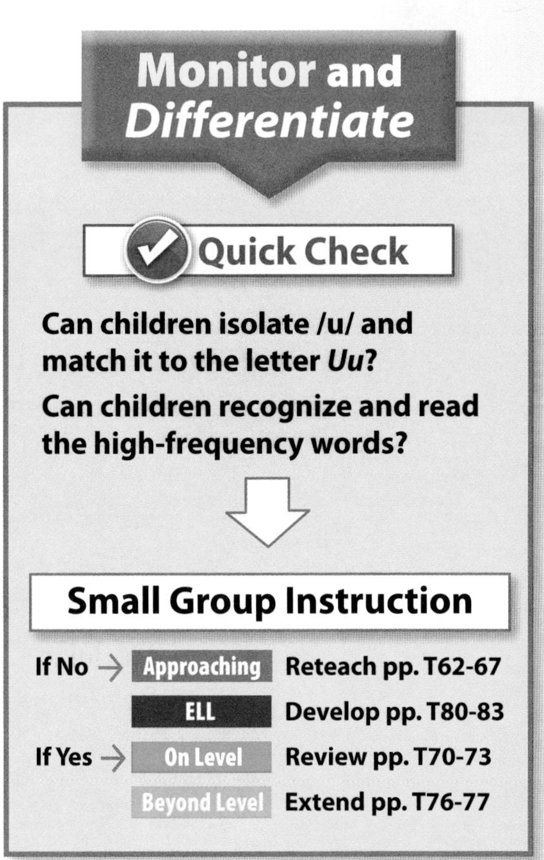

Monitor and Differentiate
Quick Check
Can children isolate /u/ and match it to the letter *Uu*?
Can children recognize and read the high-frequency words?
Small Group Instruction
If No → Approaching Reteach pp. T62-67
ELL Develop pp. T80-83
If Yes → On Level Review pp. T70-73
Beyond Level Extend pp. T76-77

Language Arts

Shared Writing

OBJECTIVES

Use a combination of drawing, dictating, and writing to compose informative/explanatory texts in which they name what they are writing about and supply some information about the topic. **W.K.2**

Use frequently occurring nouns and verbs. **L.K.1b**

- Recall facts about animals
- Identify action words

ACADEMIC LANGUAGE

- *action words, inform*
- Cognates: *informar*

Writing Trait: Word Choice

1 **Model** Explain to children that writers write about things they know about. Writers choose words that explain their ideas clearly.

→ Display the **Photo Card** for *dolphin*. Write and read: *Dolphins swim in the sea. My sentence tells about what dolphins do.*

2 **Guided Practice/Practice** Display the Photo Card for *rabbit*. Ask children to describe how a rabbit moves. Write their ideas on the board. (A rabbit hops. A rabbit jumps.)

Write an Animal Card

Focus and Plan Tell children that this week they will write about an animal they know about and create an animal card for it.

Brainstorm Ask children to think about an animal they know about, for example, a squirrel. Create a word web about the way a squirrel acts. Write children's responses in the outer circles of the web.

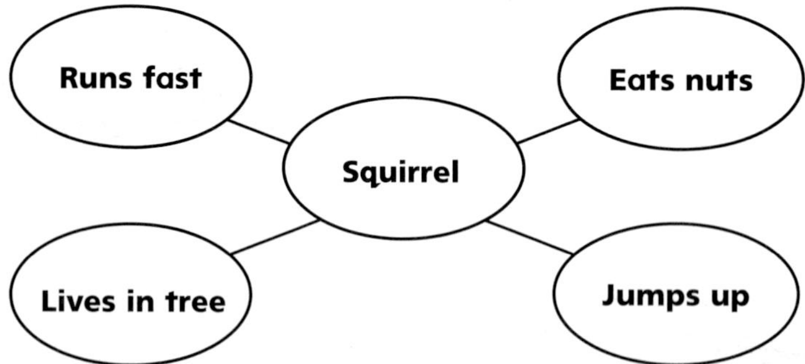

Write Model creating an Animal Card using the information in the web. Draw a picture on an index card of a squirrel. Write and read: *The squirrel eats nuts.*

Model writing other sentences about squirrels, using the word web. Read aloud the sentences with children.

Go Digital

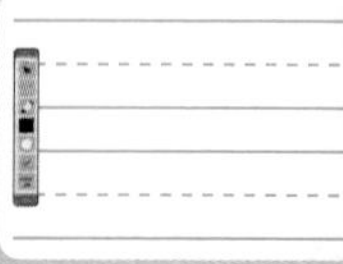

Writing

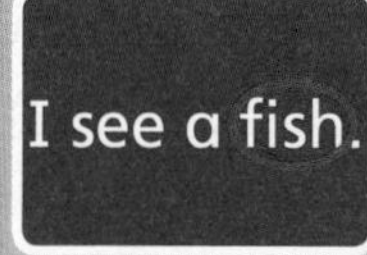

Grammar

Grammar

Action Words (Verbs)

1 Model Explain that an action word tells what is happening. It tells what a person, an animal, or a thing is doing. Ask students to watch you as you jump on two feet for a few seconds.

→ Write and read aloud: *I jump fast.* Explain that *jump* is the action word in the sentence. It is the word that tells what you do. Circle *jump.*

2 Guided Practice/Practice Have one girl in the class clap loudly. Write and read aloud this sentence: *The girl claps loudly.* Ask: *What does the girl do?* (clap) *Is* girl *an action word? How do you know?* (No. It tells who does the action, not what action is done.) Have a child circle the action word, *claps.* Say: Claps *is the action word in the sentence. It tells what the girl does.*

Explain that the action word ends in *-s* when it tells about one naming word, such as *girl.* When the naming word is *I* the action word does not end in *-s.*

Model how to use action words in other sentences. Say and write: *Sandy jumps. Sandy runs. Sandy skips.* Explain that *Sandy* is the name of the person who does each action. The action word in each sentence tells what Sandy does. Underline the action word in each sentence. Say: *The action words* jumps, runs, *and* skips *tell what Sandy does. They are action words.* Ask children to tell why these action words end in *-s.*

Talk About It

Have partners practice using action words with pantomime. One child pantomimes an action, and the partner names the action word.

ENGLISH LANGUAGE LEARNERS SCAFFOLD

Beginning

Explain Demonstrate different movements, such as clapping your hands, walking, and hopping. Have children describe each action that you do. Correct the meaning of children's responses as needed.

Intermediate

Practice Write and read: *She walks to school.* Have children raise a hand when you read the action word in the sentence. Repeat with additional sentences. Allow children ample time to respond.

Advanced/Advanced High

Practice Have children say action words to describe to you what they do on the playground. For example, a child might say *kicking* when talking about playing soccer. Restate children's responses in order to develop their oral language proficiency.

Daily Wrap Up

- Review the Essential Question and encourage children to discuss it, using the new oral vocabulary words. *How are baby animals alike and different?*
- Prompt children to share the skills they learned. How might they use those skills?

WHOLE GROUP
DAY 2

Materials

Reading/Writing Workshop Big Book
UNIT 7

Literature Big Book
ZooBorns!

Visual Vocabulary Cards
appearance
behavior

Photo Cards
bus
nut
sun
thumb

Response Board

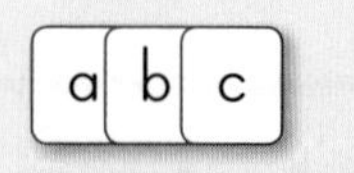
Word-Building Cards

Sound-Spelling Card
umbrella

High-Frequency Word Cards
for
have

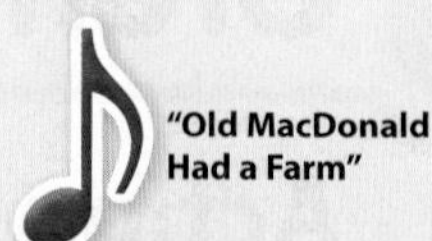
Retelling Cards

"Old MacDonald Had a Farm"

Build the Concept

Oral Language

OBJECTIVES

CCSS Use words and phrases acquired through conversations, reading and being read to, and responding to texts. **L.K.6**

CCSS Use frequently occurring nouns and verbs. **L.K.1b**

Develop oral vocabulary

ACADEMIC LANGUAGE

- *same, different*
- Cognates: *diferente*

ESSENTIAL QUESTION

How are some animals alike and how are they different?

Remind children that this week they are learning about baby animals. With so many different kinds of animals, it is interesting to see how their behavior and appearance are the same and different. Ask children to tell about two animals that have different behaviors.

Sing "Old MacDonald Had a Farm" with children.

Phonological Awareness

Onset/Rime Blending

Point out that "Old MacDonald" tells about sounds that animals make. In the song, the chick says "chick." Explain that the word *chick* has two parts. The first sound is /ch/. The second sound is /ik/. We can blend the two sounds together to say the word: /ch/ /ik/, *chick*. Invite children to choose another animal sound and say its two parts. Then they can blend the sounds to make the word.

Review Oral Vocabulary

Use the **Define/Example/Ask** routine to review the oral vocabulary words **appearance** and **behavior**. Prompt children to use the words in sentences.

Visual Vocabulary Cards

Go Digital

Visual Glossary

Category Words

Category Words: Animal Parts

❶ **Model** Use *ZooBorns!* to discuss animals parts: *ears,* page 6; *hair,* page 9; *beak,* page 10; *skin,* page 14; *teeth,* page 17; *fur,* page 20; *paws,* page 30; *legs* and *tongue,* page 33. Read aloud the text on page 6. Point to the fennec fox's ears. *This fox has big ears. What does he do with his ears?* (He listens.) *Where are your ears? Point to your ears.* Repeat with other animal parts in the book.

❷ **Guided Practice/Practice** Display a picture of an animal from the Big Book. Point to different parts of the animal, and have children identify each one. Then ask what the animal does with each body part. Encourage children to answer using complete sentences. (The lion uses its mouth to eat.)

Vocabulary Strategy: Compound Words

❶ **Model** Read this sentence from page 14 of *ZooBorns!* "One Day I'll grow into all this extra skin." Point out that the word *into* is made up of two smaller words: *in* and *to*. Point out other examples in *ZooBorns!* of compound words: *dinnertime,* page 10; *zookeepers* pages 18, 26; *sometimes* page 21.

❷ **Guided Practice/Practice** Tell children that you will say some words. Ask them to raise their hands if the word has two smaller words. When children raise their hands, have them identify the two smaller words.

backpack (back, pack)
umbrella
applesauce (apple, sauce)
bedtime (bed, time)
popcorn (pop, corn)
lookout (look, out)

anything (any, thing)
everybody (every, body)
elephant
downstairs (down, stairs)
football (foot, ball)
wonderful

ELL

ENGLISH LANGUAGE LEARNERS

Understand Help children understand animal parts such as fur, feathers, and tails. Look through books and magazines to find pictures of different animals, such as bird, lions, and elephants. Then discuss each animal part as you point to each one. Have children repeat the words in their native language and in English.

LET'S MOVE!

Tell children that you will call out different animal parts. Have them point to that animal part on their own bodies and then act out the animal's movement.

WHOLE GROUP
DAY 2

Listening Comprehension

Literature Big Book

OBJECTIVES

With prompting and support, ask and answer questions about key details in a text. **RI.K.1**

CCSS Actively engage in group reading activities with purpose and understanding. **RI.K.10**

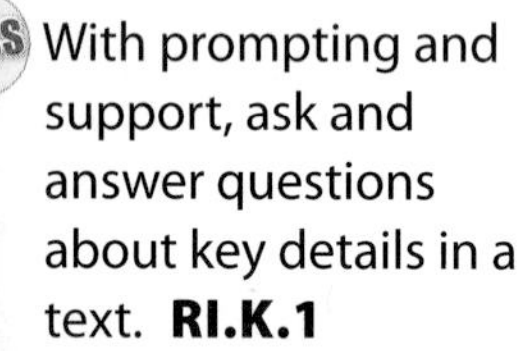

- Strategy: Reread
- Skill: Connections within Text: Compare and Contrast

ACADEMIC LANGUAGE

- *informational text, facts*
- Cognates: *texto informativo*

Reread Literature Big Book

Genre: Informational Text

Display *ZooBorns!* Remind children that informational texts include facts about real animals or people. They often have photographs. *How do you know that* ZooBorns! *is an informational text?* (It tells facts about real animals and shows photographs of them.) Have children point to evidence in the text and the pictures to show that the story is informational text.

Strategy: Reread

Remind children that good readers sometimes reread to help them understand a book. *When you don't understand what you just read, you can reread and find details that will help you understand.*

Skill: Connections Within Text: Compare and Contrast

Explain to children that as they read it is helpful to think about how things are the same and how they are different. Comparing people, animals, or places can help them understand what they are reading. *In this selection we will read about lots of different baby animals.* As you read, have children listen for evidence in the text that tells how the baby animals are alike and different. Use the prompts to model filling in the compare and contrast graphic organizer.

Access Complex Text

Lack of Prior Knowledge Many of these animals will be unfamiliar to children. To guide their understanding, list the names. Then invite children to find the matching photo in the book.

→ Turn to pages 6–7 and point to the illustration. Have children repeat: *fennec fox.* Repeat with additional unfamiliar animals.

Go Digital

ZooBorns!

Retelling Cards

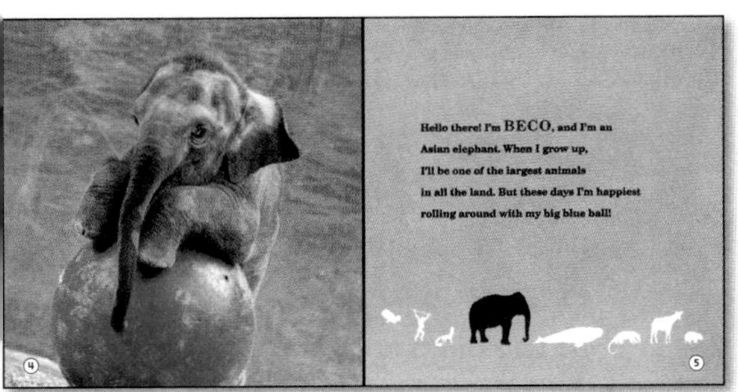

Hello there! I'm BECO, and I'm an Asian elephant. When I grow up, I'll be one of the largest animals in all the land. But these days I'm happiest rolling around with my big blue ball!

PAGES 4–5

COMPARE AND CONTRAST

Think Aloud As I read I will pay attention to how the baby animals are alike and different. I'll add some details to my chart so I can compare the elephant to another animal: *big ears, big feet, trunks.* Later I will choose another animal to compare.

pp. 4–5
in all the land: Explain that this phrase means "everywhere." Point to a globe or world map, sweep your hand across, and say *in all the land.*

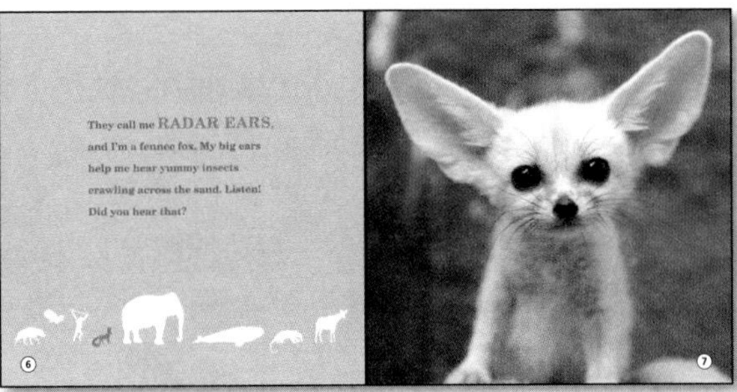

They call me RADAR EARS, and I'm a fennec fox. My big ears help me hear yummy insects crawling across the sand. Listen! Did you hear that?

PAGES 6–7

KEY DETAILS

Why does the fennec fox hear so well? (Its ears are very big, and they stick out so they catch sound easily.)

pp. 6–7
yummy: Make certain children understand that *yummy* means "tasty." Using toy food or illustrations of food, pretend to eat. Rub your stomach, and say, *Yummy!* Have children echo and mimic.

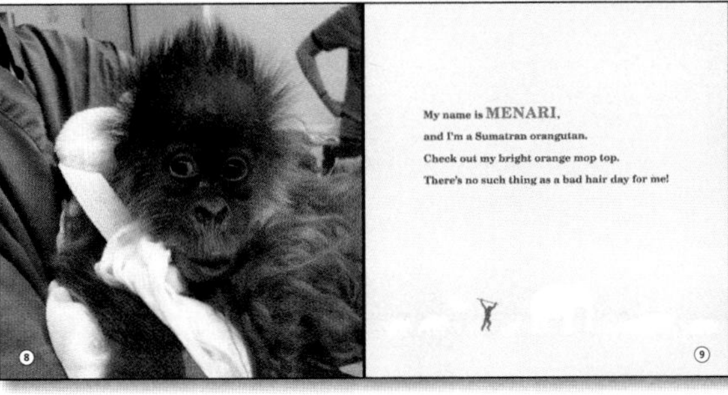

My name is MENARI, and I'm a Sumatran orangutan. Check out my bright orange mop top. There's no such thing as a bad hair day for me!

PAGES 8–9

COMPARE AND CONTRAST

Think Aloud This orangutan has bright orange hair. That is different from the fennec fox. The fennec fox had white fur.

pp. 8–9
mop top: If you have a mop available, put it on the head of a stuffed animal, as you say *mop top.* Tell children that this is a funny way of talking about messy hair.

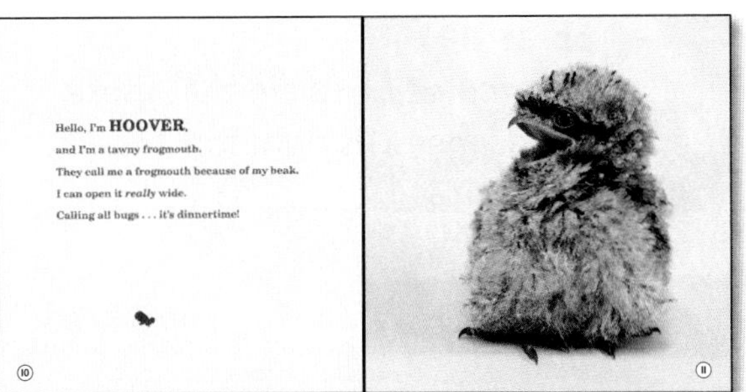

Hello, I'm HOOVER, and I'm a tawny frogmouth. They call me a frogmouth because of my beak. I can open it *really* wide. Calling all bugs . . . it's dinnertime!

PAGES 10–11

REREAD

Think Aloud The picture shows a baby bird, but I read something about a frog. I will reread to understand. Oh, the bird is called a tawny frogmouth because of its beak. I see that its beak looks a little like a frog's mouth.

pp. 10–11
wide: Make certain children understand the meaning of *wide* relating to a mouth. Say: *Open wide.* Then open your mouth as wide as you can. Have children echo and mimic.

Listening Comprehension

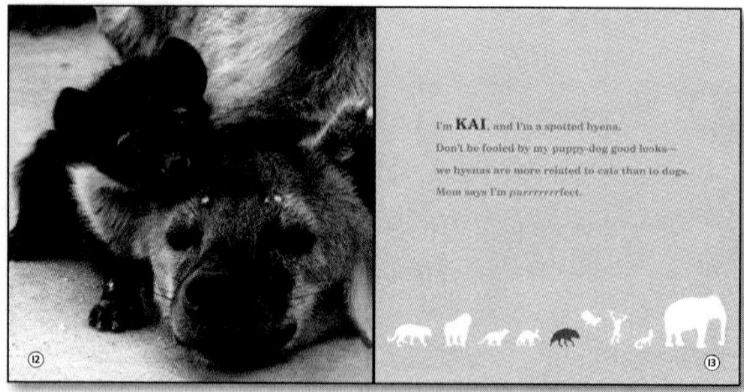

PAGES 12–13

CONCEPTS OF PRINT

Read the word *purrrrrrrr*fect. Track the print. Point out that the letter *r* is repeated many times, so you make the /r/ sound for longer. *The first part of the word is slanted, so I will say it in a stronger way. Listen.* Read the word again. Have children repeat with you.

pp. 12–13
spotted: Point to the spots on the hyena as you say *spotted.* Have children echo and mimic. Point out additional illustrations of spotted things in the classroom.

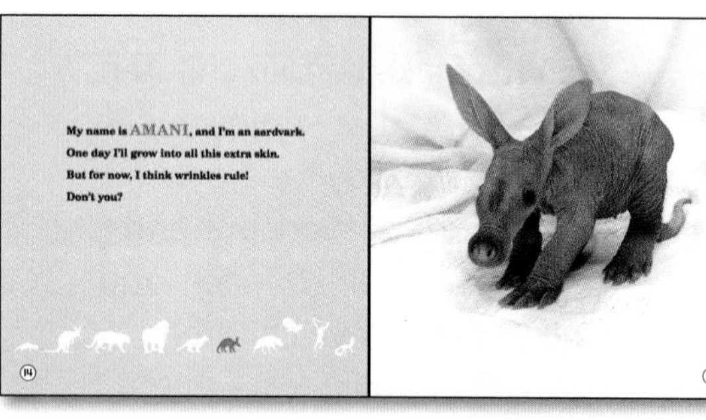

PAGES 14–15

HIGH-FREQUENCY WORDS

Have children point to and read aloud the word *for.*

MULTIPLE MEANINGS

We know that a rule *tells us how to behave. What do you think* rule *means on this page?* (to be really good or the best)

pp. 14–15
wrinkles: Point to the wrinkles on the aardvark as you say *wrinkles.* Have children echo and mimic.

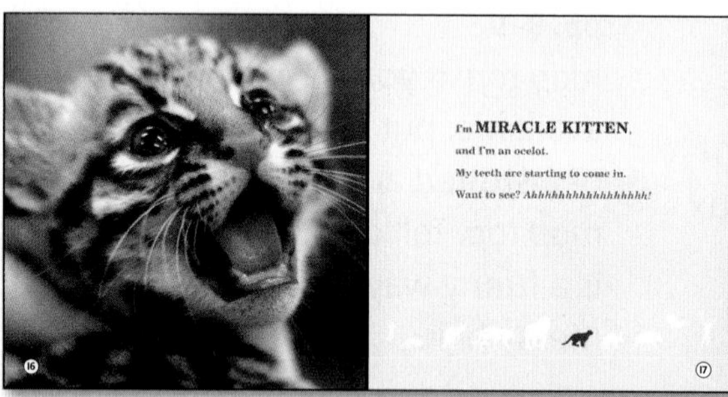

PAGES 16–17

REREAD

What kind of baby animal is this? Let's reread to find out. Reread the page and emphasize the word *ocelot.* Ask children again. (an ocelot)

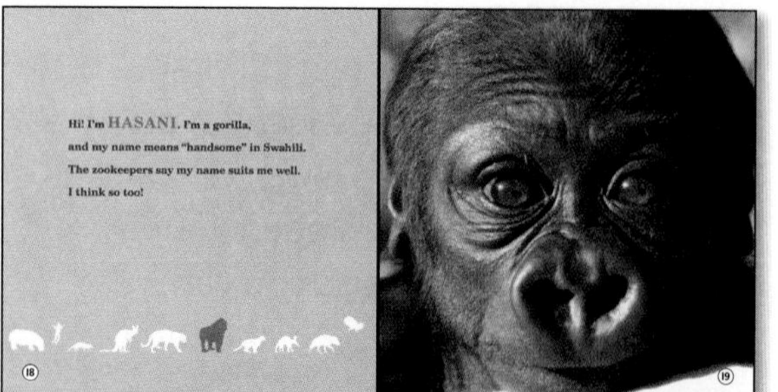

PAGES 18–19

COMPARE AND CONTRAST

How is the baby gorilla the same as the the baby orangutan? How is it different? Flip back to page 8 to remind children. (Possible answers: Their eyes and noses look alike. They have different color hair.)

pp. 18–19
suits me well: Explain that these words mean "is right for."

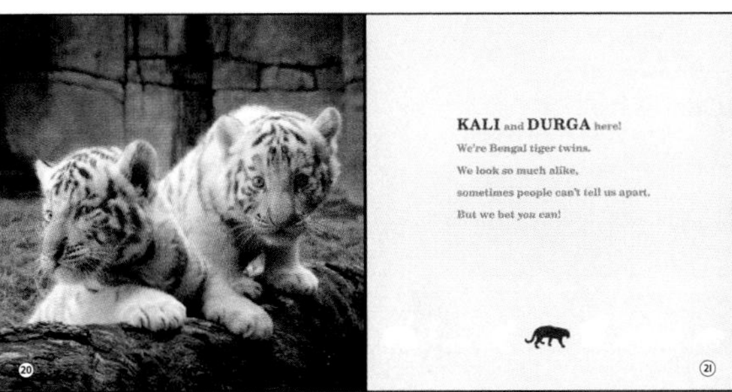

PAGES 20–21

PHONICS

Reread page 21. Have a volunteer point to and read the word that has the /u/ sound at the beginning. (us)

MAKE CONNECTIONS

The tigers look alike, *or almost the same. Do you know other animals that look alike? What do they look like?*

PAGES 22–23

KEY DETAILS

How does the photograph help you understand why the kangaroo needs the blanket? (The photograph shows that the kangaroo has no fur.)

pp. 22–23
blankie: Blankie is the same as *blanket*. Young children sometimes call their blanket a blankie.

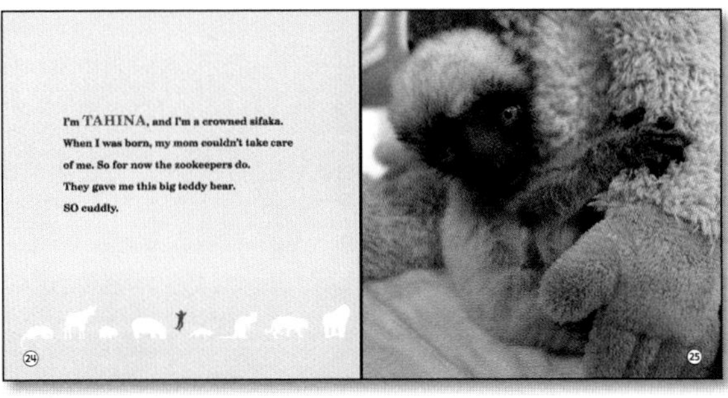

PAGES 24–25

COMPARE AND CONTRAST

How is this animal's fur like a crown? (The fur sits on its head like a crown.) *How is this fur different from a crown?* (The fur is part of the animal's head, and it is soft.)

pp. 24–25
cuddly: Something that is cuddly is nice and soft. Cuddle a stuffed toy as you say *cuddly. This animal is cuddly.* Have children echo and mimic.

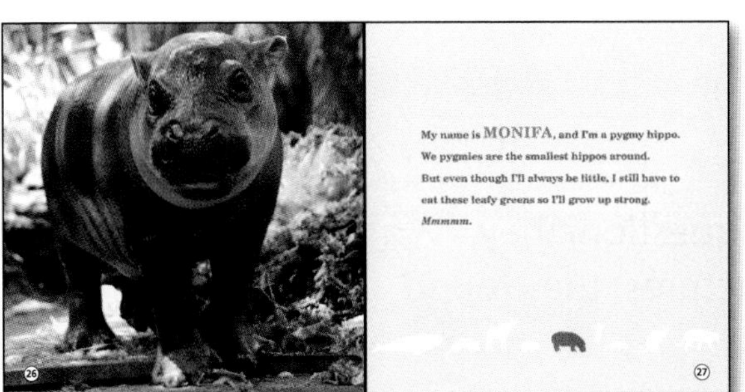

PAGES 26–27

HIGH-FREQUENCY WORDS

Ask a child to point to *have* and read it aloud.

OPPOSITES

This is the smallest *kind of hippo. What word means the opposite of* smallest? (biggest) Then point out the word *strong. What word means the opposite of* strong? (weak)

Listening Comprehension

PAGES 28–29

COMPARE AND CONTRAST

After reading these pages, flip back to pages 4–5. *How is the wombat like the elephant?* (grey color, both babies) *How is it different?* (little nose, little ears, small paws) *Let's add our answers to the compare and contrast chart.*

PAGES 30–31

REREAD

Is this baby animal a zebra? (no) *Is it a giraffe?* (no) *Let's reread to find out what animal it is.* Reread and emphasize the animal name. *What kind of animal is it?* (okapi)

pp. 30–31

throw in: Point out that these words mean the same as "add." Put a pencil and a crayon on a table. As you put a paperclip next to them, say *Now let's throw in a paperclip.*

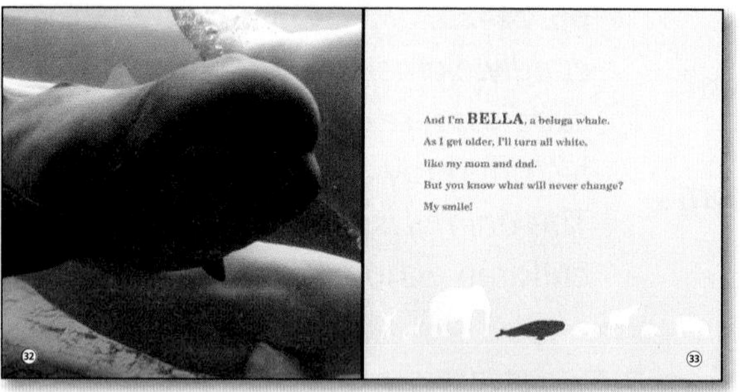

PAGES 32–33

AUTHOR'S PURPOSE

Why do you think the authors wrote this book? (Possible answer: They wrote it to tell fun facts about unusual animals.)

Text Evidence

Explain Remind children that when they answer a question, they need to show where in the book (both words and pictures) they found the answer.

Discuss *Which animals have soft fur? How do you know?* (Possible answer: The crowned sifaka on pages 24–25 is cuddly and looks soft.)

Connections Within Text: Compare and Contrast

Review Skill Review comparing and contrasting by using the completed graphic organizer to talk about the similarities and differences between the baby elephant and the baby wombat. Encourage children to give more examples.

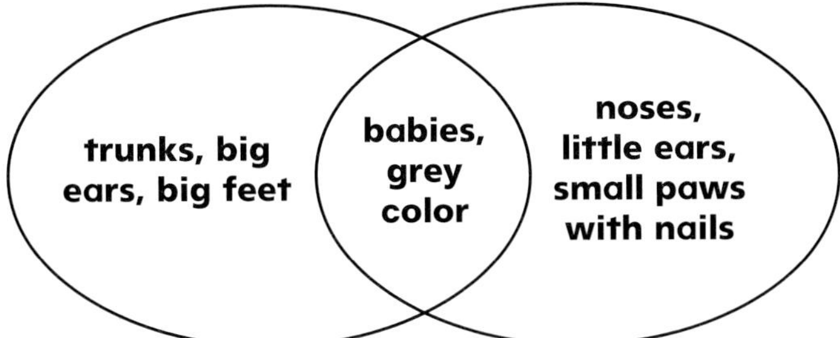

Guided Retelling

Tell children that they will use the **Retelling Cards** to retell the story.

- Display Retelling Card 1. Based on children's needs, use either the Guided or ELL retelling prompts. The ELL prompts contain support for children based on levels of language acquisition. Repeat with the rest of the cards, using the prompts as a guide.
- Choose a place in the book and have children discuss how those pages told something interesting about an animal's appearance or behavior. Have them support with details from the text.

Model Fluency

Remind children of the way you read the word *purrrrrfect* earlier in the lesson. Have children practice saying the words with you as the animals would say them on pages 13, 17, and 27.

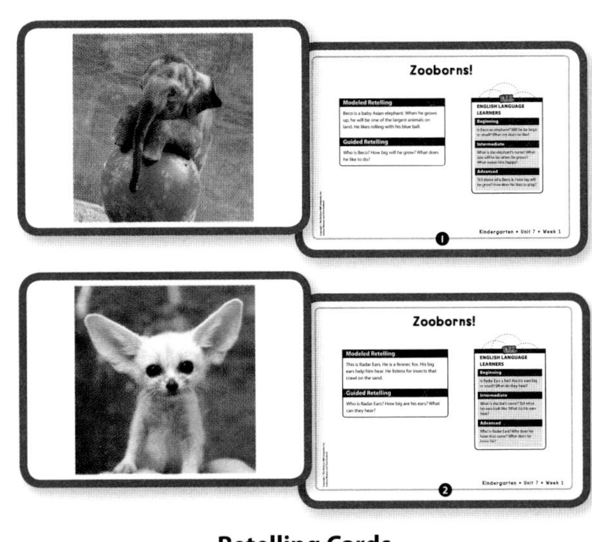

Retelling Cards

YOUR TURN PRACTICE BOOK p. 187

Word Work

Quick Review

Build Fluency: Sound-Spellings: Show the following **Word-Building Cards:** *a, b, c, d, e, f, h, i, k, l, m, n, o, p, r, s, t, u.* Have children chorally say each sound. Repeat and vary the pace.

MINILESSON 5 Mins

Phonemic Awareness

OBJECTIVES

CCSS Isolate and pronounce the initial, medial vowel, and final sounds in three-phoneme words. **RF.K.2d**

CCSS Associate the long and short sounds with common spellings (graphemes) for the five major vowels. **RF.K.3b**

CCSS Read common high-frequency words by sight. **RF.K.3c**

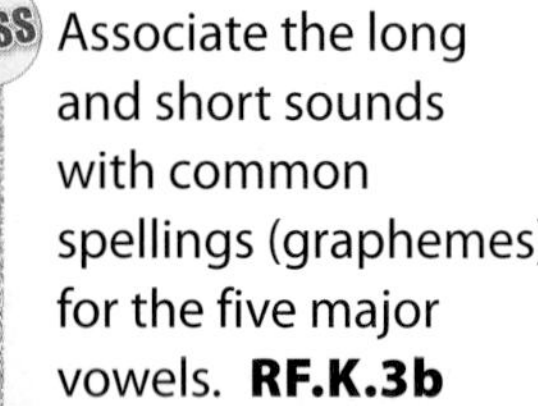

Phoneme Isolation

Photo Card

1 Model Introduce /u/ in the medial position. Listen for /u/ in the middle of this word: bug. Bug *has /u/ in the middle, /b/ /u/ /g/. Say the sound with me: /u/. Say the word with me:* bug. Then say *cup, pup, luck* and have children repeat. Emphasize medial /u/.

2 Guided Practice/Practice Display and name each **Photo Card** *bus, nut, sun, thumb. Say each picture name with me. Tell me the sound in the middle of the word.* Guide practice with the first word.

MINILESSON 5 Mins

Phonics

Review Short *u*

1 Model Display the *Umbrella* **Sound-Spelling Card**. *This is the letter* u. *The letter* u *stands for the sound /u/ as in the word* umbrella. *What is the letter?* (u) *What sound does the letter* u *stand for?* (/u/)

2 Guided Practice/Practice Have children listen as you say some words. Ask them to write the letter *u* on their **Response Boards** if the word begins with /u/. Do the first word with children.

until top umpire hat upon until

Repeat and have children listen for medial /u/.

nut shirt much hug get cub

Go Digital

Phonemic Awareness

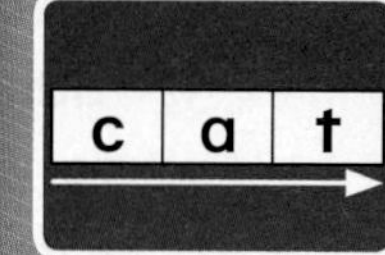

Phonics

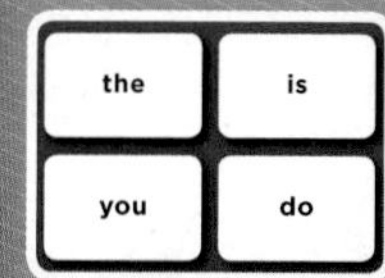

High-Frequency Word Routine

Handwriting

ENGLISH LANGUAGE LEARNERS

High-Frequency Words: Build Meaning Reinforce the use of the word *for* by saying the sentences and demonstrating them.

- Here is a book *for* you.
- What did you eat *for* lunch?
- Say the answer *for* the first question.
- I will open the door *for* you.

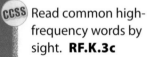

Blend Words with Short *u*

1. **Model** Place **Word-Building Cards** *u* and *p* in a pocket chart. Point to the *u*. This is the letter *u*. The letter *u* stands for /u/. Say /u/. *This is the letter* s. *The letter* s *stands for /s/. Say /s/. Listen as I blend the two sounds together: /uuusss/,* us. *Now blend the sounds with me to read the word.*

2. **Guided Practice/Practice** Change Word-Building Card *s* to *p* to make *up*. Point to the letter *u* and have children say /u/. Point to the letter *p* and have children say /p/. Then move your hand from left to right under the word and have children blend and read the word *up*. Add Word-Building Card *c* in front of *up* to make the word *cup* and have children blend the word *cup*. Repeat with *pup*.

High-Frequency Words

for, have

for

High-Frequency Word Cards

1. **Guided Practice** Display the **High-Frequency Word Card** *for*. Use the **Read/Spell/Write** routine to teach the word. Ask children to close their eyes, picture the spelling of the word in their minds, and then write it the way they see it. Have children self-correct by checking the High-Frequency Word Card.

   Repeat the routine for the high-frequency word *have*.

2. **Practice** Add *for* and *have* to the cumulative word bank.
   - → Have partners create sentences using the words.
   - → Have children count the number of letters in each word and then write *for* and *have* again.

Cumulative Review Review *my, are, he, with, is, little, she, was.*

- → Repeat the **Read/Spell/Write** routine. Mix the words and have children chorally say each one.

Monitor and *Differentiate*

Quick Check

Can the children isolate /u/ and match it to the letter *Uu*?

Can children recognize and read the high-frequency words?

Small Group Instruction

If No →	Approaching	Reteach pp. T62-67
	ELL	Develop pp. T80-83
If Yes →	On Level	Review pp. T70-73
	Beyond Level	Extend pp. T76-77

Shared Read

Reading/Writing Workshop Big Book and Reading/Writing Workshop

OBJECTIVES

 Read common high-frequency words by sight. **RF.K.3c**

 Read emergent-reader texts with purpose and understanding. **RF.K.4**

ACADEMIC LANGUAGE

- *predict*
- Cognates: *predecir*

MINILESSON 10 Mins

Read "A Pup and a Cub"

Model Skills and Strategies

Model Concepts About Print Read the sentences on page 9. Then discuss sentence boundaries. *There are two sentences on this page. Notice that each sentence begins with a capital letter and ends with a punctuation mark called a period.* Together, count the number of words in each sentence. *The first sentence has four words in it. The second sentence has seven words in it.* Invite volunteers to come up to the **Big Book** and tell where each sentence in the selection begins and ends. Then have them count the words in each sentence.

Predict Read the title together and look at the photograph. Ask children to predict what the selection will be about.

Read Have children chorally read the story with you. Point to each word as you read it together. Help children sound out the decodable words and say the sight words. If children have difficulty, provide corrective feedback and guide them page by page using the student **Reading/Writing Workshop**.

Ask the following:

- → *Look at page 8. What is the season? What animal do you see?* (spring; a wolf pup)
- → *Look at page 11. How is a wolf pup different than a puppy dog?* (Possible answer: A wolf pup lives in the wild. A puppy dog is a pet and can live in a house with a family of people.)
- → *Look at page 13. What does this lion cub enjoy doing?* (Possible answer: napping in the hot sun)

Go Digital

"A Pup and a Cub"

"A Pup and a Cub"

A Pup and a Cub
I am a pup.
I **have** a mom and a dad.

I am in a pack.
We sit in a den.
I am not a pet.
I have not met a pet pup!

I am a cub.
Mom, dad, and sis see me.
I sit on a rock in the sun.
I nap in the sun a lot!

Sis and I have fun.
We can go up, up!

A pup can run **for** fun.
A cub can run **for** fun.

READING/WRITING WORKSHOP, pp. 8–15

Rereading

Have small groups use the **Reading/Writing Workshop** to reread "A Pup and a Cub." Then review the skills and strategies using the *Phonics* and *Words to Know* pages that come before the selection.

- Have children compare and contrast the similarities and differences between a wolf pup and a lion cub. If necessary, encourage them to reread portions of the text to find the answers. In addition, have them look closely at the photographs to make comparisons between the animals.
- Have children use page 7 to review high-frequency words *for* and *have*.
- Have children use page 6 to review that the letter *u* stands for the sound /u/. Have them identify and name each picture. Guide them to blend the sounds to read the words.

ENGLISH LANGUAGE LEARNERS

Reinforce Vocabulary Display the **High-Frequency Word Cards** *for, have, is, are.* Point to classroom objects and groups of children as you use the high-frequency word in sentences, such as the following: *This is a pencil. What is a pencil for?* (A pencil is for writing.) *This is a smock. When do you wear a smock?* (I wear a smock when I paint.) *What does a clock tell you?* (A clock tells time.) *Are you sitting in your chairs?* (Yes, we are sitting in our chairs.)

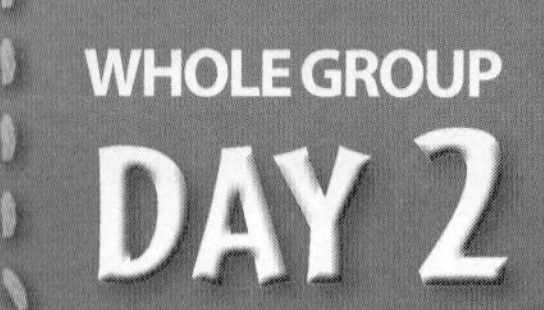

Language Arts

MINILESSON 10 Mins

Interactive Writing

OBJECTIVES

CCSS Use a combination of drawing, dictating, and writing to compose informative/explanatory texts in which they name what they are writing about and supply some information about the topic. **W.K.2**

CCSS Use frequently occurring nouns and verbs. **L.K.1b**

- Make Animal Cards
- Use verbs

ACADEMIC LANGUAGE

- *information, action words*
- Cognates: *información*

Writing Trait: Word Choice

Review Remind children that they can use action words when they write to share information. Write and read: *A bird flies to its nest. I chose the action word* flies *to describe what the bird does.*

Write an Animal Card

Discuss Display the animal web from Day 1. Read aloud the information on the web. Talk about other animals that children know about, such as cats, dogs, hamsters, frogs, and so on. Guide children to choose one animal to write about, such as a cat.

Model/Apply Grammar Tell children that you will work together to make an animal card about a cat. Remind children that they should use action words to describe what a cat does.

I have seen a cat lick its paws. What kinds of actions have you seen a cat do? Write children's responses on the board.

Write Draw a picture of a cat on an index card. Under the picture, write the sentence frame: *The cat* _____.

Guide children to complete the sentence frame, using one of their responses. (The cat plays with a ball.) Write the words. Share the pen with children and have them write the letters they know.

Go Digital

Writing

I see a fish.

Grammar

Grammar

Action Words (Verbs)

1 Review Remind children that action words tell what a person, an animal, or a thing does. *I can use action words to tell what my dog does. My dog runs. My dog jumps. My dog digs. What action words did I use?* (runs, jumps, digs) Runs, jumps, *and* digs *are all action words. They tell what my dog does.*

→ Read the following sentence: *My dog chases me.* Have children chorally repeat the sentence. *What is the action word in the sentence?* (chases) *How do you know?* (It tells what the dog does.)

2 Guided Practice Write the following sentence frame on a sentence strip and read it aloud: *Mike ______ fast.* Write and read aloud the following words: *ball, runs, cat.* Ask children to point to the action word that can be used in the sentence. (runs) *How do you know that* runs *is the correct word?* (*Runs* is an action word. It tells what Mike does.) *Why won't the words* ball *and* cat *work in the sentence?* (because *ball* and *cat* are naming words, not action words) Remind children that *runs* ends with *-s* because it tells what one noun does.

3 Practice Pair children with a partner. Have partners think of action words they know. Tell them to choose one action word and draw a picture together to show the action.

Talk About It

Have partners work together to orally generate sentences with action words. Challenge them to create sentences with more than one verb.

ENGLISH LANGUAGE LEARNERS

Describe It Display the **Big Book** page showing the baby elephant. Provide a sentence frame, such as *The elephant* ____. Ask children to tell you what an elephant can do. For example: *The elephant plays with a ball.* Write the sentences on the board and have children underline the action word in each sentence.

Daily Wrap Up

- Discuss the Essential Question and encourage children to use the oral vocabulary words. *How are animals alike and different?*
- Prompt children to review and discuss the skills they used today. How do those skills help them?

WHOLE GROUP
DAY 3

Materials

Reading/Writing Workshop Big Book
UNIT 7

Visual Vocabulary Cards
exercise
plenty
wander

Interactive Read-Aloud Cards

Word-Building Cards

Puppet

Photo Cards
bus
nut
sun
thumb
umbrella
umpire
under
up

High-Frequency Word Cards
are
for
have
he
in
little
my
she
was
with

Think Aloud Cloud

"My Umbrella"

Build the Concept

Oral Language

OBJECTIVES

CCSS With prompting and support, identify basic similarities and differences between two texts on the same topic (e.g., in illustrations, descriptions, or procedures). **RI.K.9**

CCSS Identify real-life connections between words and their use. **L.K.5c**

Develop oral vocabulary

ACADEMIC LANGUAGE
- *informational text*
- Cognates: *texto informativo*

ESSENTIAL QUESTION

Remind children that this week they are talking and learning about how animals are alike and different. Guide them to discuss the Essential Question, using information from the **Big Book** and the weekly song. Remind children that "Old MacDonald Had a Farm" describes different animal sounds. Sing and have children join in.

Oral Vocabulary

Review last week's oral vocabulary words, as well as *appearance* and *behavior* from Day 1. Then use the **Define/Example/Ask** routine to introduce *exercise, wander,* and *plenty*.

Oral Vocabulary Routine

Define: When you **exercise**, you use an action to improve your body.

Example: I exercise when I run and play outside.

Ask: How do you like to exercise on the playground?

Visual Vocabulary Cards

Define: When you **wander**, you move around with no specific place to go.

Example: We like to wander through the mall and look at the stores.

Ask: Why would a dog wander through a neighborhood?

Define: When there is **plenty** of something, there is a large amount, or enough.

Example: There are plenty of balls in the gym.

Ask: What do we have plenty of in our classroom?

Go Digital

Visual Glossary

"Baby Farm Animals"

Think Aloud Cloud

Listening Comprehension

Read the Interactive Read Aloud

Genre: Informational Text

Interactive Read-Aloud Cards

Tell children you will be reading an informational text. Remind them that *informational text* gives true information about a person, place, or thing. Display the **Interactive Read-Aloud Cards**.

Read aloud the title. Point out that many different kinds of baby animals might live on a farm.

Strategy: Reread

Remind children that good readers reread to help them understand. Information might not be clear to them at first, but reading it again can help them understand it. Children might reread the same page or a page they have already read. The **Think Aloud Cloud** can help them reread to understand more about baby animals.

Think Aloud I read that baby animals are alike. I also read that baby animals are different. How can they be both alike and different? I'll reread the first page to try to figure this out. I understand now. They are alike because they live on a farm. They are different because they do not look or sound quite the same. Rereading helps me understand how baby animals are alike and different.

Read "Baby Farm Animals," and model the strategy of rereading.

Make Connections

Guide partners to connect "Baby Farm Animals" with *ZooBorns!* Discuss the similarities and differences between the two selections. *How are all the animals in the two selections alike?* (They are young babies.) *How are they different?* (Possible answer: The *ZooBorns!* animals are in a zoo. The animals in "Baby Farm Animals" are on a farm.)

ELL

ENGLISH LANGUAGE LEARNERS

Reinforce Meaning As you read "Baby Farm Animals," make meaning clear by pointing to specific animals, places, or objects in the illustrations, demonstrating word meanings, paraphrasing text, and asking children questions. For example, on Card 1, point to the chicks and say: *These are chicks. They are baby chickens.* Repeat with other baby animals in the text.

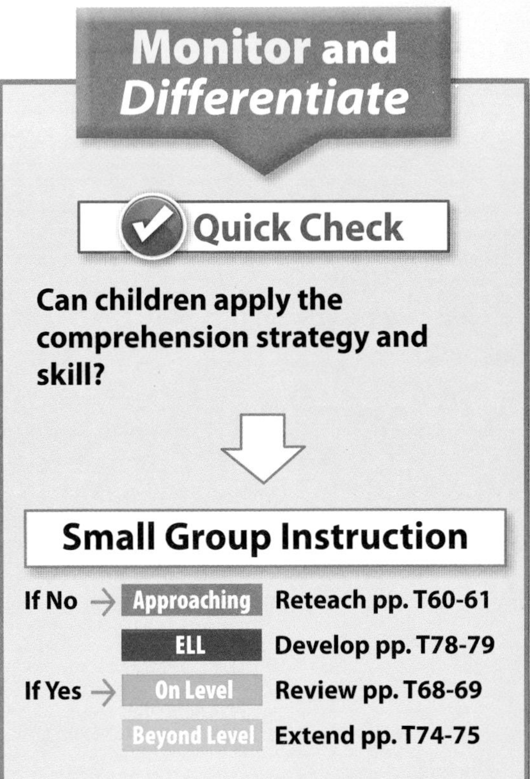

Monitor and Differentiate

Quick Check

Can children apply the comprehension strategy and skill?

Small Group Instruction

If No →	Approaching	Reteach pp. T60-61
	ELL	Develop pp. T78-79
If Yes →	On Level	Review pp. T68-69
	Beyond Level	Extend pp. T74-75

WHOLE GROUP
DAY 3

Word Work

Quick Review

Build Fluency: Sound-Spellings: Display the following **Word-Building Cards:** *b, c, e, f, h, k, l, r, u.* Have children chorally say each sound. Repeat and vary the pace.

MINILESSON 5 Mins

Phonemic Awareness

Puppet

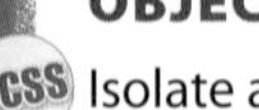

OBJECTIVES

CCSS Isolate and pronounce the initial, medial vowel, and final sounds in three-phoneme words. **RF.K.2d**

CCSS Demonstrate basic knowledge of one-to-one letter-sound correspondences by producing the primary or many of the most frequent sounds for each consonant. **RF.K.3a**

CCSS Associate the long and short sounds with common spellings (graphemes) for the five major vowels. **RF.K.3b**

Phoneme Blending

1 **Model** Use the puppet to demonstrate how to blend phonemes to make words. *The puppet is going to say sounds in a word. Listen: /u/ /s/. It can blend those sounds to make a word: /uuusss/,* us. *When the puppet blends the sounds together, it makes the word* us. *Listen as the puppet blends more sounds to make words.* Model phoneme blending with the following:

/u/ /p/ *up*   /b/ /u/ /s/ *bus*   /t/ /u/ /g/ tug

2 **Guided Practice/Practice** Have children blend sounds to make words. *The puppet is going to say sounds in a word. Listen as it says each sound. Repeat the sounds, then blend them to say the word.* Guide practice with the first word.

/p/ /u/ /p/ /s/ *pups*   /m/ /u/ /d/ *mud*   /r/ /u/ /g/ rug
/k/ /u/ /p/ /s/ *cups*   /d/ /u/ /m/ /p/ *dump*   /l/ /u/ /k/ luck

Review initial /u/. Play and sing "My Umbrella." Have children clap when they hear initial /u/. Demonstrate as you sing with them.

Go Digital

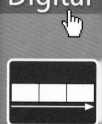

Phonemic Awareness

Phonics

Handwriting

Phonics

Word-Building Card

Review Short *u*

1 Model Display **Word-Building Card** *u. This is the letter* u. *The letter* u *can stand for /uuu/, the sound you hear at the beginning of* umbrella. *Say the sound with me: /uuu/. I will write the letter* u *because* umbrella *has /u/ at the beginning.* Repeat the routine using the word *run*. Point out that *run* has /u/ in the middle of the word.

2 Guided Practice/Practice Tell children that you will say some words that have the /u/ sound in the middle and some words that do not. Have children say /u/ and write the letter *u* on their **Response Boards** when they hear /u/ in the middle of a word. Guide practice with the first word.

hum	up	red	but	bus	tub
bit	rub	bat	mud	duck	ten

Blend Words with Short *u* and *b, f, r, d, s, n, f, t, r, c*

1 Model Display Word-Building Cards *c, u, t. This is the letter* c. *It stands for /k/. This is the letter* u. *It stands for /u/. This is the letter* t. *It stands for /t/. Let's blend the three sounds together: /k/ /u/ /t/, /kuuut/. The word is* cut. Repeat with *tub, up, pup*

2 Guided Practice/Practice Write the following words. Have children read each word, blending the sounds. Guide practice with the first word: */m/ /u/ /d/, /muuud/. The word is* mud.

mud us bun fun up nut run sun

Write these sentences and prompt children to read the connected text, sounding out the decodable words: *I like the mud. It is fun to run. We like the sun.*

Corrective Feedback

Sound Error Model the sound that children missed, then have them repeat. For example, say: *My turn.* Tap under the letter *u* in the word *mud* and ask: *Sound? What's the sound?* Return to the beginning of the word. *Let's start over.* Blend the word again.

YOUR TURN PRACTICE BOOK p. 188

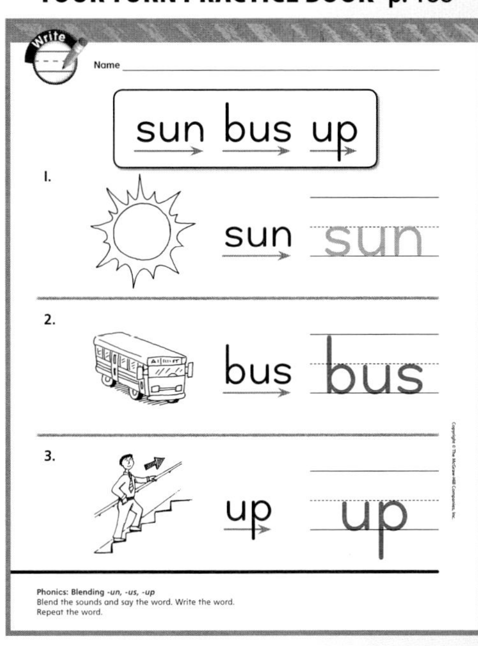

Word Work

Phonics

Photo Cards

OBJECTIVES

CCSS Read common high-frequency words by sight. **RF.K.3c**

Sort names of objects by initial and medial /u/u

ACADEMIC LANGUAGE

sort

Picture Sort

1. **Model** Remind children that the letter *u* can stand for /u/. Place **Word-Building Card** *u* at the top center of a pocket chart. *What is this letter?* (u) *What sound does this letter stand for?* (/u/)

   Hold up the **Photo Card** for *up*. *Here is the picture for* up. Up *has the /u/ sound at the beginning. Listen, /uuup/.* Place the photo card on the left side of the pocket chart. *I will place* up *on this side of the chart because the /u/ sound is at the beginning of* up.

   Use the same routine for letter *u* and *nut*, reminding children that the /u/ sound is in the middle of the word. Place the *nut* photo card on the opposite side as the Photo Card for *up*.

2. **Guided Practice/Practice** Have children sort the Photo Cards *bus, thumb, sun, umbrella, umpire, under*. Have them say the word and tell whether /u/ is at the beginning or in the middle of the word. Then have them tell where the Photo Card should be placed: under the *up* Photo Card for initial /u/ or under the *nut* Photo Card for medial /u/.

Photo Cards

Go Digital

Phonics

the | is | you | do

High-Frequency Word Routine

High-Frequency Words

for, have

1 Guided Practice Display the **High-Frequency Word Card** *have*. Review the word using the **Read/Spell/Write** routine. Repeat the routine, using the word *for*.

2 Practice Point to the High-Frequency Word Card *have* and have children read it. Repeat with *for* and last week's words *my, are, he, with, in, little, she, was*.

Build Fluency

Word Automaticity Write the following sentences and have children chorally read aloud as you track the print. Repeat several times.

We run *for* fun.
I *have* a nut.
I *have* a bun *for* you.
You *have* a hat *for* the sun.

Read for Fluency Distribute pp. 189–190 of the **Your Turn Practice Book** and help children assemble their Take-Home Books. Chorally read the Take-Home Book with children. Then have children reread the book to review high-frequency words and build fluency.

YOUR TURN PRACTICE BOOK pp. 189–190

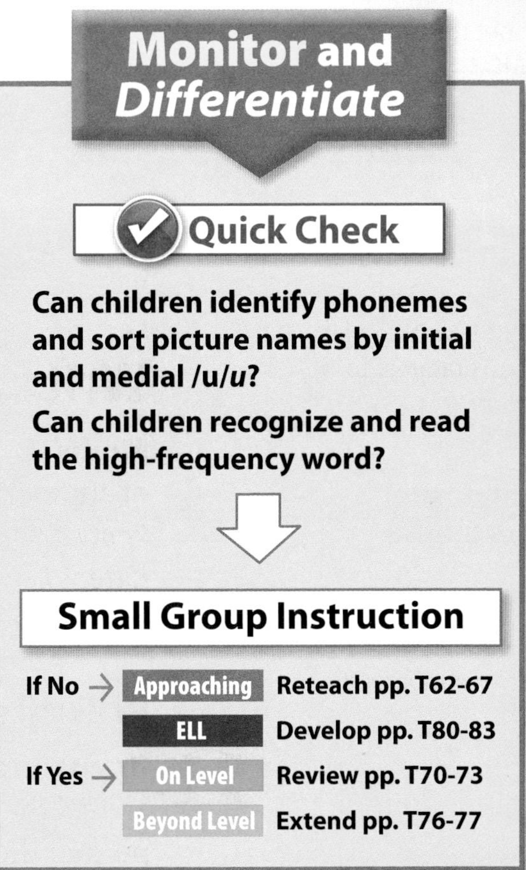

Monitor and Differentiate
Quick Check
Can children identify phonemes and sort picture names by initial and medial /u/u?
Can children recognize and read the high-frequency word?
Small Group Instruction
If No → Approaching Reteach pp. T62-67
ELL Develop pp. T80-83
If Yes → On Level Review pp. T70-73
Beyond Level Extend pp. T76-77

Language Arts

Reading/Writing Workshop Big Book

OBJECTIVES

CCSS Use a combination of drawing, dictating, and writing to compose informative/explanatory texts in which they name what they are writing about and supply some information about the topic. **W.K.2**

CCSS Use frequently occurring nouns and verbs. **L.K.1b**

- Write informative text
- Apply writing trait and grammar to writing

ACADEMIC LANGUAGE

- *information, action word, verb*
- Cognates: *información, verbo*

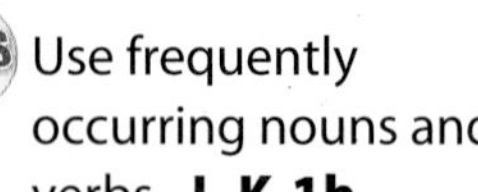

Independent Writing

Writing Trait: Word Choice

1 Practice Tell children that today they will create an Animal Card that includes two or three sentences about an animal they choose.

2 Guided Practice Share the Readers to Writers page in the **Reading/Writing Workshop**. Read the model sentences aloud.

Readers to Writers

Word Choice

Read Emma's animal card. Emma tells about what wolf pups can do.

Emma's model

Wolf pups can run fast. The pups like to play. They howl, too.

Read Together

Verbs

A verb is a word that tells what a person or thing does.

A bear cub climbs up a tree.

A rabbit hops in a garden.

READING/WRITING WORKSHOP BIG BOOK, pp. 18–19

Write an Animal Card

Model Display the web from Day 1. On chart paper, write the name of another familiar animal, such as a kitten. *I have a pet kitten so I know a lot about kittens. I will write sentences to tell about kittens.* Write: *Kittens like to play with string. This is one fact I know about kittens.* Read the sentence aloud, tracking the print.

Prewrite

Brainstorm Have children work with a partner to choose a pet or an animal they are familiar with to write about. Ask children to tell their partner the facts that they know about the animal they chose.

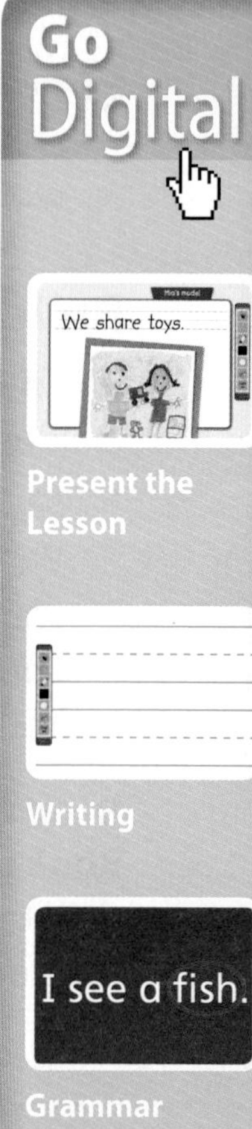

Draft

Ask children to draw a picture of their animal. Guide them in writing the name of the animal below the picture. Then ask them to write one or two sentences about the animal. Help children write their sentences.

Apply Writing Trait As children write and draw, ask them to tell you more information about the animal they chose. Encourage children to include some of that information in their sentences.

Apply Grammar Tell children to point to the action words in their sentences and tell who or what does each action.

ENGLISH LANGUAGE LEARNERS

Use Verbs Use the Photo Card for *mouse* for support. Have children draw a picture of the mouse doing something that a mouse might do. For example, children might draw a mouse eating cheese. Have children dictate a sentence to tell what the mouse is doing. Write the sentence below the picture and read it aloud with children.

Grammar

Action Words (Verbs)

1. **Review** Remind children that action words, also called verbs, tell the actions in sentences. Write and read: *I blow a bubble.*

   Point out that *blow* is an action word that tells what the person is doing. *It is a verb. A verb tells the action in a sentence.* Remind students that when the naming word is *I* the action word does not end in *-s*.

2. **Guided Practice/Practice** Write and read aloud the sentence *The bubble pops. What does the bubble do?* (It pops.) *Which word is the action word in the sentence?* (pops) Ask them to tell you how they know *pops* is the action word in the sentence. (It tells what the bubble does.) Repeat with the sentence: *The bubble floats away.* Ask children to tell why the action words *pops* and *floats* end in *-s*.

   Display and read the **Photo Cards** for *baby, cow,* and *helicopter.* Have children work with a partner. Have each pair of children choose one Photo Card and talk about what a baby, cow, or helicopter can do. Have pairs say sentences about the photos using action words, such as *The helicopter flies in the sky.*

Talk About It

Have partners work together to describe how different animals move. Remind them to use action words to tell what each animal does.

Daily Wrap Up

- Review the Essential Question and encourage children to discuss, using the oral vocabulary words *appearance* and *behavior. How are some animals alike? How are they different?*
- Prompt children to review and discuss the skills they used today. Guide them to give examples of how they used each skill.

WHOLE GROUP
DAY 4

Materials

Reading/Writing Workshop Big Book
UNIT 7

Literature Big Book
ZooBorns!

Visual Vocabulary Cards
for
have

Interactive Read-Aloud Cards

Word-Building Cards

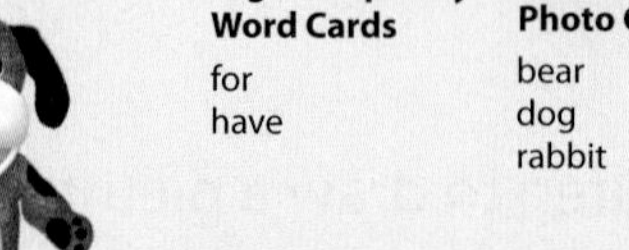
Puppet

High-Frequency Word Cards
for
have

Photo Cards
bear
dog
rabbit

Extend the Concept

Oral Language

OBJECTIVES

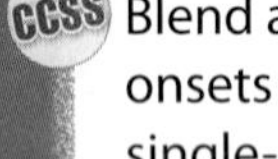

CCSS Use words and phrases acquired through conversations, reading and being read to, and responding to texts. **L.K.6**

CCSS Blend and segment onsets and rimes of single-syllable spoken words. **RF.K.2c**

Develop oral vocabulary

ESSENTIAL QUESTION

Remind children that this week they have been talking and reading about the ways baby animals are alike and different. Have them sing "Old MacDonald" and say the different animal sounds. *How is the frogmouth in* ZooBorns! *like the chick in "Old MacDonald Had a Farm"?*

Phonological Awareness

Onset/Rime Blending

Have children say the word *quack* from "Old MacDonald Had a Farm." *The word quack has a beginning sound and an end sound. Listen: /kw/ /ak/ We blend the sounds together to say the word,* quack. Repeat the routine, segmenting other words from the song: /f/ /ärm/, farm; /p/ /igz/, pigs; /d/ /uks/, ducks

Review Oral Vocabulary

Reread the Interactive Read Aloud

Use the **Define/Example/Ask** routine to review the oral vocabulary words *appearance, behavior, exercise, wander,* and *plenty*. Then have children listen as you reread "Baby Farm Animals."

→ *Which baby animal has a beak and might wander near a barn?* (chick)

→ *Why does a duckling need plenty of water?* (to help it grow)

Go Digital

Visual Glossary

"Baby Farm Animals"

Category Words

Category Words: Animal Parts

1 Explain/Model Have children draw one of the following animal parts on an index card: *tail, teeth, paws, ears, eyes, nose, legs, feet.* Say the name of each animal part with children. *I am going to read a story. When you hear an animal part word, hold up your card.*

> *The lion cubs liked to chase each other's* tails. *Sometimes they would playfully bite each other with their* teeth *or swipe each other with their paws. The mother lion wanted her cubs to keep their* ears *and* eyes *open for danger. Sometimes she would nudge them with her* nose. *When the cubs got tired, they stopped to rest their* legs *and* feet.

2 Guided Practice Display pictures of wild and domestic animals from books and magazines. Distribute paper and crayons. Have children draw pictures of one of the animals. When they are finished, have children share their pictures pointing out the different animal parts.

Vocabulary Strategy: Compound Words

1 Model Remind children about special words that are made up of two words. Say *cook* and *book*. Tell children that we can put those words together to make one word: *cookbook*.

2 Guided Practice/Practice Tell children that you will say some two words. Have them listen to both words and put them together to make one word. Guide practice with the first word.

door, bell (doorbell)
base, ball (baseball)
sun, burn (sunburn)
tooth, brush (toothbrush)
hair, cut (haircut)
cup, cake (cupcake)
in, side (inside)
tug, boat (tugboat)
ant, eater (anteater

LET'S MOVE!

Play Simon Says, naming animal parts in the directions. Simon says, flap your wings. *Simon says, wag your tail. Simon says, stick out your beak. Point to your ears.*

ENGLISH LANGUAGE LEARNERS

Use Visuals Point to the **Photo Cards** for *dog, bear,* and *rabbit.* Help children identify the animal parts in each picture. Point to each animal's ears, paws, and fur. Name each animal part as you point to the pictures. Review other animal-part words, such as *eyes, nose,* and *tail,* and write each one on the board.

YOUR TURN PRACTICE BOOK p. 191

Listening Comprehension

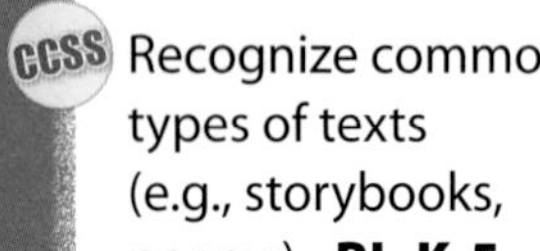

Literature Big Book

OBJECTIVES

CCSS Recognize common types of texts (e.g., storybooks, poems). **RL.K.5**

CCSS Ask and answer questions about unknown words in a text. **RL.K.4**

- Recognize the literary element alliteration to learn features of poetry
- Apply the comprehension strategy: Reread
- Make connections across texts

ACADEMIC LANGUAGE

- *sound, poem*
- Cognates: *sonido, poema*

Read Poetry

Genre: Poetry

Display the poems on pages 34–36 of the **Big Book** and read aloud the titles. Ask children to tell which type of text this is. (poems) Remind them that poems are a kind of creative writing. Poets often use words that rhyme, or have the same ending sounds.

Set a Purpose for Reading

Read aloud page 34. Tell children to listen as you continue reading the poems so they can learn more about baby animals.

Strategy: Reread

Remind children that good readers reread part of a text if there is something they do not understand. Point to page 34. Reread the last line. Point to the word *he's. If I don't know who he is, I can reread one line, or the whole poem if I need to. When I reread the first line, I know that the word* he's *refers to the baby goat.*

Literary Element: Alliteration

Explain Tell children that many poems use words that begin with the same sound. Poets like to use words in new and creative ways to help share their thoughts and feelings. Read aloud the first line of "Kitty Caught a Caterpillar" on page 36. *The poet uses the same beginning sound with* kitty, caught, *and* caterpillar. *Which sound is this?* (/k/)

Apply Read aloud the fourth line of "Kitty Caught a Caterpillar." *Which words have the same beginning sound?* (turtle, tiny, tail) *Which sound is this?* (/t/)

Go Digital

ZooBorns!

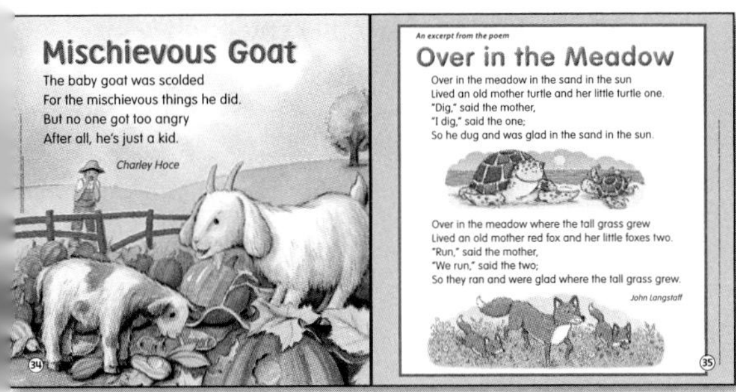

LITERATURE BIG BOOK **PAGES 34–35**

LITERARY ELEMENT

Reread the first line of the last stanza on page 35. Have children identify the words with the same beginning sounds. (grass, grew)

Ask and Answer Questions Have children ask a partner about an unknown word, such as *mischievous*. The partner will use clues to figure out the meaning and answer the question.

LITERATURE BIG BOOK **PAGE 36**

REREAD

Point to the word *her* in the last line. *Let's reread a part of the poem to find out who the word* her *refers to.* Reread the last four lines of the poem. *Yes, the word* her *refers to Kitty.*

Retell and Respond

Have children discuss the selection by asking these questions:

→ *What did the little foxes do with their mother?* (run)

→ *What caught the kitty?* (a bumblebee)

Make Connections

Have children recall the selections they read this week.

→ *How were the baby Asian elephant and the pygmy hippo alike?* (They both have four legs and their skin is gray and rough.) How were they different? (The elephant has a trunk, and the hippo doesn't.)

Write About It Write one way the baby lamb and the piglet were alike, and one way they were different. Draw a picture to show one of these.

ENGLISH LANGUAGE LEARNERS

Reinforce Meaning As you read aloud the text, make the meaning clear by pointing to details in the illustrations. Ask children questions to elicit language.

CONNECT TO CONTENT

Comparing Baby Animals Review with children the baby animals in the poems (goat, turtle, fox, kitty). Have partners compare how the two baby animals in "Over in the Meadow" are alike and different.

STEM

WHOLE GROUP
DAY 4

Word Work

Quick Review

Build Fluency: Sound-Spellings: Show the following **Word-Building Cards:** *a, b, c, d, e, f, h, i, k, l, m, n, o, p, r, s, t, u.* Have children chorally say each sound. Repeat and vary the pace.

MINILESSON 5 Mins

Phonemic Awareness

Puppet

OBJECTIVES

CCSS Distinguish between similarly spelled words by identifying the sounds of the letters that differ. **RF.K.3d**

CCSS Add or substitute individual sounds (phonemes) in simple, one-syllable words to make new words. **RF.K.2e**

CCSS Read common high-frequency words by sight. **RF.K.3c**

Phoneme Deletion

1 Model *The puppet can take sounds away from words to make new words. Listen as it says a word:* cup. *Say the word with the puppet:* cup. *Now listen as it says* cup *without /k/:* up. *Say the word:* up. Cup *without /k/ is* up. Repeat with *bus/us.*

2 Guided Practice/Practice Have children delete initial sounds to make new words. Guide practice with the first word.

Say sat. *Now say* sat *without /s/.* (at)
Say his. *Now say* his *without /h/.* (is)
Say wax. *Now say* wax *without /w/.* (ax)
Say train. *Now say* train *without /t/.* (rain)
Say sand. *Now say* sand *without /s/.* (and)

MINILESSON 5 Mins

Phonics

Blend Words with Short *u, a, i* and *t, b*

1 Guided Practice Display **Word-Building Cards** *t, u, b.* Point to the letter *t. This is the letter* t. *The letter* t *stands for /t/. Say /t/. This is the letter* u. *The letter* u *stands for /u/. Listen as I blend the two sounds together /tuuu/. This is the letter* b. *The letter* b *stands for /b/. Listen as I blend the three sounds /tuuub/,* tub. *Now you say it. Let's change the* u *to* a. Use the same routine to blend the word *tab.*

2 Practice Write *bat, but* and *bit.* Have children blend the words. Point to the words and ask which letters are the same. (b, t) Ask children to tell which letters are different. (a, u, i) Discuss the sound each letter stands for and how it changes the word. Repeat with *run, fun, sun.*

Go Digital

Phonemic Awareness

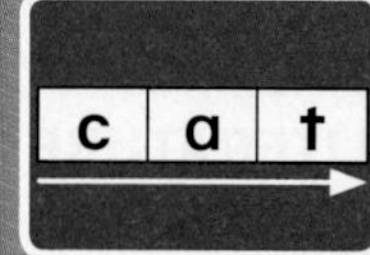

Phonics

Handwriting

Visual Glossary

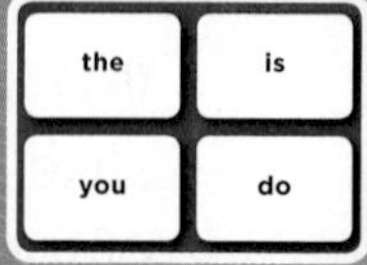

High-Frequency Word Routine

Dictation

Review Dictate each sound for the children to spell. Have children repeat the sound and then write the letter that stands for the sound.

/u/ /n/ /t/ /p/ /b/ /k/ /h/ /m/ /d/

Dictate the following words for children to spell: *cut, nut, duck, tuck, tub, rub, run, fun*. Model for children how to segment each word to scaffold the spelling. *When I say the word* cut, *I hear three sounds: /k/ /u/ /t/. I know the letter* c *stands for /k/, the letter* u *stands for /u/, and the letter* t *stands for /t/. I will write letters* c, u, t *to spell the word* cut.

When children finish, write the letters and words for them to self-correct.

High-Frequency Words

Practice Say the word *for* and have children write it. Then display the **Visual Vocabulary Card** *for*. Follow the Teacher Talk routine on the back.

Visual Vocabulary Cards

Repeat for the word *have*.

Build Fluency Build sentences in the pocket chart using the **High-Frequency Word Cards** and **Photo Cards**. Use an index card to create a punctuation card for a period. Have children chorally read the sentences as you track the print. Then have them identify the words *have* and *for*.

I *have* a cat *for* you.
We *have* a gem *for* you.
Do you *have* a guitar?

High-Frequency Words Practice

Have partners create sentences using the words *have* and *for*.

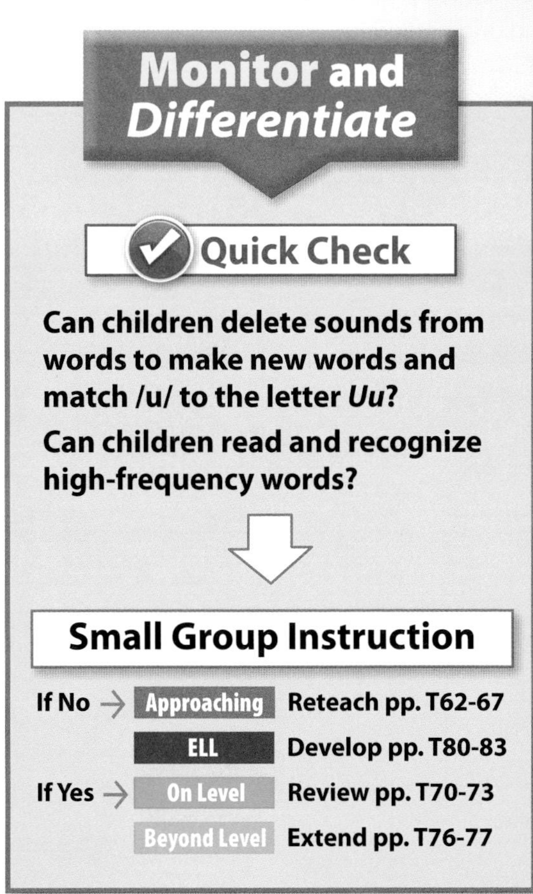

Monitor and Differentiate

Quick Check

Can children delete sounds from words to make new words and match /u/ to the letter *Uu*?

Can children read and recognize high-frequency words?

Small Group Instruction

If No →	Approaching	Reteach pp. T62-67
	ELL	Develop pp. T80-83
If Yes →	On Level	Review pp. T70-73
	Beyond Level	Extend pp. T76-77

WHOLE GROUP
DAY 4

Shared Read

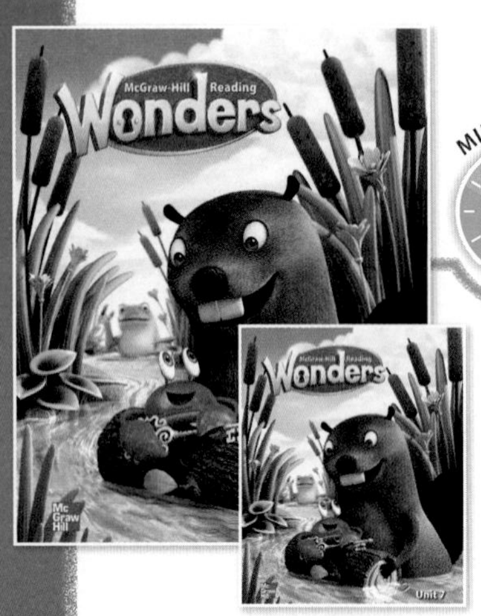

Reading/Writing Workshop Big Book and Reading/Writing Workshop

OBJECTIVES

CCSS Read common high-frequency words by sight. **RF.K.3c**

CCSS Read emergent-reader texts with purpose and understanding. **RF.K.4**

MINILESSON 10 Mins

Read "A Pup and a Cub"

Model Skills and Strategies

Model Concepts About Print Reinforce sentence boundaries by turning to page 13 and discussing each sentence. *The first sentence begins with the word* I *and starts with a capital letter. It ends with a period after the word* sun. *The second sentence also begins with the word* I *and ends with an exclamation point.* Invite children to find sentence boundaries by pointing to the capital letters at the start of each sentence and the punctuation marks that end each sentence. Then count the words in each sentence. Finally, count the number of sentences on each page.

Reread Invite children to chorally reread the story. Children should sound out the decodable words and say the sight words. Offer support as needed using the student **Reading/Writing Workshop**.

Ask the following:

- *Look at page 10. What is a group of wolves called? Where do they live?* (a pack; a den)
- *Look at page 12. How many lions are in this family?* (four in all)
- *Look at page 15. What is something that wolf pups and lion cubs enjoy doing for fun?* (They like to run.)

Go Digital

"A Pup and a Cub"

"A Pup and a Cub"

A Pup and a Cub
I am a pup.
I have a mom and a dad.

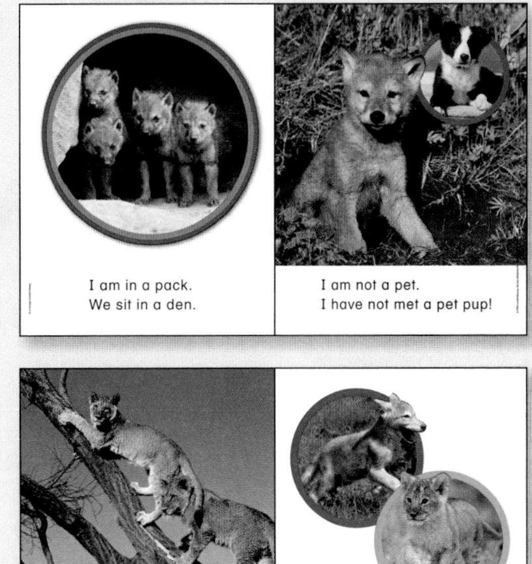

I am in a pack.
We sit in a den.
I am not a pet.
I have not met a pet pup!
Sis and I have fun.
We can go up, up!
A pup can run for fun.
A cub can run for fun.

I am a cub.
Mom, dad, and sis see me.
I sit on a rock in the sun.
I nap in the sun a lot!

READING/WRITING WORKSHOP 7, pp. 8–15

Fluency: Expression

1. **Explain** Tell children that as you read the story, you will be reading with expression. Mention that as you read, you will look at the punctuation at the end of sentences to tell you how to change the tone of your voice.

2. **Model** Model reading the selection "A Pup and a Cub." Read the text fluently and with emotion. Change your inflection as you read sentences that end with periods and exclamation points.

3. **Guided Practice** Read each sentence and invite children to echo you, encouraging them to change their inflection as indicated by the punctuation. Then encourage them to chorally read the story with expression.

Language Arts

Independent Writing

OBJECTIVES

 With guidance and support from adults, recall information from experiences or gather information from provided sources to answer a question. **W.K.8**

CCSS Use frequently occurring nouns and verbs. **L.K.1b**

- Write informative text
- Use verbs in sentences

ACADEMIC LANGUAGE

- *revise, verb*
- Cognates: *revisar, verbo*

Write an Animal Card

Revise

Distribute the children's draft Animal Cards from Day 3.

Apply Writing Trait: Word Choice Explain that as writers revise, they make sure they have chosen the correct action words. Write and read: *walk, slither, crawl, hop. I want to write a sentence about how cows move.* Write and read the sentence frame: *Cows ______. Which action word completes the sentence?* (walk) *How do you know?* (A cow walks. It doesn't slither, crawl, or hop.)

Then have children reread the sentences they wrote on Day 3 and check for the following:

→ Did I give information about the animal I chose?

→ Did I use strong action words to tell what the animal does?

→ Did I draw a picture of the animal?

Apply Grammar Review that action words are verbs that tell the action in a sentence. *What action words did you use in your sentences?*

COLLABORATE

Peer Edit Have children work in pairs to do a peer edit, in which they read their partner's draft. Ask partners to check that their sentences describe the pictures drawn and include action words about the animal they chose. Provide time for children to make revisions to their sentences.

Final Draft

After children have edited their own papers and finished their peer edits, have them write their final draft on an index card. Explain that they should try to write letters carefully and leave spaces between words so that readers can read their writing. Remind children that there should be more space between words than between letters in a word. As children work, conference with them to provide guidance.

Go Digital

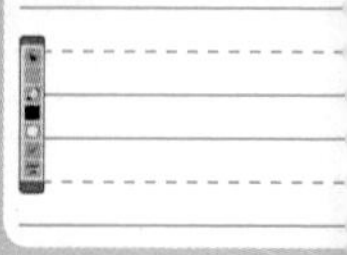

Writing

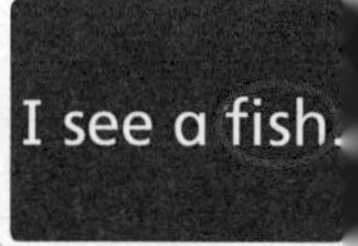

Grammar

Grammar

Action Words (Verbs)

1 Review Write and read aloud this sentence: *Sam writes stories. Which word is an action word?* (writes) *How do you know that it is an action word?* (It tells what Sam does.)

2 Guided Practice Write the following sentences and read them aloud: *Julia reads a book. Ramon plays a game.* Ask children to circle the action word in each sentence. Ask volunteers to explain how they know that *reads* and *plays* are action words.

We know that reads *and* plays *are action words because they tell what the person does in each sentence.* Use a self-stick note to cover the action word in each sentence. *If we take away the word* reads, *then we don't know what Julia does with the book. If we take away the word* plays, *then we don't know what Ramon does with the game.*

3 Practice Write this sentence frame and read it aloud: *Marta ______ a bike.*

Have children work with a partner to choose the correct action word to complete the sentence. (rides) Have children work together to complete the sentence frame with the correct word. Remind children that the action word ends in *-s* in this sentence. It tells about one naming word, *Marta*.

Talk About It

Have partners work together to orally generate sentences with action words about things they do after school. Challenge them to create sentences with more than one verb.

ENGLISH LANGUAGE LEARNERS

Photo Cards and Sentences Provide sentences that go with images on the **Photo Cards**. As you read a sentence aloud, hold up a Photo Card as you say the action and you tell the person or thing doing the action. For example: *The man talks.* Model correct pronunciation as needed.

Daily Wrap Up

- Review the Essential Question and encourage children to discuss it, using the oral vocabulary words.
- Prompt children to discuss the skills they practiced and learned today. Guide them to share examples of each skill.

www.connected.mcgraw-hill.com
RESOURCES
Research and Inquiry

Wrap Up the Week
Integrate Ideas

RESEARCH AND INQUIRY

Baby Animals

OBJECTIVES

Participate in shared research and writing projects (e.g., explore a number of books by a favorite author and express opinions about them). **W.K.7**

With guidance and support from adults, recall information from experiences or gather information from provided sources to answer a question. **W.K.8**

ACADEMIC LANGUAGE
research, inquiry

Animal Features Report

Review the steps in the research process. Tell children that today, they will do a research project with a partner to make a report about an animal.

STEP 1 Choose a Topic

Guide children to think of different animals. List the animals in the first column of a five-column chart. Work with children to identify four features, such as size, number of legs, how it moves, and what it eats. Tell partners to pick an animal to research from the list in column one.

STEP 2 Find Resources

Review how to locate and use resources. Guide children to use selections from the week. Provide other print reference sources and online ones. Have children use the Research Process Checklist online.

STEP 3 Keep Track of Ideas

Help children note the features they are researching on a sheet of paper. As they gather information, they can draw pictures or write words next to each feature.

Collaborative Conversations

Ask and Answer Questions As children engage in partner, small-group, and whole-class discussions, encourage them to:

- ask questions to clarify ideas they do not understand.
- ask for help in getting information.
- wait after asking a question to give others a chance to think before they respond.
- answer questions with complete ideas, not one-word answers.

The eagle is a big bird.
It has two legs and two wings.
It flies and eats meat.

STEM

STEP 4 Create the Project: Animal Features Report

Explain the characteristics of the project:

- **Information** Reports give facts about a topic. Partners will research facts about their animal for the report.
- **Text** Have partners summarize their research in a written report. Provide these sentence frames:

  The _______ is _______. It has _______ legs. It _____ and eats_______.
- **Illustration** Have partners include a picture of the animal in their report.

Have partners work together to write their report. Help them to add facts. Encourage children to use the computer to write and publish their report.

- Encourage children who can generate more writing to do so.
- Prompt children to include details in their illustration.
- Have children use their reports to compare and contrast the animals.

ELL ENGLISH LANGUAGE LEARNERS SCAFFOLD

Beginning	Intermediate	Advanced/Advanced High
Actively Engage As partners present their research, prompt them to act out how animals move.	**Describe** Prompt children to include details in their illustrations and to be ready to talk about them when they share with the class. In particular, guide children to focus on details related to how the animal moves.	**Expand** Encourage children to use longer sentences that tell more about how the animal moves. For example: *A giraffe uses its long legs to walk and run.* To steer children toward these ideas, as partners work, ask questions about the animal's body parts or about *how* the animal moves (i.e., quickly, slowly, smoothly, and so on).

WHOLE GROUP

DAY 5

Materials

Literature Big Book
ZooBorns!

Interactive Read-Aloud Cards

Word-Building Cards

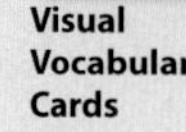
Visual Vocabulary Cards
for
have

High-Frequency Word Cards
are
for
have
he
my
with

Puppet

Response Boards

"My Umbrella"

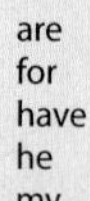

Integrate Ideas

TEXT CONNECTIONS

Connect to Essential Question

OBJECTIVES

With prompting and support, identify basic similarities in and differences between two texts on the same topic (e.g., illustrations, descriptions, or procedures). **RI.K.9**

Participate in collaborative conversations with diverse partners about *kindergarten topics and texts* with peers and adults in small and larger groups. **SL.K.1**

- Make connections among texts
- Make connections to the world

Text to Text

Remind children that all week they have been reading selections about different kinds of baby animals. Tell them that now they will connect the texts, or think about how the selections are alike. Model comparing *ZooBorns!* with another selection from the week.

Think Aloud In *ZooBorns!* I learned about lots of different kinds of baby animals that all live in zoos. In "Baby Farm Animals" I learned about different baby animals that live on farms. Both selections are about baby animals.

Guide children to compare an animal they saw and read about in *ZooBorns!* and an animal from one of the poems in the paired selection. Have them tell how the animals are alike and different.

Text to Self

Have two children each name a favorite animal. Then invite other children to tell how those two animals are alike and different. Continue with two other animals named by children.

Text to World

Guide children to talk about animals that they see in the community. *What kinds of animals do you see? Are they wild animals or pets? How are they alike and different?*

TALK ABOUT READING

Analyze and Explain

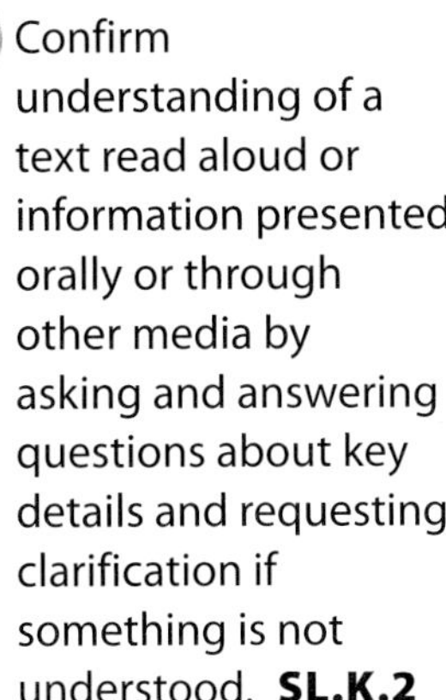

OBJECTIVES

CCSS Confirm understanding of a text read aloud or information presented orally or through other media by asking and answering questions about key details and requesting clarification if something is not understood. **SL.K.2**

Becoming Readers

Talk with children about the genres, strategy, and skill they have learned about this week. Prompt them to discuss how this knowledge helps them to read and understand selections.

→ Remind children that one genre they learned about is informational text. Recall with them some characteristics of informational text.

→ Discuss the strategy of rereading. *How did rereading the poems, such as "The Mischievous Goat," help you to understand the poem more fully?*

→ Talk about how the children learned to make connections within a text. *Each page of* ZooBorns! *shows a different baby animal. How did comparing and contrasting the pictures of those animals help you learn about and understand the animals?*

RESEARCH AND INQUIRY

Baby Animals

OBJECTIVES

CCSS Participate in shared research and writing projects (e.g., explore a number of books by a favorite author and express opinions about them). **W.K.7**

Wrap Up the Project

COLLABORATE

Guide children to discuss the information in their animal report. What other details could they add? Encourage children to use words and phrases they learned this week. Have children use the Presenting and Listening checklists online.

STEM

Word Work

Quick Review

Build Fluency: Sound-Spellings: Show the following **Word-Building Cards:** *a, b, c, d, e, f, h, i, k, l, m, n, o, p, r, s, t, u.* Have children chorally say the sounds. Repeat and vary the pace.

Phonemic Awareness

Puppet

OBJECTIVES

CCSS Spell simple words phonetically, drawing on knowledge of sound-letter relationships. **L.K.2d**

CCSS Read common high-frequency words by sight. **RF.K.3c**

Delete phonemes to make new words

Phoneme Deletion

1 **Model** *The puppet can take sounds away from words to make new words. Listen as it says a word:* feet. *Say the word with the puppet:* feet. *The sound at the beginning of feet is /f/. Listen as the puppet says* feet, *without /f/:* eat. *The word* feet *without /f/ is* eat. Repeat with *Gus/us.*

2 **Guided Practice/Practice** Have children delete the initial sound and say the new word. Guide practice with the first word.

Say sit. *Now say* sit *without /s/.* (it)
Say hat. *Now say* hat *without /h/.* (at)
Say cup. *Now say* cup *without /k/.* (up)
Say cold. *Now say* cold *without /k/.* (old)
Say tray. *Now say* tray *without /t/.* (ray)
Say sled. *Now say* sled *without /s/.* (led)

MINILESSON 5 Mins

Phonics

Read Words with Short *u* and *f, b, r, c*

1 **Guided Practice** Remind children that the letter *u* can stand for the sound /u/. Display **Word-Building Cards** *u, s.* Point to the letter *u. The letter* u *stands for the sound /u/. Say /uuu/. The letter* s *stands for /s/. Say /sss/. Let's blend the sounds to make the word: /uuusss/* us. *Now let's add* b *to the beginning.* Blend and read *bus.*

2 **Practice** Write these words and sentences for children to read:

sun fun bun run tub sub cub rub

I like fun. Pat can run.
I have a bun for you. The cub has fun in the sun.

Remove words from view before dictation.

Review /u/*u*. Have children write *u* on their **Response Boards**. Play and sing "My Umbrella" Have children hold up and show the letter *u* on their boards when they hear initial /u/. Demonstrate as you sing.

Go Digital

Phonemic Awareness

Phonics

Handwriting

High-Frequency Word Cards

Dictation

1 Review Dictate the following sounds for children to spell. As you say each sound, have children repeat it and then write the letter that stands for the sound.

/u/ /t/ /b/ /a/ /k/ /p/ /n/ /s/

Dictate the following words for children to spell. Model for children how to use **Sound Boxes** to segment each word to scaffold the spelling. *I will say a word. You will repeat the word, then think about how many sounds are in the word. Use your Sound Boxes to count the sounds. Then write one letter for each sound you hear.*

tub tab up cub cap bun but us

Then write the letters and word for children to self-correct.

MINILESSON 5 Mins

High-Frequency Words

for, have

Visual Vocabulary Cards

1 Review Display **Visual Vocabulary Card** *for*. Have children **Read/Spell/Write** the word *for*. Then choose a Partner Talk activity.

Repeat the routine for the word *have*.

Distribute one of the following **High-Frequency Word Cards** to children: *my, are, he, with, for, have*. Tell children that you will say some sentences. *When you hear the word that is on your card, stand and hold up the word card.*

I *have* a pet for you.
He can sing for you.
We *are* at the house.
She will go *with* me to the store.
Will you read *for* me?
My big ball is red.

2 Build Fluency: Word Automaticity Display High-Frequency Word Cards *my, are, he, with, for, have*. Point to each card, at random, and have children read the word as quickly as they can.

Monitor and *Differentiate*

Quick Check

Can children delete initial phonemes to make new words and recognize words with /u/ and match it to letter *Uu*?

Can children read and recognize high-frequency words?

Small Group Instruction

If No →	Approaching	Reteach pp. T62-67
	ELL	Develop pp. T80-83
If Yes →	On Level	Review pp. T70-73
	Beyond Level	Extend pp. T76-77

Language Arts

Independent Writing

OBJECTIVES

 Speak audibly and express thoughts, feelings, and ideas clearly. **SL.K.6**

 Add drawings or other visual displays to descriptions as desired to provide additional detail. **SL.K.5**

Present an informative text

ACADEMIC LANGUAGE

- *present, publish*
- Cognates: *presente*

Write an Animal Card

Prepare

Tell children that they will present their finished Animal Cards from Day 4 to the class. Hold up an example from Day 4 and read it aloud, tracking the print. Use words to describe the drawing clearly. *I read the sentences clearly so that everyone could understand what I was saying. I talked about the animal drawing clearly so that everyone could understand what I was saying.*

Present

Have children take turns standing up and reading their sentences aloud and talking about their drawings. Remind children to speak clearly. Encourage the rest of the class to listen carefully to the person speaking and to speak clearly when asking questions about the presentation.

Evaluate

Have children discuss their own presentations and evaluate their performances, using the presentation rubric. Use the teacher's rubric to evaluate children's writing.

Publish

After children have finished presenting, collect the Animal Cards. Display the Animal Cards on a bulletin board under the heading "Animal Information." Encourage children to read and look at the drawings on their classmates' Animal Cards when they have free time.

Go Digital

Writing

I see a fish.

Grammar

Grammar

Action Words (Verbs)

1 **Review** Write and read aloud this sentence: *Lauren hits the ball. Which word is an action word?* (hits) *What does it tell you?* (what Lauren does)

2 **Review Practice** Write these sentence frames:

Tracy ______ the soccer ball.
Marco ______ the flowers.
Tom ______ the ladder.

Have children work with a partner to choose an action word to complete each sentence. (kicks; picks, smells; climbs) Then have partners copy the sentence frames and complete each one, using an action word that makes sense. (Tracy kicks the soccer ball. Marco picks/smells the flowers. Tom climbs the ladder.) Help children complete the sentences as needed. Ask children to tell why these action words end in *-s*.

Have children circle the verbs in their sentences. Gather the sentences and store them in a folder for a center or review activity.

Wrap Up the Week

- Review blending words with initial and medial /u/*u*. Remind children that a verb is an action word in a sentence.
- Use the **High-Frequency Word Cards** to review the Words to Know.
- Remind children that when they write, they should choose action words that will describe what the person or thing is doing.

Approaching Level

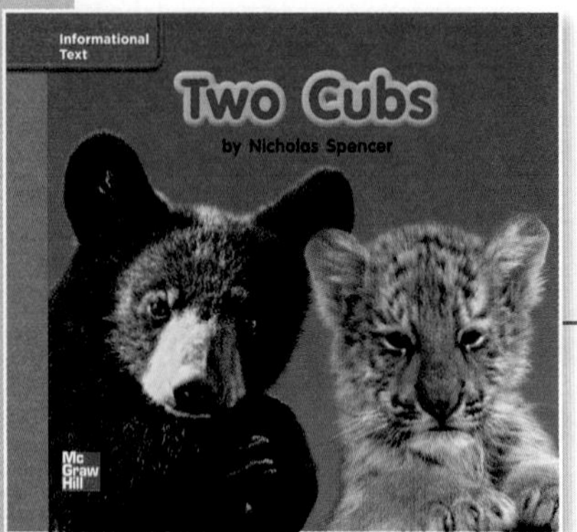

Leveled Reader

OBJECTIVES

With prompting and support, describe the connection between two individuals, events, ideas, or pieces of information in a text. **RI.K.3**

Name the author and illustrator of a text and define the role of each in presenting the ideas or information in a text. **RI.K.6**

Read emergent-reader texts with purpose and understanding. **RF.K.4**

Leveled Reader: *Two Cubs*

Before Reading

Preview and Predict

Point to and read each word in the title and in the author's name. Share with children that many baby animals are called "cubs," such as bears, lions, and tigers. Preview the photographs with children. Ask: *What do you think this book is about?*

Review Genre: Informational Text

Explain to children that informational text gives facts and information about a topic. Say: *One way we can tell that this book is an informational text is that it uses photographs of real tiger and bear cubs.*

Model Concepts of Print

Have children turn to page 2 and put their finger on where the sentence starts. Say: *How many words are in this sentence?* (four)

Review High-Frequency Words

Point out the word *have* on page 2, and read it with children. Ask them to locate *have* on other pages.

Essential Question

Set a purpose for reading: *Let's find out how these tiger and bear cubs are alike and different.*

During Reading

Guided Comprehension

As children read *Two Cubs*, monitor and provide guidance by correcting blending and modeling the strategy and skill.

Go Digital

Leveled Readers

Strategy: Reread

Remind children that if they do not understand one part of the text, they can reread it to help them better understand what is happening.

Skill: Connections Within Text (Compare and Contrast)

Explain to children that as they read it is helpful to think about how things are the same and how they are different. Comparing people, animals, or places can help them understand what they are reading.

Think Aloud I know this selection is about how the cubs are alike and different. The text on page 3 tells me something about them that is the same. The details in the photo show me how the ears are the same—they stick up—and how they are different—they are different colors. I will use the text and the photos to help me find out how these cubs are alike and different.

As children read the book, guide them to identify details in the pictures and text that help them compare and contrast the features of the bear and tiger cubs.

After Reading

Respond to Reading

- *What is this book about?* (comparing bear and tiger cubs)
- *How are bear cubs and tiger cubs the same?* (ears that stick up, sharp teeth, dark noses, feet with claws, thick fur, etc.)
- *How are they different?* (eyes are a different color; tigers have a long tail; their feet are a different shape; their fur is not the same color)

Retell

Have children take turns retelling. Help children make a personal connection. Ask: *Are the cubs more alike or more different? Why?*

Model Fluency

Read the book aloud, pausing after each page to have children chorally repeat.

Apply Have children practice reading with partners as you observe and provide needed assistance.

LITERACY ACTIVITIES

Have children complete the activities on the inside back cover of the reader.

Level Up

IF Children read *Two Cubs* **Approaching Level** with fluency and correctly answer the Respond to Reading questions,

THEN Tell children that they will read another story about how animals are alike and how they are different.

- Have children page through *Animal Bodies* **On Level** with you and identify the body parts being compared and contrasted in the book.
- Have children read the story, monitoring their comprehension and providing assistance as necessary.

Approaching Level

Phonological Awareness

ONSET/RIME BLENDING

TIER 2

OBJECTIVES

CCSS Demonstrate understanding of spoken words, syllables, and sounds (phonemes). **RF.K.2**

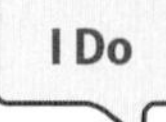

Tell children that the word *chicks* in the song "Old McDonald Had a Farm" has two parts and that each part has a sound. *The puppet can say the first sound in* chicks: /ch/. *The second sound is /iks/.* Have the puppet blend the sounds: /ch/ /iks/, *chicks.*

Listen as the puppet says the sounds in another word: /kw/ /ak/, quack. *Repeat the sounds and the word after the puppet: /kw/ /ak/,* quack.

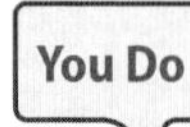

Ask children to blend the word parts to make a word. Have the puppet say the following: /d/ /uks/ (ducks); /k/ /ouz/ (cows); /m/ /ü/ (moo).

PHONEME ISOLATION

TIER 2

OBJECTIVES

Isolate and pronounce the initial, medial vowel, and final sounds (phonemes) in three-phoneme words. **RF.K.2d**

Display the *Up* **Photo Card**. *This is* up. *The first sound I hear in* up *is /u/.* Have children repeat the word with you, emphasizing the initial sound. Then have children say the first sound with you: /u/. Repeat with the *Bus* Photo Card, emphasizing the medial sound.

Display the *Under* Photo Card. Name the photo and have children say the name. *What is the first sound in* under? Say the sound together. Repeat with the *Nut* Photo Card, emphasizing the medial sound.

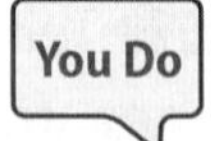

Show the *Umbrella* Photo Card. Have children name it and say the initial sound of the picture name. Repeat with the *Sun* Photo Card and the medial sound.

You may wish to review Phonological Awareness and Phonemic Awareness with ELL using this section.

PHONEME BLENDING

OBJECTIVES

CCSS Isolate and pronounce the initial, medial vowel, and final sounds (phonemes) in three-phoneme words. **RF.K.2d**

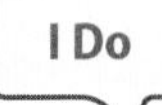

The puppet is going to say the sounds in a word. Listen: /u/ /p/. *The puppet can blend these sounds together:* /uuu/ /p/, /uuup/, up.

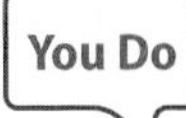

Now the puppet is going to say the sounds in another word. Say the sounds with the puppet: /u/ /s/. *Let's blend the sounds together:* /uuu/ /ssss/, /uuusss/, us. Repeat with *bun* and *under*.

Have children blend sounds to form words. Practice together: /uuu/ /p/, /uuup/, *up*. Then have children practice blending the following sounds to say the words.

/s/ /u/ /n/ sun   /u/ /n/ /t/ /ī/ untie   /m/ /u/ /d/ mud

PHONEME DELETION

OBJECTIVES

Demonstrate understanding of spoken words, syllables, and sounds (phonemes). **RF.K.2**

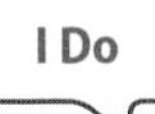

The puppet can take the sound away from one word to make a new word. Listen to the puppet say a word: bus. *Say the word with the puppet:* bus. *Now the puppet will take* /b/ *away from* bus. *The new word is* us. Have children say *us* with the puppet.

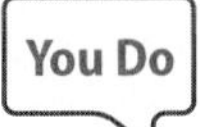

Have children say *bus* and take /b/ away to make *us*. Guide them to do the same with *cup* and *up*.

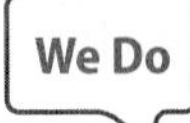

Guide children with phoneme deletion. *Say* slow. *Now say slow without /s/.* (low) Repeat the routine with the following: *rat* to at; *fin* to *in; cluck* to *luck; brake* to *rake; glove* to *love; bus* to *us*.

ELL ENGLISH LANGUAGE LEARNERS

For the **ELLs** who need **phonics, decoding,** and **fluency** practice, use scaffolding methods as necessary to ensure children understand the meaning of the words. Refer to the Language Transfer Handbook for phonics elements that may not transfer in students' native languages.

Approaching Level

Phonics

SOUND-SPELLING REVIEW

TIER 2

OBJECTIVES

Associate the long and short sounds with common spellings (graphemes) for the five major vowels. **RF.K.3b**

Display the **Word-Building Card** *h*. Say the letter name and the sound it stands for: *h*, /h/. Repeat for *e, f, r, b, l, k,* and *c*.

Display Word-Building Cards one at a time and together say the letter name and the sound that each letter stands for.

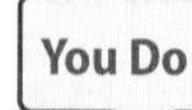
Display Word-Building Cards one at a time and have children say the letter name and the sound that each letter stands for.

CONNECT *u* TO /u/

TIER 2

OBJECTIVES

Demonstrate basic knowledge of one-to-one letter-sound correspondences by producing the primary or many of the most frequent sounds for each consonant. **RF.K.3a**

Display the *Umbrella* **Sound-Spelling Card**. *The letter* u *can stand for /u/ at the beginning of* umbrella. *What is this letter? What sound does it stand for? I will write* u *when I hear /u/ in these words: up, at, under, undo, empty.*

The word until *begins with /u/. Let's write* u. Guide children to write *u* when they hear a word that begins with /u/. Say: *until, uncle, apple, itch, ugly.*

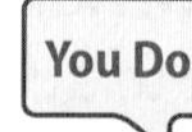
Say the following words and have children write the letter *u* if a word begins with /u/: *us, it, under, edge, on, up.*

RETEACH

OBJECTIVES

Know and apply grade-level phonics and word analysis skills in decoding words. **RF.K.3**

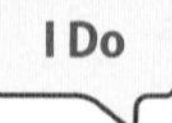
Display **Reading/Writing Workshop**, p. 6. The letter *u* stands for the /u/ sound you hear at the beginning of *umbrella*. Say *umbrella,* emphasizing /u/.

Have children name each picture in row 1. Say the word again, emphasizing /u/. Repeat for row 2, emphasizing the medial sound /u/.

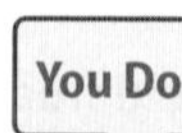
Guide children in reading the words in row 3. Then have them read the words in row 4, offering assistance as needed.

BLEND WORDS WITH /u/ *u*

OBJECTIVES

CCSS Isolate and pronounce the initial, medial vowel, and final sounds (phonemes) in three-phoneme words. **RF.K.2d**

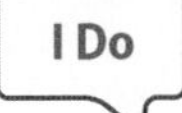

Display the **Word-Building Cards** *s, u,* and *n. This is the letter* s. *It stands for* /s/. *This is the letter* u. *It stands for* /u/. *This is the letter* n. *It stands for* /n/. *Listen as I blend all three sounds:* /sssuuunnn/, sun. *The word is* sun. Repeat for *up*.

Now let's blend more sounds to make words. Make the word *us*. *Let's blend:* /uuusss/, us. Have children blend to read the word. Repeat with the word *bug*. *Let's blend:* /buuug/, bug.

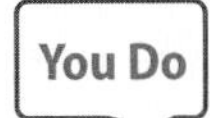

Distribute Word-Building Cards with *b, u, s, c, p,* and *t*. Write: *bus, us, cup, up, but*. Have children form the words and then blend and read the words.

REREAD FOR FLUENCY

OBJECTIVES

CCSS Read emergent-reader texts with purpose and understanding. **RF.K.4**

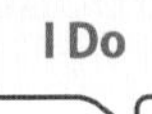

Turn to p. 8 of **Reading/Writing Workshop** and read aloud the title. *Let's read the title together*. Page through the book. Ask children what they see in each picture. Ask children to find the word *have* on pp. 9 and 11 and the word *for* on p. 15.

Then have children open their books and chorally read the story. Have children point to each word as they read. Provide corrective feedback as needed. After reading, ask children to think of something that the cub does for fun.

Have children reread "A Pup and a Cub" with a partner for fluency.

BUILD FLUENCY WITH PHONICS

Sound/Spelling Fluency

Display the following Word-Building Cards: *h, e, f, r, b, l, k, c,* and *u*. Have children chorally say each sound. Repeat and vary the pace.

Fluency in Connected Text

Write the following sentences. *The sun is up for us. We have to go to the bus. Do you have a cup for me?* Have children read the sentences and identify the words with /u/.

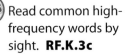

Approaching Level

High-Frequency Words

TIER 2

RETEACH WORDS

OBJECTIVES

Read common high-frequency words by sight. **RF.K.3c**

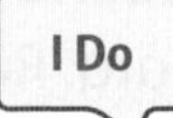

Display the **High-Frequency Word Card** *for* and use the **Read/Spell/Write** routine to reteach the word. Repeat for *have.*

Have children turn to p. 7 of **Reading/Writing Workshop** and discuss the first photo. Then read aloud the first sentence. Reread the sentence with children. Then distribute index cards with the word *have* written on them. Have children match their word cards with the word *have* in the sentence. Use the same routine for *for* and the other sentence on the page.

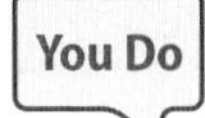

Write the sentence frame *I have* _____ *for my pet*. Have children copy the sentence frame on their **Response Boards**. Then have partners work together to read and orally complete the frame by talking about what they might give to a pet. Reteach previously introduced high-frequency words using the **Read/Spell/Write** routine.

CUMULATIVE REVIEW

OBJECTIVES

Read common high-frequency words by sight. **RF.K.3c**

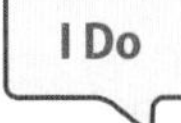

Display the **High-Frequency Word Cards** *I, can, the, we, see, a, like, to, and, go, you, do, my, are, he, with, is, little, she, was, for,* and *have*. Use the **Read/Spell/Write** routine to review words. Use the High-Frequency Word Cards and **Word-Building Cards** to create sentences such as *Do you have it? You and I are on the bus.*

Use the **Read/Spell/Write** routine with children to review words. Invite a volunteer to write the words on the board. Offer help as needed. Then guide children to create a sentence as a class using the High-Frequency Word Cards and Word-Building Cards.

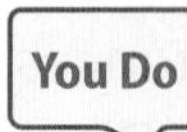

Have partners use the High-Frequency Word Cards and Word-Building Cards to create short sentences.

Oral Vocabulary

REVIEW WORDS

OBJECTIVES

CCSS Identify real-life connections between words and their use. **L.K.5c**

Develop oral vocabulary: *appearance, behavior, exercise, wander, plenty*

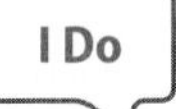

Use the **Define/Example/Ask** routine to review words. Use the following definitions and provide examples:

appearance The way that something looks is its **appearance**.

behavior **Behavior** is the way a person or an animal acts.

exercise When you **exercise**, you do an activity to improve your body.

wander When you **wander**, you move around without a particular place to go.

plenty When there is **plenty** of something, there is enough.

Ask questions to build understanding. *How would you describe a duck's appearance? When have you seen someone show good behavior? Why do we need to exercise? Where would be a good place to wander around? What is something you have plenty of at home?*

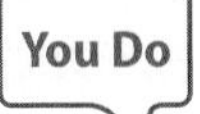

Have children complete these sentence frames: *I like the appearance of a ______. A dog shows good behavior when it ______. My favorite way to get exercise is to ______. We should not wander away from our families when we go out because ______. A chick needs plenty of ______.*

Comprehension

SELF-SELECTED READING

OBJECTIVES

With prompting and support, ask and answer questions about key details in a text. **RI.K.1**

Apply the strategy and skill to reread the text

Read Independently

Help children select a nonfiction text with photographs for sustained silent reading. Remind children that they can better understand information when they read again. Explain that they can use photographs to help them figure out how things are alike and how they are different.

Read Purposefully

Before reading, ask children to select a photograph that includes two things they want to compare. Remind them to read again if they don't understand something. After reading, guide children to compare the photographs: *The two things are alike because ______. They are different because ______. Reading again helped me understand how ______.*

On Level

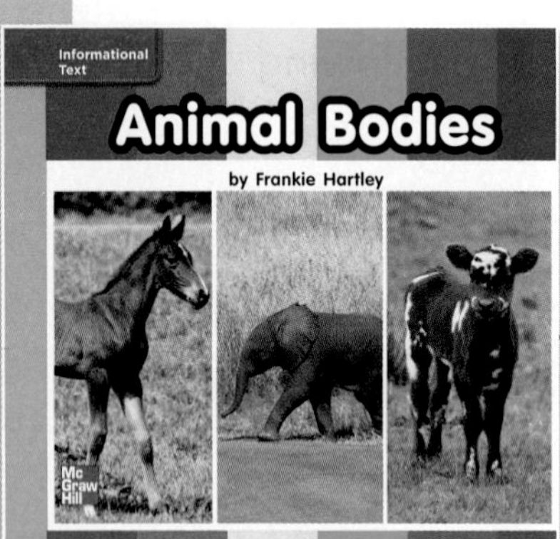

Leveled Reader

OBJECTIVES

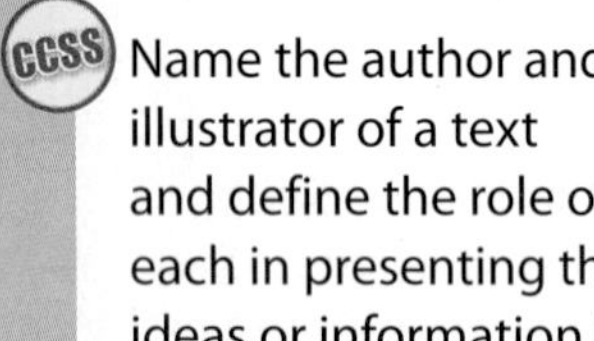

With prompting and support, describe the connection between two individuals, events, ideas, or pieces of information in a text. **RI.K.3**

Name the author and illustrator of a text and define the role of each in presenting the ideas or information in a text. **RI.K.6**

Read emergent-reader texts with purpose and understanding. **RF.K.4**

Leveled Reader: *Animal Bodies*

Leveled Readers

Before Reading

Preview and Predict

Show children the cover of the book. Have children point to and read the title with you. Point out the author's name. Ask: *What does the author do?* Guide children through the photos on each page. Ask: *What do you think this book is comparing?*

Review Genre: Informational Text

Point out that this is an informational text that gives us ideas and facts about a topic. Say: *You can tell this is an informational text because it has photographs of real animals and it gives us facts about the animals.*

Model Concepts of Print

Have children point to the sentence on page 2. Ask: *What does the first word in the sentence start with?* (a capital letter) *What does the sentence end with?* (a period) *How many words are there in this sentence?* (four)

Review High-Frequency Words

Point out the word *have* on page 2, and read it with children. Ask them to locate *have* on the other pages.

Essential Question

Remind children of the Essential Question: *How are some animals alike and how are they different?* Set a purpose for reading: *Let's read to find out how animal body parts are alike and how they are different.*

During Reading

Guided Comprehension

As children read *Animal Bodies*, monitor and provide guidance by correcting blending and modeling the strategy and skill.

Strategy: Reread

Remind children that if they do not understand one part of the text, they can reread it to help them better understand what is happening.

Skill: Connections Within Text (Compare and Contrast)

Explain to children that as they read it is helpful to think about how things are the same and how they are different. Model how to use the text and the photos to compare and contrast the animals.

Think Aloud The words on page 2 tell me that these animals have feet. That is one way they are alike. But the photo shows me that the feet are different. Some are paws and some are hooves. Using both the text and the photos to see how things are the same and how they are different helps me understand more about what I read.

As children read the book, guide them to identify details in the pictures and text that help them compare and contrast the animals.

After Reading

Respond to Reading

→ *According to this book, what body parts do some animals not have?* (feet, trunks, tails)

→ *Which animals do not have feet?* (worms, snakes, fish)

→ *What do you have that is different from all the animals in this book?* (hands, two feet)

→ *What do you have that is the same?* (eyes, ears, nose, etc.)

Retell

Have children take turns retelling. Help children make a personal connection by asking: *What other animals have body parts that are different from ours?*

Model Fluency

Read the book aloud, pausing after each page to have children chorally repeat.

Apply Have children practice reading with partners as you observe and provide needed assistance.

LITERACY ACTIVITIES

Have children complete the activities on the inside back cover of the reader.

Level Up

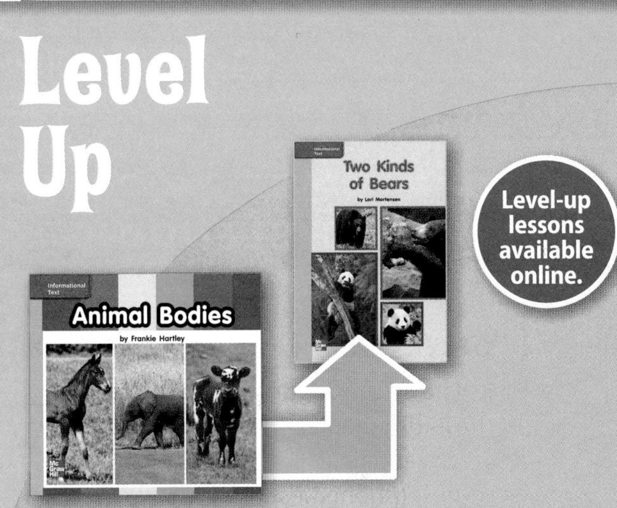

IF Children read *Animal Bodies* On Level with fluency and correctly answer the Respond to Reading questions,

THEN Tell children that they will read another story about how animals are alike and how they are different.

- Have children page through *Two Kinds of Bears* Beyond Level as you guide them to compare and contrast the animals' features and characteristics.
- Have children read the story, monitoring their comprehension and providing assistance as necessary.

On Level

Phonemic Awareness

PHONEME ISOLATION

OBJECTIVES

CCSS Isolate and pronounce the initial, medial vowel, and final sounds (phonemes) in three-phoneme words. **RF.K.2d**

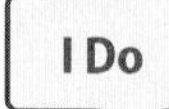

Display the *Under* **Photo Card**. *This is* under. *The first sound is* /u/. *Say it with me.* Repeat with medial /u/ and the *Nut* Photo Card.

Say *uncle* and have children repeat it. *What is the first sound in* uncle? Say the sound together. *What is the middle sound in* sun? Repeat with *until, undo, bus,* and *jump*.

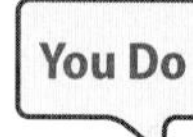

Say these words and have children isolate /u/: *us, up, cut, bug, duck,* and *cub*. Have them tell if /u/ is the initial or medial sound.

PHONEME BLENDING

OBJECTIVES

CCSS Isolate and pronounce the initial, medial vowel, and final sounds (phonemes) in three-phoneme words. **RF.K.2d**

Place the *Up, Sun, Bus, Juggle,* and *Jump* Photo Cards facedown. Choose a card. Do not show it to children. *These are the sounds in the word* up: /u/ /p/. *I will blend the sounds:* /uuup/, up. *The word is* up. Show the picture.

Choose another picture and say the sounds in the word. Together say and blend the sounds to say the word. Then show the picture.

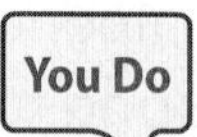

Continue choosing Photo Cards. Say the sounds and have children blend the sounds and say the words.

PHONEME DELETION

OBJECTIVES

CCSS Demonstrate understanding of spoken words, syllables, and sounds (phonemes). **RF.K.2**

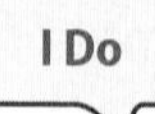

The puppet can say a word and take the first sound away to make a new word. Listen: bus. *Bus without /b/ is us.*

Listen as the puppet says another word: cup. *What new word does the puppet make by taking away /k/ from* cup? Have children repeat both words.

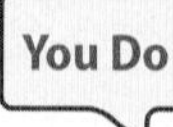

Say snow. *Now say snow without /s/.* (no) Repeat routine with the following: *bus* to *us; stop* to *top; flake* to *lake; struck* to *truck; clean* to *lean.*

Phonics

REVIEW PHONICS

OBJECTIVES

CCSS Demonstrate basic knowledge of one-to-one letter-sound correspondences by producing the primary or many of the most frequent sounds for each consonant. **RF.K.3a**

Display **Reading/Writing Workshop**, p. 6. Point to the *Umbrella* **Sound-Spelling Card**. *What letter stands for the /u/ sound you hear at the beginning of* umbrella? *The letter is* u.

Have children say the name of each picture in rows 1 and 2. Then ask them to identify the words with /u/ at the beginning and in the middle.

Have children read each word in rows 3 and 4. Repeat, asking them to raise their hands if they hear /u/ in the middle of the word and keeping their hands lowered if they hear /u/ in the beginning of the word.

PICTURE SORT

OBJECTIVES

CCSS Demonstrate basic knowledge of one-to-one letter-sound correspondences by producing the primary or many of the most frequent sounds for each consonant. **RF.K.3a**

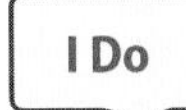

Display **Word-Building Cards** *u* and *o* in a pocket chart. Then show the *Sun* **Photo Card**. Say /s/ /u/ /n/, *sun*. Tell children that the sound in the middle is /u/. *The letter* u *stands for* /u/. *I will put the sun under the letter* u. Show the *Rock* Photo Card. Say /r/ /o/ /k/, *rock*. Tell children that the middle sound is /o/. *The letter* o *stands for* /o/. *I will put the Photo Card for* rock *under the* o.

Show the *Bus* Photo Card and say *bus*, /b/ /u/ /s/. Have children repeat. Then have them tell the sound they hear in the middle of *bus*. Ask them if they should place the photo under the *u* or the *o*.

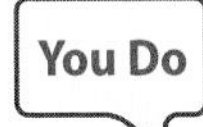

Continue the activity using the *Box, Butter, Dog, Doll, Fox, Juggle, Jump, Mop,* and *Nut* Photo Cards. Have children say the picture name and the sounds in the name. Then have them place the card under the *u* or *o*.

On Level

Phonics

BLEND WORDS WITH SHORT *u*

OBJECTIVES

Isolate and pronounce the initial, medial vowel, and final sounds (phonemes) in three-phoneme words. **RF.K.2d**

Use **Word-building Cards** or write *c, u, b. This is the letter* c. *It stands for* /k/. *Say it with me:* /k/. *This is the letter* u. *It stands for* /u/. *Say it with me:* /uuu/. *This is the letter* b. *It stands for* /b/. *Say it with me:* /b/. *I'll blend the sounds together to read the word:* /kuuub/, cub.

Write *up* and *fun*. Guide children to blend the words sound by sound to read each word.

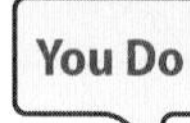

Write the following words. Have children blend the sounds to read each word.

us run sun mud tub duck luck

REREAD FOR FLUENCY

OBJECTIVES

CCSS Read emergent-reader texts with purpose and understanding. **RF.K.4**

I Do

Turn to "A Pup and a Cub" on p. 11 in **Reading/Writing Workshop** and read aloud the second sentence. Tell children that they should make their voices sound exciting when they read a sentence that ends with an exclamation point. Have children repeat the sentence after you. Work with children to read for accuracy and expression.

Reread p. 11. Then have children chorally read the page with you. Continue chorally reading the remainder of the pages.

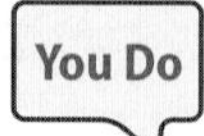

Have partners read "A Pup and a Cub." Provide time to listen as children read the pages. Comment on their accuracy and expression and provide corrective feedback by modeling proper fluency.

High-Frequency Words

REVIEW WORDS

OBJECTIVES

CCSS Read common high-frequency words by sight. **RF.K.3c**

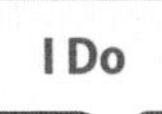

Use the **High-Frequency Word Cards** *for* and *have* with the **Read/Spell/Write** routine to review the words.

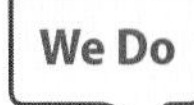

Have children turn to p. 7 of **Reading/Writing Workshop**. Discuss the photographs and read aloud the sentences. Point to the word *have* and have children read it. Then chorally read the sentences. Have children frame the word *have* in the sentence and read the word. Repeat the routine with the word *for*.

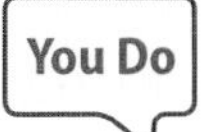

Say the word *have*. Ask children to close their eyes, picture the word, and write it as they see it. Have children self-correct. Repeat the routine with the word *for*.

Reteach previously introduced high-frequency words using the **Read/Spell/Write** routine.

Fluency Point to the **High-Frequency Word Cards** *I, can, the, we, see, a, like, to, and, go, you, do, my, are, he, with, is, little, she, was, have,* and *for* in random order. Have children chorally read. Repeat at a faster pace.

Comprehension

SELF-SELECTED READING

OBJECTIVES

CCSS With prompting and support, ask and answer questions about key details in a text. **RI.K.1**

Apply the strategy and skill to reread the text.

Read Independently

Have children select a nonfiction text with photographs for sustained silent reading. Remind children that they can reread when they don't understand part of a text. This can help them figure out how things are alike and how they are different.

Read Purposefully

Before reading, ask children to point out two photographs that show the same character or place. Tell them to read to find out more about how they are alike and how they are different. Remind children to read again when they don't understand something. After reading, have children identify similarities and differences in the photographs. Ask them to explain how rereading helped them compare and contrast.

Beyond Level

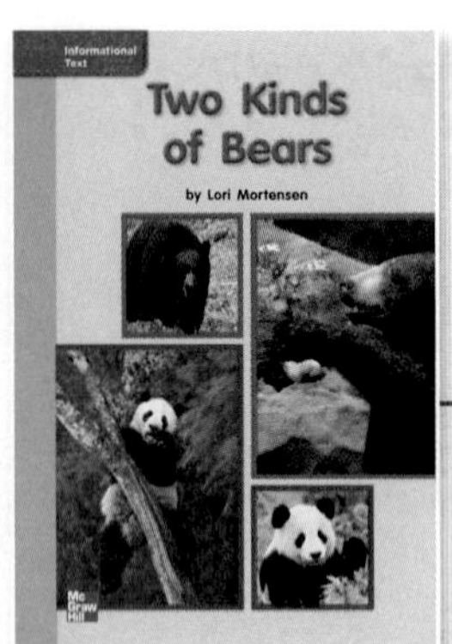

Leveled Reader

OBJECTIVES

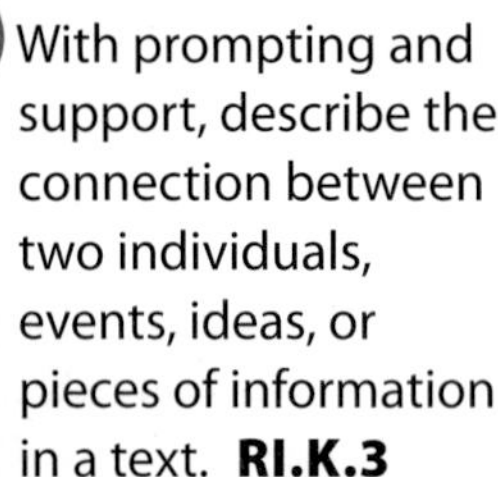

With prompting and support, describe the connection between two individuals, events, ideas, or pieces of information in a text. **RI.K.3**

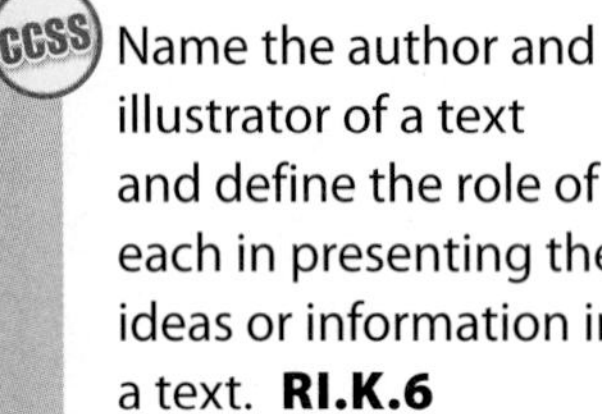

Name the author and illustrator of a text and define the role of each in presenting the ideas or information in a text. **RI.K.6**

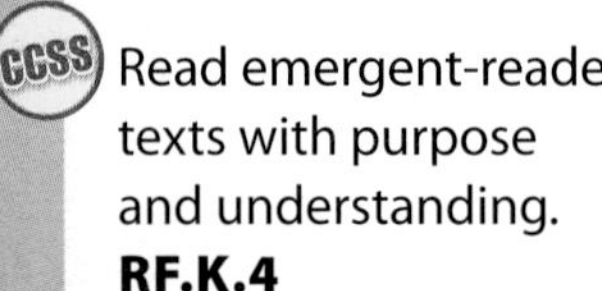

Read emergent-reader texts with purpose and understanding. **RF.K.4**

Leveled Reader: *Two Kinds of Bears*

Go Digital

Leveled Readers

Before Reading

Preview and Predict

Show children the cover of the book. Read aloud the title with children. Ask them to point to the name of the author and ask them to tell what the author does. Preview the photos on the cover and title page. Ask children to predict what the book is about. Preview the rest of the pages with children and point out the photographs and captions.

Review Genre: Informational Text

Explain to children that informational text gives details and facts about real things. Most informational text has photos and captions. Captions give information about the photos. Ask: *How can you tell that this is an informational text?* (It uses photos of real animals.) Encourage children to give specific examples from the book to support their answers.

Essential Question

Remind children of the Essential Question: *How are some animals alike and how are they different?* Help children set a purpose for reading by saying: *Let's find out what makes black bears and giant pandas the same and what makes them different.*

During Reading

Guided Comprehension

As children read *Two Kinds of Bears*, monitor and provide guidance by correcting blending and modeling the strategy and skill. Remind children to read the captions.

Strategy: Reread

Remind children that if they do not understand one part of the text, they can reread it to help them better understand what is happening.

Skill: Connections Within Text (Compare and Contrast)

Explain to children that as they read it is helpful to think about how things are the same and how they are different. Comparing people, animals, or places can help them understand what they are reading.

Think Aloud When I read page 3, I learn that both panda and black bears are alike because they have fur. The text also tells me that they are different because panda bears have black and white fur and black bears have brown fur. The photos show me that both bears have thick fur. The caption tells me that they have different colored fur.

Guide children to use the photos, captions, and text to identify the comparisons and contrasts between the two bears. Have children point to evidence in the text to support their statements.

After Reading

Respond to Reading

→ *Which type of bear eats only bamboo?* (pandas)

→ *Why don't some black bears eat in the winter?* (There is no food in the cold weather.)

→ *What do they do instead?* (sleep in their dens until spring)

→ *Which type of bear has more than one cub?* (black bears)

→ *How are these bears alike?* (Possible answer: They are both bears, they both have furs, claws, and teeth.)

Retell

Have children take turns retelling. Invite them to use the photos, if needed, for support. Help children make a personal connection by asking: *What is the most interesting thing you learned about black bears and giant pandas?*

LITERACY ACTIVITIES

Have children complete the activities on the inside back cover of the reader.

Gifted and Talented

EVALUATING Ask children to recall the different facts they learned about black bears and giant pandas. Challenge them to make a Venn diagram showing the characteristics that are the same and those that are different.

HAVE children tell what else they would like to know about bears (e.g., other types, which ones live in their area or state) and where they could find more information.

Beyond Level

Phonics

REVIEW

OBJECTIVES

Know and apply grade-level phonics and word analysis skills in decoding words. **RF.K.3**

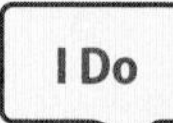

Display **Reading/Writing Workshop**, p. 6. Point to the *Umbrella* **Sound-Spelling Card**. *What is the sound at the beginning of* umbrella? *What letter can stand for /u/? The letter is* u.

Have children say the name of each picture in rows 1 and 2. Then ask children to say more words that begin with /u/ or have /u/ in the middle.

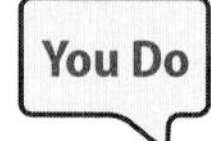

Have partners read each word in rows 3 and 4. Ask them to write them on their **Response Boards**, underlining the letter in each word that stands for /u/.

Fluency Have children reread the story "A Pup and a Cub" for fluency.

Innovate Have children create a new page for "A Pup and a Cub" using the sentence frame: *I _____ for fun.*

REVIEW

OBJECTIVES

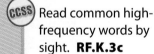

Read common high-frequency words by sight. **RF.K.3c**

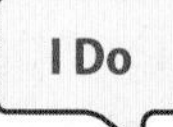

Create **High-Frequency Word Cards** for *run* and *today*. Introduce the words using the **Read/Spell/Write** routine.

Display the High-Frequency Word Cards *we, can, and, have,* and *I*. Have children help you complete the following sentence frames using the High-Frequency Word Cards: _____ *can run and have fun. I can see* _____ *today!*

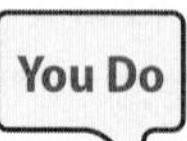

Have partners write sentences using the high-frequency words *run* and *today* on their Response Boards. Have them read their sentences.

Vocabulary

ORAL VOCABULARY: SYNONYMS

OBJECTIVES

CCSS With guidance and support from adults, explore word relationships and nuances in word meanings. **L.K.5**

Develop oral vocabulary: Synonyms

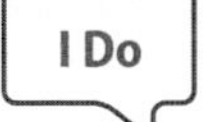

Review the meanings of the oral vocabulary words *plenty* and *wander*. Explain that a synonym is a word that means almost the same thing as another word.

A synonym for plenty *is* enough. *You have plenty when there is enough of something*. There was enough food at the party for everyone.

A synonym for wander *is* roam. *To roam is to walk around with no place special to go*. The children like to roam around the playground.

Have partners think of sentences about a trip to a farm using the words *enough* and *roam.*

Have children share their sentences with the group.

Extend Challenge children to work with a partner to generate three or four more synonyms for *enough* and *roam*. Then have partners tell a story about wild animals using some of the words.

Comprehension

SELF-SELECTED READING

OBJECTIVES

CCSS With prompting and support, ask and answer questions about key details in a text. **RI.K.1**

Apply the strategy and skill to reread the text.

Read Independently

Have children select a nonfiction text with photographs for sustained silent reading. Remind them that rereading can help them understand the text better. Tell them to reread as they make comparisons about the book's settings, events, and characters.

Read Purposefully

Before reading, ask children to choose three interesting photographs from the book. Tell them to note details as they read that will help them compare photographs. After reading, ask children to compare and contrast the photographs, explaining how they are alike and how they are different. Have children explain how rereading helped them make these comparisons. Then ask them to explain why rereading is an important skill.

Independent Study Have children write a few sentences describing something they found surprising or interesting about an animal that they read this week. Ask them to create a book cover illustrating what they wrote about.

English Language Learners

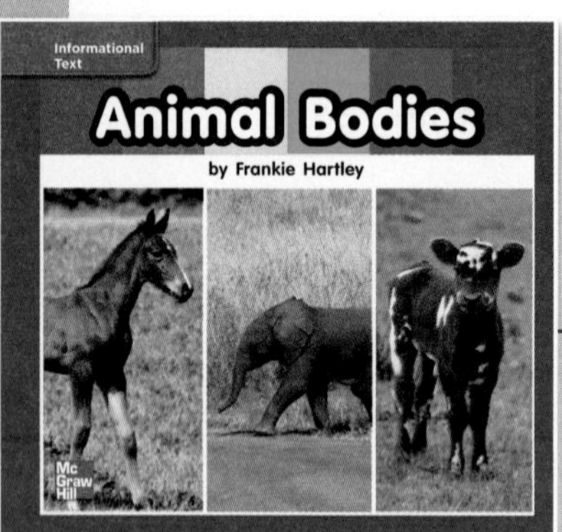

Leveled Reader

OBJECTIVES

With prompting and support, describe the connection between two individuals, events, ideas, or pieces of information in a text. **RI.K.3**

With prompting and support, ask and answer questions about unknown words in a text. **RI.K.4**

Read emergent-reader texts with purpose and understanding. **RF.K.4**

Shared Read: *Animal Bodies*

Go Digital

Leveled Readers

Before Reading

Preview and Predict

Have children point to the title on the cover as you read it aloud. Make sure children understand the English word for *body*. Ask them to point to their feet, hands, and heads. Have them look at the photo on the cover. Say: *This book is about animal body parts. What are some animal parts?* Guide children through the book to preview the photos. Reinforce the word *animals* and the body part shown on each page. Encourage children to ask for help if they do not know a word.

Essential Question

Remind children of the Essential Question: *How are some animals alike and how are they different?* Set a purpose for reading: *As we read this book about animals, think about how their body parts are alike and how they are different.*

During Reading

Interactive Question Response

Pages 2–3 Point to the photos on page 2. Ask: *What part of each animal's body do the pictures show?* (feet) *Point to your feet. Point to the label that says "feet." Let's read this page together.* Point to the photos on page 3 and ask children: *Do these animals have feet?* (No.) *That's right. These animals have no feet. Read this page with me.* Model and encourage children to point under each word as they read.

Pages 4–5 Point to the photo on page 4. Ask: *What do we call this body part? It's a trunk. These animals have trunks. Point to the label on the picture that says "trunks." Do you have trunks? What do you have instead of a trunk?* (a nose) *Let's read this page.* Point to page 5. Ask: *Do these animals have trunks? That's right. These animals have no trunks. Let's read this page together.* Continue to model tracking beneath the print as you read with children.

Pages 6–7 Turn to page 6. Ask: *What do these animals have that makes them the same?* (tails) *Point to the label in the picture that says "tails." Let's read this page together.* Have children turn to page 7. Ask: *Do these animals have tails?* (No.) Read the page with children.

Page 8 Ask children to look at the photo and labels on page 8. Ask: *What do we have that makes us different from the animals in this book?* (hands) *Show me your hands. What sentence could we think of for this page?* (Possible answers: People have hands; this child has hands.)

After Reading

Respond to Reading

→ *What is this book about?* (how animals' bodies are alike and different)

→ *What is something that some animals have that others don't?* (feet, trunks, tails)

→ *What do we have that none of the animals in this book have?* (hands)

Retell

Ask children to look back through the book and take turns retelling. Prompt and support their retelling by providing needed labels and by modeling simple sentence structures they can use to respond.

Model Fluency

Read the sentences one at a time as you track beneath the print, pointing to each word. Have children orally repeat.

Apply Have children read with partners as you monitor. Encourage them to use the photos on each page and prompt them to point beneath each word as they read to reinforce the basic concepts of left to right progression and one-to-one matching of spoken words to print.

LITERACY ACTIVITIES

Have children complete the activities on the inside back cover of the reader.

Level Up

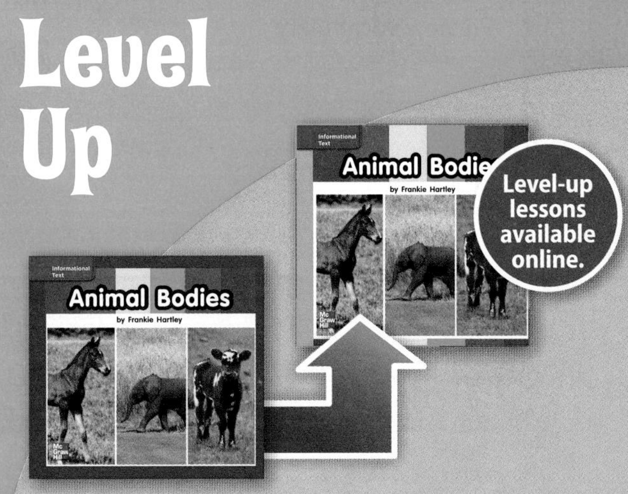

IF Children read *Animal Bodies* **ELL Level** with fluency and correctly answer the Respond to Reading questions,

THEN Tell children that they will read a more detailed version of the story.

- Have children page through *Animal Bodies* **On Level** with you and describe each picture in simple language.
- Have children read the story, monitoring their comprehension and providing assistance as necessary.

English Language Learners

Vocabulary

PRETEACH ORAL VOCABULARY

OBJECTIVES

Speak audibly and express thoughts, feelings, and ideas clearly. **SL.K.6**

LANGUAGE OBJECTIVE

Preview vocabulary

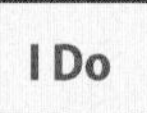

Display the images from the **Visual Vocabulary Cards** and follow the routine to preteach the oral vocabulary words.

Display each image again and explain how it illustrates or demonstrates the word. Model using sentences to describe the image.

Display the word *behavior* again and have children talk to a partner about how the card demonstrates the word.

Beginning	Intermediate	Advanced/High
Prompt children by asking them about common animal behaviors.	Encourage partners to talk about different *behaviors* that people can have.	Ask children to use each word in sentences of their own.

PRETEACH ELL VOCABULARY

OBJECTIVES

Speak audibly and express thoughts, feelings, and ideas clearly. **SL.K.6**

LANGUAGE OBJECTIVE

Preview ELL vocabulary

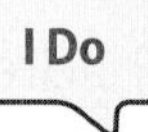

Display the images from the **Visual Vocabulary Cards** one at a time to preteach the ELL vocabulary words *feature* and *detail*. Follow the routine. Say each word and have children repeat it. Define each word in English.

Display each image again and explain how it illustrates or demonstrates the word. Model using sentences to describe the image.

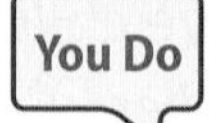

Display the word *detail* again and have children say it. Encourage children to talk about some of the details the picture shows.

Beginning	Intermediate	Advanced/High
Use each word in a sentence. Ask children to repeat each word and sentence.	Have partners talk about things that have a lot of detail.	Use the word *detail* in a sentence and have children use it in a sentence of their own.

High-Frequency Words

REVIEW WORDS

OBJECTIVES

CCSS Read common high-frequency words by sight (e.g., *the, of, to, you, she, my, is, are, do, does*). **RF.K.3c**

LANGUAGE OBJECTIVE

Review high-frequency words

Display the **High-Frequency Word Cards** for *for* and *have*. Read the words. Use the **Read/Spell/Write** routine to teach the words. Have children write the words on their **Response Boards**.

Write a sentence frame that uses the week's high-frequency words. Track the print as children read and complete the sentence: *I have a gift for* ______.
Provide children with examples of how to complete the sentence frame.

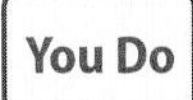

Display a sentence that uses the high-frequency words *for* and *have*. Ask children to point to the words and say them aloud. Then work with children to read and say the entire sentence aloud.

Beginning	Intermediate	Advanced/High
Use the words in another sentence together and have children repeat the sentence orally.	Help partners locate the words in the selections and read the sentences aloud.	Ask children to complete the sentence frame *I have a gift for* ____ in several different ways.

REVIEW CATEGORY WORDS

OBJECTIVES

CCSS Identify real-life connections between words and their use (e.g., note places at school that are *colorful*). **L.K.5c**

LANGUAGE OBJECTIVE

Use category words

Display the **Visual Vocabulary Card** for Animal Features and say the words aloud. Define the words in English and then in Spanish, if appropriate, identifying any cognates.

Point to each animal feature on the card and say each word aloud. Ask children to repeat each word after you. Tell children that these words name animal parts.

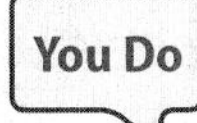

Allow children to look more closely at pictures of animals in the selections. Then have them name as many body parts as they can.

Beginning	Intermediate	Advanced/High
Ask children to say the category words aloud and match each word with one of the pictures.	Help children list other examples of animal parts and point to the animal that has that part.	Have children use the category words to describe animals orally in complete sentences.

English Language Learners

Writing

SHARED WRITING

OBJECTIVES

CCSS Use a combination of drawing, dictating, and writing to narrate a single event or several loosely linked events, tell about the events in the order in which they occurred, and provide a reaction to what happened. **W.K.3**

LANGUAGE OBJECTIVE

Contribute to a shared writing project

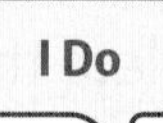

Review the word web from the Whole Group Shared Writing project that names traits of the squirrel. Then model using the information in the web to help you form a sentence: *The squirrel eats nuts.*

Have children help you choose other words from the web to write a shared sentence about the squirrel.

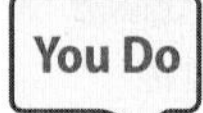

Help partners work together to write another sentence using the word web and a sentence starter: *The squirrel* ______.

Beginning	Intermediate	Advanced/High
Work with individual children to help them write a sentence.	Help children complete the sentence frame with ideas from the web in the Whole Group section.	Ask children to complete the sentence frame on their own, and then read it to a partner.

WRITING TRAIT: WORD CHOICE

OBJECTIVES

CCSS Use a combination of drawing, dictating, and writing to narrate a single event or several loosely linked events, tell about the events in the order in which they occurred, and provide a reaction to what happened. **W.K.3**

LANGUAGE OBJECTIVE

Identify the importance of word choice in writing

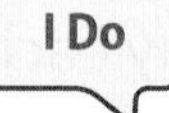

Explain that good writers must choose the best words to get their ideas across. Explain that making good word choices helps improve writing.

Read aloud the section about the fennec fox in the **Big Book** selection *ZooBorns!* Help children identify the descriptive words *radar* ears, *big* ears, and *yummy* insects. Say: *The author chooses the best words to make the page interesting and to help readers picture the fox in their minds.*

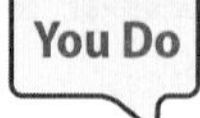

Have partners describe an animal they know, looking back at the Big Book selection for ideas.

Beginning	Intermediate	Advanced/High
Have children draw a picture of the animal. Ask questions to elicit language.	Provide the sentence frame: *Our animal has* ____.	Ask children to write a sentence describing two animals.

Grammar

ACTION WORDS (VERBS)

OBJECTIVES

CCSS Use frequently occurring nouns and verbs. **L.K.1b**

LANGUAGE OBJECTIVE

Learn to use verbs correctly

Language Transfers Handbook

Subject-verb agreement is not used in some languages, such as Cantonese, Haitian Creole, Hmong, Korean, and Vietnamese. As a result, children who speak these languages may omit *-s* in the present tense, third-person agreement. Correct them when they say *He like pizza* instead of *He likes pizza*.

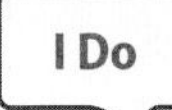

Review with children that a verb is an action word and that every sentence has a verb. Say the following sentence: *The dog runs.* Explain that *runs* is the action that the dog does. *Runs* is the verb in the sentence.

Say the following sentences. Have children verbally identify the verb. The have them say: *The action word is* ______.

The rabbit hops.

The fish swims.

The bird flies.

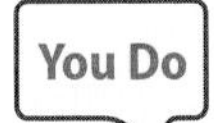

Say the following sentence:

The ______ *can* ______.

Pair children and have them orally complete the sentence frame by providing details from this week's readings. Circulate, listen in, and take note of each child's language use and proficiency.

Beginning	Intermediate	Advanced/High
Prompt discussion about how animals move by looking at pictures from the selections. Ask: *How does this animal get around?*	Ask partners to choose pictures from this week's selections to help them describe how animals move.	Ask children to think from their own experiences about how animals move and get around. Ask them to use this knowledge to complete the sentence frame.

PROGRESS MONITORING

Weekly Assessment

Use your Quick Check observations and the assessment opportunities identified below to evaluate children's progress in key skill areas.

✓ TESTED SKILLS CCSS	Quick Check Observations	Pencil and Paper Assessment
PHONEMIC AWARENESS/ PHONICS **u** /u/ (initial/medial) **RF.K.3a, RF.K.3b**	Can children isolate /u/ and match it to the letter *Uu*?	Practice Book, pp. 185–186, 188
HIGH-FREQUENCY WORDS **for** *for, have* **RF.K.3c**	Can children recognize and read the high-frequency words?	Practice Book, pp. 189–190
COMPREHENSION Connections Within Text: Compare and Contrast **RI.K.3**	As you read *ZooBorns!* with children, can they make connections within the text by comparing and contrasting?	Practice Book, p. 187

Quick Check Rubric

Skills	1	2	3
PHONEMIC AWARENESS/ PHONICS	Does not connect the sound /u/ with the letter *Uu.*	Usually connects the sound /u/ with the letter *Uu.*	Consistently connects the sound /u/ with the letter *Uu.*
HIGH-FREQUENCY WORDS	Does not identify the high-frequency words.	Usually recognizes the high-frequency words with accuracy, but not speed.	Consistently recognizes the high-frequency words with speed and accuracy.
COMPREHENSION	Does not make connections within the text by comparing and contrasting.	Usually makes connections within the text by comparing and contrasting.	Consistently makes connections within the text by comparing and contrasting.

Go Digital! www.connected.mcgraw-hill.com

Using Assessment Results

TESTED SKILLS	If ...	Then ...
PHONEMIC AWARENESS/ PHONICS	**Quick Check Rubric:** Children consistently score 1 or **Pencil and Paper Assessment:** Children get 0–2 items correct	... reteach tested Phonemic Awareness and Phonics skills using Lessons 16–17 in the ***Tier 2 Phonemic Awareness Intervention Online PDFs*** and Lesson 30 in the ***Tier 2 Phonics/ Word Study Intervention Online PDFs.***
HIGH-FREQUENCY WORDS	**Quick Check Rubric:** Children consistently score 1	... reteach tested skills by using the High-Frequency Word Cards and asking children to read and spell the word. Point out any irregularities in sound-spellings.
COMPREHENSION	**Quick Check Rubric:** Children consistently score 1 or **Pencil and Paper Assessment:** Children get 0–1 items correct	... reteach tested skill using Lessons 88–90 in the ***Tier 2 Comprehension Intervention Online PDFs.***

Response to Intervention

Use the children's assessment results to assist you in identifying children who will benefit from focused intervention.

Use the appropriate sections of the ***Placement and Diagnostic Assessment*** to designate children requiring:

Tier 2 Intervention Online PDFs

WonderWorks Intervention Program

→ Phonemic Awareness

→ Phonics

→ Vocabulary

→ Comprehension

→ Fluency

WEEKLY OVERVIEW

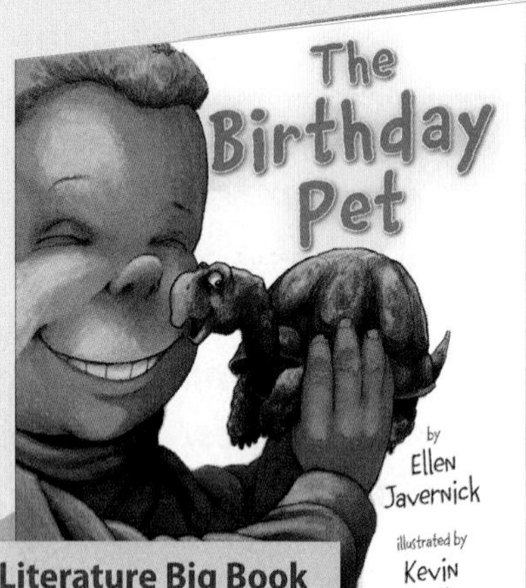

Literature Big Book

Listening Comprehension

The Birthday Pet, 3–32

Genre Fiction

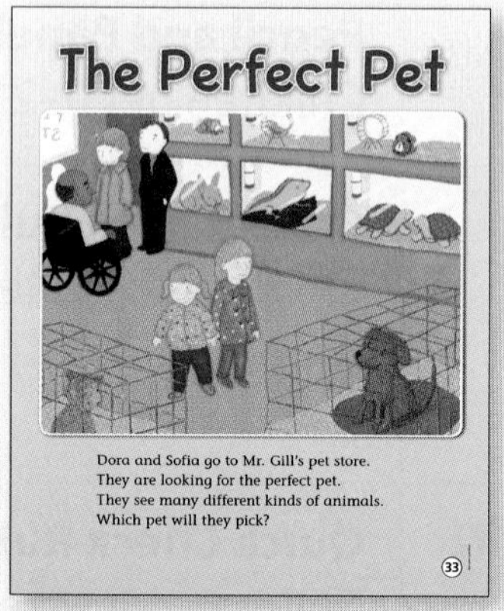

"The Perfect Pet," 33–36

Genre Fiction

Interactive Read-Aloud Cards

"The Family Pet"

Genre Informational Text

Oral Vocabulary

compared **social**

depend **train**

responsibility

Minilessons

✓ **Comprehension Strategy** .... Make, Confirm, and Revise Predictions, T95

✓ **Comprehension Skill** .... Plot: Problem and Solution, T104

Go Digital

www.connected.mcgraw-hill.com

Nathan Love

PET PALS

Essential Question

How do you take care of different kinds of pets?

Big Book and Little Book Reading/Writing Workshop

Shared Reading

Hug Gus!
I can see a big, red pup.
I pick a pup for a pet.

"I Hug Gus!" 22–29

Genre Fiction

High-Frequency Words of, they, T17

Minilessons ✓TESTED SKILLS 

✓**Phonics** .... /g/g, /w/w, T97

Writing Trait........................ Word Choice, T100

Grammar .... Verbs, T101

Differentiated Text

Approaching

On Level

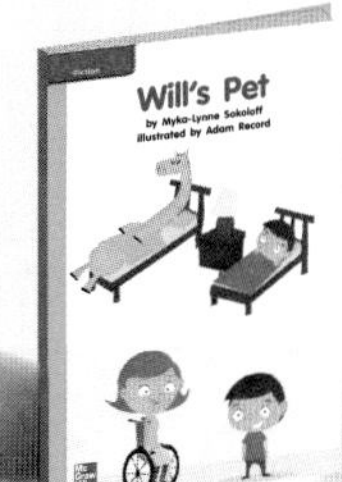

Beyond

ELL

TEACH AND MANAGE

What You Do

INTRODUCE

Weekly Concept

Pet Pals

Reading/Writing Workshop Big Book, 18–19

TEACH AND APPLY

Listening Comprehension

Big Book
The Birthday Pet
Genre Fiction
Paired Read "The Perfect Pet"
Genre Fiction

Minilessons
Strategy: Make, Confirm, and Revise Predictions
Skill: Problem and Solution

Shared Reading

Reading/Writing Workshop
"I Hug Gus"

Minilessons
/g/*g*, /w/*w*, High-Frequency Words: of, they,
Writing, Grammar

Interactive Whiteboard

Interactive Whiteboard

Mobile

What Your Students Do

WEEKLY CONTRACT

PDF Online

Online To-Do List

PRACTICE AND ONLINE ACTIVITIES

Your Turn Practice Book, pp. 193–202

Name

under | gift | goat
guitar | sock | gate
ladder | gum | kite

Phonemic Awareness: /g/
Say the name of each picture. Put a marker on each picture if its name begins with the /g/ sound.

Unit 7: The Animal Kingdom • Week 2 193

Online Activities

Leveled Readers

Mobile

DIFFERENTIATE

Small Group Instruction

Leveled Readers

Mobile

INTEGRATE

Research and Inquiry

Pet-Care Poster, pp. T134–T135

Text Connections

Compare Pets, p. T136

Talk About Reading

Becoming Readers, p. T137

Online Research

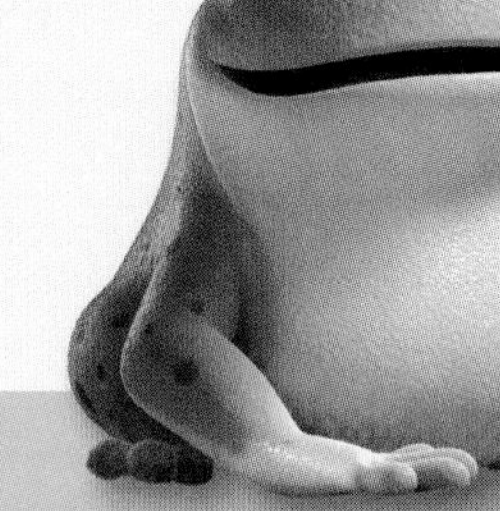

WORKSTATION CARDS

More Activities on back of cards

20 Following Rules (SOCIAL STUDIES)

1. Talk about safety.
2. Think about safety rules.

21 Put Things in Order (WRITING)

It is best to follow an order when you do something.

1. Draw a sandwich you like.
2. Label your sandwich.

cheese bread

20 Funny Fish Mural (PHONICS/WORD STUDY)

Think of words with *g* and *w*.

guitar

1. Think of words.
2. Draw a funny fish.
3. Name your funny fish.

guitar fish

Go Digital! www.connected.mcgraw-hill.com • Interactive Games and Activities • Grade K

10 Problem and Solution (READING)

A solution solves a problem.

1. Read a book.
2. Talk about a problem.
3. Draw the problem and solution.

Go Digital! www.connected.mcgraw-hill.com • Interactive Games and Activities • Grade K

Nathan Love

DEVELOPING READERS AND WRITERS

Write About Reading • Analytical Writing

Write to Sources and Research

Respond to Reading, T95, T143, T151, T157, T161

Connect to Essential Question, T95, T127

Problem and Solution, T109

Research and Inquiry, T134

Teacher's Edition

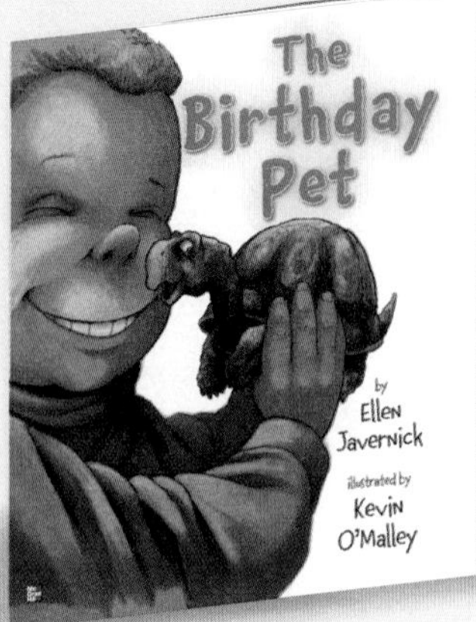

Literature Big Book
The Birthday Pet
Paired Read: *The Perfect Pet*

Interactive Whiteboard

Leveled Readers
Responding to Texts

Writing Process • Independent Writing

Informational Text
Explanatory Sentences, T122–T123, T132, T140

Conferencing Routines
Peer Conferences, T132

Interactive Whiteboard

Teacher's Edition

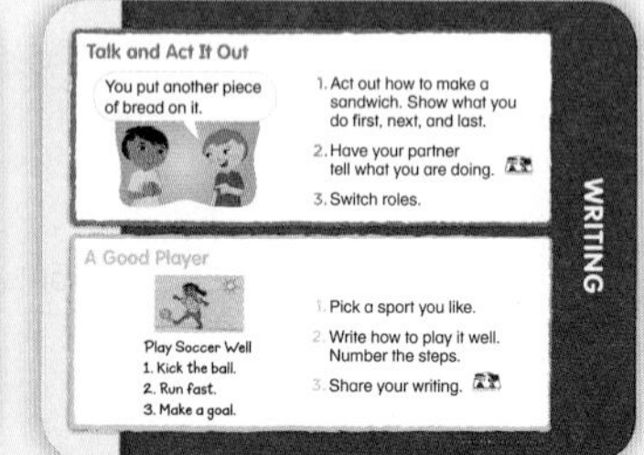

Leveled Workstation Card
Put Things in Order, Card 21

WEEK 2

Writing Traits • Shared and Interactive Writing

Writing Trait:
Word Choice
Explanatory Sentences, T100, T114

Teacher's Edition

Word Choice, p. 32
Verbs, p. 33
Reading/Writing Workshop

Interactive Whiteboard

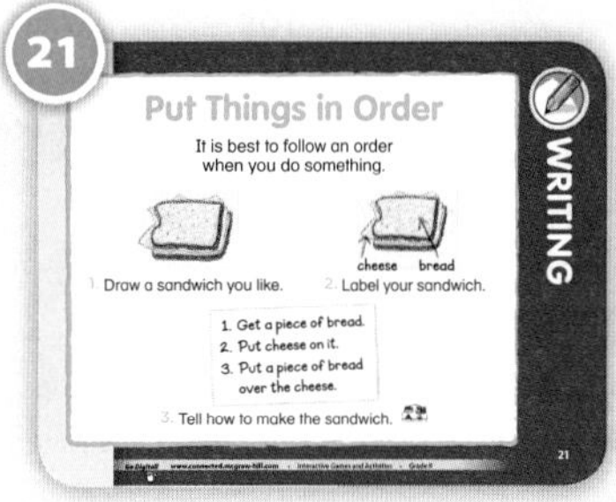

Leveled Workstation Card
Put Things in Order, Card 21

Grammar and Spelling/Dictation

Grammar
Action Words (Verbs), T101

Spelling/Dictation
Words with Short *a*, *e*, and *w*, *g*, *b*, *s*, T129, T139

Interactive Whiteboard

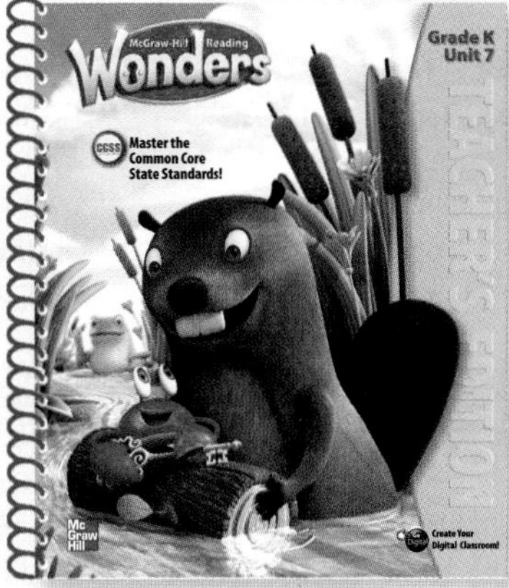
Teacher's Edition

Online Grammar Games

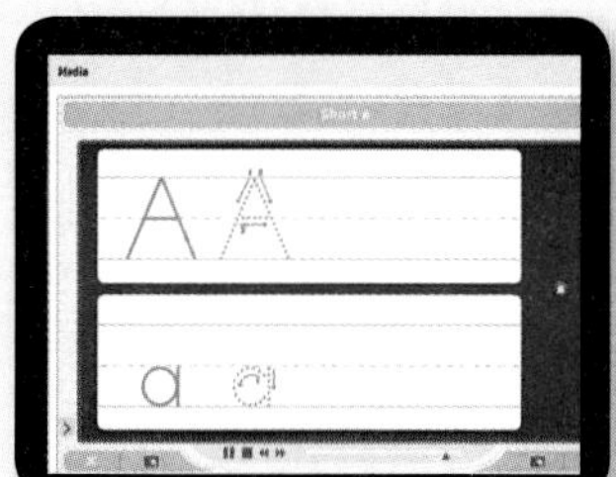
Handwriting

SUGGESTED LESSON PLAN

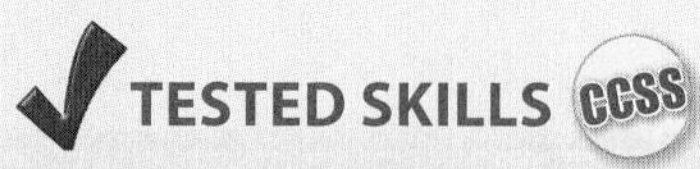

		DAY 1	DAY 2
Whole Group	**READING**		
	Teach and Model 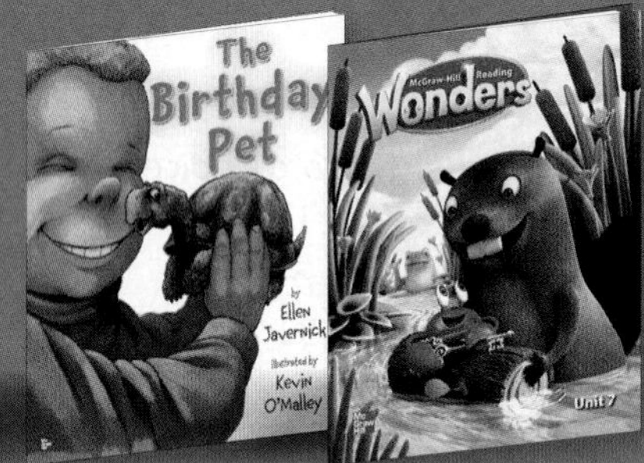 Literature Big Book Reading/Writing Workshop	**Build Background** Pet Pals, T92 **Oral Vocabulary Words** responsibility, train, T92 ✓**Listening Comprehension** • Genre: Fiction • Strategy: Make, Confirm, and Revise Predictions, T95 **Big Book** *The Birthday Pet* ✓**Word Work** **Phonemic Awareness** • Phoneme Isolation, T96 **Phonics** • Introduce /g/*g*, /w/*w*, T97 **Handwriting** Gg, Ww, T98 **High-Frequency Words** of, they, T99 **Practice** *Your Turn* 193–196	**Oral Language** Pet Pals, T102 ✓**Category Words** Pet Words, T103 ✓**Listening Comprehension** • Genre: Fiction • Strategy: Make, Confirm, and Revise Predictions, T104 • Skill: Plot: Problem and Solution, T104 • Guided Retelling, T109 • Model Fluency, T109 **Big Book** *The Birthday Pet* ✓**Word Work** **Phonemic Awareness** • Phoneme Isolation, T110 **Phonics** • Review *g* and *w*, T110 **High-Frequency Words** of, they, T111 **Shared Reading** "I Hug Gus!" T112–T113 **Practice** *Your Turn* 197
Small Group	**DIFFERENTIATED INSTRUCTION** Choose across the week to meet your student's needs.		
	Approaching Level 	**Leveled Reader** *My Cats,* T142–T43 **Phonological Awareness** Recognize and Generate Rhyme, T144  **Phonics** Sound-Spelling Review, T146 TIER 2 **High-Frequency Words** Reteach Words, T148 TIER 2	**Leveled Reader** *My Cats,* T142–T43 **Phonemic Awareness** Phoneme Isolation, T144 TIER 2 **Phonics** Connect *g* to /g/ and *w* to /w/, T146 TIER 2 **High-Frequency Words** Cumulative Review, T148
	On Level 	**Leveled Reader** *Their Pets,* T150–T151 **Phonemic Awareness** Phoneme Isolation, T152 **Phonics** Review Phonics, T153	**Leveled Reader** *Their Pets,* T150–T151 **Phonemic Awareness** Phoneme Blending, T152 **Phonics** Picture Sort, T153 **High-Frequency Words** Review Words, T155
	Beyond Level 	**Leveled Reader** *Will's Pet,* T156–T157 **Phonics** Review, T158 	**Leveled Reader** *Will's Pet,* T156–T157 **High-Frequency Words** Review, T158
	English Language Learners 	**Leveled Reader** *Their Pets,* T160–T161 **Phonological Awareness** Recognize and Generate Rhyme, T144 TIER 2 **Phonics** Sound-Spelling Review, T146 TIER 2 **Vocabulary** Preteach Oral Vocabulary, T162 **Writing** Shared Writing, T164	**Leveled Reader** *Their Pets,* T160–T161 **Phonemic Awareness** Phoneme Isolation, T144 TIER 2 **Phonics** Connect *g* to /g/ and *w* to /w/, T146 TIER 2 **High-Frequency Words** Cumulative Review, T148 **Vocabulary** Preteach ELL Vocabulary, T162
Whole Group	**LANGUAGE ARTS**		
	Writing and Grammar	**Shared Writing** Writing Trait: Word Choice, T100 Write an Explanatory Text, T100 **Grammar** Action Words (Verbs), T101	**Interactive Writing** Writing Trait: Word Choice, T114 Write an Explanatory Text, T114 **Grammar** Action Words (Verbs), T115

Go Digital

CUSTOMIZE YOUR OWN LESSON PLAN

www.connected.mcgraw-hill.com

WEEK 2

	DAY 3	DAY 4	DAY 5 Review and Assess
READING	**Oral Language** Pet Pals, T116 **Oral Vocabulary** depend, compared, social, T116 ✓**Listening Comprehension** • Genre: Informational Text • Strategy: Make Predictions, T117 • Make Connections, T117 **Interactive Read Aloud** "The Family Pet," T117 ✓**Word Work** **Phonemic Awareness** • Phoneme Blending, T118 **Phonics** • Blend Words with Short *i, a, e* and *g, w, t, p, b, s, n, l*, T119 **High-Frequency Words** of, they, T121 **Practice** *Your Turn* 198–200	**Oral Language** Pet Pals, T124 ✓**Category Words** Pet Words, T125 ✓**Listening Comprehension** • Genre: Fiction • Strategy: Make Predictions, T126 • Text Feature: Chart, T126 • Make Connections, T127 **Big Book** Paired Read: "The Perfect Pet," T126 ✓**Word Work** **Phonemic Awareness** • Phoneme Substitution, T128 **Phonics** • Blend Words with Short *e* and *w, g, b, s*, T128 **High-Frequency Words** of, they, T129 **Shared Reading** "I Hug Gus!" T130–T131 **Integrate Ideas** Research and Inquiry, T134–T135 **Practice** *Your Turn* 201	**Integrate Ideas** • Text Connections, T136 • Talk About Reading, T137 • Research and Inquiry, T137 ✓**Word Work** **Phonemic Awareness** Phoneme Substitution, T138 **Phonics** • Read Words with Short *a, e* and *g, w, b*, T138 **High-Frequency Words** of, they, T139  **Practice** *Your Turn* 202
DIFFERENTIATED INSTRUCTION	**Leveled Reader** *My Cats*, T142–T43 **Phonemic Awareness** Phoneme Blending, T145 **Phonics** Reteach, T146 **High-Frequency Words** Reteach Words, T148	**Leveled Reader** *My Cats*, T142–T43 **Phonemic Awareness** Phoneme Substitution, T145 **Phonics** Blend Words with /g/*g* and /w/*w*, T147 **Oral Vocabulary** Review Words, T149	**Leveled Reader** Literacy Activities, T143 **Phonemic Awareness** Phoneme Substitution, T145 **Phonics** Reread for Fluency, T147 Build Fluency with Phonics, T147 **Comprehension** Self-Selected Reading, T149
	Leveled Reader *Their Pets*, T150–T151 **Phonemic Awareness** Phoneme Substitution, T152 **Phonics** Blend Words with *g* and *w*, T154	**Leveled Reader** *Their Pets*, T150–T151 **Phonics** Blend Words with *g* and *w*, T154 Reread for Fluency, T154	**Leveled Reader** Literacy Activities, T151 **Comprehension** Self-Selected Reading, T155
	Leveled Reader *Will's Pet*, T156–T157 **Vocabulary** Oral Vocabulary: Synonyms, T159 Gifted and Talented	**Leveled Reader** *Will's Pet*, T156–T157 **Phonics** Innovate, T158	**Leveled Reader** Literacy Activities, T157 **Comprehension** Self-Selected Reading, T159 
	Leveled Reader *Their Pets*, T160–T161 **Phonemic Awareness** Phoneme Blending, T145 **Phonics** Reteach, T146 **High-Frequency Words** Review Words, T163 **Writing** Writing Trait: Word Choice, T164	**Leveled Reader** *Their Pets*, T160–T161 **Phonemic Awareness** Phoneme Substitution, T145 **Phonics** Blend Words with /g/*g* and /w/*w*, T147 **Vocabulary** Review Category Words, T163 **Grammar** Verbs, T165	**Leveled Reader** Literacy Activities, T161 **Phonemic Awareness** Phoneme Substitution, T145 **Phonics** Reread for Fluency, T147 Build Fluency with Phonics, T147
LANGUAGE ARTS	**Independent Writing** Writing Trait: Word Choice, T122 Write an Explanatory Text Prewrite/Draft, T122–T123 **Grammar** Action Words (Verbs), T123	**Independent Writing** Writing Trait: Word Choice, T132 Write an Explanatory Text Revise/Final Draft, T132 **Grammar** Action Words (Verbs), T133	**Independent Writing** Write an Explanatory Text Prepare/Present/Evaluate/Publish, T140 **Grammar** Action Words (Verbs), T141

DIFFERENTIATE TO ACCELERATE

Scaffold to Access Complex Text

IF the text complexity of a particular section is too difficult for children

THEN see the references noted in the chart below for scaffolded instruction to help children Access Complex Text.

	Literature Big Book	Reading/Writing Workshop	Leveled Readers
	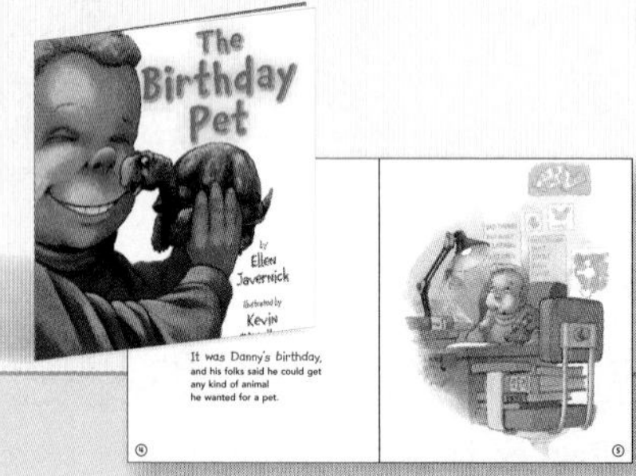		
Quantitative	*The Birthday Pet* **Lexile** 530 Paired Selection: "The Perfect Pet" **Lexile** 500	"I Hug Gus" **Lexile** 310	**Approaching Level** **Lexile** BR **On Level** **Lexile** 270 **Beyond Level** **Lexile** 190 **ELL** **Lexile** BR
Qualitative	What Makes the Text Complex? • **Organization** Recognizing Clues to Make Predictions, T104 ACT *See Scaffolded Instruction in Teacher's Edition, T104.*	What Makes the Text Complex? **Foundational Skills** • Decoding with *g, w*, T110–T111 • Identifying high-frequency words, T111	What Makes the Text Complex? **Foundational Skills** • Decoding with *g, w* • Identifying high-frequency words *of, they* *See Level Up lessons online for Leveled Readers.*
Reader and Task	The Introduce the Concept lesson on pages T92–T93 will help determine the reader's knowledge and engagement in the weekly concept. See pages T94–T95, T105–T109, T126–T127 and T134–T137 for questions and tasks for this text.	The Introduce the Concept lesson on pages T92–T93 will help determine the reader's knowledge and engagement in the weekly concept. See pages T112–T113, T130–T131 and T134–T137 for questions and tasks for this text.	The Introduce the Concept lesson on pages T92–T93 will help determine the reader's knowledge and engagement in the weekly concept. See pages T142–T143, T150–T151, T156–T157, T160–T161 and T134–T137 for questions and tasks for this text.

Nathan Love

BR = Epitome of a beginning reader

WEEK 2

Monitor and *Differentiate*

IF you need to differentiate instruction

THEN use the Quick Checks to assess children's needs and select the appropriate small group instruction focus.

Comprehension Strategy Make, Confirm, and Revise Predictions, T117

Phonemic Awareness/Phonics /g/*g*, /w/*w*, T99, T111, T121, T129, T139

High-Frequency Words *of*, *they*, T99, T111, T121, T129, T139

If No →	Approaching	**Reteach,** pp. T142–T149
	ELL	**Develop,** pp. T160–T165
If Yes →	On Level	**Review,** pp. T150–T155
	Beyond Level	**Extend,** pp. T156–T159

Level Up with Leveled Readers

IF children can read their leveled text fluently and answer comprehension questions

THEN work with the next level up to accelerate children's reading with more complex text.

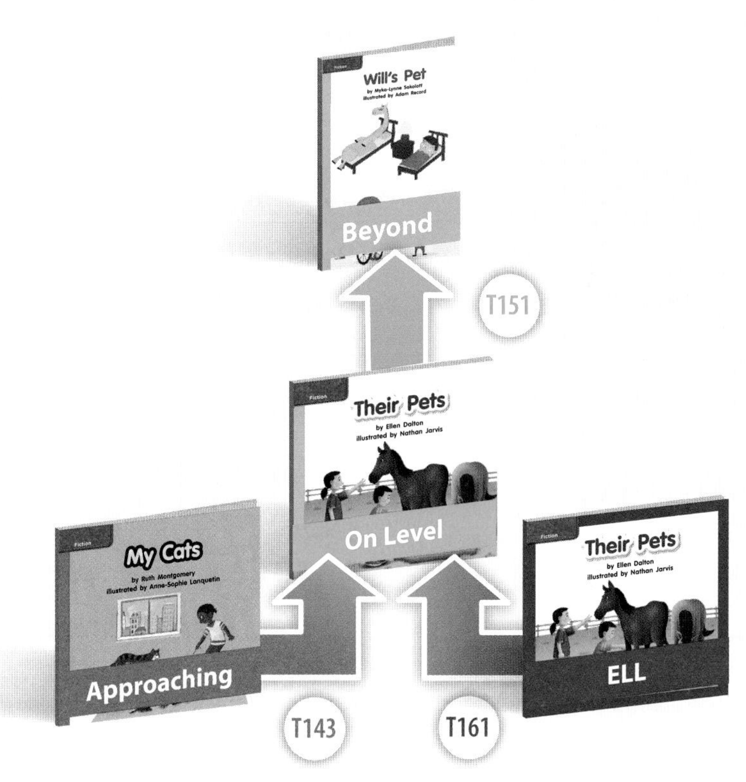

ENGLISH LANGUAGE LEARNERS SCAFFOLD

IF ELL students need additional support **THEN** scaffold instruction using the small group suggestions.

Reading-Writing Workshop / Integrate Ideas	Leveled Reader	Phonological Awareness	Phonics	Oral Vocabulary / High-Frequency Words	Writing	Grammar
Reading-Writing Workshop T93 "Animal Pals" **Integrate Ideas** T135	**Leveled Reader** T160–T161 *Their Pets*	**Phonological Awareness** Recognize and Generate Rhyme, T144 Phoneme Isolation, T144 Phoneme Blending, T145 Phoneme Substitution, T145	**Phonics,** /g/*g*, /w/*w*, T146–T147	**Oral Vocabulary,** T162 responsibility, train, compare, social, depend **High-Frequency Words,** T163 *they, of*	**Writing** Shared Writing, T164 Writing Trait: Word Choice, T164	**Grammar** T165 Verbs

Note: Include ELL Students in all small groups based on their needs.

WHOLE GROUP
DAY 1

Materials

Reading/Writing Workshop Big Book
UNIT 7

Literature Big Book
The Birthday Pet

Response Board

Visual Vocabulary Cards
responsibility train

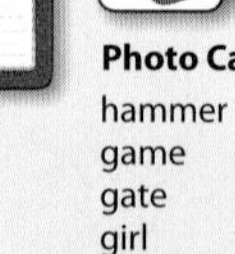
Photo Cards
hammer
game
gate
girl
gorilla
guitar
nail
sandwich
walrus
watch
water
watermelon
web
window
wolf

Sound-Spelling Cards
guitar
window

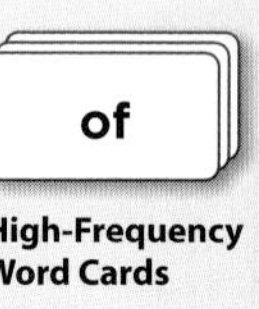

High-Frequency Word Cards
of
they

Think Aloud Cloud

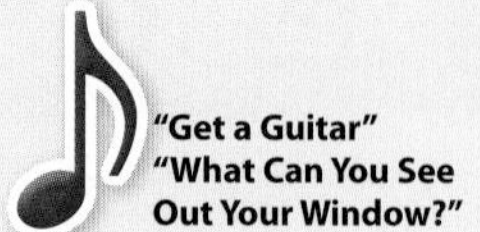
"Get a Guitar"
"What Can You See Out Your Window?"

Introduce the Concept

Build Background

Reading/Writing Workshop Big Book

OBJECTIVES

CCSS Confirm understanding of a text read aloud or information presented orally or through other media by asking and answering questions about key details and requesting clarification if something is not understood. **SL.K.2**

CCSS Identify real-life connections between words and their use. **L.K.5c**

ESSENTIAL QUESTION

How do you take care of different kinds of pets?

Read aloud the Essential Question. Tell children you are going to say a rhyme about a pet dog and its behavior.

My Carefree Dog

My dog is very carefree.
He greets everyone, you see.
So don't scream when you meet—
He is really so sweet—
And he'll soon let you
Up off the street!

Read the rhyme "My Carefree Dog" with children. *What does the dog in the rhyme do when it greets people?* (knocks people down) *Do you think this is good behavior? What should the owner do?* (Possible answer: No. Teach the dog to behave.) Tell children that this week they will read to find out how to take care of different kinds of pets.

Oral Vocabulary Words

Use the **Define/Example/Ask** routine to introduce the oral vocabulary words **responsibility** and **train**.

To introduce the theme of "Pet Pals," explain that pet owners have a responsibility to train their pets to behave. They are supposed to teach their pets to behave. *What is one way you could train a cat to behave?* (Possible answer: You could train it not to scratch the furniture.)

Go Digital

Pet Pals

Video

Visual Glossary

Visual Vocabulary Cards

Oral Vocabulary Routine

Define: Something you are supposed to do is your **responsibility**.

Example: Covering the birdcage at night is my responsibility.

Ask: What responsibility might a fish owner have?

Define: To **train** is to teach a person or animal how to do something.

Example: I will train my dog to be quiet.

Ask: What could you train a hamster to do?

Talk About It: Pet Pals

COLLABORATE

Have children talk about how pet owners take care of their pets. List their responses. Display page 21 of the **Reading/Writing Workshop Big Book** and have children do the **Talk About It** activity with a partner.

READING/WRITING WORKSHOP BIG BOOK, pp. 20–21

Collaborative Conversations

Be Open to All Ideas As children engage in partner, small group, or whole group discussions, encourage them:

- That all ideas, questions, or comments are important.
- To ask a question if something is unclear.
- To respect the opinions of others.
- To give their opinions, even if they are different from others'.

ENGLISH LANGUAGE LEARNERS SCAFFOLD

Beginning

Comprehend Explain how the children are taking care of the pet in the picture. *Are they washing the dog?* (yes) *Does this picture show the children taking care of the dog?* (yes) Allow them ample time to respond.

Intermediate

Describe Ask children to describe how the children in the picture are taking care of the dog. Elicit more details to support children's answers.

Advanced/Advanced High

Expand Have children use complete sentences to tell how pet owners can take care of other types of pets. (A cat owner can brush the cat.) Clarify children's responses as needed by providing vocabulary.

Listening Comprehension

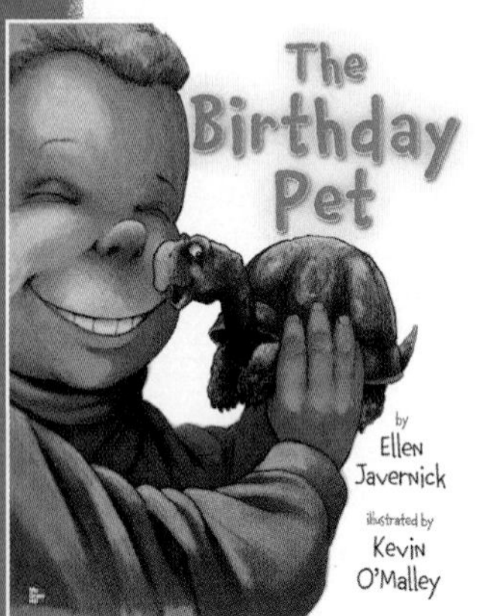

Literature Big Book

OBJECTIVES

With prompting and support, name the author and illustrator of a story and define the role of each in telling the story.
RL.K.6

Actively engage in group reading activities with purpose and understanding.
RL.K.10

- Recognize characteristics of fiction
- Strategy: Make, confirm, and revise predictions

ACADEMIC LANGUAGE

- *character, predict*
- Cognates: *predecir*

Read the Literature Big Book

Connect to Concept: Pet Pals

Tell children that they will now read a story about taking care of different kinds of pets. *What are some ways that you know of to take care of pets?*

Concepts of Print

Directionality and Punctuation Display page 11 of the **Big Book**. Read the page aloud, tracking the print with your finger. Remind children that we read from left to right and top to bottom. Point to the first set of ellipses on the page as you say: *These marks tell us to pause—or wait a bit—before we continue reading.* Model reading aloud, pausing for the ellipses.

Genre: Fiction

Model *The Birthday Pet* is a fiction story. Remind children of these characteristics of fiction:

- The events and characters are made up.
- A character usually solves—or figures out—a problem by the end of the story.

Story Words Preview these words before reading:

beady: round and small
gnawed: chewed
absurd: very, very silly

Set a Purpose for Reading

- Identify and read aloud the title and the names of the author and illustrator. Then have children name the author and illustrator and explain the role of each in telling the story.
- Ask children to listen as you read aloud the Big Book to will find out about different kinds of pets.

Go Digital

The Birthday Pet

Think Aloud Cloud

Strategy: Make, Confirm, and Revise Predictions

Explain Tell children that as good readers read, they think about what might happen next. This is called *making a prediction*. Then they check to see if they were correct. If they were not right, they think about what really did happen next. This helps them to think about how to make a better prediction the next time they read.

As you display the cover, have children predict what the story will be about. Encourage children to make predictions as you read the story.

Think Aloud Listen as I read aloud page 7. Hmmmm, I read that Danny's dad tells Danny he shouldn't get a turtle. I wonder what he will get him? I know that some other pets are dogs and cats. I also read the word log. Log rhymes with dog, so I predict that Dad will get Danny a dog. I'll turn the page to see if I am right. Turn the page, and read aloud: dog. I was right. I figured it out!

Model As you read, use the **Think Aloud Cloud** to model the strategy.

Think Aloud Let's reread pages 20 and 21. I read that Danny's sister got him a bird. I wonder if he will like this pet? I know that he has not liked the other pets that his family has given him. He really wants a turtle. I predict that he will not like the bird either.

As you continue reading, pause to have children make predictions. Ask: *What do you predict will happen at the end?*

Respond to Reading

After reading, prompt children to name the pets that Danny's family brought home. Discuss the ways that predicting helped children understand and enjoy the story. Then have children draw and label a picture of a pet they would like to have.

Make Connections

Revisit the concept behind the Essential Question *How do you take care of different kinds of pets?* by paging through the **Big Book** and having children describe specific animal needs.

Write About It Write about one of Danny's pets. Tell why he did or did not like it.

ENGLISH LANGUAGE LEARNERS SCAFFOLD

Beginning

Listen Read aloud page 7. Then say: *I want to guess what pet Dad will get. Dad talks about a log. I think the pet will have the same end sound as* log. *Does* dog *have the same end sound as* log? (yes) *Do you think Dad will get Danny a dog?* (yes) Turn the page, and ask: *Did Dad get Danny a dog?* (yes) Allow children ample time to respond.

Intermediate

Demonstrate Understanding Read aloud page 7. Then ask: *What pet do you think Dad will get?* (dog) *Why do you think so?* (*Dog* rhymes with *log*.) Repeat correct answers slowly and clearly to the class.

Advanced/Advanced High

Discuss Read aloud page 7. Ask: *How does the word* log *help you figure out the pet Dad will get?* (Possible answer: I think Dad will get a pet with a name that rhymes with *log*. I think Dad will get a dog.) Restate children's responses, adding details in order to develop their oral language proficiency.

Word Work

Quick Review

Review /u/: Ask children to tell the initial sound of the *umpire* and *umbrella* Photo Cards.

Build Fluency: Sound-Spellings: Show the following **Word-Building Cards:** *a, b, c, d, e, f, h, i, k, l, m, n, o, p, r, s, t, u.* Have children chorally say each sound. Repeat and vary the pace.

Phonemic Awareness

OBJECTIVES

CCSS Isolate and pronounce the initial, medial vowel, and final sounds in three-phoneme words. **RF.K.2d**

CCSS Demonstrate basic knowledge of one-to-one letter-sound correspondences by producing the primary or many of the most frequent sounds for each consonant. **RF.K.3a**

ENGLISH LANGUAGE LEARNERS

Pronunciation
Display and have children name Photo Cards from this lesson to reinforce phonemic awareness and word meanings. Point to the *girl* Photo Card and ask: *What do you see?* (a girl) *What is the sound at the beginning of the word* girl? (/g/) Repeat using the *watch* Photo Card. Reinforce the initial /g/ and /w/ sounds using the *game, goat, water* and *web* Photo Cards.

Phoneme Isolation

Photo Cards

1 Model Display the **Photo Card** for *guitar. Listen for the sound at the beginning of* guitar. Guitar *has the /g/ sound at the beginning. Say the sound with me: /g/.* Say *girl* and *give* and have children repeat. Emphasize /g/.

Repeat with /w/ using the *window* Photo Card and *will* and *win*.

Let's play a song. Listen for words with /g/ at the beginning. Play "Get a Guitar," and have children listen for /g/. *Let's listen to the song again and clap when we hear words that begin with /g/.* Play and/or sing the letter song again, encouraging children to join in. Have children clap when they hear a word that begins with /g/.

Repeat with /w/ and "What Can You See Out Your Window?"

2 Guided Practice/Practice Display and name each Photo Card: *gorilla, gate, girl. Say each picture name with me. Tell me the sound at the beginning of the word.* Guide practice with the first word.

Repeat with /w/ and the *walrus*, *wolf*, and *watermelon* Photo Cards.

ARTICULATION SUPPORT

Demonstrate how to say /g/. Open your mouth a little. Hold the back of your tongue on the top of your mouth, near your throat. Use your voice, and push your tongue forward a little. Place your hand on your throat. Can you feel your throat move? Say *gum, goat, gas* and have children repeat. Emphasize /g/.

Demonstrate how to say /w/. Push out your lips. They should be very close together, but not touching. Then, as you use your voice, open your mouth. The corners of your mouth should move back a little, too. Say *wet, win, wag* and have children repeat. Emphasize /w/ when you say the words.

Go Digital

Phonemic Awareness

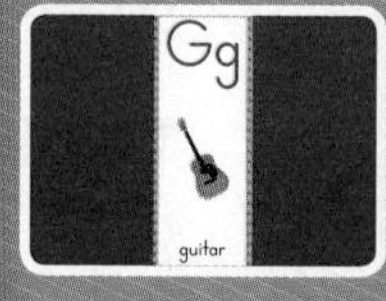

Phonics

Phonics

Sound-Spelling Card

Introduce /g/*g* and /w/*w*

1. **Model** Display the *Guitar* **Sound-Spelling Card**. *This is the* guitar *card. The sound is /g/. The /g/ sound is spelled with the letter* g. *Say it with me: /g/. This is the sound at the beginning of* guitar. *Listen: /g/, /g/, /g/,* guitar. *What is the name of this letter?* (g) *What sound does this letter stand for?* (/g/)

   Display the song "Get a Guitar" (see **Teacher's Resource Book** online). Read or sing the song with children. Reread the title and point out that the words *Get* and *Guitar* both begin with the letter *g*. Model placing a self-stick note below the *g* in *Get* and *Guitar.*

2. **Guided Practice/Practice** Read each line of the song. Stop after each line and ask children to place self-stick notes below words that begin with *G* or *g* and say the letter name.

   Repeat Steps 1–2 with /w/*w* and the *Window* Sound-Spelling Card.

Get a Guitar

Get a guitar and you can sing a song.
Get a guitar and you can play it all day long.
Join the band and have some fun.
Sing and play till the day is done.
Get a guitar and you can sing a song.

What Can You See Out Your Window?

What can you see out your window?
Can you see a bird flying in the sky?
What can you see out your window?
Can you see people hurrying by?
Can you watch the willow tree waving goodbye?
Can you hear the wind blowing branches on high?
What can you see out your window?
Can you watch winter snowflakes as they gently fall?
What can you see out your window?
Make a wish at the wonder of it all.

ELL ENGLISH LANGUAGE LEARNERS

Phoneme Variations in Language: Speakers of Hmong, Cantonese, Korean, and Khmer may have difficulty perceiving and pronouncing /g/. Emphasize the /g/ sound and demonstrate correct mouth position. Speakers of Spanish, Hmong, and Khmer may have difficulty perceiving and pronouncing /w/. Emphasize the /w/ sound and demonstrate correct mouth position.

Corrective Feedback

Sound Error Say: *My turn. Window. /w/ /w/ /w/. Now it's your turn.* Have children say the words *window* and *win* and isolate the initial sound. Repeat for /g/*g*.

YOUR TURN PRACTICE BOOK pp. 193–196

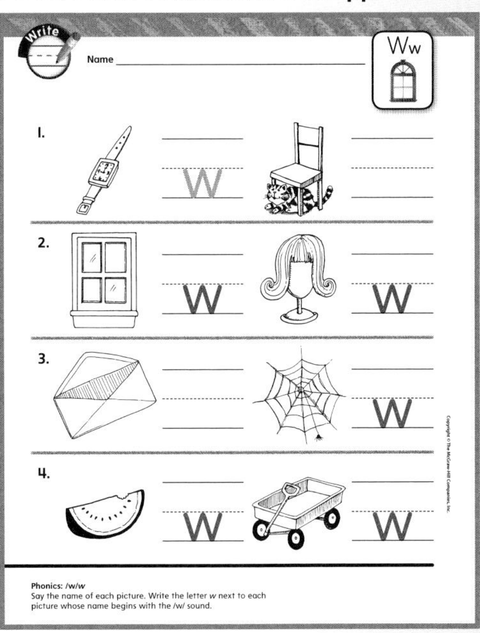

Word Work

Handwriting: Write *Gg* and *Ww*

MINILESSON 5 Mins

OBJECTIVES

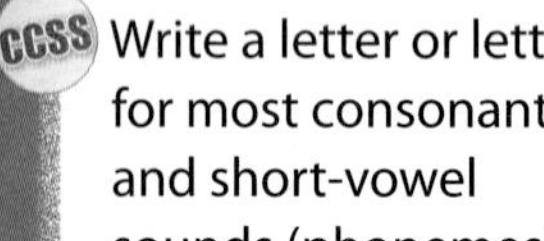

CCSS Write a letter or letters for most consonant and short-vowel sounds (phonemes). **L.K.2c**

CCSS Read common high-frequency words by sight. **RF.K.3c**

ACADEMIC LANGUAGE

uppercase, lowercase

Daily Handwriting

Throughout the week teach uppercase and lowercase letters *Gg* and *Ww* using the Handwriting models. At the end of the week, have children use **Your Turn Practice Book** page 202 to practice handwriting.

1 Model Say the handwriting cues below as you write and then identify the upper and lowercase forms of *Gg*. Then trace the letters on the board and in the air as you say the sounds.

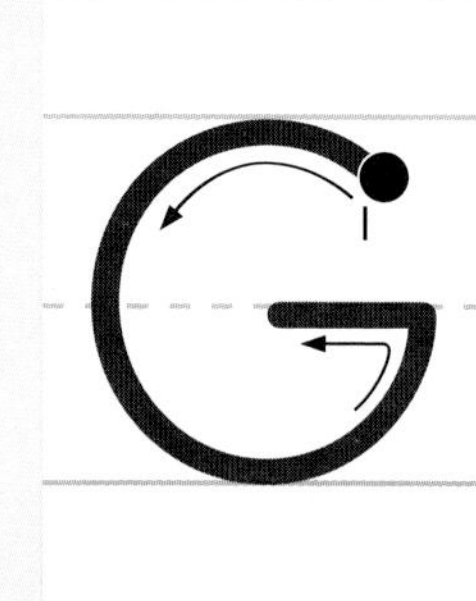

Circle back and around. Push up to the dotted line, and straight in.

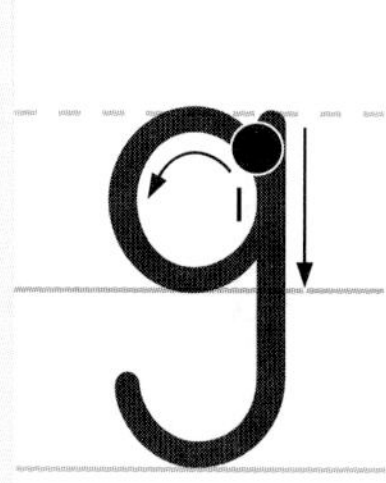

Circle back, then around all the way. Straight down past the bottom line, and curl back.

2 Guided Practice/Practice

- Say the cues together as children trace the letter with their index fingers. Have them identify the uppercase and lowercase forms of the letters.
- Have them write *G* and *g* in the air as they say /g/ multiple times.
- Distribute **Response Boards**. Observe children's pencil grip and paper position, and correct as necessary. Have children say the appropriate sound every time they write the letter.

Repeat Steps 1–2 with *Ww*.

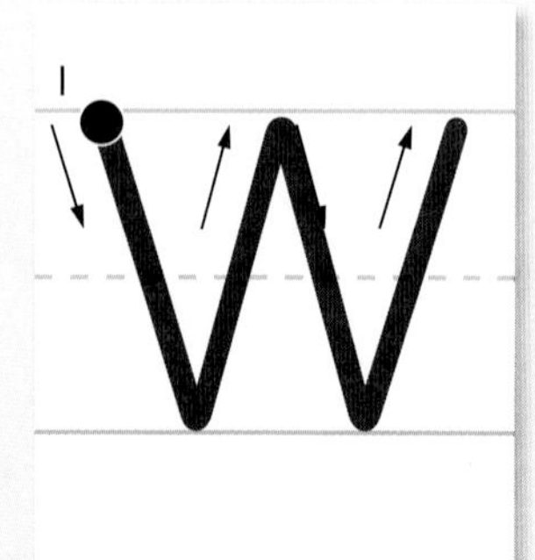

Slant down, slant up. Slant down, slant up.

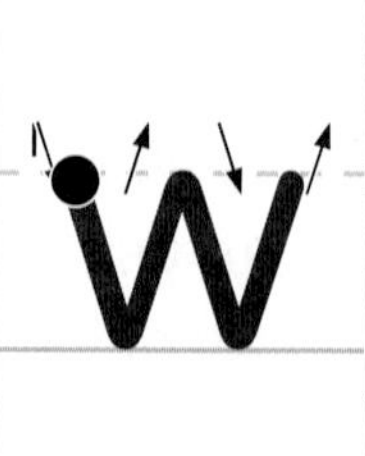

Slant down, slant up. Slant down, slant up.

Go Digital

Handwriting

High-Frequency Word Routine

High-Frequency Words

of, they

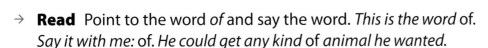

of

High-Frequency Word Cards

1 Model Display page 4 of the **Big Book** *The Birthday Pet*. Read the sentence and point to the word *of*. Then display the **High-Frequency Word Card** *of* and use the **Read/Spell/Write** routine to teach the word.

- **Read** Point to the word *of* and say the word. *This is the word* of. *Say it with me:* of. *He could get any kind* of *animal he wanted.*
- **Spell** *The word of is spelled o-f. Spell it with me.*
- **Write** *Let's write the word* of *in the air as we say each letter: o-f.*
- Point out to children that the letters *o* and *f* in the word *of* are different from the /o/ and /f/ sounds in *pop* and *fan*.
- COLLABORATE Have partners create sentences using the word.

Repeat the routine to introduce *they* using the sentence on page 9 of *The Birthday Pet.*

2 Guided Practice/Practice Build sentences using the **High-Frequency Word Cards**, **Photo Cards**, and teacher-made punctuation cards. Have children point to the high-frequency words *of* and *they*. Use these sentences.

They like the toys.
They can see a sky of blue.
They can juggle nine of the toys.

Also online

They see the .

High-Frequency Words Practice

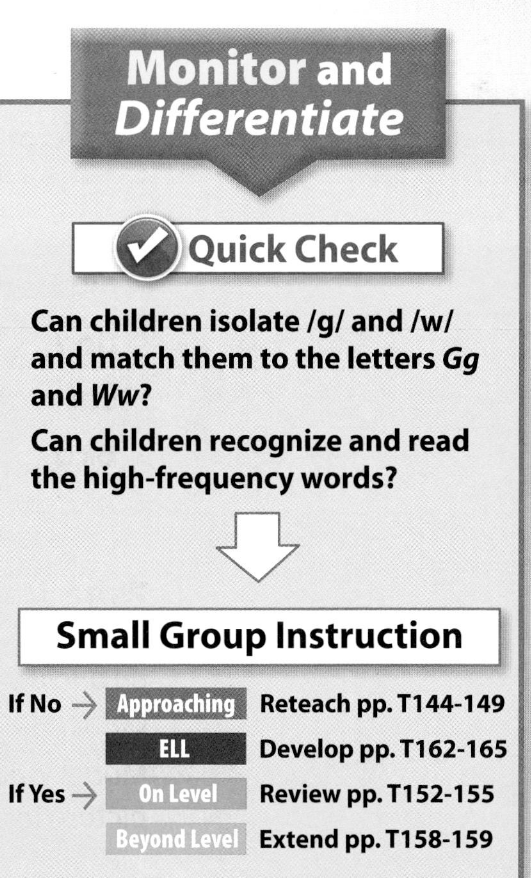

Monitor and *Differentiate*

Quick Check

Can children isolate /g/ and /w/ and match them to the letters *Gg* and *Ww*?

Can children recognize and read the high-frequency words?

Small Group Instruction

If No →	Approaching	Reteach pp. T144-149
	ELL	Develop pp. T162-165
If Yes →	On Level	Review pp. T152-155
	Beyond Level	Extend pp. T158-159

Language Arts

Shared Writing

OBJECTIVES

 Use a combination of drawing, dictating, and writing to compose informative/explanatory texts in which they name what they are writing about and supply some information about the topic. **W.K.2**

 Use frequently occurring nouns and verbs. **L.K.1b**

- Identify pets
- Identify action words

ACADEMIC LANGUAGE

- *explain, action words*
- Cognates: *explicar*

Writing Trait: Word Choice

1 Model Explain that sometimes we write to tell how to do something or to tell how something works.

→ Display and read the labels for the **Photo Cards** *hammer* and *nail. I can write about how to use a hammer to put a nail in wood. Hold the nail with the pointed end on the wood. Carefully hit the flat part of the nail with the hammer. Keep hitting the nail with the hammer until the nail goes all the way into the wood.*

2 Guided Practice/Practice Display and read the label for the **Photo Card** for *sandwich*. Help children tell what they know about making a sandwich, and write their ideas on the board.

Write an Explanatory Text

Focus and Plan Tell children that this week they will learn how to write sentences about taking care of a pet.

Brainstorm Ask children to name animals that make good pets. Have children tell what they know about taking care of those pets.

Pets

dog	fish
cat	hamster
bird	turtle

Write Model writing a sentence about a pet on the list. Write and read: *A ______ is a good pet. I can write a sentence about one of the pets on our list.* Draw a picture of a hamster. *A hamster can make a good pet.* Complete the sentence frame and read it aloud.

Model writing sentences about other pets, using the pet list. Draw a picture for each animal. Read aloud the sentences with children.

Go Digital

Writing

Grammar

Grammar

Action Words (Verbs)

1 **Model** Explain that an action word tells what is happening in a sentence. It tells what a person, animal, or thing is doing. Ask students to watch you as you open a book.

→ Write and read aloud: *I opened the book.* Explain that *opened* is the action word in the sentence and that it is the word that tells what you did. Circle *opened. I'm not opening the book now. I already opened it. I did it in the past. To show that an action happened in the past, we can sometimes add -ed to the end of the word.*

2 **Guided Practice/Practice** Have a child jump in place. While the child is jumping, write and read aloud this sentence: *[Name] jumps on the floor. What word tells what [Name] is doing?* (jumps) Have the child stop jumping. Write and read aloud: *[Name] jumped on the floor. [Name] is not jumping right now. He/she did that in the past. What word in the sentence tells the action? How do you know?* (jumped; it tells what he/she did.) Have a child circle the action word *jumped.* Jumps *and* jumped *are the action words in the sentences.* Jumps *is used to tell what [Name] is doing now.* Jumped *is used to tell what [Name] did in the past.*

Model how to use past-tense action words in other sentences. Say and write: *Andy walked far.* Explain that *Andy* is the name of the person who did the action. The *-ed* at the end of *walked* tells that he did the action in the past. Underline the action word.

Talk About It

Have partners practice using past-tense action words with pantomime. One child pantomimes an action; the partner identifies the action with the past-tense form of the verb. For example: *You smiled.*

ELL

ENGLISH LANGUAGE LEARNERS SCAFFOLD

Beginning

Explain Have children work in small groups. Have one child act out an action, such as *clap.* Have the other children in the group say the action word. Model for children how to say the past-tense version of the action word. Restate children's responses in order to develop their oral language proficiency.

Intermediate

Practice Write a sentence, such as *I walk to the park.* Read the sentence aloud as you track each word with a finger. Have a child add *-ed* to *walk* to make it past tense. Read the new sentence aloud together. Repeat with additional sentences.

Advanced/Advanced High

Practice Have children work in pairs. Have each child tell their partner a few things they did last night. Write a few of the sentences. Have children circle the past-tense action words in the sentences. Correct the meaning of children's responses as needed.

Daily Wrap Up

- Review the Essential Question and encourage children to discuss it, using the new oral vocabulary words. *How do people choose a pet?*
- Prompt children to share the skills they learned. How might they use those skills?

WHOLE GROUP
DAY 2

Materials

Reading/Writing Workshop Big Book
UNIT 7

Literature Big Book
The Birthday Pet

Visual Vocabulary Cards
responsibility
train

Retelling Cards

Sound-Spelling Card
window
guitar

Photo Cards
dog

Word-Building Cards

High-Frequency Word Cards
of
they

Build the Concept

MINILESSON 10 Mins

Oral Language

OBJECTIVES

CCSS Use words and phrases acquired through conversations, reading and being read to, and responding to texts. **L.K.6**

CCSS Sort common objects into categories (e.g., shapes, foods) to gain a sense of the concepts the categories represent. **L.K.5a**

Develop oral vocabulary

ACADEMIC LANGUAGE

- *rhyme*
- Cognates: *rima*

ESSENTIAL QUESTION

How do you take care of different kinds of pets?

Remind children that this week they are learning about ways to take care of pets. Point out that owning a pet means having the responsibility of taking care of it. Tell children that families must train pets. Training helps keep a pet safe, and it helps other people stay safe when they are near a pet.

Say the rhyme "My Carefree Dog" with children.

Phonological Awareness

Recognize and Generate Rhyme

Remind children that rhyming words have the same end sound. *These words from "My Carefree Dog" have the same end sound:* meet, sweet, street. Have children repeat: *meet, sweet, street. Why do these words rhyme?* (They have the same end sound.) Challenge children to say a rhyming word for each word below.

set *make* *can* *tub* *rock* *ten* *jam* *seed*

Review Oral Vocabulary

Use the **Define/Example/Ask** routine to review the oral vocabulary words **responsibility** and **train**. Prompt children to use the words in sentences.

Visual Vocabulary Cards

Go Digital

Visual Glossary

Category Words

Category Words: Pets

1 Model Use the **Big Book** *The Birthday Pet* to discuss pets. Explain that a pet is an animal you keep in your home and care for. Discuss the pets from each illustration. *A rabbit can be a pet. How do you care for a pet rabbit? What do you think it's like to have a pet rabbit?* Chant the following jingle:

Mom says that I can get a pet, but what kind should I get?
A snake, a rat, a dog, a cat? It's hard to pick one I have not met!

→ Help children identify the pets in the jingle. Discuss which pet they would prefer and why.

2 Guided Practice/Practice Make up riddles about pets and ask children to figure out which pet you are describing. *I live in a cage. I sit on a branch. I have feathers and a beak. Which pet am I?* (a bird)

→ Ask children how pets are different from other animals. (Possible answers: They live indoors; You can play with them; You take care of them.)

Vocabulary Strategy: Word Categories/Prepositions

1 Model Explain that words that have something in common can be grouped into categories based on their job in a sentence. One type of word is called a preposition. Prepositions are usually short words such as *to, for, with, of, for, from,* and *in.* Prepositions tell the position or place of something. Use p. 16 of *The Birthday Pet* to model how to recognize and use prepositions.

Think Aloud In *The Birthday Pet,* the preposition *in* can be found in this phrase: *when it gnawed in the night*. The preposition *in* connects the word *night* to the word *gnawed.* The preposition *in* tells when the gnawing took place.

2 Guided Practice/Practice Help children find other prepositions in the book. Make a list of the prepositions. Then talk about how the prepositions link words in the following sentence:

The kitten was cuddly, but it made Danny sneeze, and he always had to get it down ***from*** *the trees.* (p. 12)

Work with children to make up sentences about training a pet. Be sure each sentence includes a preposition. Have children identify the preposition in the sentences.

ENGLISH LANGUAGE LEARNERS

Discuss Provide books and magazines to help children find pictures of pets. Ask children to identify the pet. Discuss what it is like to have this pet. Have children repeat the name of each pet in English and in their native language.

LET'S MOVE!

Count to three and then say a pet word. Children should act out something that a pet would do. Continue until you have named all the pets in the Big Book.

Listening Comprehension

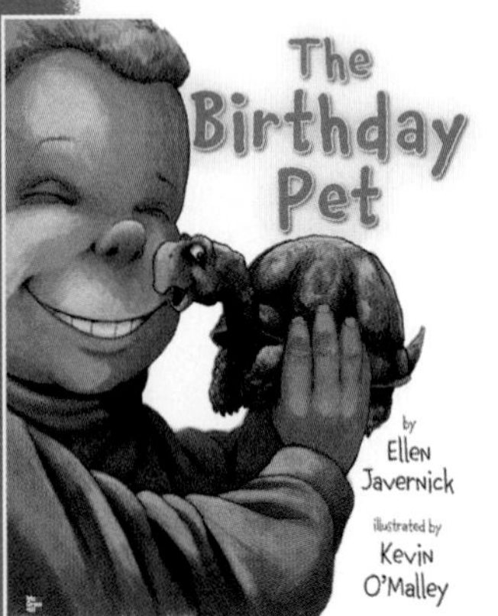

Literature Big Book

Reread Literature Big Book

Genre: Fiction

Display *The Birthday Pet.* Remind children that fiction books tell make-believe stories. In fiction stories, a character usually solves, or figures out, a problem. *How do you know that* The Birthday Pet *is fiction?* (The story is make-believe, and Danny finally solves the problem of getting the perfect pet.) Have children point to evidence in the text and the illustrations to show that the story is fiction.

Strategy: Make, Confirm, and Revise Predictions

Remind children that good readers make predictions, or figure out what they think will happen next, as they read. *How can you tell if your predictions are right?* (You can read what comes next.)

Skill: Plot: Problem and Solution

Remind children that characters are the people or animals in a story. The setting is the time and place of story events. The plot is how the characters figure out—or solve—a big problem. Have children repeat these terms: *character, setting, plot.* As you read, have children listen for evidence in the story that tells about the problem and solution in the plot. Use the prompts to fill in the graphic organizer.

Access Complex Text

Organization This book is organized with a clue for prediction at the end of most spreads—and an opportunity to confirm the prediction on the following page. As you read, guide children in recognizing the clues in text and art.

→ Review page 7 again with children, asking them to recall how they predicted what would be on the next page.

OBJECTIVES

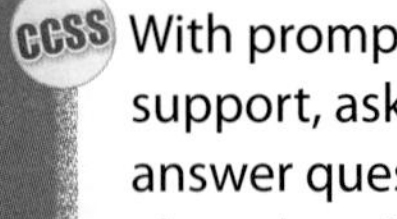

CCSS With prompting and support, ask and answer questions about key details in a text. **RL.K.1**

CCSS Confirm understanding of a text read aloud or information presented orally or through other media by asking and answering questions about key details and requesting clarification if something is not understood. **SL.K.2**

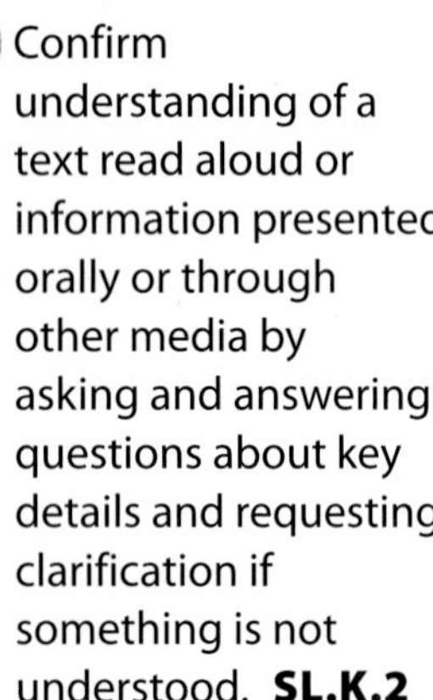

- Strategy: Make, Confirm, and Revise Predictions
- Skill: Character, Setting, and Plot

ACADEMIC LANGUAGE

- *predictions, plot*
- Cognates: *predicciones*

Go Digital

The Birthday Pet

Retelling Cards

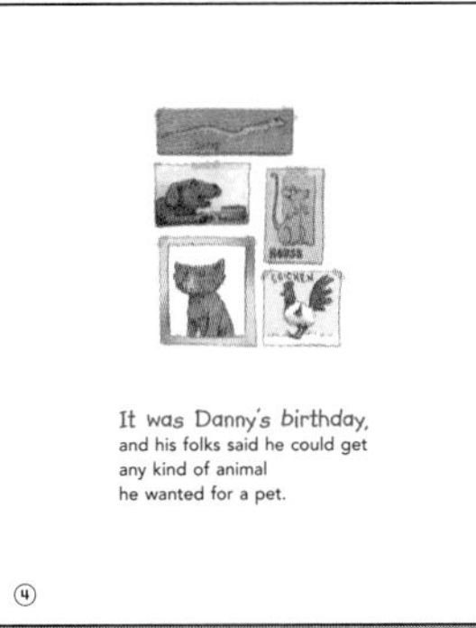

PAGES 4–5

MAKE, CONFIRM, AND REVISE PREDICTIONS

What animal do you think Danny will ask his family to get him for his birthday? Why do you think that? (Answers may vary. Possible answer: a turtle, because he is holding one on the cover.)

pp. 4–5

Reinforce the names of the animals shown on page 4. Have children join you in pointing to and naming each animal: *snake, dog, mouse, cat, chicken.*

PAGES 6–7

KEY DETAILS

Point out and read the notes in the illustration. *What details do the notes tell you about why Danny wants a turtle?* (A turtle is fun to watch. It doesn't get fur all over the place. It is quiet. It doesn't run away.)

pp. 6–7

sits like a log: Tell children this means to just sit and do nothing. Sit quietly, sigh, and say: *I sit like a log.* Have children echo and mimic.

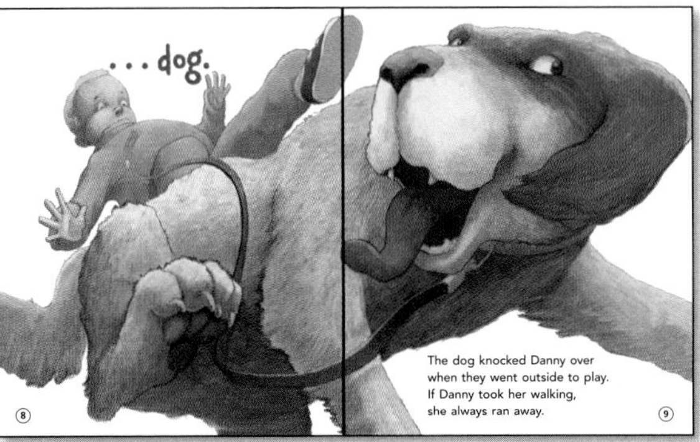

PAGES 8–9

HIGH-FREQUENCY WORDS

Have children point to and read aloud the high-frequency word **they**.

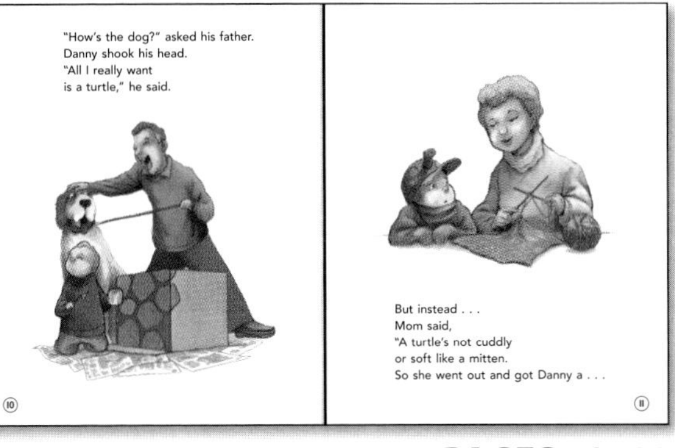

PAGES 10–11

PLOT: PROBLEM AND SOLUTION

What is Danny's big problem in this story? (He wants a turtle for his birthday but his family is giving him different animals.) *Let's add this to our problem and solution chart.*

pp. 10–11

All I really want: Tell children this phrase means the same as "the only thing I want."

Listening Comprehension

ELL

PAGES 12–13

CONCEPTS OF PRINT

Think Aloud I see that the author shows the word *kitten* in big red letters. And the author did the same thing for the word *dog*. I think the author is doing this to make the names of the pets stand out.

pp. 12–13

sneeze: Pantomime a sneeze for children as you cover your nose and mouth. Then say *sneeze*. Have children echo and mimic.

PAGES 14–15

MAKE AND REVISE PREDICTIONS

Which pet do you predict Danny's brother will get for him? (Possible answer: rat) *Why?* (*Rat* rhymes with *that*—and there is a rat on his brother's shirt.)

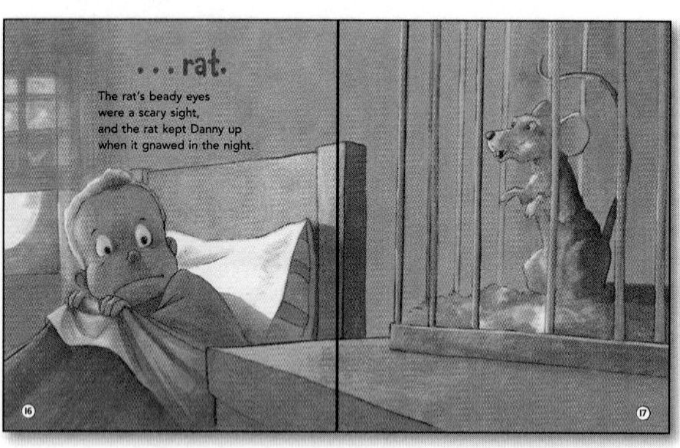

PAGES 16–17

PROBLEM AND SOLUTION

What is the problem with the rat? (It keeps Danny awake at night. Its eyes are scary.)

pp. 16–17

beady: Point to the rat's eye as you say *beady*. Have children repeat. If possible, show children a bead and explain that a beady eye is round and shiny.

PAGES 18–19

CHARACTER

How does Danny feel about the rat? How do you know? (He is unhappy about it. He looks sad in the picture and he shakes his head when his brother asks about it.)

pp. 18–19

shook his head: Demonstrate shaking your head left to right and say *no*. Have children echo and mimic. Explain that this can also mean that someone is unhappy.

PAGES 20–21

HIGH-FREQUENCY WORDS

Have children point to and read aloud the high-frequency word **of**.

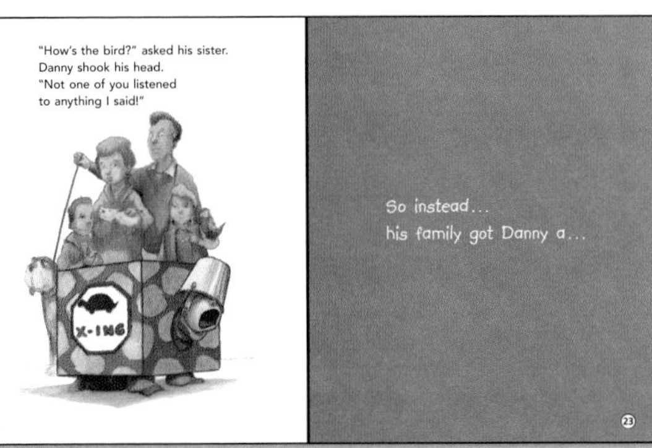

PAGES 22–23

CHARACTERS

Who are the different characters in this story? (Danny, his sister and brother, and his mom and dad) Some students might count the turtle or other animals as characters, too, even though they have only small parts in the story.

pp. 22–23

X-ING: Point out the traffic sign on the box. Tell children that *X-ING* means "crossing." *The sign means that turtles cross the road here.* Walk across the room as you say: *I am crossing the room.* Invite children to echo and mimic.

PAGES 24–25

PLOT: PROBLEM AND SOLUTION

How did Danny take care of his problem? (He convinced his family to get him a turtle.) *Let's add this to our problem and solution chart.*

pp. 24–25

show-and-tell: If children are not familiar with show-and-tell, explain that this is a time when children bring things from home and tell the class about them.

PAGES 26–27

KEY DETAILS

How does Danny feel about his turtle? (Possible responses: He is proud of her. He is very happy to have her.) *How can you tell?* (I can tell by the look on his face.)

pp. 26–27

peekaboo: Demonstrate how to play peekaboo as you say *Peekaboo!* Have children echo and mimic.

Listening Comprehension

He fed her bugs and lettuce, and he made a turtle gym.

Danny thought the turtle was the perfect pet for him.

28 29

PAGES 28–29

REREAD

Think Aloud *I know that Danny has a pet now. And I know this means he has responsibilities. I wonder if he is taking care of his responsibilities. I'll read again to figure this out.* Read aloud pages 28–29. *He gives her food to eat. I can see him training her with the hoop. He is being responsible.*

So Dad kept the dog, his brother kept the rat,

his sister kept the bird, and Mom kept the cat.

30 31

PAGES 30–31

KEY DETAILS

What happened to the other pets that Danny's family gave to him? (Danny's dad is taking care of the dog; his brother is taking care of the rat; his sister is taking care of the bird; his mother is taking care of the cat.)

Danny kept the turtle, and that was the end of that!

32

PAGE 32

AUTHOR'S PURPOSE

Why do you think the author wrote this book? (Possible answer: He wanted to tell a fun story about a boy who wanted a turtle for a pet, but no one listened to him.)

Text Evidence

Explain Remind children that when they answer a question they need to show where in the book (both words and pictures) they found the answer.

Discuss *Which animal in the story is the hardest to take care of? Why do you think so?*

Plot: Problem and Solution

Review Skill Remind children that when they read fiction stories, they can look for a big problem and solution. Discuss the problem and solution in *The Birthday Pet* using the graphic organizer. Encourage children to give more examples.

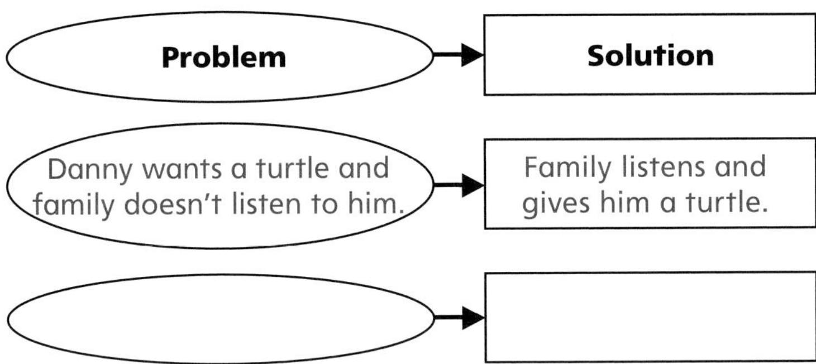
Problem
Solution
Danny wants a turtle and family doesn't listen to him.
Family listens and gives him a turtle.

Guided Retelling

Tell children that they will use the **Retelling Cards** to retell the story.

- Show Retelling Card 1. Based on children's needs, use the Modeled, Guided or ELL retelling prompts. The ELL prompts contain support for English language learners based on levels of language acquisition. Repeat with cards 2–4, using the prompts as a guide.
- Have children choose a pet from the story and tell about it.

Model Fluency

Remind children that it is important to read the words just as the characters would say them. On page 15, model reading the conversation between Danny and his brother, using two different voices. Have children echo and mimic. Repeat for other conversations in the book.

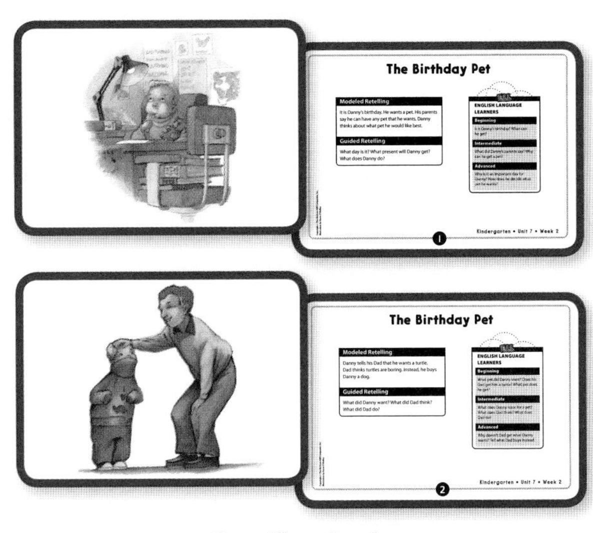
The Birthday Pet
The Birthday Pet

Retelling Cards

YOUR TURN PRACTICE BOOK p. 193

Name ______

under	gift	goat
guitar	sock	gate
ladder	gum	kite

Phonemic Awareness: /g/
Say the name of each picture. Put a marker on each picture if its name begins with the /g/ sound.

WHOLE GROUP

DAY 2

Word Work

Quick Review

Build Fluency: Sound-Spellings: Show the following **Word-Building Cards:** *a, b, c, d, e, f, g, h, i, k, l, m, n, o, p, r, s, t, u, w.* Have children chorally say each sound. Repeat and vary the pace.

Phonemic Awareness

Phoneme Isolation

1 Model Display the *guitar* **Photo Card** and remind children that *guitar* begins with /g/. Have children say /g/. Then display the *dog* Photo Card. Tell children that /g/ can also appear at the end of a word. Display the **Photo Card** *dog. Listen for /g/ at the end of this word:* dog. Emphasize final /g/. *Say the sound with me: /g/.* Then say the following words and have children repeat: *flag, egg, bug.*

2 Guided Practice/Practice Say each of the following words and have children repeat. Have them say /g/ if they hear the sound at the end of the word. Guide children with the first word.

leg game big gate rug frog wig

OBJECTIVES

CCSS Isolate and pronounce the initial, medial vowel, and final sounds in three-phoneme words. **RF.K.2d**

CCSS Demonstrate basic knowledge of one-to-one letter-sound correspondences by producing the primary or many of the most frequent sounds for each consonant. **RF.K.3a**

CCSS Read common high-frequency words by sight. **RF.K.3c**

Phonics

Review *g* and *w*

Gg Ww guitar window

Sound-Spelling Cards

1 Model Display the *Window* **Sound-Spelling Card**. *This is the letter* w. *The letter* w *stands for /w/ as in the word* window. *What is the letter?* (w) *What sound does the letter* w *stand for?* (/w/)

Repeat for /g/*g* using the *Guitar* Sound-Spelling Card.

2 Guided Practice/Practice Have children listen as you say some words. Ask them to write the letter *w* on their **Response Boards** if the word begins with the sound /w/, or the letter *g* if the word begins with the sound /g/. Do the first two words with children.

give win go will wipe girl web gone

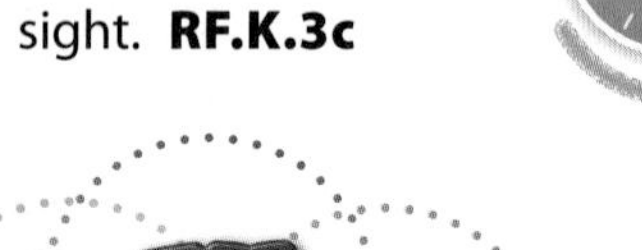

ENGLISH LANGUAGE LEARNERS

High-Frequency Words: Build Meaning Reinforce the use of the word *of* by saying these sentences and demonstrating them.

- *I* came out *of* the room.
- Choose one *of* the books.
- *She* likes all *of* the colors.
- Which one *of* you likes this book?

Go Digital

Phonemic Awareness

c a t

Phonics

the is you do

High-Frequency Word Routine

Handwriting

Blend Words with *g* and *w*

1 Model Place **Word-Building Cards** *w, i,* and *n* in a pocket chart. Point to the *w. This is the letter* w. *The letter* w *stands for /w/. Say /w/. This is the letter* i. *The letter* i *stands for /i/. Say /i/. This is the letter* n. *The letter* n *stands for /n/. Say /n/. Listen as I blend the three sounds together: /wiiinnn/. Now blend the sounds with me to read the word.*

2 Guided Practice/Practice Change Word-Building cards to *w, i, g.* Point to the letter *w* and have children say /w/. Point to the letter *i* and have children say /i/. Point to the letter *g* and have children say /g/. Then move your hand from left to right under the word and have children blend and read the word *wig.* Repeat with *wag, tag, tug, bug, web, wet, get.*

High-Frequency Words

of, they

of

High-Frequency Word Cards

1 Guided Practice Display the **High-Frequency Word Cards** *of* and *they.* Use the **Read/Spell/Write** routine to teach each word. Ask children to close their eyes, picture the spelling of the word in their minds, and then write it the way they see it. Have children self-correct by checking the High-Frequency Word Card.

2 Practice Add the High-Frequency words to the word bank.

COLLABORATE

→ Have partners create sentences using the words.

→ Have children count the number of letters in each word and then write *of* and *they* again.

Cumulative Review Review *for* and *have.*

→ Repeat the **Read/Spell/Write** routine. Mix the words and have children chorally say each one.

Monitor and *Differentiate*

Quick Check

Can children isolate /g/ and /w/ and match the sounds to the letters *Gg* and *Ww*?

Can children recognize and read the high-frequency words?

Small Group Instruction

If No →	Approaching	Reteach pp. T144-149
	ELL	Develop pp. T162-165
If Yes →	On Level	Review pp. T152-155
	Beyond Level	Extend pp. T158-159

Shared Read

Reading/Writing Workshop Big Book and Reading/Writing Workshop

OBJECTIVES

CCSS Read common high-frequency words by sight. **RF.K.3c**

CCSS Read emergent-reader texts with purpose and understanding. **RF.K.4**

ACADEMIC LANGUAGE

- *predict*
- Cognates: *predecir*

MINILESSON 10 Mins

Read "I Hug Gus!"

Model Skills and Strategies

Model Concepts About Print Point out the punctuation in the title and in each sentence of the story. *As I read, I see different kinds of punctuation, such as a period and an exclamation point. For example, the title "I Hug Gus!" ends with an exclamation point. The exclamation point is a clue to read the title with expression or feeling.* Invite volunteers to take turns coming up to the **Big Book** and pointing to the punctuation in each sentence.

Predict Read the title together. Encourage children to describe the illustration. Invite them to tell where the story will take place and what it might be about.

Read Have children chorally read the story with you. Point to each word as you read it together. Help children sound out the decodable words and say the sight words. If children have difficulty, provide corrective feedback and guide them page by page using the student **Reading/Writing Workshop**.

Ask the following questions:

→ *Look at pages 22–23. What does Gus look like?* (He is a big, red pup.)

→ *Look at page 25. What does Gus like to do?* (Possible answer: play with a ball; run)

→ *Look at page 28. What is the boy doing?* (He is giving Gus a bath.)

Go Digital

"I Hug Gus!"

"I Hug Gus!"

I Hug Gus!
I can see a big, red pup.
I pick a pup for a pet.

My big pup and a cat tug.
They tug and have fun.
Gus is a big, red pup.
Gus can run, run and win!

Gus is on top **of** the bed.
He can sit up and beg.
Gus and I are on a rug.
Gus can tug, tug, tug!

I rub Gus in the tub.
Gus is wet, wet, wet!
I tuck Gus in a big bed.
I can hug, hug, hug Gus!

READING/WRITING WORKSHOP, pp. 22–29

Rereading

Have small groups use the **Reading/Writing Workshop** to reread "I Hug Gus!" Then review the skills and strategies using the *Phonics* and *Words to Know* pages that come before the selection.

- As children read, pause occasionally and have them make predictions. As they read on, encourage them to confirm or revise their prediction based on what they read and see in the illustrations. As they make their predictions, discuss the character, setting, and plot.
- Have children use page 21 to review the high-frequency words *they* and *of*.
- Have children use page 20 to review that the letters *g* and *w* stand for the sounds /g/ and /w/ respectively. Encourage them to identify and name each picture that includes the sounds /g/ and /w/. Guide them to blend the sounds to read the words.

ENGLISH LANGUAGE LEARNERS

Reinforce Vocabulary Display the **High-Frequency Word Cards** *they, of, have, little.* Point to classroom objects and different children as you use the high-frequency word in sentences such as the following: *Do you take care of our class pet?* (Yes, we take care of our class pet.) *I see Hugo and Pam. Are they smiling?* (Yes, they are smiling.) *Do you have a notebook?* (Yes, we have a notebook.) *Is the eraser big or little?* (The eraser is little.)

Language Arts

Interactive Writing

OBJECTIVES

CCSS Use a combination of drawing, dictating, and writing to compose informative/explanatory texts in which they name what they are writing about and supply some information about the topic. **W.K.2**

CCSS Use frequently occurring nouns and verbs. **L.K.1b**

- Write about caring for pets
- Use verbs

ACADEMIC LANGUAGE

- *explain, action words*
- Cognates: *explicar*

Writing Trait: Word Choice

Review Remind children that sometimes writers write to explain how to do things. *I know how to do lots of things. I can write to explain how to brush my teeth. First, I put toothpaste on my toothbrush. Next, I make circles with the brush. I brush every part of each tooth.* Write the sentences and read them aloud.

Write an Explanatory Text

Discuss Display and read aloud the list of pets the children made and the sample sentences from Day 1. Talk about other animals that can be pets. Guide children to choose one pet to write about, such as a bird.

Model/Apply Grammar Tell children that you will work together to write sentences telling how to care for a pet bird. Remind them that they should use action words to tell what a person does to care for the bird.

Draw a picture of a bird. Under the bird, write the sentence: *A bird is a pet.* Then, write a sentence telling one thing to do to take care of a bird. *I give the bird fresh water.* Read the sentence aloud and point to each word.

Which word in the sentence is an action word? (give) *How do you know?* (It tells what I do.)

Write Have children help you write additional sentences about how to care for a pet bird. Write this sentence frame: *I ______ the bird twice a day.*

Guide children to complete the sentence frame. (I feed the bird twice a day.) Write the word. Share the pen with children and have them write the letters they know. Guide children to complete additional sentence frames about taking care of a pet bird.

Go Digital

Writing

I see a fish.

Grammar

Grammar

Action Words (Verbs)

1 Review Remind children that action words can tell what a person, an animal, or a thing does or did in the past. Say: *I can use action words to tell what I did at the park last week. I jumped. I played hopscotch. I kicked a ball. What action words did I use?* (jumped, played, kicked) Jumped, played, *and* kicked *are all action words. They each have* -ed *added to the end of the word, so they tell actions that happened in the past.*

→ Say the following sentence: *The train started.* Have children chorally repeat the sentence. Ask: *What is the action word in the sentence?* (started) *How do you know?* (It tells what the train did.)

2 Guided Practice Write the following sentence frame on a sentence strip and read it aloud: *Terri ______ slowly.* Write and read aloud the following words: *walked, banana, talked.* Tell children that two of those words can be used in the sentence. Ask children to point to one of the action words that can be used in the sentence. (talked, walked) Ask: *How do you know that* walked *is a correct word?* (*Walked* is an action word. It tells what Terri did.) *How do you know that* talked *is a correct word?* (*Talked* is an action word. It tells what Terri did.) Ask: *Why doesn't* banana *work in the sentence?* (*Banana* is the name of a fruit. It doesn't tell an action.)

3 Practice Have children work with a partner. Have partners think of action words they know. Ask each pair to choose one action word and draw a picture together to show that action. Have children dictate a caption for the picture. Ask partners to add an *-ed* at the end of the action word to make the action something that happened in the past.

Talk About It

Have partners tell about the games they like to play. Ask them to describe to one another how they play the game. Have children identify the action words in their sentences.

ENGLISH LANGUAGE LEARNERS

Use Visuals Display the **Big Book** page that shows what happened when Danny got a dog. Ask children to tell you what the dog did to Danny. For example: "The dog knocked Danny over." Write the sentences on the board and have children underline the action word in each sentence.

Daily Wrap Up

- Discuss the Essential Question and encourage children to use the oral vocabulary words. *How do you take care of pets?*
- Prompt children to review and discuss the skills they used today. How do those skills help them?

Materials

Reading/Writing Workshop Big Book
UNIT 7

Visual Vocabulary Cards
compared
depend
social

Interactive Read-Aloud Cards

Word-Building Cards

of

High-Frequency Word Cards
of
they

Photo Cards
game
gate
girl
goat
gorilla
walrus
watch
water
watermelon
web

Puppet

I predicted ______ because...

Think Aloud Clouds

Build the Concept

Oral Language

OBJECTIVES

Actively engage in group reading activities with purpose and understanding.
RI.K.10

CCSS Identify real-life connections between words and their use.
L.K.5c

Develop oral vocabulary

ACADEMIC LANGUAGE

- *informational text*
- Cognates: *texto informativo*

ESSENTIAL QUESTION

Remind children that this week they are talking and learning about how to take care of different kinds of pets. Guide children to discuss the Essential Question, using information from the **Big Book** and the weekly poem. Remind children that "My Carefree Dog" describes a pet dog. Say the rhyme and have children join in.

Oral Vocabulary

Review last week's oral vocabulary words, as well as *responsibility* and *train* from Day 1. Then use the **Define/Example/Ask** routine to introduce *depend, compared,* and *social.*

Oral Vocabulary Routine

Define: When you **depend** on someone, you trust that person.

Example: I depend on my big brother to take me to school.

Ask: If you had a dog as a pet, how would it depend on you?

Visual Vocabulary Cards

Define: If you have **compared** two things, you found out how they were alike and how they were different.

Example: I compared the basketball to the tennis ball when I said they were both round, but one was bigger than the other.

Ask: If you compared a dog and a cat, what would you say?

Define: If you are **social**, you like being around people a lot.

Example: He was so social that he spoke to everyone at the party.

Ask: How can you tell when someone is being social?

Go Digital

Visual Glossary

"The Family Pet"

I predicted ______ because...

Think Aloud Cloud

Listening Comprehension

Read the Interactive Read Aloud

Genre: Informational Text

Tell children that you will be reading an informational text. Guide them to recall that *informational texts* give true information, or facts, about a topic. Display the **Interactive Read-Aloud Cards**.

Interactive Read-Aloud Cards

Read aloud the title. Point out that different kinds of pets must be cared for in different ways.

Strategy: Make, Confirm, and Revise Predictions

Tell children that good readers make predictions as they read, which means they try to figure out what will happen next. They can use information from the words and the photos to help them predict what will happen. Model the strategy of making predictions by using the **Think Aloud Cloud**.

Think Aloud On the first card, I read that the selection is going to tell about three families with pets. I see cats on the first card. I think about other pets that I know about: dogs, fish, birds, and snakes. I predict that the author will tell about some of these pets. I'll keep reading to see if I am correct.

Read "The Family Pet," pausing to model the strategy of making, confirming, and revising predictions. Encourage children to share their predictions.

Make Connections

Guide partners to connect "The Family Pet" with *The Birthday Pet*. Discuss what both selections tell about how to take care of pets. Remind children that *The Birthday Pet* is a fiction story, and that "The Family Pet" is informational text.

ENGLISH LANGUAGE LEARNERS

Reinforce Meaning As you read "The Family Pet," make meaning clear by pointing to specific people, places, or objects in the photographs, demonstrating word meanings, paraphrasing text, and asking children questions. For example, on Card 1, point to the cat. Say: *This is a cat*. Repeat with the pets on other cards.

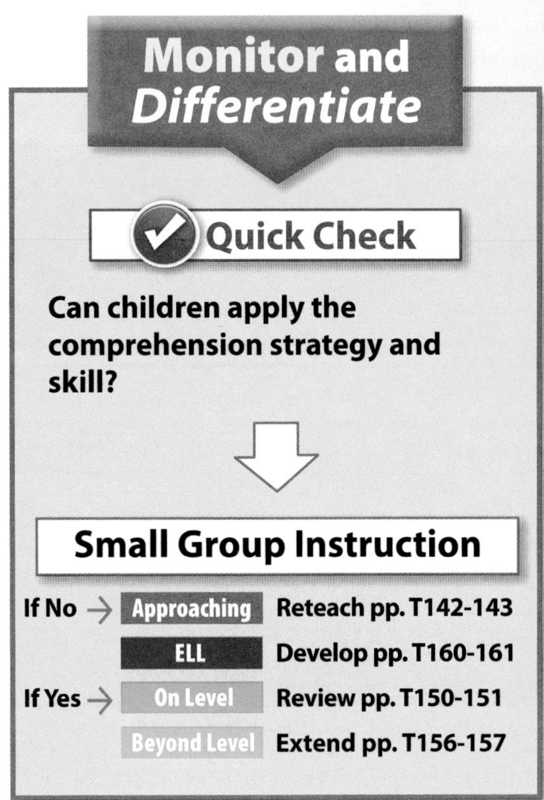

Monitor and Differentiate

Quick Check

Can children apply the comprehension strategy and skill?

Small Group Instruction

If No →	Approaching	Reteach pp. T142-143
	ELL	Develop pp. T160-161
If Yes →	On Level	Review pp. T150-151
	Beyond Level	Extend pp. T156-157

Word Work

Quick Review

Build Fluency: Sound-Spellings: Show the following **Word-Building Cards:** *a, b, c, d, e, f, g, h, i, k, l, m, n, o, p, r, s, t, u, w.* Have children chorally say each sound. Repeat and vary the pace.

Phonemic Awareness

Puppet

OBJECTIVES

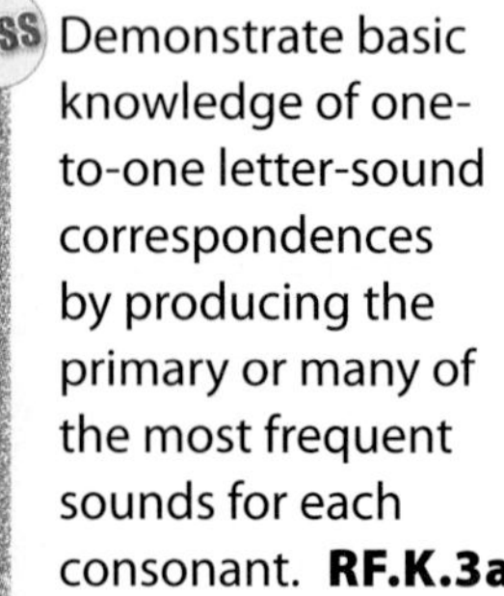

CCSS Isolate and pronounce the initial, medial vowel, and final sounds (phonemes) in three-phoneme words. **RF.K.2d**

CCSS Demonstrate basic knowledge of one-to-one letter-sound correspondences by producing the primary or many of the most frequent sounds for each consonant. **RF.K.3a**

CCSS Associate the long and short sounds with common spellings (graphemes) for the five major vowels. **RF.K.3b**

Read and blend words with *g, w*

Phoneme Blending

1 Model *The **puppet** is going to say sounds in a word /g/ /i/ /v/. It can blend those sounds to make a word: /giiivvv/* give. *Listen as it blends more sounds to make a word.* Repeat for /w/ using the word *win.* Model blending with the following:

/g/ /e/ /t/ get /t/ /a/ /g/ tag /w/ /i/ /g/ wig

2 Guided Practice/Practice Tell children that the puppet will say the sounds in a word. *Listen to the puppet as it says each sound. Repeat the sounds, then blend them to say the word.* Guide practice with the first word.

/w/ /a/ /g/ wag /g/ /a/ /p/ gap /w/ /a/ /ks/ wax
/g/ /i/ /v/ give /w/ /e/ /b/ web /g/ /u/ /m/ gum

Review /g/ and /w/. Play and sing "Get a Guitar." Have children clap when they hear initial /g/. Demonstrate as you sing with them. Repeat with /w/ and "What Can You See Out Your Window?"

Go Digital

Phonemic Awareness

Phonics

Handwriting

Phonics

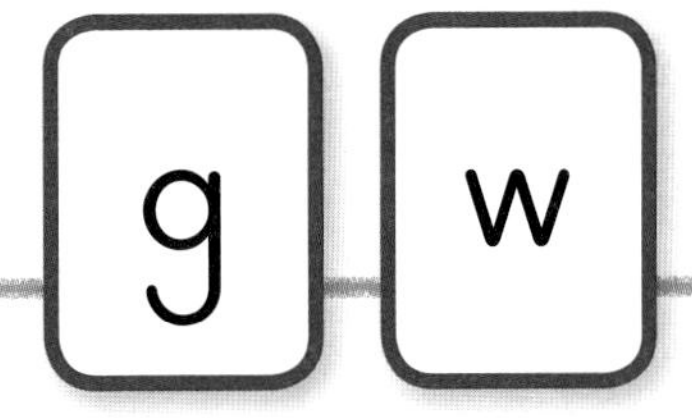

Word-Building Cards

Review *g* and *w*

1 Model Display **Word-Building Card** *g. This is the letter* g. *The letter* g *stands for /g/, the sound you hear at the beginning of* gate *and at the end of* bug. *Say the sound with me: /g/. I will write the letter* g *because* gate *has /g/ at the beginning and* bug *has /g/ at the end.* Repeat for initial /w/*w* using the word *wait.*

2 Guided Practice/Practice Tell children that you will say some words that have /g/ or /w/ at the beginning. Have children say /g/ and write the letter *g* on their **Response Boards** if the word begins with /g/, and to say /w/ and write the letter *w* if the word begins with /w/. Guide practice with the first word.

water give gain walrus web game win gone

Blend Words with Short *a, i, u, e*

1 Model Display Word-Building Cards *g, e, t. This is the letter* g. *It stands for /g/. This is the letter* e. *It stands for /e/. This is the letter* t. *It stands for /t/. Let's blend the three sounds together: /geeet/. The word is* get. Repeat with *gap, gab, gas, win, wet, web.*

2 Guided Practice/Practice Write the following words. Have children read each word, blending the sounds. Guide practice with the first word.

rug bug wag wig get wet web gum

Write these sentences and prompt children to read the connected text, sounding out the decodable words: *The bag had a pack of gum in it. He got wet. You can get the web.*

Corrective Feedback

Sound Error Model the sound that children missed, then have them repeat. For example, say: *My turn.* Tap under the letter *a* in the word *gag* and ask: *Sound?* (/a/) *What's the sound?* (/a/) Return to the beginning of the word. *Let's start over.* Blend the word again.

Extend the Lesson

Blends with /l/

Listen as I say this word: glad. *The beginning sounds are /g/ /l/. Say the sounds and blend them with me: /g/ /l/, /gl/. The /gl/ sounds are spelled with the letters* g *and* l. Place the Word-Building Cards *g, l, a, d* in a pocket chart. Model blending and then read the word with children. Repeat with *glass.* Use the same routine to teach *cl* using the words *clap, clam, club.*

YOUR TURN PRACTICE BOOK p. 198

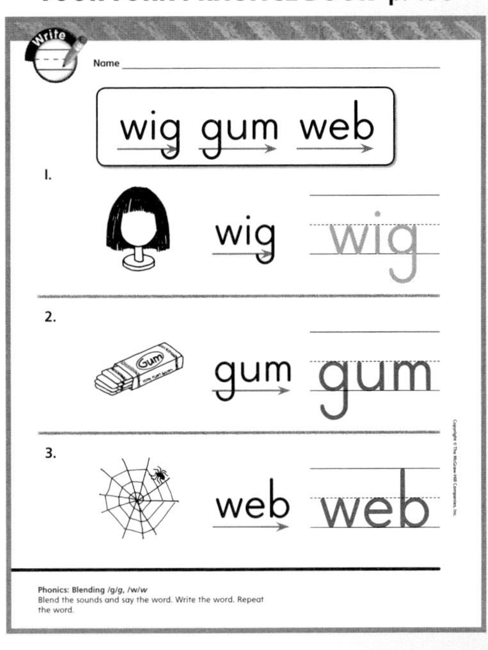

Write
Name
wig gum web
1.
wig
wig
2.
gum
gum
3.
web
web
Phonics: Blending /g/g, /w/w
Blend the sounds and say the word. Write the word. Repeat the word.

Word Work

Phonics

OBJECTIVES

CCSS Read common high-frequency words by sight. **RF.K.3c**

Sort picture names by initial /g/*g* or initial /w/*w*

ACADEMIC LANGUAGE
sort

Picture Sort

Photo Cards

1 Model Remind children that the letter *g* can stand for /g/ and the letter *w* stands for /w/. Place **Word-Building Card** *g* on the left side of a pocket chart. *What is this letter?* (g) *What sound does this letter stand for?* (/g/) Continue the routine placing letter *w* on the right side of the pocket chart.

Hold up the **Photo Card** for *game. Here is the picture for* game. Game *has the /g/ sound at the beginning. Listen, /gām/. I will place* game *under the letter* g *because the letter* g *stands for /g/.* Continue the same routine for *water.*

2 Guided Practice/Practice Display and name the following Photo Cards: *gate, girl, goat, gorilla, walrus, watch, watermelon, web.* Have children say the word and tell if it begins with /w/ or /g/. Have them tell under which letter the Photo Card should be placed. Guide practice with the first word.

Photo Cards

Go Digital

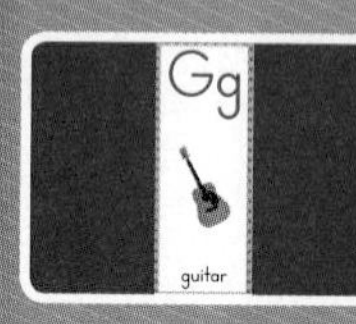

Phonics

the	is
you	do

High-Frequency Word Routine

High-Frequency Words

of, they

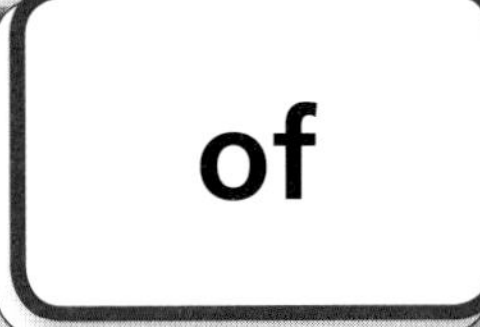

High-Frequency Word Cards

1. **Guided Practice** Display the **High-Frequency Word Cards** *of* and *they*. Review the words using the **Read/Spell/Write** routine.

2. **Practice** Point to the High-Frequency Word Card *of* and have children read it. Repeat with *they* and last week's words *for* and *have.*

Build Fluency

Word Automaticity Write the following sentences and have children chorally read aloud as you track the print. Repeat several times.

They can run with you.
It is a lot of fun.
They are in the hut.
The pack *of* gum is wet.

Read for Fluency Distribute pages 199–200 of the **Your Turn Practice Book** and help children assemble their Take-Home Books. Chorally read the Take-Home Books with children. Then have children reread the books to review high-frequency words and build fluency.

YOUR TURN PRACTICE BOOK pp. 199–200

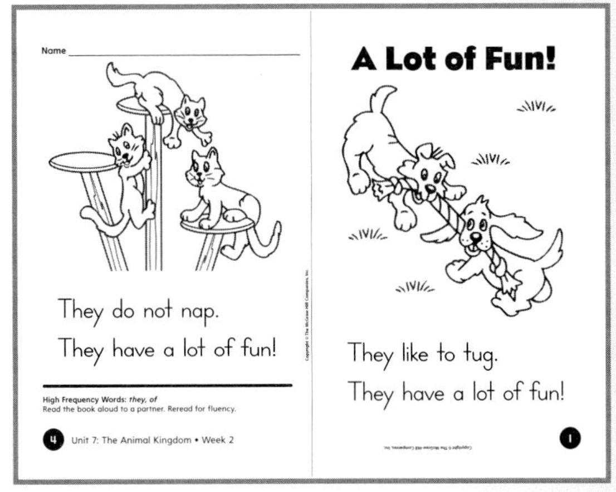

Monitor and Differentiate
Quick Check
Can children identify initial phonemes and sort words by initial /g/*g* and /w/*w*?
Can children recognize and read the high-frequency word?
Small Group Instruction
If No → Approaching Reteach pp. T144-149
ELL Develop pp. T162-165
If Yes → On Level Review pp. T152-155
Beyond Level Extend pp. T158-159

Language Arts

Reading/Writing Workshop Big Book

OBJECTIVES

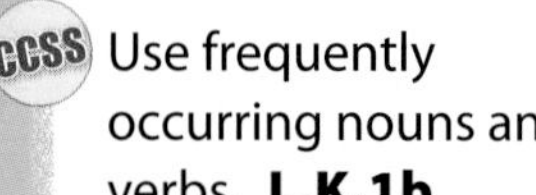

CCSS Use a combination of drawing, dictating, and writing to compose informative/explanatory texts in which they name what they are writing about and supply some information about the topic. **W.K.2**

CCSS Use frequently occurring nouns and verbs. **L.K.1b**

- Write explanatory text
- Apply writing trait and grammar to writing

ACADEMIC LANGUAGE

- *explain, action word, verb*
- Cognates: *explicar, verbo*

MINILESSON 10 Mins

Independent Writing

Writing Trait: Word Choice

1 Practice Tell children that today they will write sentences telling how to take care of a pet of their choice.

2 Guided Practice Share the Readers to Writers page in the **Reading/Writing Workshop**. Read the model sentences aloud.

READING/WRITING WORKSHOP BIG BOOK, pp. 32–33

Write an Explanatory Text

Model Display the list from Day 1. Write the name of a pet from the list, such as *cat*. Say: *I know how to take care of a cat. I will write sentences to explain how to take care of a cat.* Write: *I feed the cat twice a day. One important thing to remember is that a cat needs to be fed regularly.* Read the sentence aloud, tracking the print.

Prewrite

COLLABORATE

Brainstorm Have children work with a partner to choose a pet to write about. Ask children to tell their partner what they know about taking care of that pet.

Draft

Ask children to draw a picture of the pet they chose. Guide them in writing the name of the pet below the picture. Then ask them to write one or two sentences, telling how they would take care of the pet. Help children write their sentences.

Apply Writing Trait As children write and draw, ask them to explain how they would take care of the pet they chose.

Apply Grammar Tell children to point to the action words in their sentences and tell who or what does each action.

ENGLISH LANGUAGE LEARNERS

Understand Action Words
Use the Photo Card for *otter* for support. Have children draw a picture of the otter doing something. For example, children might draw an otter swimming. Have children dictate a sentence to tell what the otter is doing in the picture. Write the sentence below the picture and read it aloud with children.

Grammar

Action Words (Verbs)

1 **Review** Write and read aloud these sentences: *I jump high. I jumped high. Jump is an action word that tells what I do.* Jumped *is the action word in the second sentence. It tells an action that happened in the past. It has* -ed *added to the end of the word.*

2 **Guided Practice/Practice** Write and read aloud: *Sue jumped over the log.* Ask: *What did Sue do?* (jumped over the log) *Which word is the action word in the sentence?* (jumped) Ask children to tell you how they know *jumped* is the action word in the sentence. (It tells what Sue did.) *Is the action happening now, or did it happen in the past? How do you know?* (The action happened in the past. I know because *jumped* ends with *-ed*.)

Display and name the **Photo Cards** for *fox, giraffe, goat,* and *octopus.* Have children work with a partner. Have each pair of children choose one Photo Card and talk about what the animal that they chose can do. Have pairs say sentences about the photos using action words, such as *The fox walked in the snow.* Encourage children to use past-tense verbs when possible.

Talk About It

Have one partner pantomime an action they would do to care for a pet. Ask the other partner to identify the action. Then, have children switch roles.

Daily Wrap Up

- Review the Essential Question and encourage children to discuss it, using the oral vocabulary words *responsibility* and *train. What can you do to train a pet?*
- Prompt children to review and discuss the skills they used today. Guide them to give examples of how they used each skill.

WHOLE GROUP

DAY 4

Materials

Reading/Writing Workshop Big Book
UNIT 7

Literature Big Book
The Birthday Pet

Visual Vocabulary Cards
responsibility
train
depend
compared
social
of
they

Interactive Read-Aloud Cards

Word-Building Cards

Puppet

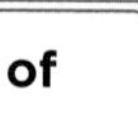

High-Frequency Word Cards
of
they

Photo Cards
fish
kitten
mouse
turtle

Extend the Concept

MINILESSON 10 Mins

Oral Language

OBJECTIVES

CCSS Recognize and produce rhyming words. **RF.K.2a**

CCSS Use words and phrases acquired through conversations, reading and being read to, and responding to texts. **L.K.6**

Develop oral vocabulary

ESSENTIAL QUESTION

Remind children that this week they have been talking and reading about ways to take care of different kinds of pets. Have them recite "My Carefree Dog" and think about how they would take care of a dog. How does the boy take care of his turtle in *The Birthday Pet*?

Phonological Awareness

Recognize and Generate Rhyme

Remind children that rhyming words have the same end sound. Say: *The words* meet *and* sweet *have the same end sound. Say them with me:* meet, sweet. Then say the following word pairs and have children raise their hands if the words rhyme: *see/free; cat/sat; cat/cake; take/cake.* Then challenge children to name a rhyming word for each of the following words: *bat* (rat); *tip* (rip); *rack* (pack); *pet* (net).

Review Oral Vocabulary

Reread the Interactive Read Aloud Use the **Define/Example/Ask** routine to review the oral vocabulary words *responsibility, train, depend, compared,* and *social*. Then have children listen as you reread "The Family Pet."

→ *What does a pet depend on you for?* (food, water, love)

→ *Why do the Johnsons want a social animal?* (They want to cuddle and play with it; they want to train it.)

Go Digital

Visual Glossary

"The Family Pet"

Category Words

Category Words: Pet Words

1 Explain/Model Have the **Photo Cards** for *fish, kitten, turtle,* and *mouse* ready to display. Tell children you are going to read a story. *When I hold up a Photo Card, say the pet word with me.*

Molly loved to look at the different animals at the pet store. First, she visited the [hold up *fish* card] *tank. Next, she saw the* [hold up *kitten* card]. *Then she watched the* [hold up *turtle* card]. *Last, she looked in the* [hold up *mouse* card] *cage. When it was time to leave, Molly said good-bye to each pet. "Good-bye* [hold up *fish* card], *good-bye* [hold up *kitten* card], *good-bye* [hold up *turtle* card], *good-bye* [hold up *mouse* card]*!"*

2 Guided Practice Write two pet words on the board, such as *fish* and *dog*. Guide children to compare and contrast the animals. (Possible answers: Both animals have tails. Fish do not have legs; dogs have legs. Fish live in water; dogs do not.)

→ Display the Photo Cards for *fish, kitten, dog, mouse,* and *turtle*. Have children takes turns choosing one of the pet words and using it in a sentence.

Vocabulary Strategy: Word Categories/Prepositions

1 Model Remind children that some words can be grouped into the category of prepositions. Tell children that prepositions often show the position or place of something. Discuss the following sentence from *The Birthday Pet*: "Danny thought it over before he went to bed." *The word* to *is a preposition. It connects the words* went *and* bed. *It helps tell where Danny went. He went to bed.*

2 Guided Practice/Practice Help children think of prepositional phrases such as *through the door, on the bed, in the middle,* and *to the park*. Point out examples from *The Birthday Pet* if necessary. Have children take turns using the prepositional phrases to make sentences that relate to caring for a pet.

ENGLISH LANGUAGE LEARNERS

Expand Have children draw pictures of different kinds of pets. Help them label their drawings with the correct pet word. Prompt children to describe the pets they drew.

LET'S MOVE!

Assign groups a pet word. Then give groups directions with pet words: *Birds, fly to the play area. Dogs, walk to the computers.*

YOUR TURN PRACTICE BOOK p. 201

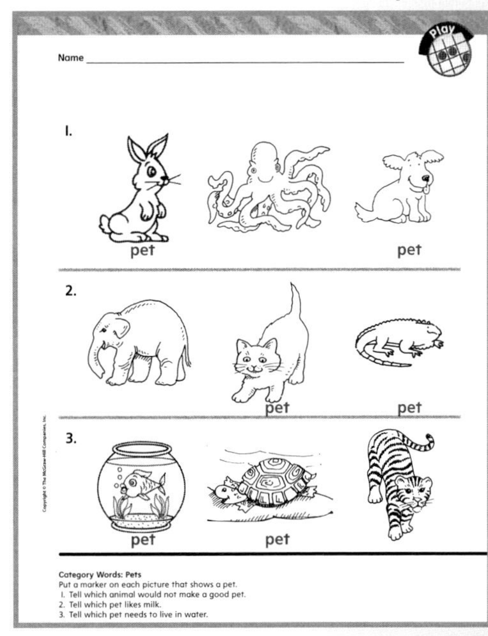
Name

1. pet pet

2. pet pet

3. pet pet

Category Words: Pets
Put a marker on each picture that shows a pet.
1. Tell which animal would not make a good pet.
2. Tell which pet likes milk.
3. Tell which pet needs to live in water.

Listening Comprehension

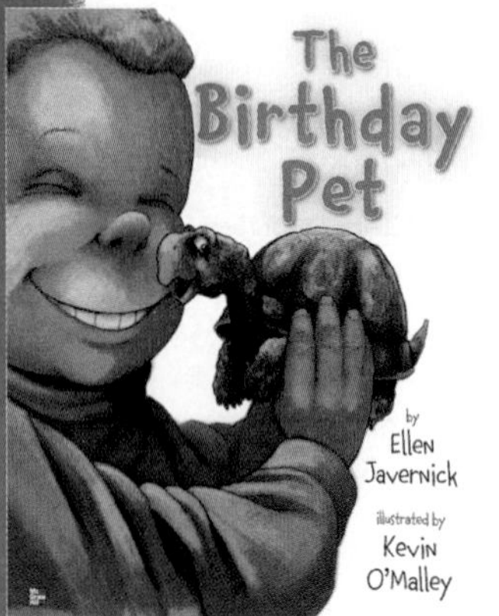

Literature Big Book

OBJECTIVES

CCSS With prompting and support, ask and answer questions about key details in a text. **RL.K.1**

- Understand the characteristics of fiction
- Use the text feature chart to gather information
- Apply the comprehension strategy: Make Predictions
- Make connections across texts

ACADEMIC LANGUAGE

- *chart, prediction*
- Cognates: *predicciones*

Read "The Perfect Pet"

Genre: Fiction

Display "The Perfect Pet" on pages 33–36 of the **Big Book** and read aloud the title. Remind children that fiction stories have made-up characters and events.

Set a Purpose for Reading

Read aloud the first two sentences on page 33. Tell children to listen as you continue reading the story, so they can learn which pet the family will pick.

Strategy: Make Predictions

Remind children that good readers make, change, and check predictions as they read. Read aloud the last two lines on page 33. *What kind of animal do you think would be the perfect pet? How would you take care of the pet?*

Text Feature: Chart

Explain Point to the chart on page 36. Explain that information in the chart tells who will take care of the pet each day. *This chart shows a length of time. How much time is shown?* (one week) Read aloud the days of the week with children.

Apply Read aloud the text for Monday and Tuesday on the chart. *What kind of information is written on this chart?* (who does each kind of chore and when) *Why is it a good idea to have a chart to take care of a pet?* (Possible answers: It is a fair way of sharing chores. A chart is a good reminder so no one will forget.)

Go Digital

The Birthday Pet

LITERATURE BIG BOOK PAGE 33

HIGH-FREQUENCY WORDS

Have children identify and read aloud the high-frequency words *they* and *of*.

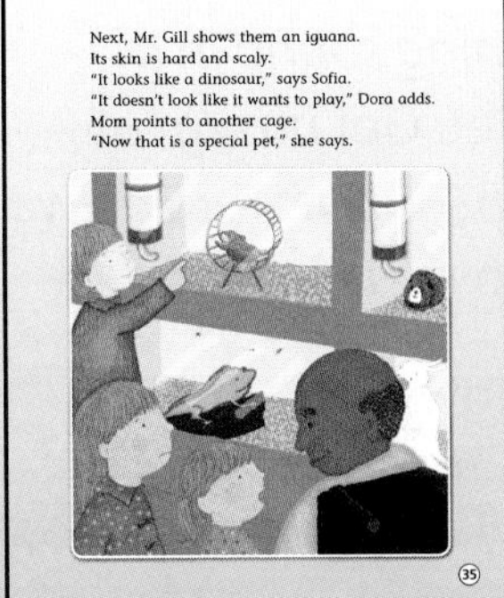

LITERATURE BIG BOOK PAGES 34–35

MAKE PREDICTIONS

Which pet do you predict the girls will take home? Why? (Possible answers: The girls will bring a hamster home. The illustration shows their mother pointing to a hamster cage.)

LITERATURE BIG BOOK PAGE 36

KEY DETAILS

What rules do the girls have to follow to care for their new pet? (They will need to follow their posted schedule to make sure the hamster is fed and watered and the cage is kept clean.)

ENGLISH LANGUAGE LEARNERS

Reinforce Meaning As you read aloud the text, make the meaning clear by pointing to details in the illustrations. Ask children questions and elicit language.

Retell and Respond

Have children discuss the selection by asking the following questions:

→ *How will Dora and Sofia keep track of their chores?* (on a chart)

→ *Why didn't they get an iguana?* (It was scaly and looked unfriendly.)

Make Connections

Have children recall the selections they read this week.

→ *Which pet did Danny want for his birthday?* (a turtle)

Write About It Write about a pet from "The Family Pet."

CONNECT TO CONTENT

Pet Rules Review with children the kinds of animals the family saw in the pet store (puppy, bird, iguana, rabbit, turtle, hamster). Have partners discuss the kind of animal they would like as a pet. Ask them to think about the rules that they would need to take care of the animal as a pet.

WHOLE GROUP

DAY 4

Word Work

Quick Review

Build Fluency: Sound-Spellings: Show the following **Word-Building Cards:** *a, b, c, d, e, f, g, h, i, k, l, m, n, o, p, r, s, t, u. w.* Have children chorally say each sound. Repeat and vary the pace.

Phonemic Awareness

Puppet

OBJECTIVES

CCSS Distinguish between similarly spelled words by identifying the sounds of the letters that differ. **RF.K.3d**

CCSS Add or substitute individual sounds (phonemes) in simple, one-syllable words to make new words. **RF.K.2e**

CCSS Read common high-frequency words by sight. **RF.K.3c**

Phoneme Substitution

1 **Model** Use the *puppet* to model phoneme substitution. *The puppet can change the beginning sound in a word to make a new word. Listen to this word:* get. *Get has /g/ at the beginning. Say* get, */g/. Let's change /g/ to /n/. What word do we have? We have the word* net. Repeat with *got* to make *hot.*

2 **Guided Practice/Practice** Have children follow directions to make new words. Give them ample time to respond. Guide practice with the first word.

Say give. *Change /g/ to /l/. What word do you have?* (live)
Say wave. *Change /w/ to /s/. What word do you have?* (save)
Say peach. *Change /p/ to /r/. What word do you have?* (reach)
Say wet. *Change /w/ to /l/. What word do you have?* (let)
Say game. *Change /g/ to /s/. What word do you have?* (same)
Say duck. *Change /d/ to /t/. What word do you have?* (tuck)

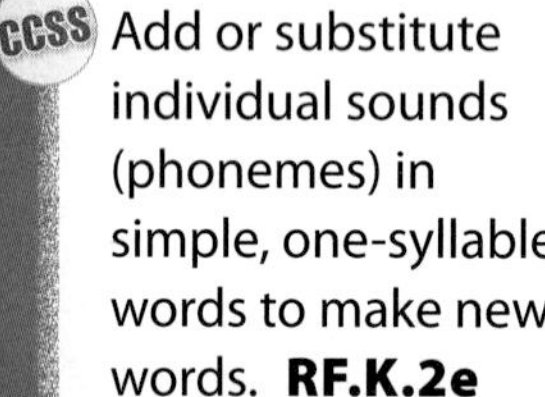

Phonics

Blend Words with Short *e* and *w, g, b, s*

1 **Guided Practice** Display **Word-Building Cards** *w, e, t.* Point to the letter *w. This is the letter* w. *The letter* w *stands for /w/. Say /w/. This is the letter* e. *The letter* e *stands for /e/. Listen as I blend the two sounds together /weee/. This is the letter* t. *The letter* t *stands for /t/. Listen as I blend the three sounds /weeet/,* wet. *Now you say it. Let's change the* w *to* g. Use the same routine to blend the word *get.*

2 **Practice** Write *wet, bet, get, set.* Have children blend the words. Ask children which letters are the same. (e, t) Ask children to tell which letters are different. (w, b, g, s) Discuss the sound each letter stands for and how it changes the word.

Go Digital

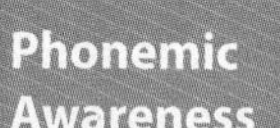

Phonemic Awareness

Phonics

Handwriting

Visual Glossary

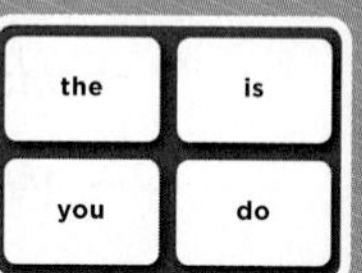

High-Frequency Word Routine

Dictation

Review Dictate each sound for children to spell. Have children repeat the sound and then write the letter that stands for the sound.

/g/ /w/ /b/ /a/ /s/ /t/ /l/

Dictate the following words for children to spell: *bag, sag, get, gas, wig, will.* Model for children how to segment each word to scaffold the spelling. *When I say the word* bag, *I hear three sounds: /b/ /a/ /g/. I know the letter* b *stands for /b/, the letter* a *stands for /a/, and the letter* g *stands for /g/. I will write the letters* b, a, g, *the word* bag.

When children finish, write the letters and words for them to self-correct.

Extend the Lesson

Blends with *l*

Use Word-Building Cards *s, l, i, p*. Point to the letters *s, l*. Tell children that when they blend these letters, they should say each sound: /s/ /l/. Blend and read the word and have children repeat. Continue blending *slap, clap, clock, click, slick, slim, slam.*

High-Frequency Words

Visual Vocabulary Cards

Practice Say the word *of* and have children write it. Then display the **Visual Vocabulary Card** *of*. Follow the Teacher Talk routine on the back.

Repeat for the word *they*.

Build Fluency Build sentences in the pocket chart using the **High-Frequency Word Cards** and **Photo Cards**. Use an index card to create a punctuation card for a period. Have children chorally read the sentences as you track the print. Then have them identify the words *of* and *they*.

They have a box **of** toys.
They have a yo-yo.
They have a map **of** the city.

COLLABORATE Have partners create sentences using the words *of* and *they*.

Monitor and *Differentiate*

Quick Check

Can children substitute initial phonemes to make new words and match /g/ and /w/ with the letters *Gg* and *Ww*?

Can children read and recognize high-frequency words?

Small Group Instruction

If No →	Approaching	Reteach pp. T144-149
	ELL	Develop pp. T162-165
If Yes →	On Level	Review pp. T152-155
	Beyond Level	Extend pp. T158-159

Shared Read

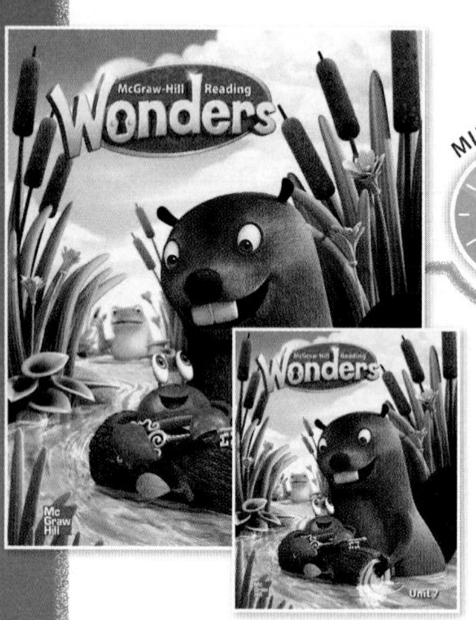

Reading/Writing Workshop Big Book and Reading/Writing Workshop

OBJECTIVES

CCSS Read common high-frequency words by sight. **RF.K.3c**

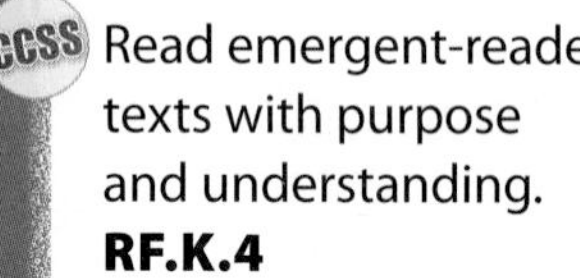

CCSS Read emergent-reader texts with purpose and understanding. **RF.K.4**

MINILESSON 10 Mins

Read "I Hug Gus!"

Model Skills and Strategies

Model Concepts About Print Begin reading the story. Point out the punctuation at the end of each sentence. *When I read, I notice that after the last word in each sentence, there is a punctuation mark. It can be a period or an exclamation point.* Then invite volunteers to come up to the **Big Book**. Have them point to and identify the punctuation at the end of each sentence. Have them point to the spaces between sentences to acknowledge the sentence boundaries.

Reread Invite children to chorally reread the story. Children should sound out the decodable words and say the sight words. Offer support as needed using the student **Reading/Writing Workshop**.

Ask the following:

- *Look at page 24. What animals are pictured on the page? What are they doing?* (a cat and a puppy; playing tug)
- *Look at page 26. What is Gus doing? What does he want?* (Gus is standing up on his hind legs on top of his bed. He wants the boy to give him a treat.)
- *Look at page 29. What is the boy doing?* (He is hugging Gus. He is tucking Gus into bed.)

Go Digital

"I Hug Gus!"

"I Hug Gus!"

I Hug Gus!
I can see a big, red pup.
I pick a pup for a pet.

My big pup and a cat tug.
They tug and have fun.
Gus is a big, red pup.
Gus can run, run and win!

Gus is on top **of** the bed.
He can sit up and beg.
Gus and I are on a rug.
Gus can tug, tug, tug!

I rub Gus in the tub.
Gus is wet, wet, wet!
I tuck Gus in a big bed.
I can hug, hug, hug Gus!

READING/WRITING WORKSHOP 7, pp. 22–29

Fluency: Intonation

1. **Explain** Tell children that as you read the story, you will change the tone of your voice when reading sentences that end with a period or an exclamation point. Point out different kinds of punctuation in the story.

2. **Model** Model reading page 25 of "I Hug Gus!" Read each sentence with the proper intonation and expression. Then point to the punctuation mark at the end of the second sentence. *When I read each sentence, the tone of my voice sounds different. When there is a period at the end of the sentence, I am making a statement. When there is an exclamation point at the end of the sentence, I read it with more emotion.* Read each sentence with appropriate intonation. Then point out differences in intonation by reading other sentences in the story that end with a period or an exclamation point.

3. **Guided Practice** Read each sentence in the story and have children echo you. Encourage children to repeat each sentence using proper intonation and expression. Then invite the class to choral read the story as you listen for proper intonation.

Language Arts

Independent Writing

OBJECTIVES

With guidance and support from adults, recall information from experiences or gather information from provided sources to answer a question. **W.K.8**

CCSS Use frequently occurring nouns and verbs. **L.K.1b**

- Revise explanatory sentences
- Use verbs in sentences

ACADEMIC LANGUAGE
revise

Write an Explanatory Text

Revise

Distribute the children's draft sentences with drawings from Day 3.

Apply Writing Trait Word Choice Explain that as writers revise, they make sure they have chosen the correct action words. Write and read aloud: *eats, drinks, hops.* Say: *I want to write a sentence that tells about taking care of a pet rabbit.* Then, write: *A rabbit ______ lettuce.* Read the sentence frame, pointing to each word. As a class, read the sentence frame with each of the words. *Which action word completes the sentence?* (eats) *How do you know?* (The only thing a rabbit does with lettuce is eat it. A rabbit doesn't drink or hop lettuce.) Read the sentence with the correct action word aloud. Then have children reread the sentences they wrote on Day 3 and check for the following:

- Did I explain how to take care of a pet?
- Did I use the right action words?
- Did I draw a picture of the pet?

Apply Grammar Review that action words are verbs that tell what someone or something is doing. *What action words did you use in your sentences?*

Peer Edit Have children work in pairs to do a peer edit, in which they read their partner's draft. Ask partners to check that their sentences describe their pictures. Have children check that they chose appropriate action words to explain how to take care of their pet. Provide time for children to make revisions to their sentences.

Final Draft

After children have edited their own papers and finished their peer edits, have them write their final draft. Remind children to use a period at the end of each sentence. As children work, conference with them to provide guidance.

Go Digital

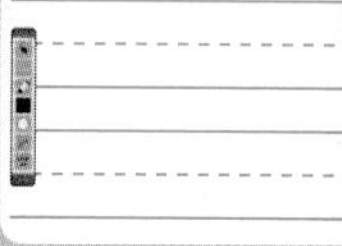

Writing

Grammar

Grammar

Action Words (Verbs)

1 Review Write and read aloud this sentence: *Amelia walked to school.* Ask: *Which word is an action word?* (walked) *How do you know that it is an action word?* (It tells what Amelia did.) *Is the action happening now, or did it happen in the past?* (in the past) *How do you know?* (*walked* ends with *-ed*.)

2 Guided Practice Say these sentences aloud: *Andrew sings a song. Walter plays the guitar.* Ask children to tell which word in each sentence is the action word. (sings, plays) Ask volunteers to explain how they know that *sings* and *plays* are action words.

Say: *We know that* sings *and* plays *are action words because they tell what the person does in each sentence. We know that the actions are happening now because each word ends with* -s. *Action words that tell about one naming word end in* -s.

3 Practice Write and read aloud: *Mary ______ the tree.*

Have children work with a partner to choose an action word to complete the sentence. (climbs, climbed) Ask partners to read aloud the sentence.

Have partners think of action words. As one child says an action word, the other child says a sentence using the word. Tell them to say each action word in the present and then in the past. If children use verbs that are irregular in the past tense, such as *swims/swam, runs/ran,* and so on, praise them for knowing these past-tense words. Point out that not all action words that tell about the past end with *-ed*.

Talk About It

Have partners think of sentences, using past tense action words. Encourage them to think about things they did yesterday.

ENGLISH LANGUAGE LEARNERS

Photo Cards and Sentences Provide sentences that go with images on the **Photo Cards**. As you say a sentence aloud, hold up a Photo Card as you say the action and the person or thing doing the action, such as *The dog barked.* Then have children repeat saying the sentences. Ask children to name the action word in each sentence.

Daily Wrap Up

- Review the Essential Question and encourage children to discuss it, using the oral vocabulary words.
- Prompt children to discuss the skills they practiced and learned today. Guide them to share examples of each skill.

WHOLE GROUP

DAY 4

Go Digital

www.connected.mcgraw-hill.com
RESOURCES
Research and Inquiry

Wrap Up the Week
Integrate Ideas

RESEARCH AND INQUIRY

SOCIAL STUDIES

Pet Pals

OBJECTIVES

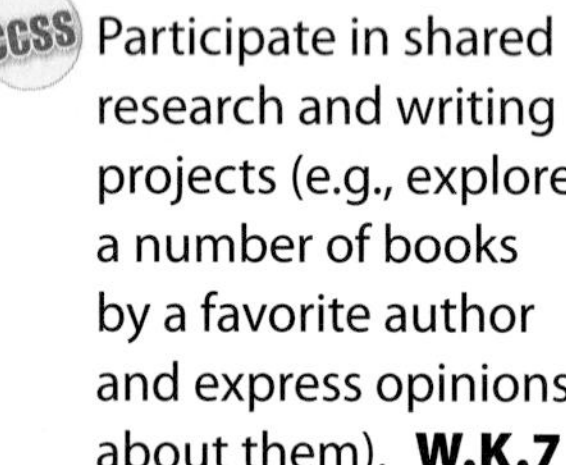

CCSS Participate in shared research and writing projects (e.g., explore a number of books by a favorite author and express opinions about them). **W.K.7**

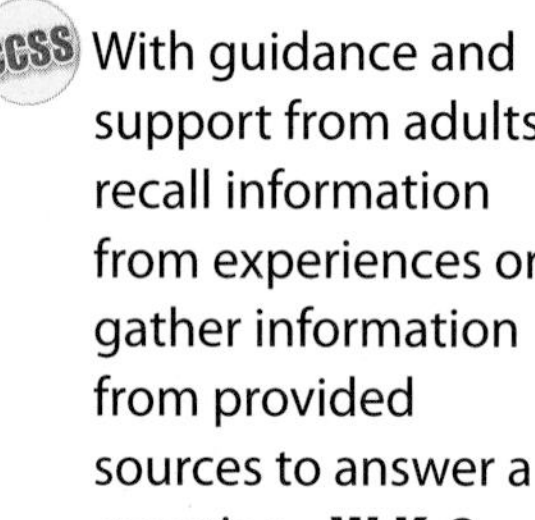

CCSS With guidance and support from adults, recall information from experiences or gather information from provided sources to answer a question. **W.K.8**

ACADEMIC LANGUAGE

research, inquiry, reference

Make a Poster

Tell children that today, as part of a small group, they will make a poster about pet care. Review the steps in the research process.

STEP 1 Choose a Topic

Guide groups to think about a pet they would like to have. Tell them to think about the rules they would have to follow to care for the pet.

STEP 2 Find Resources

Review how to locate and use resources. Guide children to use selections from the week, the Internet, and books from the school library. Children can also use their own experiences as resources. Have children use the Research Process Checklist online.

STEP 3 Keep Track of Ideas

Have children collaborate in their small group to list the information they collected by drawing pictures or writing words. They may also wish to print out pages from Web sites. Help children with the names of animals and other content-related words.

Collaborative Conversations

Be Open to All Ideas As children engage in partner, small-group, and whole-class discussions, tell them to:

- listen carefully because all ideas, questions, or comments are important.
- ask a question if something is unclear.
- respect the opinions of others.
- give their opinions, even if they are different from those of other people.

We have a cat. We brush our pet.

STEP 4 Create the Project: Pet-Care Poster

Explain the characteristics of the project:

→ **Information** A poster can give information. This poster will give information about pet care.

→ **Text** Explain that each poster will have sentences that name the animal and tell how to care for it. Provide these sentence frames:

We have a ______. We ______ our pet.

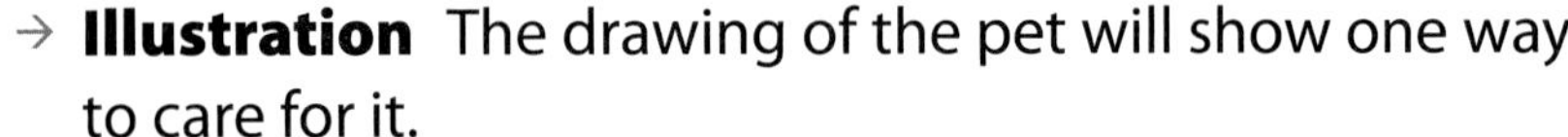

→ **Illustration** The drawing of the pet will show one way to care for it.

Have group members work together to sort through the information they have collected and decide on the pet care tip they will use as the subject of their poster.

→ Guide children to write complete sentences.

→ Encourage children who can generate more writing to do so.

→ Prompt children to include details in their illustration.

ENGLISH LANGUAGE LEARNERS SCAFFOLD

Beginning

Elaborate Allow children to point to and identify details on posters with single-word names. Restate (or have more fluent partners restate) the information using a complete sentence; then elicit more information and, again, refashion the child's answer in a complete sentence.

Intermediate

Identify As partners work on their posters, prompt them to talk about and identify all of the details they are adding to their illustration. Tell children to anticipate questions such as these: *What is the pet doing? What does the pet play with? How does the pet's [skin or fur] feel?*

Advanced/Advanced High

Describe Direct children to include describing words as they tell about the details in their poster. For example: *Our pet has thick fur. He has a loud bark.*

WHOLE GROUP
DAY 5

Materials

Reading/Writing Workshop Big Book
UNIT 7

Literature Big Book
The Birthday Pet

Word-Building Cards

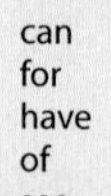
Visual Vocabulary Cards
of
they

High-Frequency Word Cards
can
for
have
of
see
they

Puppet

Response Boards

Integrate Ideas

TEXT CONNECTIONS

Connect to Essential Question

OBJECTIVES

With prompting and support, compare and contrast the adventures and experiences of characters in familiar stories. **RL.K.9**

Participate in collaborative conversations with diverse partners about *kindergarten topics and texts* with peers and adults in small and larger groups. **SL.K.1**

- Make connections among texts
- Make connections to the world

Text to Text

Remind children that all week they have been reading selections about caring for pets. Tell them that now they will connect the texts, or think about how the selections are alike. Model comparing *The Birthday Pet* with another selection from the week.

COLLABORATE

Think Aloud In *The Birthday Pet,* I learned about how a boy wanted a turtle for a pet. In "The Perfect Pet," I learned about how two sisters looked for a new pet and got a hamster. Turtles and hamsters are very different, but at the end of both stories the characters take care of their new pets.

Guide children to compare the experiences of the characters, people and pets from this week's selections including the Leveled Readers.

Text to Self

Have children discuss what they have done to care for a pet. Help them focus on the importance of basic pet care such as food, water, exercise, grooming or cleaning, and "play time."

Text to World

Talk about the pets that children see in the community. They may be at zoos, animal parks, pet stores, or animal shelters. Have children tell about how they see people caring for those animals.

TALK ABOUT READING

Analyze and Explain

OBJECTIVES

CCSS Confirm understanding of a text read aloud or information presented orally or through other media by asking and answering questions about key details and requesting clarification if something is not understood. **SL.K.2**

Becoming Readers

Talk with children about the genres, strategy, and skill they have learned about this week. Prompt them to discuss how this knowledge helps them to read and understand selections.

- → Remind children that one genre they learned about is fiction. Recall with them some characteristics of fiction.
- → Talk about the strategy of making, confirming, and revising predictions. *In* The Birthday Pet*, were you right about what pet the boy would choose? How did making predictions help make the reading more interesting?*
- → Discuss how thinking about the problem and solution helps readers understand a story. *What problem does the boy have in* The Birthday Pet*? How is the problem solved? How did looking for the problem and solution keep you interested in the story?*

RESEARCH AND INQUIRY

Pet Pals

OBJECTIVES

CCSS Participate in shared research and writing projects (e.g. explore a number of books by a favorite author and express opinions about them). **W.K.7**

Wrap Up the Project

COLLABORATE

Guide partners to share information they've learned about pet care. Encourage children to use words and phrases they learned this week. Have children use the Presenting and Listening checklists online.

WHOLE GROUP
DAY 5

Word Work

Quick Review

Build Fluency: Sound-Spellings: Show the following **Word-Building Cards:** *a, b, c, d, e, f, g, h, i, k, l, m, n, o, p, r, s, t, u, w.* Have children chorally say the sounds. Repeat and vary the pace.

MINILESSON 5 Mins

Phonemic Awareness

OBJECTIVES

CCSS Add or substitute individual sounds (phonemes) in simple, one-syllable words to make new words. **RF.K.2e**

CCSS Spell simple words phonetically, drawing on knowledge of sound-letter relationships. **L.K.2d**

CCSS Read common high-frequency words by sight. **RF.K.3c**

Phoneme Substitution

1 **Model** *The puppet can change the beginning sound in a word to make a new word. Listen to this word:* wet. Wet *has the /w/ sound at the beginning. Say* wet, */w/. What word do we have when we change /w/ in* wet *to /g/? We have* get. Repeat with *hit* changing it to *bit.*

2 **Guided Practice/Practice** Have children follow the directions to make new words. Guide practice with the first word.

Say got. Change /g/ to /h/. *What word do you have?* (hot)
Say wag. Change /w/ to /b/. *What word do you have?* (bag)
Say gate. Change /g/ to /w/. *What word do you have?* (wait)
Say wig. *Change /w/ to /p/. What word do you have?* (pig)

MINILESSON 5 Mins

Phonics

Read Words with Short *a, e,* and *g, w, b*

1 **Guided Practice** Remind children that the letter *g* stands for the sound /g/. Display **Word-Building Cards** *g, e, t.* Point to the letter *g. The letter* g *stands for the sound /g/. The letter* e *stands for the sound /e/. Say /eee/. The letter* t *stands for /t/. Say /t/. Let's blend the sounds to make the word: /geeet/* get. *Now let's change the* g *to* w. Blend and read *wet* with children.

2 **Practice** Write these words and sentences for children to read:

gap sap tap wet set get bag wag

I can tap the top. Can you get the hat?
The wet bag sags. Will you see him?

Remove words before dictation.

Review initial /g/*g* and /w/*w*. Have children write *g* on their **Response Boards**. Play and sing "Get a Guitar" Have children hold up and show the letter *g* when they hear initial /g/. Demonstrate as you sing with children. Repeat with /w/*w* and "What Can You See Out Your Window?"

Go Digital

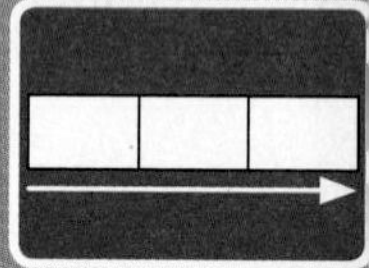

Phonemic Awareness

Phonics

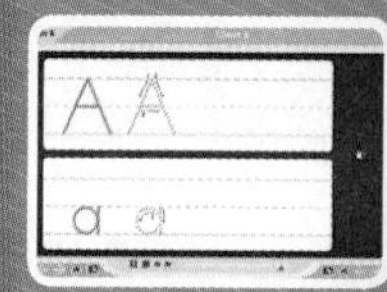

Handwriting

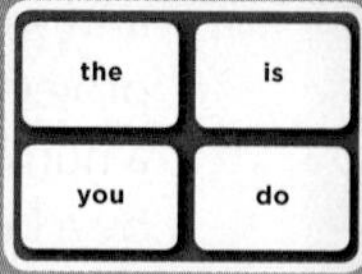

High-Frequency Word Cards

Dictation

1 Review Dictate the following sounds for children to spell. As you say each sound, have children repeat it and then write the letter that stands for the sound.

/w/ /i/ /g/ /e/ /t/ /l/ /b/ /a/

Dictate the following words for children to spell. Model for children how to use sound boxes to segment each word to scaffold the spelling. *I will say a word. You will repeat the word, then think about how many sounds are in the word. Use your* ***Sound Boxes*** *to count the sounds. Then write one letter for each sound you hear.*

will wet get bag big gap wig gas sag

Then write the letters and words for children to self-correct.

MINILESSON 5 Mins

High-Frequency Words

of, they

Visual Vocabulary Cards

1 Review Display **Visual Vocabulary Card** *of.* Have children **Read/Spell/Write** the word *of.* Then choose a Partner Talk activity.

Repeat the routine for the word *they.*

Distribute one of the following **High-Frequency Word Cards** to children: *they, have, of, for, can, see.* Tell children that you will say some sentences. *When you hear the word that is on your card, stand and hold up the word card.*

They *have* one of the books.
They can see him.
They are in the back *of* the house.
I opened the door *for* the dog.
He *can* ride his bicycle.
I *see* the park from my house.

2 Build Fluency: Word Automaticity Display the High-Frequency Word Cards *they, have, of, for, can, see.* Point to each card, at random, and have children read the word as quickly as they can.

Monitor and *Differentiate*

Can children substitute initial phonemes to make new words and recognize words with /g/ and /w/ and match them to the letters *Gg* and *Ww*?

Can children read and recognize high-frequency words?

Small Group Instruction

If No →	Approaching	Reteach pp. T144-149
	ELL	Develop pp. T162-165
If Yes →	On Level	Review pp. T152-155
	Beyond Level	Extend pp. T158-159

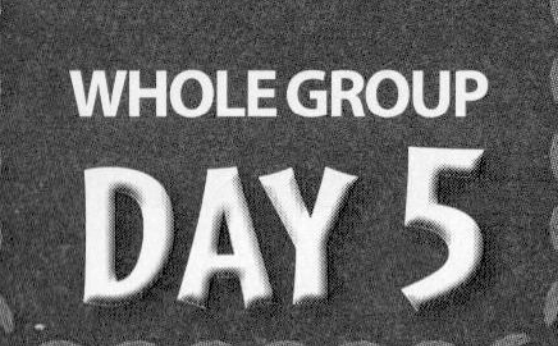

Language Arts

Independent Writing

OBJECTIVES

Speak audibly and express thoughts, feelings, and ideas clearly. **SL.K.6**

CCSS Use frequently occurring nouns and verbs. **L.K.1b**

Present an explanatory text

ACADEMIC LANGUAGE

- *present, publish*
- Cognates: *presente*

Write an Explanatory Text

Prepare

Tell children that they will present to the class their finished pet-care directions from Day 4. Hold up an example from Day 4 and read it aloud, tracking the print. Use words to describe the drawing clearly. Say: *I read the sentences clearly so that everyone could understand what I was saying. I talked about the pet drawing clearly and pointed out items in the picture so everyone would know what I drew.*

Present

Have children take turns standing up and reading their sentences aloud and talking about their drawings. Remind children to speak clearly. Encourage the rest of the class to listen carefully to the person speaking and to wait until the end of the presentation to raise their hands and ask questions.

Evaluate

Have children discuss their own presentations and evaluate their performances, using the presentation rubric. Use the teacher's rubric to evaluate children's writing.

Publish

After children have finished presenting, collect the pet-care directions. Bind the directions together to create a class book called *Pet Care*. Place the book in the reading area so children can read it independently or with a partner.

Go Digital

Writing

I see a fish.

Grammar

Grammar

Action Words (Verbs)

1 **Review** Write and read aloud these sentences: *Katie plays hockey. She hits the puck.* Ask: *Which words are action words?* (plays, hits) *What do these action words tell you?* (The words *plays* and *hits* tell me what Katie did.)

2 **Review Practice** Write these sentence frames on sentence strips:

We ______ soccer yesterday.
Justin ______ the ball.
Meg ______ the ball to Matt.
Matt ______ up high.

Read the sentence frames aloud. Write these action words on index cards: *jumps, jumped; kicks, kicked; pass, passed; play, played.* Display the cards and read the words aloud. Have children work with a partner to choose an action word to complete each sentence. Tell them that more than one word may be correct in some sentences.

Then have partners complete a sentence frame with an index card. Ask them to explain why they chose these words. Guide them to see that the word *yesterday* in the first sentence is a clue to use action words that tell about the past.

Gather the sentence strips and cards and store them in a folder for a center or review activity.

Wrap Up the Week

- Review blending words with initial and final /g/*g* and initial /w/*w*. Remind children that action words tell about what people or things are doing.
- Use the **High-Frequency Word Cards** to review the Words to Know.
- Remind children that when they write, they should choose action words that will make their writing more interesting.

Approaching Level

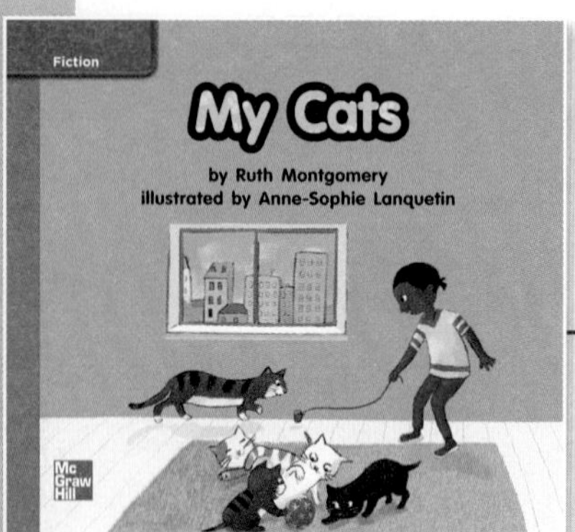

Leveled Reader

OBJECTIVES

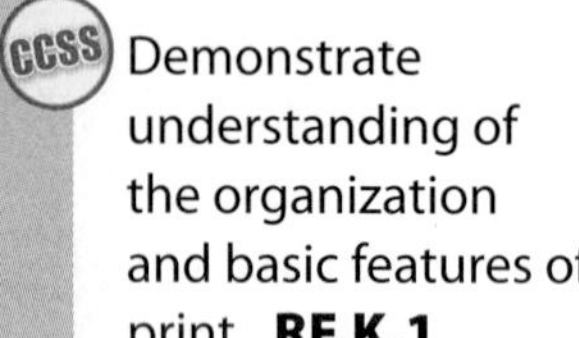

With prompting and support, identify characters, settings, and major events in a story. **RL.K.3**

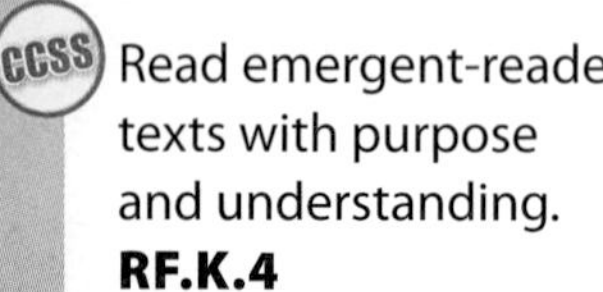

Demonstrate understanding of the organization and basic features of print. **RF.K.1**

Read emergent-reader texts with purpose and understanding. **RF.K.4**

Leveled Reader: *My Cats*

Go Digital

Leveled Readers

Before Reading

Preview and Predict

Point to and read each word in the title and in the author's and illustrator's name. Ask children to tell what they see in the cover illustration. Ask: *What do you think this book is about?* Preview the illustrations in the book to help children confirm their predictions or make new ones.

Review Genre: Fiction

Review with children that fiction stories have made-up characters, events, and settings. Ask them to say who they think will be the main character in the book.

Model Concepts of Print

Have children point to the sentence on page 2. Say: *This is a sentence. It begins with a capital letter and ends with a period.* Point to each word. Say: *There are three words in this sentence.*

Review High-Frequency Words

Point out the word *They* on page 2, and read it with children. Ask them to locate *They* on other pages.

Essential Question

Remind children of the Essential Question: *How do you take care of different kinds of pets?* Set a purpose for reading: *As we read this book, think about how you would take care of a pet.*

During Reading

Guided Comprehension

As children whisper-read *My Cats*, monitor and provide guidance by correcting blending and modeling the strategy and skill.

Strategy: Make, Confirm, and Revise Predictions

Explain to children that making predictions as they read will make them better readers. Explain that readers ask themselves what they think will happen next and then read to find out if they were right.

Skill: Character, Setting, Plot

Remind children that thinking of who the story is about, where the story takes place, and what is happening helps us make sense of what we read.

Think Aloud The first two pages give me an idea of the character and the setting. The character is a young girl. The story takes place at her home. I think the events in the story will be about how she takes care of her cats. I can find out about the characters, setting, and plot from the words on the page and from the illustrations.

As children read the book, guide them to identify the characters, the setting, and plot. Assist them in using the pictures to understand that the girl is taking care of a mother cat and her kittens.

After Reading

Respond to Reading

- *Who is this story about?* (a girl and her cats)
- *Where does this story take place?* (in the girl's house)
- *What happens at the end of the story?* (The girl and her mother are sitting with some of the cats on the couch.)

Retell

Have children take turns retelling the story. Help them make a personal connection by asking: *What kind of pet do you have or would you like to have? How would you take care of it?*

Model Fluency

Read the story aloud, pausing after each page to have children chorally repeat.

Apply Have children practice reading with partners as you observe and provide needed assistance.

LITERACY ACTIVITIES

Have children complete the activities on the inside back cover of the reader.

Level Up

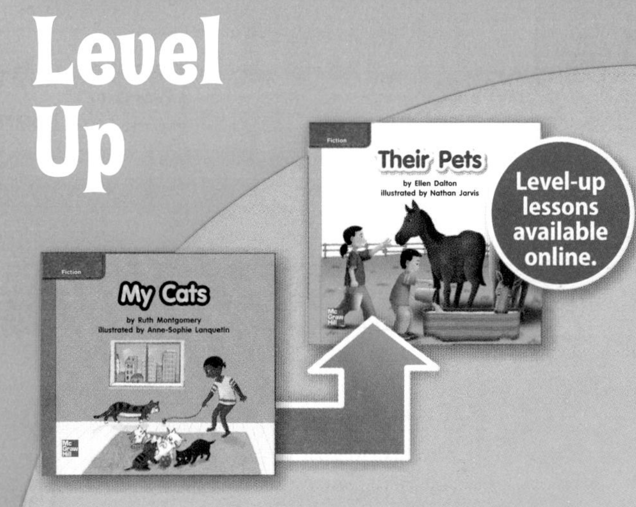

IF Children read *My Cats* Approaching Level with fluency and correctly answer the Respond to Reading questions,

THEN Tell children that they will read another story about taking care of pets.

- Have children page through *Their Pets* On Level with you, helping them identify the main characters, the story's setting, and what is happening.
- Have children read the story, monitoring their comprehension and providing assistance as necessary.

Approaching Level

Phonological Awareness

RECOGNIZE AND GENERATE RHYME

TIER 2

OBJECTIVES

CCSS Recognize and produce rhyming words. **RF.K.2A**

I Do

Remind children that rhyming words have the same ending sounds. Reread "My Carefree Dog" and point out that the words *carefree* and *see* rhyme because they have the same ending sound. List new words that rhyme with *carefree* and *see,* such as *me, tree,* or *key*.

We Do

Say the words *meet, sweet,* and *street* from "My Carefree Dog." *These words rhyme. They all have the same ending sounds*. Have children repeat the words after you, emphasizing /ēt/.

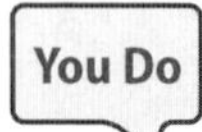
You Do

Say the following words and have children name words that rhyme with them: *sat, nut, can, pen, seat*.

PHONEME ISOLATION

TIER 2

OBJECTIVES

CCSS Isolate and pronounce the initial, medial vowel, and final sounds (phonemes) in three-phoneme words. **RF.K.2d**

I Do

Display the *Girl* **Photo Card**. *This is a girl. The first sound I hear in* girl *is* /g/. Have children repeat the word with you, emphasizing the initial sound. Then have children say the first sound with you: /g/. Repeat for initial /w/ using the *Wolf* Photo Card.

We Do

Display the *Goat* Photo Card. Name the photo and have children say the name. *What is the first sound in* goat*?* (/g/) Say the sound together. Repeat using the *Gate* Photo Card. Repeat for /w/ using the Photo Cards for *Window* and *Whale*.

You Do

Show the *Game* Photo Card. Have children name it and say the initial sound of the picture name. Repeat with the *Gorilla* Photo Card. Repeat for /w/ using the *Watch* and *Walrus* Photo Cards.

Repeat the routine for final /g/ using the *Dog* Photo Card in *I Do*. Ask children to name the final sound. (/g/) In *We Do,* have children tell where the /g/ sound is in *dog*. (at the end) In *You Do,* have children name the /g/ sound and its position in the words *mug* and *tag*.

You may wish to review Phonological Awareness and Phonemic Awareness with ELL using this section.

PHONEME BLENDING

OBJECTIVES

CCSS Isolate and pronounce the initial, medial vowel, and final sounds (phonemes) in three-phoneme words. **RF.K.2d**

The puppet will say the sounds in a word. Listen: /g/ /e/ /t/. The puppet can blend these sounds together: /g/ /eee/ /t/, /geeet/, get. Repeat with *web.*

Now the puppet is going to say the sounds in another word. Say the sounds with the puppet: /g/ /u/ /m/. Let's blend the sounds together: /g/ /uuu/ /mmm/, /guuummm/, gum. Repeat with *wet.*

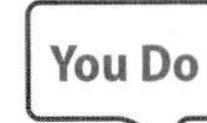

Have children blend sounds to form words. Practice together: /g/ /i/ /v/, *give.* Then have children practice blending the following sounds to say the words: /g/ /o/ /t/ got; /g/ /a/ /s/ gas; /w/ /i/ /n/ win; /w/ /a/ /g/ wag.

Repeat the routine for final /g/ and the sounds in the words /r/ /i/ /g/; /h/ /o/ /g/; /n/ /a/ /g/.

PHONEME SUBSTITUTION

OBJECTIVES

CCSS Add or substitute individual sounds (phonemes) in simple, one-syllable words to make new words. **RF.K.2e**

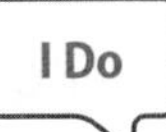

The puppet can change the beginning sound in a word to make a new word. Listen as the puppet says a word: gum. Gum *has the /g/ sound at the beginning. Listen as the puppet changes the /g/ sound to /h/:* hum.

Listen as the puppet says a word: win. *What word does the puppet make when it changes /w/ in* win *to /f/?* Together say the word *fin.* Repeat with *get/wet.*

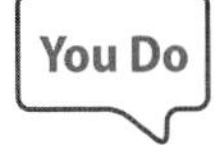

Guide children with phoneme substitution. *Say* get. *Change /g/ to /w/. What word do you have?* (wet) Repeat the routine with the following: /g/ in *got* to /h/ (hot); /w/ in *wall* to /f/ (fall); /w/ in *wax* to /t/ (tax); /k/ in *keep* to /w/ (weep); /g/ in *gate* to /l/ (late); /g/ in *goat* to /b/ (boat).

ELL ENGLISH LANGUAGE LEARNERS

For the **ELLs** who need **phonics, decoding,** and **fluency** practice, use scaffolding methods as necessary to ensure children understand the meaning of the words. Refer to the Language Transfer Handbook for phonics elements that may not transfer in students' native languages.

Approaching Level

Phonics

SOUND-SPELLING REVIEW

TIER 2

OBJECTIVES

CCSS Demonstrate basic knowledge of one-to-one letter-sound correspondences by producing the most frequent sounds for each consonant. **RF.K.3a**

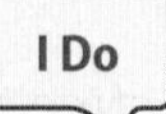

Display **Word-Building Card** *u*. Say the letter name and the sound it stands for: *u*, /u/. Repeat for *h, e, f, r, b, l, k,* and *c*.

Display Word-Building Cards one at a time and together say the letter name and the sound that each letter stands for.

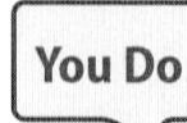

Display Word-Building Cards one at a time and have children say the letter name and the sound that each letter stands for.

CONNECT *g* TO /g/ AND *w* TO /w/

OBJECTIVES

Demonstrate basic knowledge of one-to-one letter-sound correspondences by producing the primary or many of the most frequent sounds for each consonant. **RF.K.3a**

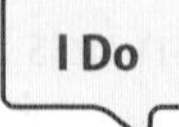

Display the *Guitar* **Sound-Spelling Card**. *The letter* g *stands for /g/ at the beginning of* guitar. *What is this letter? What sound does it stand for? I will write* g *when I hear /g/* in these words: *girl, see, game, fan, gum*.

The word get *begins with /g/. Let's write g*. Guide children to write *g* when they hear a word that begins with /g/. Say: *gap, pan, go, gills, rock, cub*. Repeat for final /g/ using the words *hog, rug, deck, man, leg*.

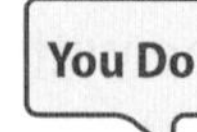

Have children write *g* if a word begins or ends with /g/: *dog, pit, big, gab, get*. Repeat for initial /w/ using the *Window* Sound-Spelling Card and these words: *wet, wind, toy, we, tree, walk, pop, with*.

RETEACH

CCSS Know and apply grade-level phonics and word analysis skills in decoding words. **RF.K.3**

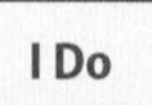

Display **Reading/Writing Workshop**, p. 20. Review *g* and *w*. *The letter* g *stands for /g/ as in* guitar. Repeat with *window* and /w/.

Have children name each picture in row 1. Repeat the name, emphasizing /g/. Repeat for row 2, emphasizing initial /w/.

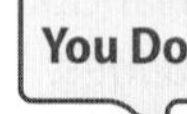

Guide children in reading the words in row 3. Then have them read the words in row 4, offering assistance as needed.

BLEND WORDS WITH /g/ *g* AND /w/ *w*

OBJECTIVES

CCSS Isolate and pronounce the initial, medial vowel, and final sounds (phonemes) in three-phoneme words. **RF.K.2d**

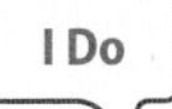

Display **Word-Building Cards** *g, e,* and *t. This is the letter* g. *It stands for* /g/. *This is the letter* e. *It stands for* /e/. *This is the letter* t. *It stands for* /t/. *Listen as I blend all three sounds:* /geeet/, get. *The word is* get. Repeat for *dog*.

Now let's blend more sounds to make words. Make the word *gum*. *Let's blend:* /guuummm/, gum. Have children blend to read the word. Repeat with the word *got*. *Let's blend:* /gooot/, got.

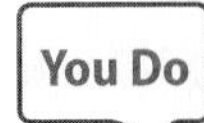

Distribute sets of Word-Building Cards with *g, a, b, o, u,* and *f*. Write: *gab, go, bug, fog*. Have children form the words and then blend and read the words.

Repeat the routine for /w/*w* using the words *wet, wig, we, wed, win, wag,* and *web*.

REREAD FOR FLUENCY

OBJECTIVES

Read emergent-reader texts with purpose and understanding. **RF.K.4**

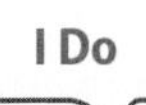

Turn to p. 22 of **Reading/Writing Workshop** and read aloud the title. *Let's read the title together*. Page through the book. Ask children what they see in each picture. Ask children to find the word *they* on p. 24 and *of* on p. 26.

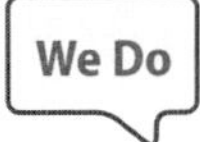

Then have children open their books and chorally read the story. Have children point to each word as they read. Provide corrective feedback as needed. After reading, ask children to recall what Gus likes to do.

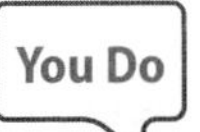

Have children reread "I Hug Gus!" with a partner for fluency.

BUILD FLUENCY WITH PHONICS

Sound/Spelling Fluency

Display the following Word-Building Cards: *h, e, f, r, b, l, k, ck, u, g,* and *w*. Have children chorally say each sound. Repeat and vary the pace.

Fluency in Connected Text

Write the following sentences. *Get the big red bag for me. The web is wet. Nick got to hug the dog*. Have children read the sentences and identify the words with /g/ and /w/.

Approaching Level

High-Frequency Words

TIER 2

RETEACH WORDS

OBJECTIVES

 Read common high-frequency words by sight. **RF.K.3c**

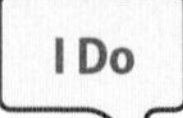 Display **High-Frequency Word Card** *they* and use the **Read/Spell/Write** routine to reteach the word. Repeat for *of*.

 Have children turn to p. 21 of **Reading/Writing Workshop** and discuss the first photo. Then read aloud the first sentence. Reread the sentence with children. Then distribute index cards with the word *they* written on them. Have children match their word cards with the word *they* in the sentence. Use the same routine for *of* and the other sentence on the page.

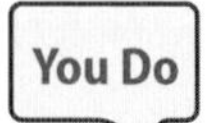 Write the sentence frame *They have a bag of* ____. Have children copy the sentence frame on their **Response Boards**. Then have partners work together to read and orally complete the frame by talking about something from a supermarket that could be in the bag. Reteach previously introduced high-frequency words using the **Read/Spell/Write** routine.

CUMULATIVE REVIEW

OBJECTIVES

 Read common high-frequency words by sight. **RF.K.3c**

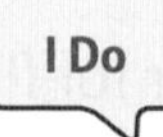 Display the **High-Frequency Word Cards** *I, can, the, we, see, a, like, to, and, go, you, do, my, are, he, with, is, little, she, was, for, have, they,* and *of*. Use the **Read/Spell/Write** routine to review words. Use the High-Frequency Word Cards to create sentences, such as *She is a red cat. I have a can of pens.*

 Use the **Read/Spell/Write** routine with children to review words. Invite a volunteer to write the words on the board. Offer help as needed. Then guide children to create a sentence as a class using the High-Frequency Word Cards and **Word-Building Cards**.

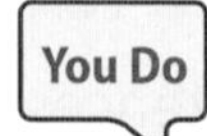 Have partners use the High-Frequency Word Cards and Word-Building Cards to create short sentences. Then have them write the sentences on their Response Boards.

Oral Vocabulary

REVIEW WORDS

OBJECTIVES

Identify real-life connections between words and their use. **L.K.5c**

Develop oral vocabulary: *responsibility, train, depend, compared, social.*

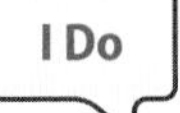

Use the **Define/Example/Ask** routine to review words. Use the following definitions and provide examples:

responsibility	Something you are supposed to do is your **responsibility**.
train	To **train** is to teach a person or an animal how to do something.
depend	When you **depend** on someone, you trust that person.
compared	If you have **compared** two things, you found out how they were alike and how they were different.
social	If you are **social**, you like being around people a lot.

Ask questions to build understanding. *What is a responsibility you have at home? What can you train a dog to do? Who is someone you depend on? What are two kinds of weather that can be compared? How can you tell if someone is being social in your neighborhood?*

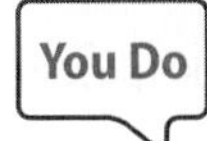

Have children complete these sentence frames: *One responsibility of a gardener is to ____. It would be fun to train a cat to ____. I can depend on my classmates to ____. If you compared a car to a bicycle, you could say that ____. A good place to be social is ____.*

Comprehension

SELF-SELECTED READING

OBJECTIVES

CCSS With prompting and support, ask and answer questions about key details in a text. **RL.K.1**

Apply the strategy and skill to reread the text.

Read Independently

Help children select an illustrated story for sustained silent reading. Tell children that they should think about what will happen to the people and animals in the story as they read. Explain that they can use the title of the book and the pictures to help them figure out what will happen.

Read Purposefully

Before reading, ask children to point to an illustration and tell what they think is happening in the picture. Then ask them to say what they think might happen. After reading, ask children if they were right about their predictions. If they were not right, help them to revise their predictions.

On Level

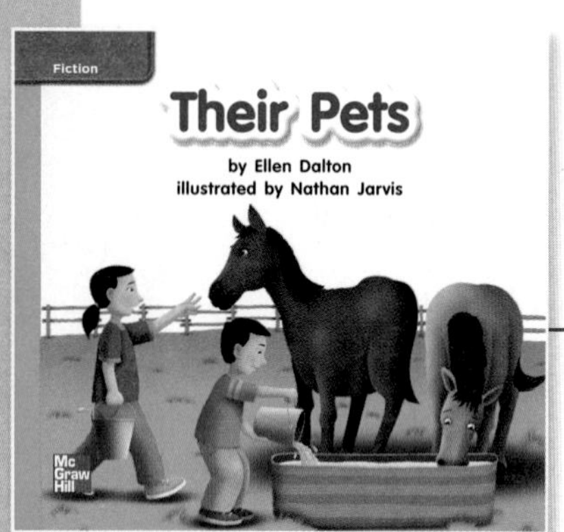

Leveled Reader

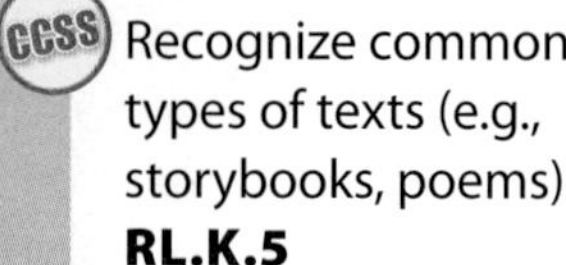

OBJECTIVES

With prompting and support, identify characters, settings, and major events in a story. **RL.K.3**

Recognize common types of texts (e.g., storybooks, poems). **RL.K.5**

Read emergent-reader texts with purpose and understanding. **RF.K.4**

Leveled Reader: *Their Pets*

Leveled Reader

Before Reading

Preview and Predict

Point to and read the title and the names of the author and illustrator. Ask children to use the cover illustration to help them predict what the book is about. Preview each page of the book to introduce vocabulary and the sentence pattern. Ask: *What do the people give their pets in this book? They give their pets ______. What do you think this story is about?*

Review Genre: Fiction

Review with children that fiction is a made-up story with characters, events, and settings. Ask: *How can you tell that this book is fiction?* (The book has characters, events, and settings.)

Model Concepts of Print

Point to where to begin reading on page 3 and track beneath the print to show left-to-right progression. Turn to page 4. Ask: *Where do we begin reading on this page? Which way do we go?*

Review High-Frequency Words

Point out the word *They* on page 2, and read it with children. Ask them to locate *They* on the other pages.

Essential Question

Set a purpose for reading: *As we read this book, think about how you would take care of a pet.*

During Reading

Guided Comprehension

As children whisper-read, monitor and provide guidance by correcting blending and modeling the strategy and skill.

Strategy: Make, Confirm, and Revise Predictions

Remind children to make predictions as they read by asking themselves what will happen next and then reading to find out if they were right.

Skill: Character, Setting, Plot

Tell children that it is very important to think about who and what the story is about, what events happen, and where it takes place.

Think Aloud As I read pages 2 and 3, I find out that people walk their pets and give them baths. When I look at the illustrations on pages 2 and 3, I notice that there are different characters. The setting is also different on each page. I think this story is about different people and their pets and how they take care of them.

As children read the book, guide them to identify who the characters are, where they are, and what they are doing.

After Reading

Respond to Reading

- *What is this story about?* (how people take care of their pets)
- *What kinds of pets are in this story?* (dogs, cats, goats, rabbits, horses, birds)
- *What is the setting for the events on page 7?* (inside of a home.)

Retell

Have children take turns retelling the story, using the illustrations. Help them make a personal connection by asking: *What different kinds of pets do your friends have? How do they take care of them?*

Model Fluency

Read each page as you track from left to right below the sentence. Have children chorally repeat.

Apply Have children practice reading with partners as you observe and provide needed assistance.

LITERACY ACTIVITIES

Have children complete the activities on the inside back cover of the reader.

Level Up

IF Children read *Their Pets* **On Level** with fluency and correctly answer the Respond to Reading questions,

THEN Tell children that they will read another story about pets. This story is about a boy who wants one.

- Have children page through *Will's Pet* **Beyond Level** as you point out and explain the use of quotation marks to show a character is asking a question or making a statement.
- Have children read the story, monitoring their comprehension and providing assistance as necessary.

On Level

Phonemic Awareness

PHONEME ISOLATION

OBJECTIVES

CCSS Isolate and pronounce the initial, medial vowel, and final sounds (phonemes) in three-phoneme words. **RF.K.2d**

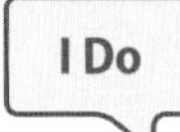

Display the *Goat* **Photo Card**. *This is a goat. The first sound is /g/. Say it with me.* Repeat for final /g/ using the *Dog* Photo Card and for /w/ using the *Window* Photo Card.

Say *girl* and have children repeat it. *What is the first sound in* girl? Say the sound together. Repeat with *get, game, win, will.* Use *log, mug* for final /g/.

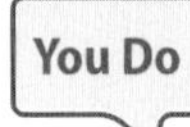

Say *got, fan, wet, pen, pit, wed,* and *wig* and have children tell the initial sound in each word. Say *wag, let,* and *beg* and tell the final sound.

PHONEME BLENDING

OBJECTIVES

Isolate and pronounce the initial, medial vowel, and final sounds (phonemes) in three-phoneme words. **RF.K.2d**

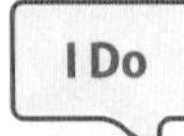

Listen as the puppet says the sounds in a word: /d/ /o/ /g/. *The puppet will blend the sounds:* /dooog/, dog. *The word is* dog. Repeat with *fig, web.*

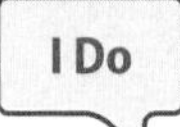

Listen as the puppet says sounds in a word: /m/ /u/ /g/. Have children repeat. *Let's blend the sounds and say the word:* /muuug/, mug. Repeat with *gate, wet.*

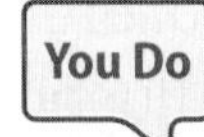

Continue choosing Photo Cards. Say the sounds and have children blend the sounds and say the words.

PHONEME SUBSTITUTION

OBJECTIVES

Add or substitute individual sounds (phonemes) in simple, one-syllable words to make new words. **RF.K.2e**

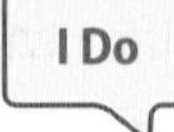

The puppet can say a word and change the first sound to make a new word. Listen: get, met. *The puppet changed the /g/ to /m/ to make* met.

Listen as the puppet says another word: rag. *What word does the puppet make if it changes /w/ in* wet *to /g/?* (get) Have children say both words.

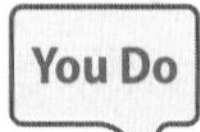

Say got. *Change /g/ to /h/. What word do you have?* (hot) Repeat routine with the following: /w/ in *wig* to /b/ (big); /g/ in *game* to /k/ (came); /w/ in *wire* to /t/ (tire); /g/ in *gold* to /h/ (hold).

Phonics

REVIEW PHONICS

OBJECTIVES

CCSS Demonstrate basic knowledge of one-to-one letter-sound correspondences by producing the primary or many of the most frequent sound for each consonant. **RF.K.3a**

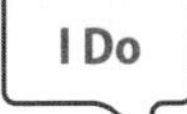

Display **Reading/Writing Workshop**, p. 20. Point to the *Guitar* **Sound-Spelling Card**. *Which letter stands for the /g/ sound you hear at the beginning of* guitar? *The letter is* g. Repeat the routine with the *Window* Sound-Spelling Card.

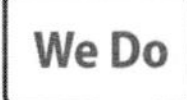

Have children say the name of each picture in rows 1 and 2. Then ask them to identify the words with /g/ at the beginning or end and the words with /w/ at the beginning.

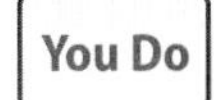

Have children read each word in rows 3 and 4. Repeat, asking them to raise their hands if they hear /g/ at the beginning of the word and pat their legs if they hear /g/ at the end of a word. Repeat the routine, having children wiggle their fingers if they hear /w/ at the beginning of a word.

PICTURE SORT

OBJECTIVES

CCSS Demonstrate basic knowledge of one-to-one letter-sound correspondences by producing the primary or many of the most frequent sounds for each consonant. **RF.K.3a**

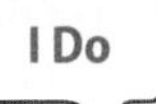

Display **Word-Building Cards** *g* and *w* in a pocket chart. Then show the *Goat* **Photo Card**. Say /g/ /ō/ /t/, *goat*. Tell children that the sound at the beginning is /g/. *The letter* g *stands for* /g/. *I will put the goat under the letter* g. Show the *Web* Photo Card. Say /w/ /e/ /b/, *web*. Tell children that the sound at the beginning is /w/. *The letter* w *stands for* /w/. *I will put web under the letter* w.

Show the *Gate* Photo Card and say *gate*, /g/ /ā/ /t/. Have children repeat. Then have them tell the sound they hear at the beginning of *gate*. Ask them if they should place the photo under the *g* or the *w*. (*g*)

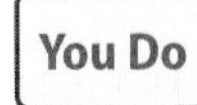

Continue the activity using the *Watch, Water, Wolf, Walrus, Window, Game, Girl, Gorilla, Grapes,* and *Guitar* Photo Cards. Have children say the picture name and the sounds in the name. Then have them place the card under the *g* or *w*.

On Level

Phonics

BLEND WORDS WITH *g* AND *w*

OBJECTIVES

Isolate and pronounce the initial, medial vowel, and final sounds (phonemes) in three-phoneme words.
RF.K.2d

Write *g, a, p. This is the letter* g. *It stands for /g/. Say it with me: /g/. This is the letter* a. *It stands for /a/. Say it with me: /aaa/. This is the letter* p. *It stands for /p/. Say it with me: /p/. I'll blend the sounds together to read the word:* /gaaap/, gap. Repeat the routine with final /g/ and the word *bug* and initial /w/ and the word *wag*.

Write *get, hog,* and *web*. Guide children to blend the words sound by sound to read each word.

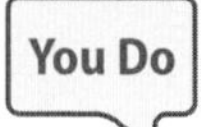

Write the following words and have children blend the words sound by sound to read each word.

bat got wig win leg get bug

REREAD FOR FLUENCY

OBJECTIVES

Read emergent-reader texts with purpose and understanding.
RF.K.4

Point to the title "I Hug Gus!" on p. 22 of **Reading/Writing Workshop** and tell children that when they read something ending in an exclamation point, they should make their voices sound excited. Work with children to read for accuracy and expression. Model reading p. 25: *When I read* "Gus is a big, red pup," *I read all the way to the end of the sentence before pausing. This makes my reading sound natural, as if I were talking*.

Reread p. 25. Then have children chorally read the page with you. Continue chorally reading the remainder of the pages.

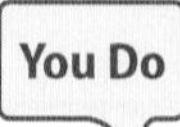

Have children read "I Hug Gus!" Provide time to listen as children read the pages. Comment on their accuracy and expression and provide corrective feedback by modeling proper fluency.

High-Frequency Words

REVIEW WORDS

OBJECTIVES

CCSS Read common high-frequency words by sight. **RF.K.3c**

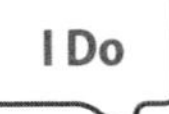

Use the **High-Frequency Word Card** *they* with the **Read/Spell/Write** routine to review the word. Repeat with *of.*

Have children turn to p. 21 of **Reading/Writing Workshop**. Discuss the photographs and read aloud the sentences. Point to the word *they* and have children read it. Then chorally read the sentence. Have children frame the word *they* in the sentence and read the word. Repeat the routine with the word *of*.

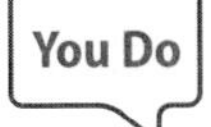

Say the word *they*. Ask children to close their eyes, picture the word, and write it as they see it. Have children self-correct. Repeat the routine with the word *of*.

Reteach previously introduced high-frequency words using the **Read/Spell/Write** routine.

Fluency Point to the High-Frequency Word Cards I, *can, the, we, see, a, like, to, and, go, you, do, my, are, he, with, is, little, she, was, have, for, they,* and *of* in random order. Have children chorally read. Repeat at a faster pace.

Comprehension

SELF-SELECTED READING

OBJECTIVES

CCSS With prompting and support, ask and answer questions about key details in a text. **RL.K.1**

Apply the strategy and skill to reread the text.

Read Independently

Have children select an illustrated story for sustained silent reading. Remind them to make predictions about the characters, events, and settings as they read. Tell children to base their predictions on their own experiences, as well as parts of the book, such as the title and illustrations.

Read Purposefully

Before reading, ask children to point out two illustrations and predict what they think will be happening to the characters at these points in the story. Remind children to base their predictions on their own experiences and the book's title and illustrations. After reading, have children explain whether their predictions were right. If their predictions were not right, allow them to revise the predictions.

Beyond Level

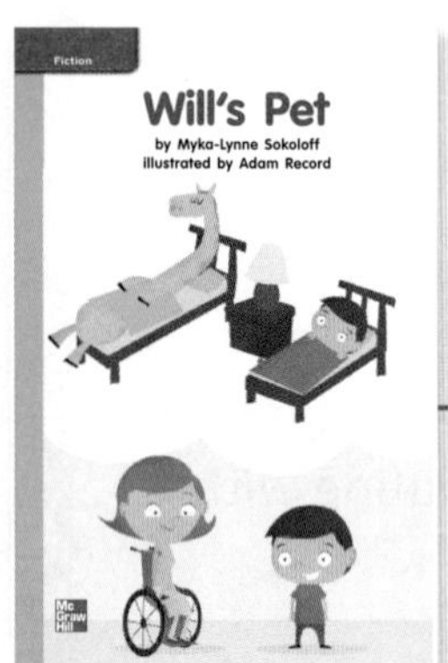

Leveled Reader

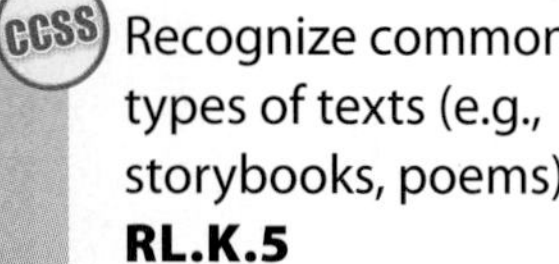

OBJECTIVES

With prompting and support, identify characters, settings, and major events in a story. **RL.K.3**

Recognize common types of texts (e.g., storybooks, poems). **RL.K.5**

Read emergent-reader texts with purpose and understanding. **RF.K.4**

Leveled Reader: *Will's Pet*

Leveled Reader

Before Reading

Preview and Predict

Hold the book so that children can see the cover illustration. Read the title. Point to the boy and say: *This is Will. What is he looking at?* Guide children on a picture walk through the book and help them identify the animals. Point out the quotation marks and explain that they show that someone is talking.

Review Genre: Fiction

Explain that fiction stories are about made-up characters and events. Ask: *What did you notice when you were looking through this book that shows you it's fiction?* (The illustrations show one of the characters imagining animals doing funny things.)

Essential Question

Remind children of the Essential Question: *How do you take care of different kinds of pets?* Help children set a purpose for reading by saying: *Let's find out how Will decides what kind of pet he should get.*

During Reading

Guided Comprehension

As children whisper-read *Will's Pet*, monitor and provide guidance by correcting blending and modeling the strategy and skill. Remind children that quotation marks mean a character is speaking.

Strategy: Make, Confirm, and Revise Predictions

Remind children to make predictions as they read by asking themselves what will happen next and then reading to find out if they were right. Explain to children that they may need to change their predictions as they continue reading.

Skill: Character, Setting, Plot (Problem and Solution)

Explain to children that they can learn about the character, setting, and plot by reading the text and looking at the illustrations. Tell children that the plot of a story is often about how the main character solves a problem.

Think Aloud On page 3, the words and pictures tell me about a problem that the main character Will has. I read that he would like a giraffe for a pet but his mother tells him a giraffe will not fit in his bed. The picture shows Will imagining the giraffe sticking out of its bed. I think Will's problem is finding the right kind of pet to have. I will keep reading to see how he solves his problem.

As children read the book, have them identify the characters, setting, and events. Help children understand that every time Will suggests an animal, his mom or dad point out a problem with having and taking care of it.

After Reading

Respond to Reading

- *Who are the main characters in this story?* (Will, Mom, Dad)
- *Where does this story take place?* (Will's house)
- *Why does Will decide not to get a porcupine?* (He wouldn't be able to pet it.)
- *What is Will's problem in the story?* (what kind of pet to get)
- *How did Will solve his problem?* (He decided to get a dog.)

Retell

Ask children to work in groups of three to retell the story by role-playing the characters and events. Help them make a personal connection by asking: *Why is it important to choose the right pet?*

LITERACY ACTIVITIES

Have children complete the activities on the inside back cover of the reader.

Gifted and Talented

EVALUATING Have children think of different kinds of animals that people keep as pets. Challenge them to include animals that need different kinds and amounts of space.

HAVE children put the animals into categories based on the amount of space they need and the type of care they require, such as large outdoor pets, caged pets, house pets, or pets that live in water.

Beyond Level

Phonics

REVIEW

OBJECTIVES

Know and apply grade-level phonics and word analysis skills in decoding words. **RF.K.3**

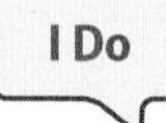

Display **Reading/Writing Workshop**, p. 20. Point to the *Guitar* **Sound-Spelling Card**. *What is the sound at the beginning of* guitar? *What letter can stand for /g/? The letter is* g. Repeat the routine with the *Window* Sound-Spelling Card.

Have children say the name of each picture in rows 1 and 2. Then ask children to share words that begin or end with /g/ or begin with /w/.

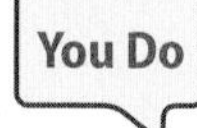

Have partners read each word in rows 3 and 4. Ask them to write the words on their **Response Boards**, underlining the letter in each word that stands for /g/ or /w/.

Fluency Have children reread the story "I Hug Gus!" for fluency.

Innovate Have children create a new page for "I Hug Gus!" by adding something else the narrator might do with Gus the cat.

REVIEW

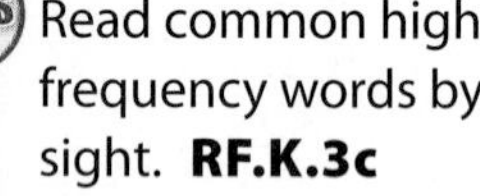

OBJECTIVES

Read common high-frequency words by sight. **RF.K.3c**

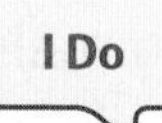

Create **High-Frequency Word Cards** for *write* and *one*. Introduce the words using the **Read/Spell/Write** routine.

Display the High-Frequency Word Cards for *they, my, to, is, the,* and *of*. Have children help you complete the following sentence frames using the High-Frequency Word Cards: *They can write to my* _____. *One of the cats is* _____!

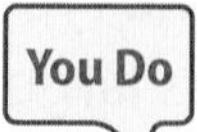

Have partners write sentences using the High-Frequency Words *write* and *one* on their Response Boards. Have them read their sentences.

Vocabulary

ORAL VOCABULARY: SYNONYMS

OBJECTIVES

With guidance and support from adults, explore word relationships and nuances in word meanings. **L.K.5**

Develop oral vocabulary: Synonyms

Review the meanings of the oral vocabulary words *responsibility* and *train*. Explain that a synonym is a word that means almost the same thing as another word.

A synonym for responsibility *is* job. *A job is something that someone needs to do.* It is my job to feed the fish.

A synonym for train *is* teach. *To teach is to show someone how to do or learn something.* The aquarium worker will teach the seal a new trick.

Work with children to create sentences using the new words *job* and *teach*.

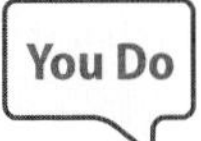

Have partners create sentences to tell about the job of a pet owner. Tell them to include the words *job* and *teach*. Have partners share their sentences.

Extend Have partners create a skit about how to take care of a pet. Challenge them to use the synonyms they learned, *job* and *teach*.

Comprehension

SELF-SELECTED READING

OBJECTIVES

CCSS With prompting and support, ask and answer questions about key details in a text. **RL.K.1**

Apply the strategy and skill to reread the text.

Read Independently

Have children select an illustrated story for sustained silent reading. Remind them that making predictions about characters, settings, and events can help them better understand and enjoy a story as they read.

Read Purposefully

Before reading, have children choose two illustrations they think will be important to the plot. Tell them to write two sentences to predict what is happening in each illustration. After reading, have children check to see if their predictions were correct. Allow them to revise their predictions. Then have children explain how they used their own experiences, as well as the book's features, to help them make their predictions.

Independent Study Have children compare and contrast how to take care of two different pets, such as a turtle and a dog. Challenge them to create a picture with labels showing how the care for each animal is alike and how it is different.

English Language Learners

Fiction
Their Pets
by Ellen Dalton
illustrated by Nathan Jarvis

Leveled Reader

OBJECTIVES

With prompting and support, identify characters, settings, and major events in a story. **RL.K.3**

Actively engage in group reading activities with purpose and understanding. **RL.K.10**

Demonstrate understanding of the organization and basic features of print. **RF.K.1**

Shared Read: *Their Pets*

Go Digital

Leveled Reader

Before Reading

Preview and Predict

Point to the title on the cover and read it aloud. Ask children to reread it with you. Point to and read the names of the author and illustrator. Have children discuss the cover illustration. Help them identify the animals shown. Make sure that children understand the English word *pet*. Guide children on a picture walk through the book. As you focus on each page, help children with the labels. Ask: *What do these animals get?* Model the response, *They get* _____. (walks, bed, hay, lettuce, etc.)

Essential Question

Remind children of the Essential Question: *How do you take care of different kinds of pets?* Set a purpose for reading: *Let's read to find out how to take care of these pets.* Remind children to look at the illustrations to help them read the words and answer the question.

During Reading

Interactive Question Response

Pages 2–3 Point to the picture on page 2. Ask: *What do these dogs get?* Encourage children to answer using the sentence frame, *They get* _____. (walks) Model as needed. Have them point to the label that says *pets*. Then read the page with children. Point to page 3. Ask: *What do these cats get?* (beds) Ask children to point to the label that says *beds*. Read the sentence with children, as they point to each word.

Pages 4–5 Turn to page 4. Point to the hay in the picture. Ask: *What do the goats get?* (They get hay.) Ask children to point to the label that says *hay* and the word in the sentence that says *hay*. Have children read the page with you. Continue to point under each word as it is read, encouraging children to do the same. Point to page 5. Ask: *What do the rabbits get?* (They get lettuce.) *Show me where it says lettuce on this page.* Continue tracking under the print as children read with you.

Pages 6–7 Direct children to page 6 and ask: *What do the horses get?* (They get water.) *Show me where it says water on this page. Read this page with me.* Turn to page 7. Say: *Look at the birds on page 7. What do they get?* (They get toys.) *Show me where it says* toys *on this page.* Continue to model the sentence pattern, as needed. Ask children to read the page with you as you point beneath the words.

Page 8 Turn to the last page. Ask: *Do you think these cats like the children?* (Yes.) *Are they friends?* (Yes.) *I think so, too. Let's read this page together.*

After Reading

Respond to Reading

- *What is this story about?* (things people give their pets)
- *What kinds of pets are in this story?* (dogs, cats, goats, rabbits, horses, birds)
- *Why do the people give their pets these things?* (so the pets will be healthy and happy)
- *What do we find out at the end of the story?* (People and their pets are friends.)

Retell

Ask children to look back through the book and take turns retelling. Prompt and support their retelling by modeling simple sentence structures they can use to respond.

Model Fluency

Read the sentences one at a time as you track beneath the print, pointing to each word. Have children orally repeat.

Apply Have children read with partners as you monitor. Encourage them to use the pictures on each page and prompt them to point beneath each word as they read.

LITERACY ACTIVITIES

Have children complete the activities on the inside back cover of the reader.

Level Up

IF Children read *Their Pets* **ELL Level** with fluency and correctly answer the Respond to Reading questions,

THEN Tell children that they will read a more detailed version of the story.

- Have children page through *Their Pets* **On Level** as you conduct a picture walk to describe each picture in simple language.
- Have children read the story, monitoring their comprehension and providing assistance as necessary.

English Language Learners

Vocabulary

PRETEACH ORAL VOCABULARY

OBJECTIVES

CCSS Speak audibly and express thoughts, feelings, and ideas clearly. **SL.K.6**

LANGUAGE OBJECTIVE

Preview vocabulary

I Do

Display the images from the **Visual Vocabulary Cards** and follow the routine to preteach the oral vocabulary words.

Display each image again and explain how it illustrates the word. Model using sentences to describe the image.

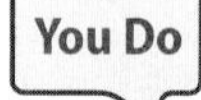

Display the word *responsibility* again and explain that a responsibility is like a job. It's something that we must do. Give children an example of a responsibility, such as putting out the garbage. Ask children to name a responsibility that they might have at home.

Beginning	Intermediate	Advanced/High
Use the words *train* and *responsibility* in the same oral sentence and ask children to repeat the sentence after you.	Have partners talk about responsibilities at home and at school.	Have children work in pairs to ask and answer questions using the words *train* and *responsibility*.

PRETEACH ELL VOCABULARY

OBJECTIVES

Speak audibly and express thoughts, feelings, and ideas clearly. **SL.K.6**

LANGUAGE OBJECTIVE

Preview ELL vocabulary

Display the images from the **Visual Vocabulary Cards** one at a time to preteach the ELL vocabulary words *provide* and *affection*. Follow the routine. Say each word, and have children repeat. Define each word in English.

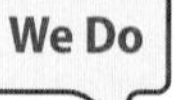

Display images again and discuss them. Model using sentences to describe each image.

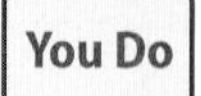

Display the word *affection* again and explain that affection is a feeling they have when they like someone or something, such as family or pets. Ask children what they feel affection for.

Beginning	Intermediate	Advanced/High
Prompt children to talk about the people and things they feel affection for.	Ask partners to *provide* a sentence that tells what they show *affection* for.	Have partners ask and answer questions using *provide* and *affection*.

High-Frequency Words

REVIEW WORDS

OBJECTIVES

CCSS Read common high-frequency words by sight (e.g., *the, of, to, you, she, my, is, are, do, does*). **RF.K.3c**

LANGUAGE OBJECTIVE

Review high-frequency words

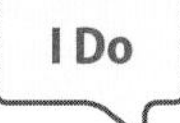

Display the **High-Frequency Word Cards** for *they* and *of*. Read the words. Use the **Read/Spell/Write** routine to teach the words. Have children write the words on their **Response Boards**.

Write a sentence frame that uses the week's high-frequency words: *They like lots of* ______. Model how to complete the sentence. Explain that the word *they* is used to replace a noun.

Display a sentence that uses the high-frequency words *they* and *of*. Ask children to point to the words and say them aloud. Then work with children to read the entire sentence aloud.

Beginning	Intermediate	Advanced/High
Tell children how to use *they* to replace a noun, such as *Trees (They) are made of wood.*	Ask partners to name more things to complete the sentence starter.	Have children use both of the words together in a sentence of their own.

REVIEW CATEGORY WORDS

OBJECTIVES

CCSS Identify real-life connections between words and their use (e.g., note places at school that are colorful). **L.K.5c**

LANGUAGE OBJECTIVE

Use category words

I Do

Write the words *rabbit, turtle, dog, kitten,* and *bird* and say the words aloud. Ask children to repeat each word after you. Define the words in English and then in Spanish, if appropriate, identifying any cognates.

Tell children that these words have to do with pets. Ask children to choose a pet that interests them most.

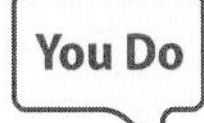

Have children choose one of the category words and draw a picture of themselves with that pet.

Beginning	Intermediate	Advanced/High
Prompt children to talk about the animal they drew.	Guide children to work together to use one or two of the category words in a sentence.	Have children choose one of the category words and describe what that animal is like.

English Language Learners

Writing

SHARED WRITING

OBJECTIVES

Use a combination of drawing, dictating, and writing to narrate a single event or several loosely linked events, tell about the events in the order in which they occurred, and provide a reaction to what happened. **W.K.3**

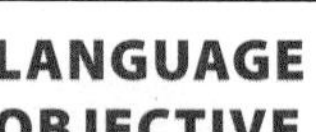

LANGUAGE OBJECTIVE

Contribute to a shared writing project

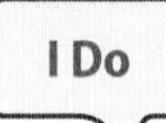

Review the chart in the Whole Group Shared Writing project for possible ideas for animals that would make good pets. Then model using one of the pets on the list to write a sentence: *A dog needs food and exercise.*

We Do Have children help you choose a pet from the chart. Talk about what this pet needs. Then have children help you write a shared sentence about how to take care of it.

You Do Provide a sentence frame and have partners write about how to care for a pet and give the pet what it needs: *A* ______ *needs* ______.

Beginning	Intermediate	Advanced/High
Provide children with pictures of pets and talk about what each one needs to live.	Have partners share their sentences.	Ask children to write a sentence about caring for a pet and then share it with a partner.

WRITING TRAIT: WORD CHOICE

OBJECTIVES

With guidance and support from adults, respond to questions and suggestions from peers and add details to strengthen writing as needed. **W.K.5**

LANGUAGE OBJECTIVE

Choose the best words in a writing exercise

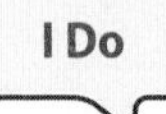

Explain that good writers choose the best words to use so their writing is clear. This includes telling someone how to do something.

Point to the **Big Book** selection *The Birthday Pet.* Say: *The author carefully chooses the right words to describe Danny's problems with pets until he gets a turtle.* Help children identify the words the author uses.

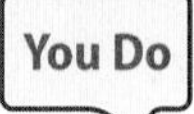

Provide a sentence frame to help children write about a pet they like and why: *I like* ______. *They can* ______.

Beginning	Intermediate	Advanced/High
Prompt children to talk about the pets they like and why they like them.	Have partners complete the sentence frame and then read it aloud.	Ask children write more than one reason why the pet is a good choice.

Grammar

ACTION WORDS (VERBS)

OBJECTIVES

CCSS Use frequently occurring nouns and verbs. **L.K.1b**

LANGUAGE OBJECTIVE

Recognize and use verbs correctly

Language Transfers Handbook

In Cantonese, Hmong, and Korean, verb forms do not change to show the number of the subject. As a result, children who speak these languages may have problems with irregular subject-verb agreement. They may say *Tom and Sue has a new car* instead of *Tom and Sue have a new car.*

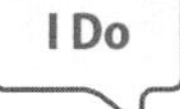

Review that a verb is a word that describes an action. Say the following sentence: *Max jumped over the puddle.* Explain that the word *jumped* tells about an action that happened in the past. Say: Jumped *is a verb. It tells about an action.*

Say the sentences. Have children repeat them after you. Then ask them to identify the verbs in each sentence: *The action word is* ______.

The dogs barked.

The cat ran.

The turtle walked.

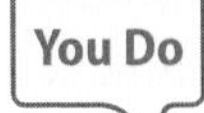

Say the following sentence frame: *The pets* ______.

Pair children and have them complete the sentence frame by providing details from this week's readings. Circulate, listen in, and take note of each child's language use and proficiency.

Beginning	Intermediate	Advanced/High
Before completing the sentence frame, brainstorm verbs that relate to pets.	Help children use the week's selections to identify actions words that tell what pets can do.	Have children use the week's selections to help them complete the sentence frame.

PROGRESS MONITORING

Weekly Assessment

Use your Quick Check observations and the assessment opportunities identified below to evaluate children's progress in key skill areas.

✓ TESTED SKILLS CCSS	Quick Check Observations	Pencil and Paper Assessment
PHONEMIC AWARENESS/ PHONICS g /g/, /w/ (initial/final g, initial w) **RF.K.3a**	Can children isolate /g/ and /w/ and match the sounds to the letters *Gg* and *Ww*?	Practice Book, pp. 193–194, 195–196, 198
HIGH-FREQUENCY WORDS they *they, of* **RF.K.3c**	Can children recognize and read the high-frequency words?	Practice Book, pp. 199–200
COMPREHENSION Character, Setting, Plot (Problem and Solution) **RL.K.3**	As you read *The Birthday Pet* with children, can they identify character, setting, and plot in the text?	Practice Book, p. 197

Quick Check Rubric

Skills	1	2	3
PHONEMIC AWARENESS/ PHONICS	Does not connect the sounds /g/ or /w/ with the letters *Gg or Ww.*	Usually connects the sounds /g/ or /w/ with the letters *Gg or Ww.*	Consistently connects the sounds /g/ or /w/ with the letters *Gg or Ww.*
HIGH-FREQUENCY WORDS	Does not identify the high-frequency words.	Usually recognizes the high-frequency words with accuracy, but not speed.	Consistently recognizes the high-frequency words with speed and accuracy.
COMPREHENSION	Does not identify character, setting, and plot in the text.	Usually identifies character, setting, and plot in the text.	Consistently identifies character, setting, and plot in the text.

Go Digital! www.connected.mcgraw-hill.com

Using Assessment Results

✓ TESTED SKILLS	If ...	Then ...
PHONEMIC AWARENESS/ PHONICS	**Quick Check Rubric:** Children consistently score 1 or **Pencil and Paper Assessment:** Children get 0–2 items correct	... reteach tested Phonemic Awareness and Phonics skills using Lessons 16–17 and 27–29 in the ***Tier 2 Phonemic Awareness Intervention Online PDFs*** and Lessons 32 and 34 in the ***Tier 2 Phonics/Word Study Intervention Online PDFs.***
HIGH-FREQUENCY WORDS	**Quick Check Rubric:** Children consistently score 1	... reteach tested skills by using the High-Frequency Word Cards and asking children to read and spell the word. Point out any irregularities in sound-spellings.
COMPREHENSION	**Quick Check Rubric:** Children consistently score 1 or **Pencil and Paper Assessment:** Children get 0–1 items correct	... reteach tested skill using Lessons 22–30 in the ***Tier 2 Comprehension Intervention Online PDFs.***

Response to Intervention

Use the children's assessment results to assist you in identifying children who will benefit from focused intervention.

Use the appropriate sections of the ***Placement and Diagnostic Assessment*** to designate children requiring:

TIER 2 Tier 2 Intervention Online PDFs

TIER 3 WonderWorks Intervention Program

→ Phonemic Awareness

→ Phonics

→ Vocabulary

→ Comprehension

→ Fluency

WEEKLY OVERVIEW

Listening Comprehension

Bear Snores On, 5–34

Genre Fantasy

"Animal Homes," 35–40

Genre Informational Text

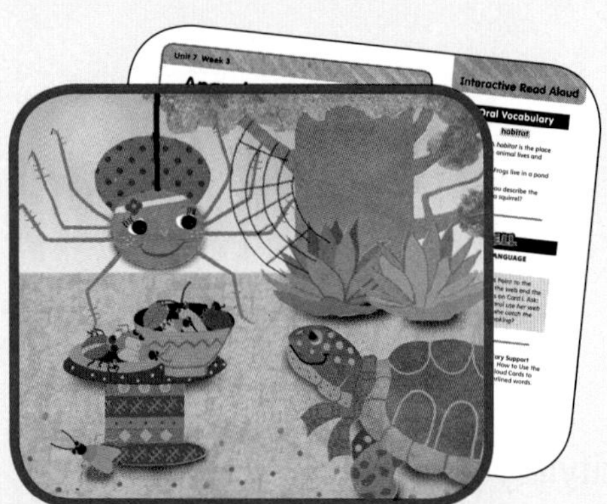

Interactive Read-Aloud Cards

"Anansi: An African Tale"

Genre Tale

Oral Vocabulary

complain
habitat
join
stubborn
wild

Minilessons

✓ **Comprehension Strategy** .... Make, Confirm, and Revise Predictions, T177

✓ **Comprehension Skill** .... Plot: Cause and Effect, T186

Go Digital

www.connected.mcgraw-hill.com

Essential Question
Where do animals live?

WEEK 3

Big Book and Little Book
Reading/Writing Workshop

Shared Reading

"A Vet in a Van," 36–43

Genre Fiction

High-Frequency Words said, want, T181

Minilessons

✓ **Phonics** .... /v/v, /ks/x, T179

Writing Trait........................ Ideas, T182

Grammar .... Verbs, T183

Differentiated Text

Approaching

On Level

Beyond

ELL

TEACH AND MANAGE

What You Do

INTRODUCE

Weekly Concept

Animal Habitats

Reading/Writing Workshop Big Book, 34–35

TEACH AND APPLY

Listening Comprehension

Big Book
Bear Snores On
Genre Fantasy
Paired Read "Animal Homes"
Genre Informational Text

Minilessons
Strategy: Make, Confirm, and Revise Predictions
Skill: Cause and Effect

Shared Reading

Reading/Writing Workshop
"A Vet in a Van"

Minilessons
/v/v, /ks/x, High-Frequency Words: said, want,
Writing, Grammar

Interactive Whiteboard

Interactive Whiteboard

Mobile

What Your Students Do

WEEKLY CONTRACT

PDF Online

Online To-Do List

PRACTICE AND ONLINE ACTIVITIES

Your Turn Practice Book, pp. 203–212

Online Activities

Leveled Readers

Mobile

WEEK 3

DIFFERENTIATE

Small Group Instruction

Leveled Readers

Mobile

INTEGRATE

Research and Inquiry

Habitat Diorama, pp. T216–T217

Text Connections

Compare Habitats, p. T218

Talk About Reading

Becoming Readers, p. T219

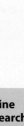

Online Research

WORKSTATION CARDS

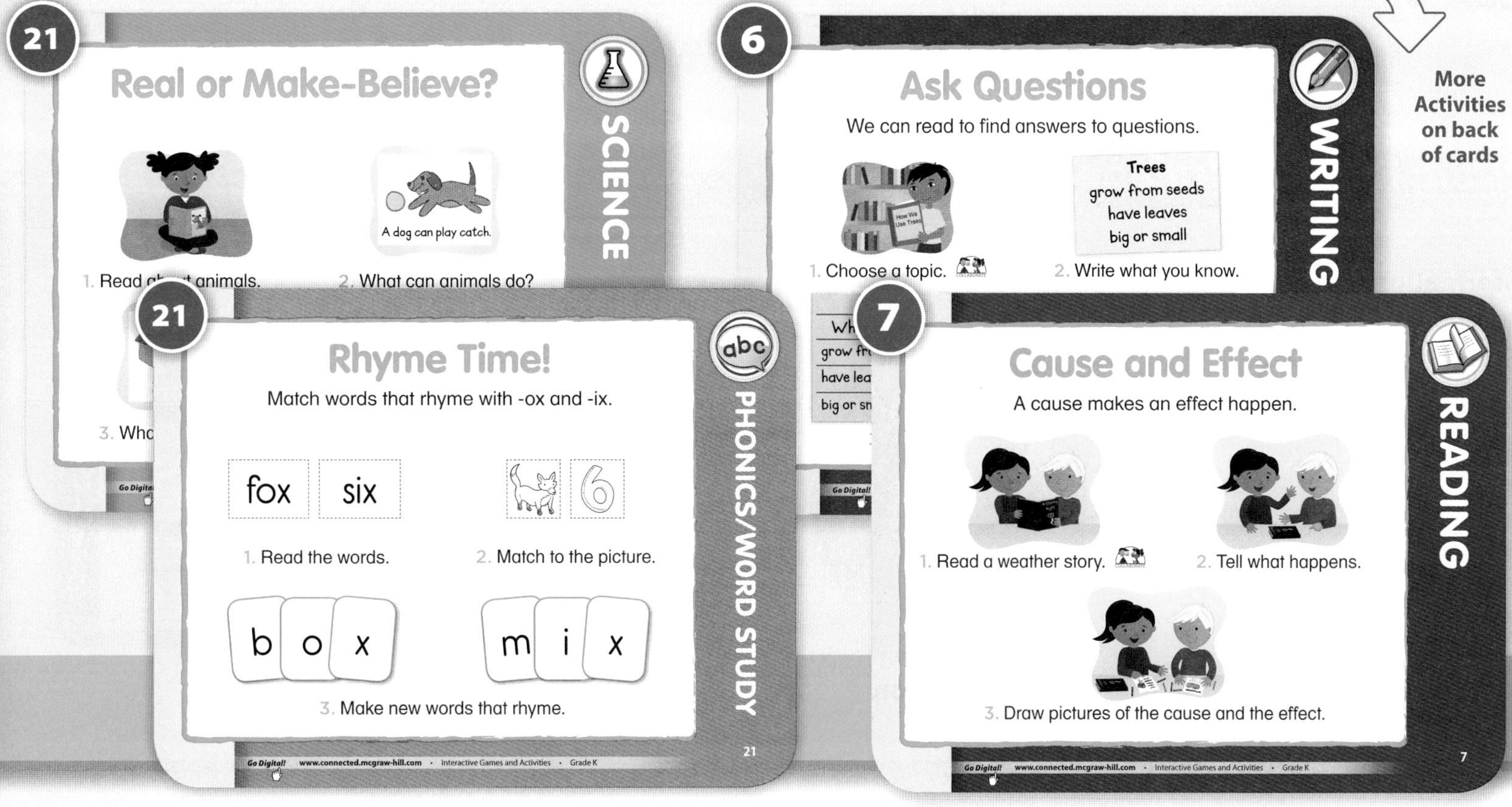

More Activities on back of cards

21 Real or Make-Believe? SCIENCE

1. Read about animals.
2. What can animals do?
3. Wha…

21 Rhyme Time! PHONICS/WORD STUDY

Match words that rhyme with -ox and -ix.

1. Read the words. (fox, six)
2. Match to the picture.
3. Make new words that rhyme. (b o x, m i x)

6 Ask Questions WRITING

We can read to find answers to questions.

1. Choose a topic.
2. Write what you know. (Trees: grow from seeds, have leaves, big or small)

7 Cause and Effect READING

A cause makes an effect happen.

1. Read a weather story.
2. Tell what happens.
3. Draw pictures of the cause and the effect.

Go Digital! www.connected.mcgraw-hill.com • Interactive Games and Activities • Grade K

DEVELOPING READERS AND WRITERS

Write About Reading • Analytical Writing

Write to Sources and Research

Respond to Reading, T177, T225, T233, T239, T243

Connect to Essential Question, T177, T209

Cause and Effect, T191

Research and Inquiry, T216

Teacher's Edition

Literature Big Book
Bear Snores On
Paired Read: *Animal Homes*

Interactive Whiteboard

Leveled Readers
Responding to Texts

Writing Process • Independent Writing

Informational Text
Questions and Answers, T204–T205, T214, T222

Conferencing Routines
Peer Conferences, T214

Interactive Whiteboard

Teacher's Edition

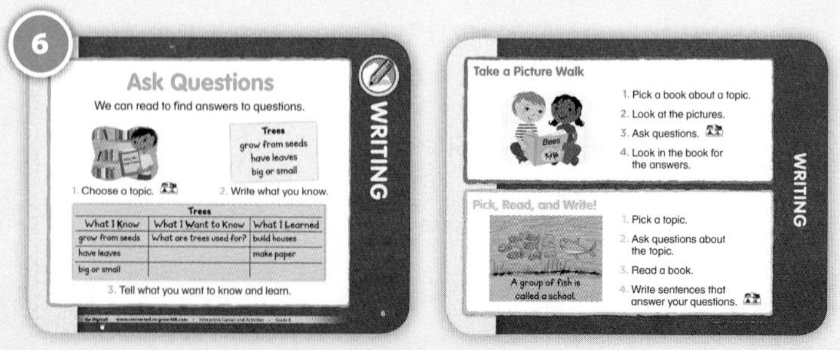

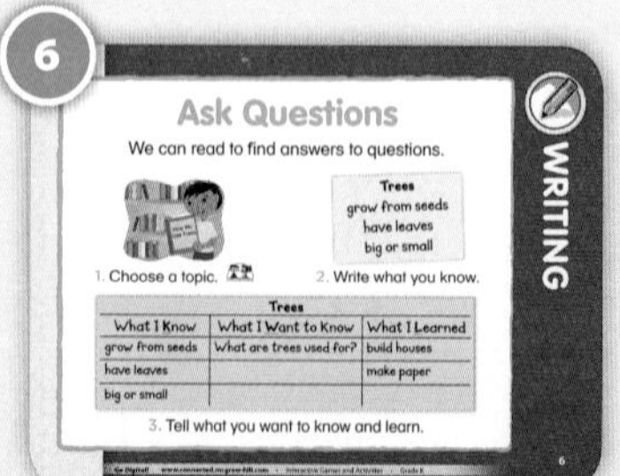

Leveled Workstation Card
Ask Questions, Card 6

WEEK 3

Writing Traits • Shared and Interactive Writing

Writing Trait:
Ideas
Questions and Answers, T182, T196

Teacher's Edition

Word Choice, p. 46

Verbs, p. 47

Reading/Writing Workshop

Interactive Whiteboard

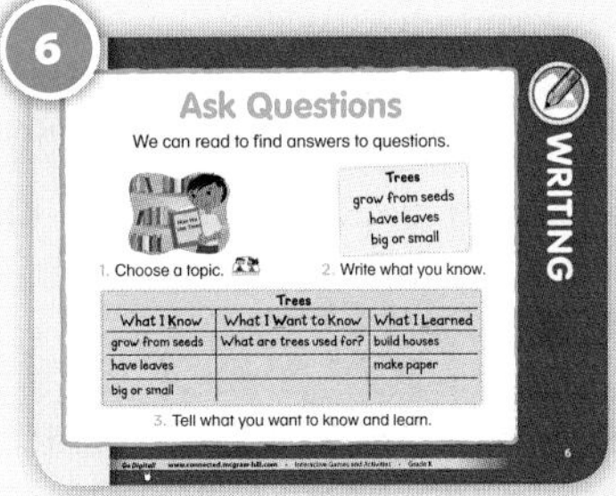

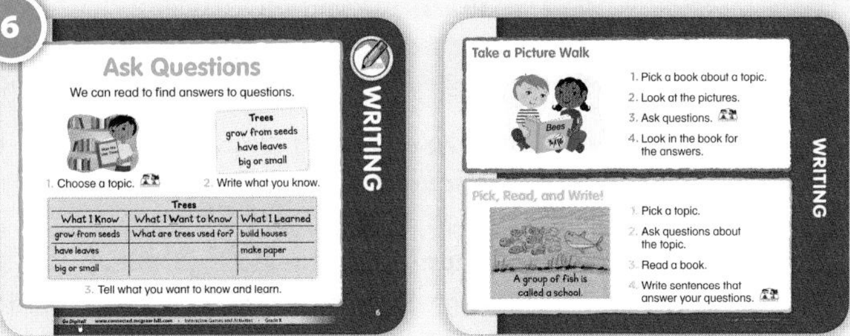

Leveled Workstation Card
Ask Questions, Card 6

Grammar and Spelling/Dictation

Grammar
Action Words (Verbs), T183

Spelling/Dictation
Words with Short *a*, *e*, *i*, and *x*, *v*, *t*, T211, T221

Interactive Whiteboard

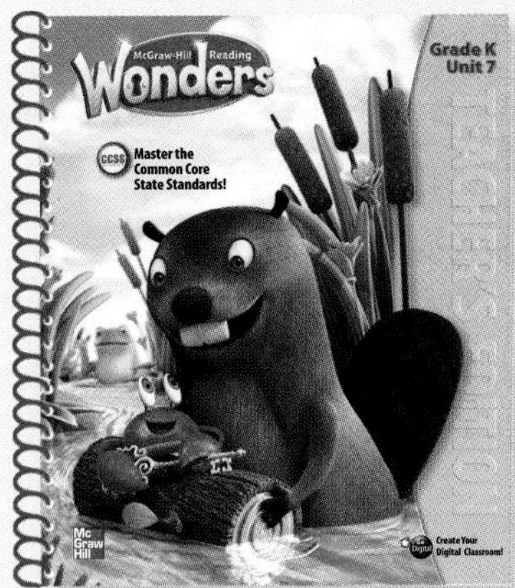

Teacher's Edition

Online Grammar Games

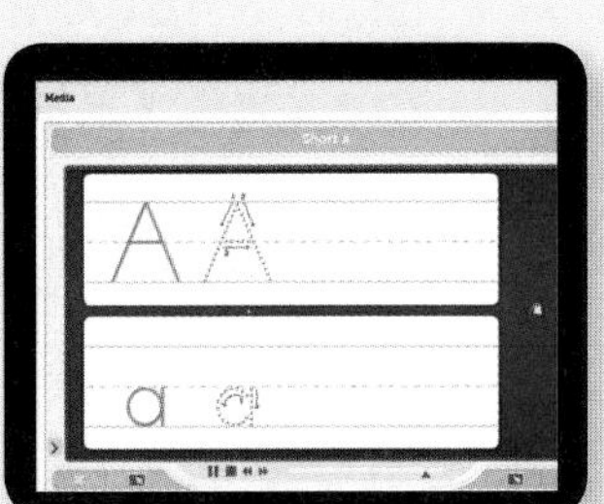

Handwriting

SUGGESTED LESSON PLAN

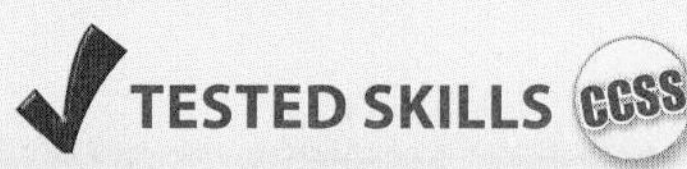

	DAY 1	DAY 2
Whole Group — **READING**		
Teach and Model Literature Big Book Reading/Writing Workshop	**Build Background** Animal Habitats, T174 **Oral Vocabulary Words** habitat, wild, T174 ✓**Listening Comprehension** • Genre: Fantasy • Strategy: Make, Confirm, and Revise Predictions, T177 **Big Book** *Bear Snores On* ✓**Word Work** **Phonemic Awareness** • Phoneme Isolation, T178 **Phonics** • Introduce /v/v, /ks/x, T179 **Handwriting** Vv, Xx, T180 **High-Frequency Words** said, want, T181 **Practice** *Your Turn* 203–206	**Oral Language** Animal Habitats, T184 ✓**Category Words** Animal Homes, T185 ✓**Listening Comprehension** • Genre: Fantasy • Strategy: Make, Confirm, and Revise Predictions, T186 • Skill: Plot: Cause and Effect, T186 • Guided Retelling, T191 • Model Fluency, T191 **Big Book** *Bear Snores On* ✓**Word Work** **Phonemic Awareness** • Phoneme Blending, T192 **Phonics** • Review *v* and *x*, T192 **High-Frequency Words** said, want, T193 **Shared Reading** "A Vet in a Van," T194–T195 **Practice** *Your Turn* 207
Small Group — **DIFFERENTIATED INSTRUCTION** Choose across the week to meet your student's needs.		
Approaching Level 	**Leveled Reader** *We Want Water,* T224–T225 **Phonological Awareness** Onset/Rime Segmentation, T226 TIER 2 **Phonics** Sound-Spelling Review, T228 TIER 2 **High-Frequency Words** Reteach Words, T230 TIER 2	**Leveled Reader** *We Want Water,* T224–T225 **Phonemic Awareness** Phoneme Isolation, T226 TIER 2 **Phonics** Connect *v* to /v/ and *x* to /ks/, T228 TIER 2 **High-Frequency Words** Cumulative Review, T230
On Level 	**Leveled Reader** *A New Home,* T232–T233 **Phonemic Awareness** Phoneme Isolation, T234	**Leveled Reader** *A New Home,* T232–T233 **Phonemic Awareness** Phoneme Blending, T234 **Phonics** Review Phonics, T235 **High-Frequency Words** Review Words, T237
Beyond Level 	**Leveled Reader** *Bird's New Home,* T238–T239 **Phonics** Review, T240	**Leveled Reader** *Bird's New Home,* T238–T239 **Phonics** Review, T240
English Language Learners 	**Leveled Reader** *A New Home,* T242–T243 **Phonological Awareness** Onset/Rime Segmentation, T226 TIER 2 **Phonics** Sound-Spelling Review, T228 TIER 2 **Vocabulary** Preteach Oral Vocabulary, T244 **Writing** Shared Writing, T246	**Leveled Reader** *A New Home,* T242–T243 **Phonemic Awareness** Phoneme Isolation, T226 TIER 2 **Phonics** Connect *v* to /v/ and *x* to /ks/, T228 TIER 2 **High-Frequency Words** Cumulative Review, T230 **Vocabulary** Preteach ELL Vocabulary, T244
Whole Group — **LANGUAGE ARTS**		
Writing and Grammar	**Shared Writing** Writing Trait: Ideas, T182 Write Questions and Answers, T182 **Grammar** Action Words (Verbs), T183	**Interactive Writing** Writing Trait: Ideas, T196 Write Questions and Answers, T196 **Grammar** Action Words (Verbs), T97

Nathan Love

WEEK 3

DAY 3	DAY 4	DAY 5 Review and Assess
READING		
Oral Language Animal Habitats, T198 **Oral Vocabulary** complain, join, stubborn, T198 ✓**Listening Comprehension** • Genre: Tale • Strategy: Make, Confirm, and Revise Predictions, T199 • Make Connections, T199 **Interactive Read Aloud** "Anansi: An African Tale," T199 ✓**Word Work** **Phonemic Awareness** • Phoneme Blending, T200 **Phonics** • Blend Words with Short *i, a, e, o* and *f, x, m, v, n, t*, T201 • Picture Sort, T202 **High-Frequency Words** said, want, T203 **Practice** *Your Turn* 208–210	**Oral Language** Animal Habitats, T206 ✓**Category Words** Animal Homes, T207 ✓**Listening Comprehension** • Genre: Informational Text • Strategy: Make Predictions, T208 • Text Feature: Glossary, T208 • Make Connections, T209 **Big Book** Paired Read: "Animal Homes," T208 ✓**Word Work** **Phonemic Awareness** • Phoneme Substitution, T210 **Phonics** • Blend Words with Short *a, e, i* and *v, x*, T210 **High-Frequency Words** said, want, T211 **Shared Reading** "A Vet in a Van," T212–T213 **Integrate Ideas** Research and Inquiry, T216–T217 **Practice** *Your Turn* 211	**Integrate Ideas** • Text Connections, T218 • Talk About Reading, T219 • Research and Inquiry, T219 ✓**Word Work** **Phonemic Awareness** Phoneme Substitution, T220 **Phonics** • Read Words with Short *a, e, i* and *x, v, t*, T220 **High-Frequency Words** said, want, T221  **Practice** *Your Turn* 212
DIFFERENTIATED INSTRUCTION		
Leveled Reader *We Want Water*, T224–T225 **Phonemic Awareness** Phoneme Blending, T227 **Phonics** Reteach, T228 **High-Frequency Words** Cumulative Review, T230	**Leveled Reader** *We Want Water*, T224–T225 **Phonemic Awareness** Phoneme Substitution, T227 **Phonics** Blend Words with /v/*v* and /ks/*x*, T229 **Oral Vocabulary** Review Words, T231	**Leveled Reader** Literacy Activities, T225 **Phonemic Awareness** Phoneme Substitution, T227 **Phonics** Reread for Fluency, T229 Build Fluency with Phonics, T229 **Comprehension** Self-Selected Reading, T231
Leveled Reader *A New Home*, T232–T233 **Phonemic Awareness** Phoneme Substitution, T234 **Phonics** Picture Sort, T235	**Leveled Reader** *A New Home*, T232–T233 **Phonics** Blend Words with *v* and *x*, T236 Reread for Fluency, T236	**Leveled Reader** Literacy Activities, T233 **Comprehension** Self-Selected Reading, T237
Leveled Reader *Bird's New Home*, T238–T239 **Vocabulary** Oral Vocabulary: Synonyms, T241 	**Leveled Reader** *Bird's New Home*, T238–T239 **Phonics** Innovate, T240	**Leveled Reader** Literacy Activities, T239 **Comprehension** Self-Selected Reading, T241 Gifted and Talented
Leveled Reader *A New Home*, T242–T243 **Phonemic Awareness** Phoneme Blending, T227 **Phonics** Reteach, T228 **High-Frequency Words** Review Words, T245 **Writing** Writing Trait: Ideas, T246	**Leveled Reader** *A New Home*, T242–T243 **Phonemic Awareness** Phoneme Substitution, T227 **Phonics** Blend Words with /v/*v* and /ks/*x*, T229 **Vocabulary** Review Category Words, T245 **Grammar** Verbs, T247	**Leveled Reader** Literacy Activities, T243 **Phonemic Awareness** Phoneme Substitution, T227 **Phonics** Reread for Fluency, T229 Build Fluency with Phonics, T229
LANGUAGE ARTS		
Independent Writing Writing Trait: Ideas, T204 Write Questions and Answers Prewrite/Draft, T204–T205 **Grammar** Action Words (Verbs), T205	**Independent Writing** Write Questions and Answers Revise/Final Draft, T214 **Grammar** Action Words (Verbs), T215	**Independent Writing** Write Questions and Answers Prepare/Present/Evaluate/Publish, T222 **Grammar** Action Words (Verbs), T223

DIFFERENTIATE TO ACCELERATE

ACT Scaffold to Access Complex Text

IF the text complexity of a particular section is too difficult for children

THEN see the references noted in the chart below for scaffolded instruction to help children Access Complex Text.

Qualitative · Quantitative · Reader and Task
TEXT COMPLEXITY

	Literature Big Book	Reading/Writing Workshop	Leveled Readers	

Quantitative	*Bear Snores On* **Lexile** 520 Paired Selection: "Animal Homes" **Lexile** 520	"A Vet in a Van" **Lexile** 230	Approaching Level **Lexile** 110 Beyond Level **Lexile** 190	On Level **Lexile** 50 ELL **Lexile** 300
Qualitative	What Makes the Text Complex? • **Purpose** Following Plot, T186 ACT *See Scaffolded Instruction in Teacher's Edition, T186.*	What Makes the Text Complex? **Foundational Skills** • Decoding with *v, x*, T192–T193 • Identifying high-frequency words, T193	What Makes the Text Complex? **Foundational Skills** • Decoding with *v, x* • Identifying high-frequency words *said, want* *See Level Up lessons online for Leveled Readers.*	
Reader and Task	The Introduce the Concept lesson on pages T174–T175 will help determine the reader's knowledge and engagement in the weekly concept. See pages T176–T177, T187–T191, T208–T209 and T216–T219 for questions and tasks for this text.	The Introduce the Concept lesson on pages T174–T175 will help determine the reader's knowledge and engagement in the weekly concept. See pages T194–T195, T212–T213 and T216–T219 for questions and tasks for this text.	The Introduce the Concept lesson on pages T174–T175 will help determine the reader's knowledge and engagement in the weekly concept. See pages T224–T225, T232–T233, T238–T239, T242–T243 and T216–T219 for questions and tasks for this text.	

WEEK 3

Monitor and *Differentiate*

IF you need to differentiate instruction

THEN use the Quick Checks to assess children's needs and select the appropriate small group instruction focus.

Comprehension Strategy Make Predictions, T199

Phonemic Awareness/Phonics /v/v, /ks/x, T181, T193, T203, T211, T221

High-Frequency Words *said, want,* T181, T193, T203, T211, T221

If No →	Approaching	**Reteach,** pp. T224–T231
	ELL	**Develop,** pp. T242–T247
If Yes →	On Level	**Review,** pp. T232–T237
	Beyond Level	**Extend,** pp. T238–T241

Level Up with Leveled Readers

IF children can read their leveled text fluently and answer comprehension questions

THEN work with the next level up to accelerate children's reading with more complex text.

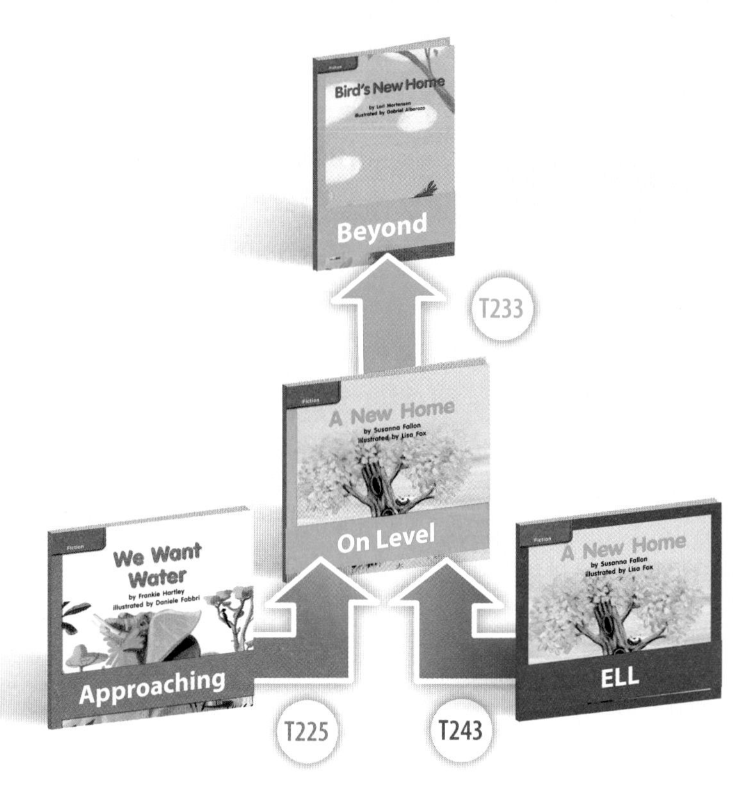

ENGLISH LANGUAGE LEARNERS SCAFFOLD

IF ELL students need additional support **THEN** scaffold instruction using the small group suggestions.

Reading-Writing Workshop	Leveled Reader	Phonological Awareness	Phonics	Oral Vocabulary	Writing	Grammar
Reading-Writing Workshop T175 "Home, Sweet Home!" **Integrate Ideas** T217	**Leveled Reader** T242–T243 *A New Home*	**Phonological Awareness** Onset/Rime Segmentation, T226 Phoneme Isolation, T226 Phoneme Blending, T227 Phoneme Substitution, T227	**Phonics,** /v/v, /ks/x, T228–T229	**Oral Vocabulary,** T244 habitat, wild, complain, stubborn, join **High-Frequency Words,** T245 *said, want*	**Writing** Shared Writing, T246 Writing Trait: Ideas,, T246	**Grammar** T247 Verbs

Note: Include ELL Students in all small groups based on their needs.

WHOLE GROUP

DAY 1

Materials

Reading/Writing Workshop Big Book
UNIT 7

Literature Big Book
Bear Snores On

Visual Vocabulary Cards
habitat
wild

Photo Cards
ax
bear
box
ox
penguin
vegetables
violin
volcano

Sound-Spelling Cards
volcano
fox

Response Board

High-Frequency Word Cards
said
want

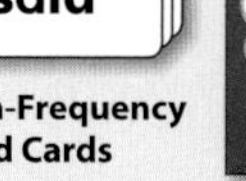

Think Aloud Cloud

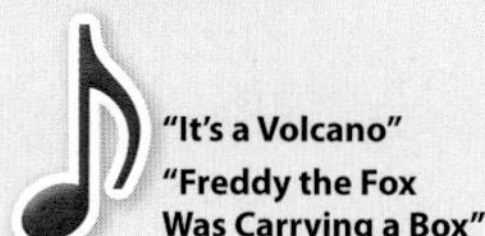

"It's a Volcano"
"Freddy the Fox Was Carrying a Box"

Introduce the Concept

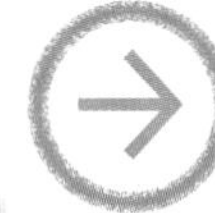

MINILESSON 10 Mins

Build Background

Reading/Writing Workshop Big Book

OBJECTIVES

CCSS Confirm understanding of a text read aloud or information presented orally or through other media by asking and answering questions about key details and requesting clarification if something is not understood. **SL.K.2**

CCSS Identify real-life connections between words and their use. **L.K.5c**

ESSENTIAL QUESTION

Where do animals live?

Read aloud the Essential Question. Tell children you are going to say a rhyme about places where people and animals live.

The Very Nicest Place

The fish lives in the brook,
The bird lives in the tree,
But home's the very nicest place
For a little child like me.

Read aloud "The Very Nicest Place" with children.

This rhyme tells you about the places where two wild animals live. Where does the fish live? (brook) Make sure children understand the word *brook. Where does the bird live?* (tree) Tell children that this week they will read to find out about more places where animals live.

Oral Vocabulary Words

Use the **Define/Example/Ask** routine to introduce the oral vocabulary words **habitat** and **wild**.

To introduce the theme of "Animal Habitats," explain that habitats are places that give animals the food, water, and other things they need to live and grow. *Where is a bear's habitat?* (a cave)

Go Digital

Animal Habitats

Video

Photos

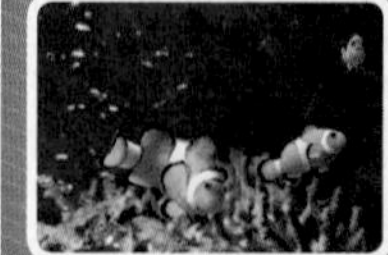

Visual Glossary

Visual Vocabulary Cards

Oral Vocabulary Routine

Define: A **habitat** is the place where an animal lives and grows.

Example: A fish must have water in its habitat.

Ask: What does a bird need in its habitat?

Define: A **wild** animal lives in nature and is not cared for by people.

Example: A wild fox lives in the woods.

Ask: What wild animal have you read about?

Talk About It: Animal Habitats

COLLABORATE

Guide children to talk about habitats for animals that live under the ground. List their responses. Display pages 34–35 of the **Reading/Writing Workshop Big Book** and have children do the **Talk About It** activity with a partner.

READING/WRITING WORKSHOP BIG BOOK, pp. 34–35

Collaborative Conversations

Provide Details As children engage in partner, small group, and whole group discussions, encourage them to:

- → Give details to express their thoughts, feelings, and ideas clearly.
- → Use details to describe people, places, things, and events.
- → Give details when asking about things they don't understand.

ENGLISH LANGUAGE LEARNERS SCAFFOLD

Beginning

Comprehend Point to the fox in the picture. Ask: *Does the fox live in the hole?* (yes) *Did the fox dig the hole?* (yes) Allow children ample time to respond.

Intermediate

Describe Ask children to describe how the fox in the picture uses the hole as a habitat. Elicit more details to support children's answers.

Advanced/Advanced High

Expand Have children use complete sentences to tell about another wild animal's habitat. (Possible answer: An owl lives in a tree.) Clarify children's responses as needed by providing vocabulary.

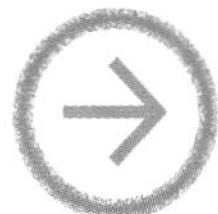

Listening Comprehension

Literature Big Book

OBJECTIVES

With prompting and support, name the author and illustrator of a story and define the role of each in telling the story. **RL.K.6**

Actively engage in group reading activities with purpose and understanding. **RL.K.10**

- Recognize characteristics of fiction
- Strategy: Make, Confirm, and Revise Predictions

ACADEMIC LANGUAGE
fantasy, events

Read the Literature Big Book

Connect to Concept: Animal Habitats

Tell children that they will now find out about more places where animals live. *What are some places that animals live?*

Concepts of Print

Directionality and Phonemic Awareness Display page 5 of the **Big Book**. Model tracking the print with your finger and sweeping from line to line as you read. Point to the word *in* and read it aloud. Then write *in* in large letters on the board. Say: *Words are made of letters. The letters stand for sounds. Listen for the sounds as I say this word slowly: /i/ /n/,* in. Have children repeat the sounds and the whole word with you. *When I read, I must say the sounds in the right order. If I said /n/ /i/, no one could understand me!*

Genre: Fantasy

Model *Bear Snores On* is a fantasy story. Share these characteristics of fantasy with children:

- The events and characters are made up by the author.
- Some events, such as animals talking, could never happen in real life.

Story Words Preview these words before reading:
brew: to make a drink, such as tea, using very hot water
dank: cold and wet with a bad smell
lair: the home of a wild animal
scuttles: moves with quick and tiny steps
stokes: how an adult pushes logs into a fire to make it burn better

Set a Purpose for Reading

- Identify and read aloud the title and the names of the author and the illustrator. *Which person wrote the words for this book?* (Karma Wilson) *Who drew the illustrations?* (Jane Chapman)
- Ask children to listen closely as you read aloud the Big Book to find out about one kind of animal habitat.

Go Digital

Bear Snores On

Think Aloud Cloud

Strategy: Make, Confirm, and Revise Predictions

Explain Remind children that good readers think about what will happen next as they read. This is called *predicting*. *After you predict, you check to see if you're right by reading more. If you are not right about what happens next, you can read again and look for clues about what is actually going to happen.* Display the cover.

Think Aloud On the cover I see a bear sleeping. I predict that the other animals in the picture will wake bear up because there are so many of them. I will start reading to find out if I am correct.

Model With the **Think Aloud Cloud**, model the strategy as you read.

Think Aloud Cover page 17. Read page 16. The badger smells something tasty and says, "Perhaps we can share." I predict that Badger will go into Bear's cave. I will keep reading to see if I'm right.

AUTHOR'S CRAFT

Rhythm, Rhyme, and Repetition Tell children that the author uses rhythm, rhyme, and repetition. Model rhythm by tapping a beat with your hand as your read page 5 aloud. Point out that *lair* and *bear* rhyme. Continue modeling rhythm and rhyme on page 6. Have children identify the rhyming words. Then point out the phrase "But the bear snores on," on page 7. *The author uses this sentence again and again during the story. The animals make so much noise but the bear keeps sleeping. When the bear finally wakes up on page 26 it is a big surprise, because we think the author is going to say "But the bear snores on" again.*

Respond to Reading

After reading, prompt children to tell about each animal that came into Bear's cave. Discuss the ways that predicting helped children understand the book. Then have children draw an animal in its habitat. Guide children to label the animal and tell about the habitat.

Make Connections

Revisit the concept behind the Essential Question *Where do animals live?* by paging through the **Big Book**.

Write About It Have children write about Bear's home.

ENGLISH LANGUAGE LEARNERS SCAFFOLD

Beginning

Listen Read aloud page 14, covering page 15. Then say: *I want to tell what will happen next. Has Bear been sleeping?* (yes) *Do you think Bear will keep sleeping?* (yes) Display page 15 and ask: *Did Bear keep sleeping?* (yes) Allow children ample time to respond.

Intermediate

Demonstrate Understanding Read aloud page 14. Then say: *What do you think Bear will be doing on the next page?* (sleeping) *Why do you think so?* (*Bear has kept on sleeping even though Mouse and Hare started a fire and cooked some food.*) Elicit more details to support children's answers.

Advanced/Advanced High

Discuss Read aloud page 14. Ask: *What helps you figure out what Bear will probably do next?* (Possible answer: I think about what happened in the story so far. Bear has been sleeping. I think Bear will probably keep sleeping.) Clarify children's responses as needed by providing vocabulary.

Word Work

Quick Review

Review /g/ /w/: Ask children to tell the initial sound of the *gate* and *water* Photo Cards.

Build Fluency: Sound-Spellings: Show the following **Word-Building Cards:** *a, b, c, d, e, f, g, h, i, k, l, m, n, o, p, r, s, t, u, w.* Have children chorally say each sound. Repeat and vary the pace.

Phonemic Awareness

OBJECTIVES

CCSS Isolate and pronounce the initial, medial vowel, and final sounds in three-phoneme words. **RF.K.2d**

CCSS Demonstrate basic knowledge of one-to-one letter-sound correspondences by producing the primary or many of the most frequent sounds for each consonant. **RF.K.3a**

Phoneme Isolation

Photo Cards

1 Model Display the **Photo Card** for *volcano. Listen for the sound at the beginning of* volcano. Volcano *has the /v/ sound at the beginning. Say the sound with me: /v/.* Say *van, vote, vest* and have children repeat. Emphasize /v/.

Repeat with final /ks/. Use the *box* Photo Card and words *mix, fix, six.*

Let's play a song. Listen for the words with /v/. Play "It's a Volcano," and have children listen for /v/. *Let's listen to the song again and clap when we hear words that begin with /v/.* Play and/or sing the letter song again, encouraging children to join in. Have children clap when they hear words that begin with /v/.

Repeat with final /ks/ using "Freddy the Fox Was Carrying a Box."

2 Guided Practice/Practice Display and name the following Photo Cards: *vegetables, violin, volcano.* Say each picture name with me. Tell me the sound at the beginning of the word. Guide practice with the first word.

Repeat with final /ks/ and the *box, ax,* and *ox* Photo Cards.

ARTICULATION SUPPORT

Demonstrate how to say /v/. Put your top front teeth on your lower lip. Keep your tongue down. Now, let a little air build up behind your teeth. Use your voice, and let the air push out your lower lip. Say *vat, vet, van* and have children repeat. Stretch /v/.

Demonstrate how to say /ks/. Begin with /k/. Open your mouth a little. Put the tongue at the top of the mouth, toward the back. Let a puff of air out as you lower your tongue. Then, move your top and bottom teeth close together, and put your tongue just behind your front teeth. Force air through your teeth, and finish with /s/. Combine /k/ and /s/ to make /ks/. Say *box, fix, six* and have children repeat. Emphasize final /ks/ as you say the word.

ENGLISH LANGUAGE LEARNERS

Pronunciation
Display and have children name Photo Cards from this lesson to reinforce phonemic awareness and word meanings. Point to the *vest* Photo Card and ask: *What do you see?* (a vest) *What is the sound at the beginning of the word vest?* (/v/) Repeat using Photo Cards with words that end with the /ks/ sound.

Go Digital

Phonemic Awareness

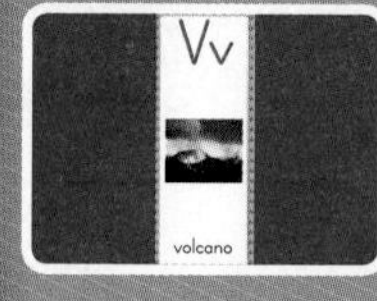

Phonics

Phonics

Introduce /v/*v* and /ks/*x*

1. **Model** Display the *Volcano* **Sound-Spelling Card**. *This is the* Volcano *card. The sound is /v/. The /v/ sound is spelled with the letter* v. *Say it with me: /v/. This is the sound at the beginning of* volcano. *Listen: /vvv/,* volcano. *What is the name of this letter?* (v) *What sound does this letter stand for?* (/v/)

   Display the song "It's a Volcano" (See **Teacher's Resource Book** online). Read or sing the song with children. Reread the title and point out that the word *volcano* begins with the letter *v*. Model placing a self-stick note below the *v* in *volcano*.

2. **Guided Practice/Practice** Read each line of the song. Stop after each line and ask children to place self-stick notes below words that begin with *V* or *v* and say the letter name.

   Repeat Steps 1–2 with final /ks/*x* and the *Fox* Sound-Spelling Card.

It's a Volcano

What is standing very still?
Is it a volcano, or is it a hill?
If it starts to shake, and it cannot stop,
It's a volcano! It's a volcano!
It's a volcano! It's a volcano!
It's a volcano and it's going to BLOW IT'S TOP!
BOOM!

Freddy the Fox Was Carrying a Box

Freddy the fox was carrying a box,
was carrying a box of six shoes and socks.
"Freddy," said I, "I wonder why,
you're carrying a box of six shoes and socks."
"Boo," said Freddy, "I'll give you a clue.
I'll give you a clue so you know what to do.
I'm carrying a box of six shoes and socks.
Four for me and two for you!"

ELL ENGLISH LANGUAGE LEARNERS

Phoneme Variations in Language: Speakers of Spanish, Cantonese, Korean, and Khmer may have difficulty perceiving and pronouncing /v/. Because /v/ is pronounced /b/ in Spanish, Spanish-speaking children may need additional practice with /v/. Provide word pairs to contrast /b/ and /v/: *bat/vat; bet/ vet; boat/vote.* Emphasize /v/ and demonstrate correct mouth position.
Speakers of Hmong and Cantonese may have difficulty perceiving and pronouncing /ks/. Emphasize the /ks/ sounds and demonstrate correct mouth position.

Corrective Feedback

Sound Error Say: *My turn. Volcano. /vvv/. Now it's your turn.* Have children say the words *very* and *vat* and isolate the initial sound. Repeat for final /ks/*x* using the words *fix* and *mix*.

YOUR TURN PRACTICE BOOK pp. 203–206

Word Work

Handwriting: Write *Vv* and *Xx*

MINILESSON 5 Mins

OBJECTIVES

CCSS Write a letter or letters for most consonant and short-vowel sounds (phonemes). **L.K.2c**

CCSS Read common high-frequency words by sight. **RF.K.3c**

ACADEMIC LANGUAGE
uppercase, lowercase

1 Model Say the handwriting cues below as you write and then identify the upper and lowercase forms of *Vv*. Then trace the letters on the board and in the air as you say the sounds.

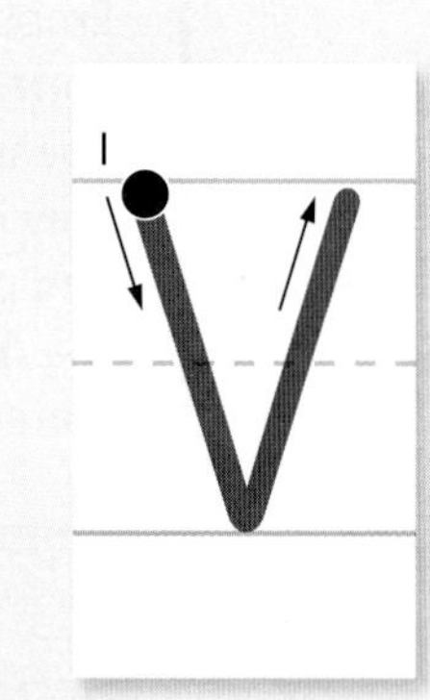

Slant down, slant up.

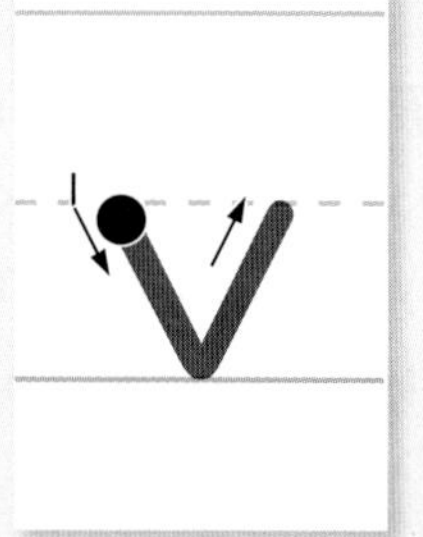

Slant down, slant up.

2 Guided Practice/Practice

- Say the cues together as children trace the letter with their index fingers. Have them identify the uppercase and lowercase forms of the letters.
- Have them write *V* and *v* in the air as they say /v/ multiple times.
- Distribute **Response Boards**. Observe children's pencil grip and paper position, and correct as necessary. Have children say the appropriate sound every time they write the letter.

Repeat Steps 1–2 with *Xx*.

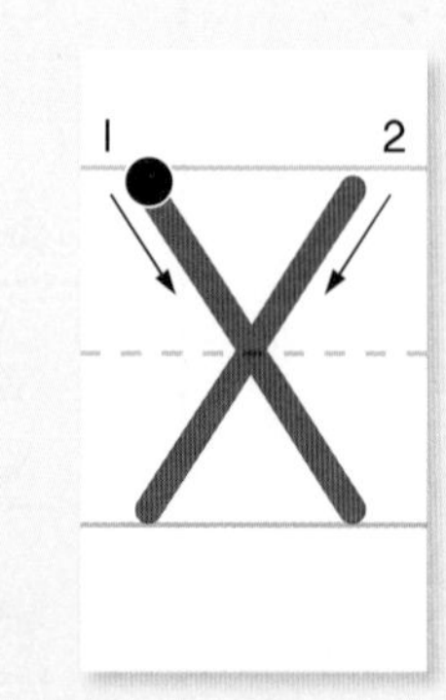

Slant down. Go back to the top. Slant down to cross.

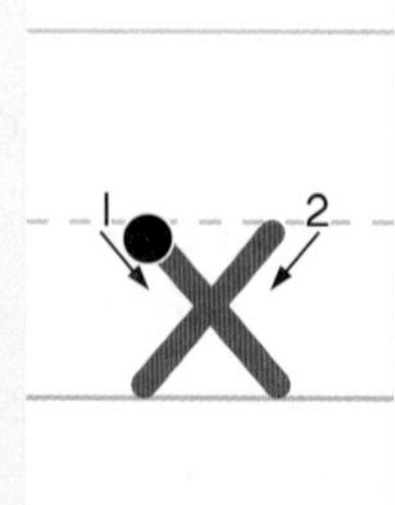

Slant down. Slant in to cross.

Daily Handwriting

Throughout the week teach uppercase and lowercase letters *Vv* and *Xx* using the Handwriting models. At the end of the week, have children use **Your Turn Practice Book** page 212 to practice handwriting.

Go Digital

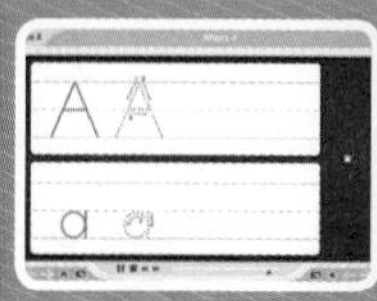

Handwriting

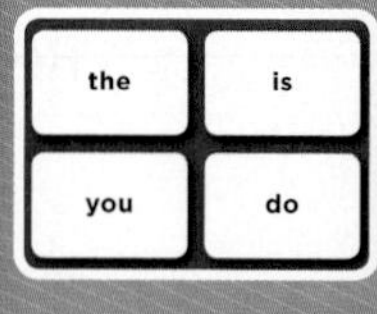

High-Frequency Word Routine

High-Frequency Words

said, want

High-Frequency Word Cards

1. **Model** Display the **High-Frequency Word Card** *said*. Use the **Read/Spell/Write** routine to teach the word.

→ **Read** Point to the word *said* and say the word. *This is the word* said. *Say it with me:* said. *Mouse* said *it was too damp in the cave.*

→ **Spell** *The word* said *is spelled s-a-i-d. Spell it with me.*

→ **Write** *Let's write* said *in the air as we say each letter: s-a-i-d.*

→ Point out that the letter *s* has the same /s/ sound as in *sat* and *d* has the same /d/ sound as in *dad*.

→ Have partners create sentences using the word.

Repeat the routine to introduce *want*. Use the sentence: *They want to sleep.* Point out that the letter *w* has the same /w/ sound as in *wet*.

2. **Guided Practice/Practice** Build sentences using the High-Frequency Word Cards, the **Photo Cards**, and teacher-made punctuation cards. Have children point to the high-frequency words *said* and *want*. Use these sentences.

He **said** they like the house.
She **said** they **want** to have soup.
I **want** my kitten.

Also online

They want the .

High-Frequency Words Practice

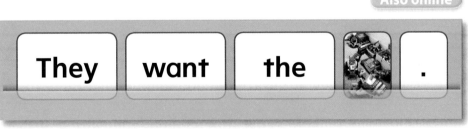

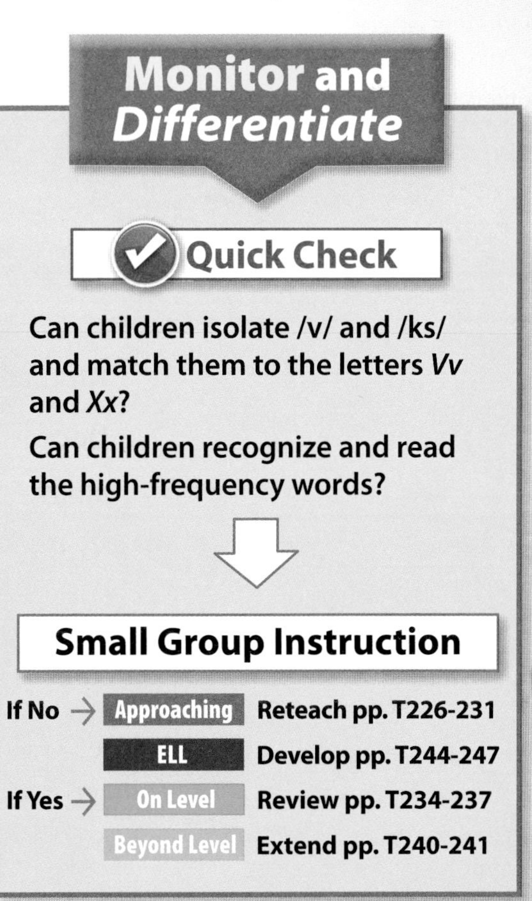

Monitor and Differentiate
Quick Check
Can children isolate /v/ and /ks/ and match them to the letters *Vv* and *Xx*?
Can children recognize and read the high-frequency words?
Small Group Instruction
If No → Approaching Reteach pp. T226-231
ELL Develop pp. T244-247
If Yes → On Level Review pp. T234-237
Beyond Level Extend pp. T240-241

Language Arts

Shared Writing

OBJECTIVES

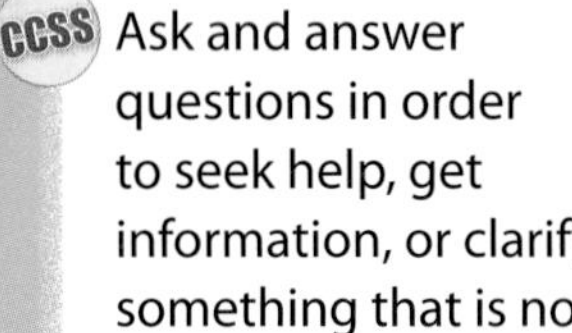
CCSS Ask and answer questions in order to seek help, get information, or clarify something that is not understood. **SL.K.3**

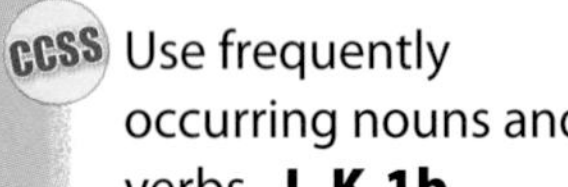
CCSS Use frequently occurring nouns and verbs. **L.K.1b**

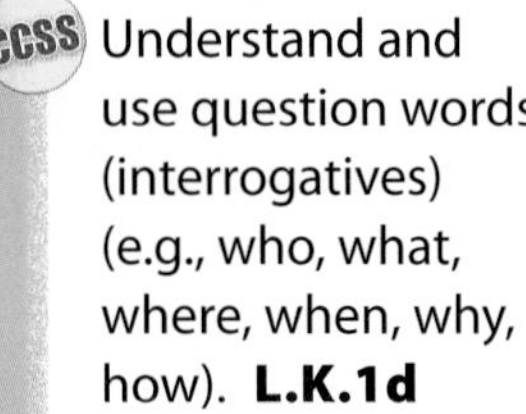
CCSS Understand and use question words (interrogatives) (e.g., who, what, where, when, why, how). **L.K.1d**

- Identify where animals live
- Identify future-tense action words

ACADEMIC LANGUAGE
questions, action words

Writing Trait: Ideas

1 Model Discuss how writers get ideas to write about. Say: *One way we can get ideas for writing is to ask questions about something. We can ask who, what, where, when, why, or how questions.*

- Display the **Photo Card** for *penguin. I can ask questions about penguins. Where do penguins live? What do they eat? How do penguins stay warm? I can look in books or talk to people to find out the answers. Then I can write what I learned about penguins.*

2 Guided Practice/Practice Display the Photo Card for *bear*. Help children think of a question they could ask about bears, using *who, what, where, when, why,* or *how*. (Why do bears sleep through the winter? Where do bears live?)

Write Questions and Answers

Focus and Plan Tell children that this week they will learn how to write questions and answers about where animals live.

COLLABORATE

Brainstorm Ask children to think about the animals in the **Big Book** as well as other animals they know about. Have children tell what they know about where those animals live. Record their ideas in a list.

Animal	Where It Lives
bear	cave
mouse	burrow
bird	nest

Write Model writing a question about an animal. Write and read: *Where does a bear live?* Point to the question mark. Explain that all questions have a question mark at the end of the sentence. *I can write an answer to the question, too.* Write and read: *A bear lives in a cave.*

Model writing questions and answers about other animals. Read aloud the sentences with children.

Go Digital

Writing

I see a fish.

Grammar

Grammar

Action Words (Verbs)

1. **Model** Explain that when we write, we can use action words to tell what will happen in the future. An action word can tell what a person, animal, or thing will do.
   - → Write and read aloud: *I will sing a song.* Circle *sing.* Explain that *sing* is the action word in the sentence. It is the word that tells what you will do. Circle *will.* Say: *I want to tell what I will do in the future, so I add the word* will *to the sentence to show that the action will happen in the future.*

2. **Guided Practice/Practice** Have children discuss events that are going to happen at school later in the day. Write and read aloud a sentence that tells what will happen. For example: *We will play outside.* Ask: *What word tells what action will happen?* (play) Say: *We are not playing outside right now. We will play outside later. Which word helps us know that this will happen in the future?* (will) Have a child circle the words *will play.* Say: Will play *tells what will happen later, in the future.*

   Model how to use future-tense action words in other sentences. Say: *Rex will go to the park.* Explain that *Rex* is the name of the person who will do the action. He is not doing the action now. He will do it in the future. Have children say more sentences about things that will happen in the future. Have them identify the action word in each sentence.

Talk About It

Have partners practice using future-tense action words by telling what they will do on the weekend. Restate children's responses in order to develop their oral language proficiency.

ENGLISH LANGUAGE LEARNERS SCAFFOLD

Beginning

Explain Write a sentence, such as *I eat an apple.* Read the sentence aloud as you pantomime the action. Add *will* before *eat* to put the sentence in the future tense. Read the new sentence aloud with children. Have children pantomime the action. Repeat with additional sentences. Allow children ample time to respond.

Intermediate

Practice Have children work in pairs. Ask partners to tell each other one thing that they will do after school. Encourage children to use complete sentences when they tell about it. For example: "I will go to the store." Model correct pronunciation as needed.

Advanced/Advanced High

Practice Have children work in pairs. Have children tell their partners where they would like to go on a vacation. Encourage children to use complete sentences. For example: "I will go to Florida." Model correct pronunciation as needed.

Daily Wrap Up

- Review the Essential Question and encourage children to discuss it, using the new oral vocabulary words. *Where are different places that animals live?*
- Prompt children to share the skills they learned. How might they use those skills?

WHOLE GROUP
DAY 2

Materials

Reading/Writing Workshop Big Book
UNIT 7

Literature Big Book
Bear Snores On

Visual Vocabulary Cards
habitat
wild

Response Board

Retelling Cards

Puppet

Word-Building Cards

Sound-Spelling Cards
volcano

High-Frequency Word Cards
are
of
said
they
want

Build the Concept

Oral Language

OBJECTIVES

CCSS Use words and phrases acquired through conversations, reading and being read to, and responding to texts. **L.K.6**

CCSS Identify real-life connections between words and their use (e.g., note places at school that are *colorful*). **L.K.5c**

Develop oral vocabulary

ACADEMIC LANGUAGE
rhyming

ESSENTIAL QUESTION
Where do animals live?

Remind children that this week they are learning about places where animals live. Point out that different animals live in different places because they need different things to live and grow.

Say the rhyme "The Very Nicest Place" with children.

Phonological Awareness

Onset/Rime Segmentation

Guide children in segmenting onset and rime using words from "The Very Nicest Place." Say: tree/me. Have children repeat *tree/me. We can break these words into parts. Listen:* me*;* /m/ /ē/. Have children repeat: *me;* /m/ /ē/. Repeat the routine with *tree;* /tr/ /ē/. Challenge children to break the words below into their parts and say the parts aloud.

jet (/j/ /et/) *take* (/t/ /āk/)

Review Oral Vocabulary

Use the **Define/Example/Ask** routine to review the oral vocabulary words **habitat** and **wild**. Prompt children to use the words in sentences.

Visual Vocabulary Cards

Go Digital

Visual Glossary

Category Words

Category Words: Animal Homes

1 Model Use the **Big Book** *Bear Snores On* to discuss words for animal homes: *cave* and *lair,* page 5; *den,* page 12. Reread the text and display the illustrations. *Bear's home is called a lair. It is in a cave. Why do you think Bear makes his home in a cave?* (It is safe. It is quiet and dark.)

Read aloud the following poem:

What is a home?
It's a place to sleep; it's a place to eat.
It's a place to be safe and put up your feet.

→ Have children discuss this question: *Why do animals need special homes?* (Possible answers: for warmth, for safety, as a place to raise babies)

2 Guided Practice/Practice Discuss other words for animal homes, such as nests, hives, tree hollows, and burrows. Make a list on the board of different names for animal homes and the animals that live in those homes.

Vocabulary Strategy: Figurative Language/Shades of Meaning

1 Model Remind children that some words and phrases can have small differences in meaning. Use *Bear Snores On* to model how to identify the shades of meaning between similar words.

Think Aloud On p. 9 in *Bear Snores On,* the word wee is in this sentence: "So he lights wee twigs with a small, hot spark." The word *wee* means very small, but *wee* is more descriptive and helps tell about the size of the tiny mouse and its tiny fire.

2 Guided Practice/Practice Have children look at the words, *scuttle* (p. 16), *nibble* and *munch* (p. 18). Use sentence clues to figure out that *scuttle* means to run with quick steps. Help children think of similar words that can be used instead of *scuttles, nibble,* and *munch.*

A badger ***scuttles*** *by, sniff-snuffs at the air.*
And they ***nibble*** *and they* ***munch*** *with a CHEW—CHOMP—CRUNCH!*

ENGLISH LANGUAGE LEARNERS

Reinforce Meaning Help children understand the names of the animals and the animal homes from the Big Book. Display and discuss the **Photo Cards** for *mouse, rabbit (hare), bear,* and *bird* to help with your discussion. Have children repeat the names of the animals in their native language and in English.

LET'S MOVE!

Reread the Big Book *Bear Snores On.* Have children act out scenes from the story. For example, on page 8, children should tiptoe around the room like the mouse.

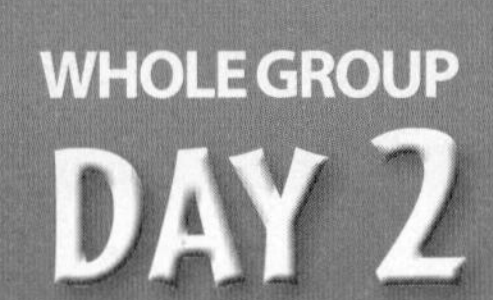

Listening Comprehension

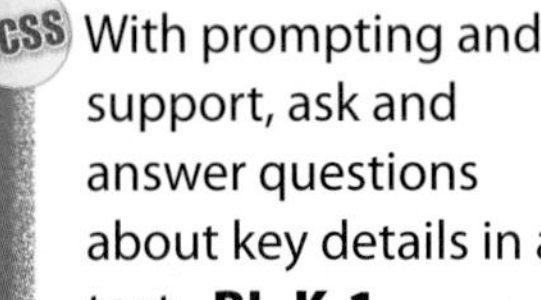

Literature Big Book

OBJECTIVES

CCSS With prompting and support, ask and answer questions about key details in a text. **RL.K.1**

CCSS With prompting and support, retell familiar stories, including key details. **RL.K.2**

- Strategy: Make, Confirm, and Revise Predictions
- Skill: Plot: Cause and Effect

ACADEMIC LANGUAGE

- *predictions, setting*
- Cognates: *prediccion*

Reread Literature Big Book

Genre: Fantasy

Display *Bear Snores On.* Guide children in recalling that fantasy books tell make-believe stories. Some events in fiction, such as animals talking, could never happen in real life. *How do you know that* Bear Snores On *is fiction?* (The animals talk.) Have children point to evidence in the text and the pictures to show that the story is fantasy.

Strategy: Make, Confirm, and Revise Predictions

Remind children that good readers make predictions—or figure out what might happen next—as they read. *How can you tell if your predictions are right?* (You can read what comes next.)

Skill: Plot: Cause and Effect

Guide children in recalling that the plot is the events that happen in the story. Tell children that to understand the plot, it helps to think about *cause* and *effect*. Tell children that an *effect* is what happens and a *cause* is why something happens. As you read, have children listen for evidence in the text that tells about causes and effects in the story. Use the prompts to help fill in the cause and effect graphic organizer.

ACT Access Complex Text

Purpose In this unit, children have read fiction and informational texts about animals. For the informational texts, they were guided to focus on facts about the animals rather than a storyline. As they read *Bear Snores On,* children might see unfamiliar animals, such as a badger, gopher, and mole. They might become confused as to whether they are to read for facts or follow a plot. Reinforce that this book is fiction, so children should focus on the story, not facts about the animals.

→ Review pages 16, 17, 18, and 20 with children, guiding them to read this book as a story, not for facts about animals.

Go Digital

Bear Snores On

Retelling Cards

PAGE 5

PLOT: CAUSE AND EFFECT

Think Aloud *I see the bear sleeping in the cave. I wonder why he is sleeping? I read that it is winter and it is cold outside. This is the cause. The* effect *is the bear sleeping.*

p. 5
great: Point out that the word *great* in this description means "very large."

PAGES 6–7

MAKE, CONFIRM AND REVISE PREDICTIONS

Think Aloud I read that the wind is howling and the night sounds are growling, but the bear keeps sleeping. I predict that it is going to be very hard to wake bear up. He can sleep with a lot of noise!

PAGES 8–9

PLOT: CAUSE AND EFFECT

Name the character on these pages. (Mouse) *What is the setting of these events?* (Bear's cave) *Why does Mouse go into the cave and light a fire?* (It is very cold outside the cave.) *Let's add this to our cause and effect chart.*

pp. 8–9
itty-bitty; wee: Guide children in understanding that these words mean "very, very, small." Display a few very small items. Have children echo and mimic as you point to each item and say: *itty-bitty (name of item); small (name of item).*

PAGES 10–11

MAKE, CONFIRM, AND REVISE PREDICTIONS

Think Aloud Bear keeps sleeping while the mouse makes a fire. My prediction that it would be hard to wake up the bear was correct!

Listening Comprehension

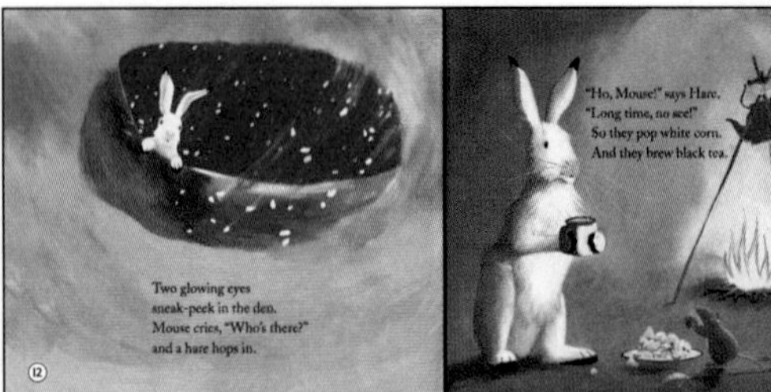

PAGES 12–13

CONCEPTS OF PRINT

Display and read aloud page 12. Ask: *Which words does Mouse say on this page?* ("Who's there?") *How do you know?* (The marks around the words show that someone is speaking.) *How do you know that Mouse is asking a question?* (The sentence ends with a question mark.)

pp. 12–13
Long time, no see: Guide children in understanding that this means Hare and Mouse have not seen each other in a long time.

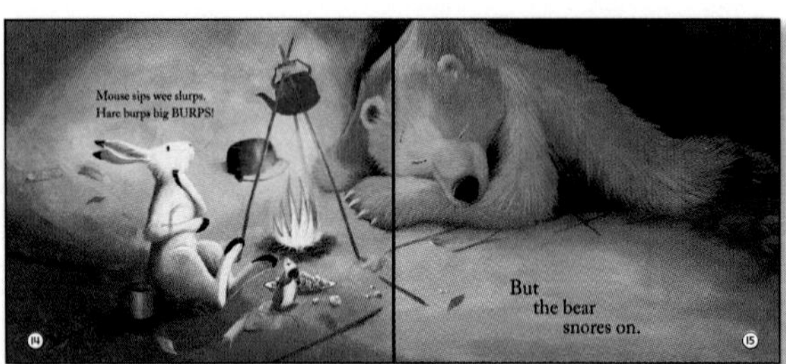

PAGES 14–15

MAKE, CONFIRM, AND REVISE PREDICTIONS

Cover page 15 as you read aloud page 14. *What do you predict Bear will do next?* (Possible answers: keep sleeping) *Why?* (because Bear is sleeping so soundly; because Bear kept sleeping earlier in the story) Uncover and read page 15.

pp. 14–15
slurps: Make a slurping sound as you say: *Slurp!* Have children echo and mimic.

PAGES 16–17

PLOT: CAUSE AND EFFECT

Have children name the character on page 16. (Badger) *What does Badger do?* (go into the cave) *Why does Badger go into the cave?* (It smells something yummy.)

pp. 16–17
divvy them up: Point out that *divvy them up* means "to share them." Display a large number of counters or other items and say: *I'm going to divvy them up.* Keep a specific number for yourself, and give several children an equal number. Say: *I divvied them up.*

PAGES 18–19

MAKE, CONFIRM, AND REVISE PREDICTIONS

What do you think will happen next? Do you think more animals will come into the cave? Why do you think so? (Possible answer: Yes, because it is cold out and the animals want to stay warm.)

pp. 18–19
nibble; munch: Show children the difference between *nibble* and *munch* by pantomiming each action after you name it. Have children echo and mimic.

PAGES 20–21

ASK AND ANSWER QUESTIONS

I read the word *mutters* on page 21. What does *mutter* mean? Let's answer the question together. The sentence says: Mole mutters, "What a night!" I know that Mole is saying "What a night!" because it is in quotation marks. *Mutters* must be another word for *says*. What is another word on this page that you can ask a question about?

pp. 20–21
clutter: Point out that the word *clutter* on this page means "get together." Motion to children to join you in a circle as you say: *Let's clutter.*

PAGES 22–23

PHONICS

Reread page 23 aloud. Invite a child to point to and read aloud the word on the page that has the /v/ sound at the beginning. (very) *Which letter makes the /v/ sound?* (v)

pp. 22–23
slumbering: Tell children that *slumbering* means "sleeping." Ask a child to pretend to sleep. Then say: *Shhh. A child is sleeping. Shhh. A child is slumbering.* Repeat the routine by having pairs echo and mimic.

PAGES 24–25

MAKE, CONFIRM AND REVISE PREDICTIONS

Think Aloud I read that a small pepper flake is going to make the bear do something. So far the bear has just kept sleeping. I think maybe the pepper will make him do something different. I predict that it will make Bear wake up.

pp. 24–25
fleck: Explain that a *fleck* is a very small piece. Rip off a tiny piece of paper, and say: *fleck of paper.* Have children echo and mimic.

PAGES 26–27

PLOT: CAUSE AND EFFECT

What does Bear do on this page? (He sneezes.) *What caused Bear to sneeze?* (the pepper that Mouse put in the stew) If children have trouble recalling, turn back to pages 24 and 25 to show them Mouse using the pepper. *Let's add this to our Cause and Effect Chart.*

pp. 26–27
freezes: Point out that *freezes* on this page means "to stop quickly and not to move at all." Demonstrate by walking across the room and then stopping suddenly and standing very still. Say: *I freeze.* Have children echo and mimic.

Listening Comprehension

PAGES 28–29

SHADES OF MEANING

Point out that when the bear wakes up he makes lots of different loud noises. Help children understand the differences between the words by acting out *snarls, roars, growls* and *grumbles* and having children echo and mimic you. Then say the words in a new order and have children act them out.

PAGES 30–31

PLOT: CAUSE AND EFFECT

Why does Mouse offer to make more tea and popcorn? (Bear is sad that he missed all the fun. Bear did not have anything to eat while all the other animals were eating.)

pp. 30–31

blubbers: Explain that *blubbers* means "to cry loudly" Demonstrate by pantomiming blubbering and saying: *I'm blubbering.* Have children echo and mimic.

PAGES 32–33

VISUALIZE

Think Aloud In the picture I see the animals having fun together. In my mind I can picture the warm fire and the smell of the stew. I picture the animals laughing. This helps me understand why they are having fun.

pp. 32–33

tall tales: Tell children that tall tales are stories about amazing things. If the class has read any tall tales, name them.

PAGE 34

AUTHOR'S PURPOSE

Why do you think the author wrote this book? (Possible answer: to tell a fun story about a bear who wakes up from a long sleep and has fun with friends)

Plot: Cause and Effect

Review Skill Remind children that when they read stories they should pay attention to why things happen. Discuss causes and effects that children heard in *Bear Snores On* using the completed graphic organizer. Encourage children to give more examples.

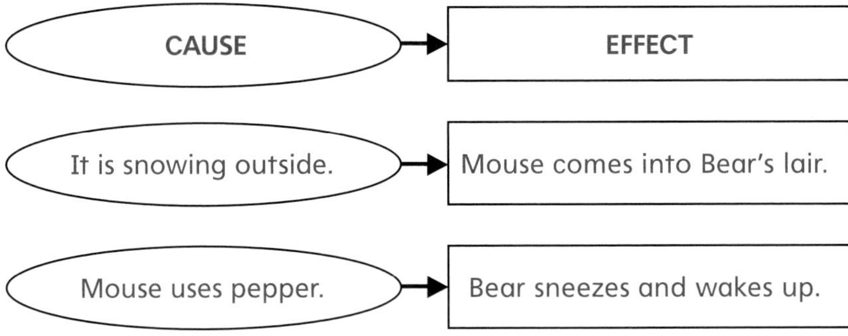

Guided Retelling

Tell children that they will use the **Retelling Cards** to retell the story.

- Show Retelling Card 1. Based on children's needs, use the Modeled, Guided or ELL retelling prompts. The ELL prompts contain support for English language learners based on levels of language acquisition. Repeat with cards 2–4, using the prompts as a guide.
- Have children choose a favorite event in the book and act it out.

Model Fluency

Read aloud the first sentence on page 28. Point out the words in all capital letters. Tell children that this means to read these words in a very loud and serious way—just the way Bear would say them. Demonstrate by reading aloud the page through the word *RUMBLES*. Have children echo. Read the rest of the page, modeling emphasis.

Retelling Cards

Text Evidence

Explain Remind children that when they answer a question they need to show where in the book (both words and pictures) they found the answer.

Discuss *What different kinds of food and drink do the animals have? How do you know?* (Popcorn, black tea, honey-nuts, stew. Rabbit and Mouse make popcorn and tea, Badger brings nuts, and they all make stew.)

YOUR TURN PRACTICE BOOK p. 207

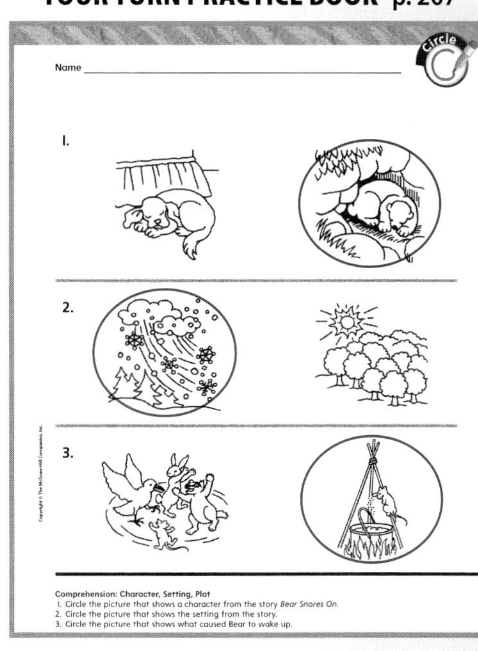

Word Work

Quick Review

Build Fluency: Sound-Spellings: Show the following **Word-Building Cards:** *a, b, c, d, e, f, g, h, i, k, l, m, n, o, p, r, s, t, u, v, w, x.* Have children chorally say each sound. Repeat and vary the pace.

Phonemic Awareness

Puppet

Phoneme Blending

1 Model *The puppet is going to say sounds in a word, /o/ /ks/. The puppet can blend those sounds to make a word: /oks/,* ox. *Listen as it blends more sounds to make a word.* Model phoneme blending with the following.

/f / /i/ /ks/, fix   /m/ /i/ /ks/, mix   /w/ /a/ /ks/, wax

2 Guided Practice/Practice Tell children that the puppet is going to say the sounds in a word. *Listen as it says each sound. Repeat the sounds, then blend them to say the word.* Guide children with the first word.

/s/ /i/ /ks/, six   /t/ /a/ /ks/, tax   /b/ /o/ /ks/, box

Repeat Steps 1–2 with /v/ with *vest, van, vat, vent, vote, vase.*

Phonics

Review *v* and *x*

1 Model Display the *Volcano* **Sound-Spelling Card.** *This is the letter* v. *The letter* v *stands for the sound /v/ as in the word* volcano. *What is the letter?* (v) *What sound does the letter* v *stands for?* (/v/) Repeat for /ks/*x* and the *Box* Sound-Spelling Card.

2 Guided Practice/Practice Have children listen as you say some words. Ask them to write the letter *v* on their **Response Boards** if the word begins with the sound /v/. Tell them to write the letter *x* if the word ends with the sound /ks/. Do the first two words with children.

very   fox   vine   vault   box   fix   wax   view

OBJECTIVES

CCSS Isolate and pronounce the initial, medial vowel, and final sounds in three-phoneme words. **RF.K.2d**

CCSS Demonstrate basic knowledge of one-to-one letter-sound correspondences by producing the primary and many of the most frequent sounds for each consonant. **RF.K.3a**

CCSS Read common high-frequency words by sight. **RF.K.3c**

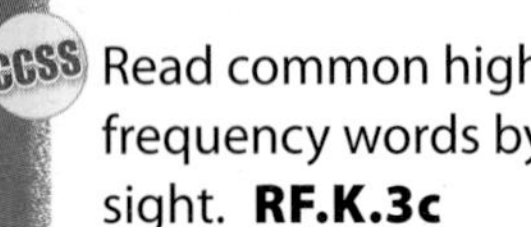

ENGLISH LANGUAGE LEARNERS

High-Frequency Words: Build Meaning Reinforce the use of the word *want* by saying these sentences and demonstrating them.

- They *want* to walk to the door.
- They *want* water.
- I *want* to sit down.
- She *wants* the book.

Go Digital

Phonemic Awareness

Phonics

High-Frequency Word Routine

Handwriting

Blend Words with *v* and *x*

1 Model Place **Word-Building Cards** *v, a,* and *n* in a pocket chart. Point to the letter *v. This is the letter* v. *The letter* v *stands for /v/. Say /v/. This is the letter* a. *The letter* a *stands for /a/. Say /a/. This is the letter* n. *The letter* n *stands for /n/. Say /n/. Listen as I blend the three sounds together: /vvvaaannn/. Now blend the sounds with me to read the word.*

2 Guided Practice/Practice Change Word-Building Cards to *v, a, t.* Point to the letter *v* and have children say /v/. Point to the letter *a* and have children say /a/. Point to the letter *t* and have children say /t/. Then move your hand from left to right under the word and have children blend and read the word *vat.*

Repeat Steps 1–2 with *x* using the words *ox, fox.*

High-Frequency Words

said, want

said

High-Frequency Word Cards

1 Guided Practice Display the **High-Frequency Word Cards** *said* and *want.* Use the **Read/Spell/Write** routine to teach each word. Ask children to close their eyes, picture the spelling of the word in their minds, and then write it the way they see it. Have children self-correct by checking the High-Frequency Word Card.

2 Practice Add the high-frequency words to the word bank.

- → Have partners create sentences using the words.
- → Have children count the number of letters in each word and then write the words *said* and *want* again.

Cumulative Review Review last week's words *they* and *of.*

Repeat the **Read/Spell/Write** routine. Mix the words and have children chorally say each one.

Monitor and *Differentiate*

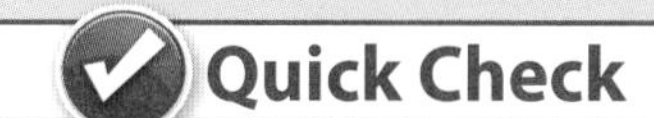

Can children blend words with /v/ and /ks/ and match them to the letters *Vv* and *Xx*?

Can children recognize and read the high-frequency words?

Small Group Instruction

If No →	Approaching	Reteach pp. T226-231
	ELL	Develop pp. T244-247
If Yes →	On Level	Review pp. T234-237
	Beyond Level	Extend pp. T240-241

Shared Read

Reading/Writing Workshop Big Book and Reading/Writing Workshop

OBJECTIVES

 Read common high-frequency words by sight. **RF.K.3c**

 Read emergent-reader texts with purpose and understanding. **RF.K.4**

ACADEMIC LANGUAGE

- *predict*
- Cognates: *predecir*

MINILESSON 10 Mins

Read "A Vet in a Van"

Model Skills and Strategies

Model Concepts About Print Point to the word *Vet* in the title of the story. Discuss how each letter stands for a sound. *This word is* vet. *I will point to each letter and say its sound: /v/ /e/ /t/:* vet. Invite volunteers to come up to the **Big Book**. Encourage them to point to and say a word, then point to the letters and sound out the word by isolating each letter sound.

Predict Read the title together. Invite children to look closely at the illustration on pages 36 and 37. Encourage them to describe what they see and predict what the story might be about.

Read Have children chorally read the story with you. Point to each word as you read it together. Help children sound out decodable words and say the sight words. If children have difficulty, provide corrective feedback and guide them page by page using the student **Reading/Writing Workshop**.

Ask the following:

- *Look at page 36. Who is the woman in the van? What does she want to see?* (The woman in the van is a vet. She wants to see a red fox.)
- *Look at page 39. What does the vet want to see now?* (She wants to see a big cat, or cheetah.)
- *Look at page 41. What does the vet see along the road?* (six pigs)

Go Digital

"A Vet in a Van"

"A Vet in a Van"

READING/WRITING WORKSHOP 7, pp. 36–43

Rereading

COLLABORATE

Have small groups use the **Reading/Writing Workshop** to reread "A Vet in a Van." Then review the skills and strategies using the *Phonics* and *Words to Know* pages that come before the selection.

- Before children reread the story, have them predict what it will be about, then confirm and revise their predictions. Occasionally stop and have them make, confirm, and revise additional predictions. Focus on the characters, setting, and plot in their predictions.
- Have children use page 35 to review the high-frequency words *said* and *want*.
- Have children use page 34 to review the letters *v* and *x* and their corresponding sounds. Guide them to blend the sounds to read the words.

ENGLISH LANGUAGE LEARNERS

Reinforce Vocabulary Display the **High-Frequency Word Cards** *said, want, of, are*. Point to objects in the classroom and groups of children as you use the high-frequency words in sentences, such as the following: *Jane said, "Hello." What did Jane say?* (Jane said, "Hello.") *I want to go outside at recess. Do you want to go outside at recess?* (Yes, we want to go outside at recess.) *This is a box of pencils. What is this?* (It is a box of pencils.) *The windows are cold. What can we say about the windows?* (The windows are cold.)

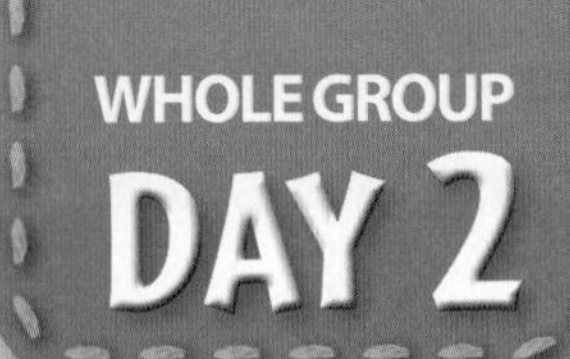

Language Arts

Interactive Writing

OBJECTIVES

 With guidance and support from adults, recall information from experiences or gather information from provided sources to answer a question. **W.K.8**

 Use frequently occurring nouns and verbs. **L.K.1b**

 Understand and use question words (interrogatives) (e.g., *who, what, where, when, why, how*). **L.K.1d**

CCSS Ask and answer questions in order to seek help, get information, or clarify something that is not understood. **SL.K.3**

- Write questions and answers
- Use future-tense verbs

ACADEMIC LANGUAGE
answer, action words

Writing Trait: Ideas

Review Remind children that asking questions can help them find ideas to write about. Guide children to recall that questions can begin with *who, what, where, when, why,* or *how.* Write and read aloud: *What is your name? I can write an answer to the question: My name is . . .*

Write Questions and Answers

Discuss Display the list of animals that the children made on Day 1, and discuss where those animals live. Read each item on the list aloud. Talk about other animals and where they live. Guide children to choose one animal to write about, such as a bird.

Model/Apply Grammar Tell children that you will work together to write questions and answers about animals. Remind them that they should use action words in their questions and answers.

Write and read aloud this sentence frame: *Where does a ______ live?* Draw a bird, such as a crow or a wren from the **Big Book**. Under the bird, write this question: *Where does a bird live? What is the name of the mark at the end of the question?* (a question mark) Then write a sentence to answer the question. *A bird lives in a nest.* Read the sentences aloud and point to each word. *Which word in each sentence is an action word?* (live, lives)

Write Have children help you write additional questions and answers about a bird. Write and read aloud the question *What does a bird eat?* Write and read this sentence frame: *A bird eats ______.*

Guide children to complete the sentence frame. (A bird eats worms.) Write the word. Share the pen with children and have them write the letters they know. Guide children to complete additional questions and answers about birds.

Go Digital

Writing

Grammar

Grammar

Action Words (Verbs)

1 Review Remind children that action words can tell what a person, animal, or thing does, did in the past, in the present, or will do in the future. Say: *I can use action words to tell what I will do this weekend. I will shop. I will clean my house. What action words did I use?* (shop, clean) Shop *and* clean *are action words. They each have the word* will *right before them in the sentence, so that tells me that the actions will happen in the future.*

→ Say: *I will ride the bus.* Have children chorally repeat the sentence. Ask: *What is the action word in the sentence?* (ride) *How do you know?* (It tells what I will do.)

2 Guided Practice Write and read: *Andy will ______ his mom.* Write and read aloud the following words: *cry, hug, leaf.* Tell children that only one of these words can be used in the sentence. Ask children to point to the action word that can be used in the sentence. (hug) Ask: *How do you know that* hug *is the correct word?* (*Hug* is an action word. It tells what Andy will do. *Cry* is an action word, but it doesn't make sense in the sentence.) Ask: *Why doesn't* leaf *work in the sentence?* (*Leaf* is a naming word. It doesn't tell the action.)

COLLABORATE **3 Practice** Have children work with a partner. Tell partners to tell each other something that they will do in the summer. Encourage children to use complete sentences, such as *I will swim in a pool.* Ask what word in the sentence tells them that this will happen in the future. (will)

Talk About It

Have partners work together to orally generate sentences with future-tense action words. Challenge them to create sentences about something they will do with their friends.

ENGLISH LANGUAGE LEARNERS

Recall Information Display the **Big Book** and show a page that shows only the bear sleeping in the cave. Ask children to tell what will happen when the bear wakes up. For example: *The bear will growl.* Write the sentence on the board and have children underline the action word.

Daily Wrap Up

- Review the Essential Question and encourage children to use the oral vocabulary words. *Why do different animals live in different places?*
- Prompt children to review and discuss the skills they used today. How do those skills help them?

WHOLE GROUP

DAY 3

Materials

Reading/Writing Workshop Big Book
UNIT 7

Visual Vocabulary Cards
complain
join
stubborn

Interactive Read-Aloud Cards

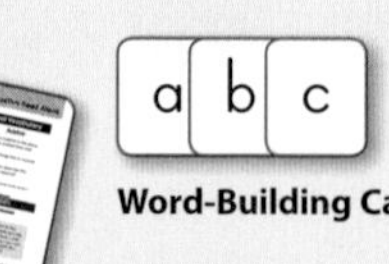

Word-Building Cards

High-Frequency Word Cards
of they
said want

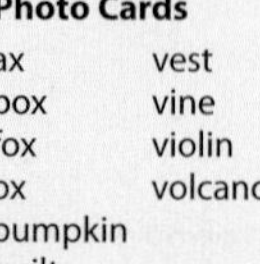

Photo Cards
ax, box, fox, ox, pumpkin, quilt, six, vegetables, vest, vine, violin, volcano

Think Aloud Cloud

Puppet

Build the Concept

Oral Language

OBJECTIVES

CCSS With prompting and support, compare and contrast the adventures and experiences of characters in familiar stories. **RL.K.9**

CCSS Identify real-life connections between words and their use. **L.K.5c**

Develop oral vocabulary

ACADEMIC LANGUAGE
tale

ESSENTIAL QUESTION

Remind children that this week they are talking and learning about places where animals live. Guide them to discuss the Essential Question, using information from the **Big Book** and the weekly poem. Ask children to think about where animals live in "The Very Nicest Place." Read the poem and have children join in.

Oral Vocabulary

Review last week's oral vocabulary words, as well as *habitat* and *wild* from Day 1. Then use the **Define/Example/Ask** routine to introduce *complain, join,* and *stubborn.*

Oral Vocabulary Routine

Define: When you **complain**, you say that you are upset about something.

Example: I heard the basketball player complain about the game.

Ask: Why might you complain about a rainy day?

Visual Vocabulary Cards

Define: When you **join** someone, you and the other person do something together.

Example: I saw the skating teacher skate over to join the skating students.

Ask: When did you join a friend to do something fun?

Define: If you are being **stubborn**, you refuse to change your mind about something.

Example: The baby was acting stubborn and wouldn't sit in her high chair.

Ask: When have you seen a dog be stubborn?

Go Digital

Visual Glossary

"Anansi: An African Tale"

Think Aloud Cloud

Listening Comprehension

MINILESSON 10 Mins

Read the Interactive Read Aloud

Genre: Tale

Tell children that you will be reading a tale, which is like a fable. Remind them that a *tale* is a fiction story from long ago. Display the **Interactive Read-Aloud Cards**.

Interactive Read-Aloud Cards

Read the title. Point out that Anansi is a spider character in many African tales.

Strategy: Make, Confirm, and Revise Predictions

Remind children that good readers make predictions as they read. They use details from the words and illustrations in a story to help them think about what might happen next. Model making predictions using the **Think Aloud Cloud**.

Think Aloud I read on Card 2 that Anansi tricked Turtle so that Turtle could not eat any food. I think that maybe Turtle will trick Anansi to teach him a lesson. I will keep reading to find out if my prediction is correct!

Read "Anansi: An African Tale." Pause to model the strategy of making, confirming, and revising predictions.

Make Connections

COLLABORATE

Guide partners to connect "Anansi: An African Tale" with *Bear Snores On*. Discuss the settings in both stories. Ask: *Where do the animals live in each story? Which animals share food?*

ELL

ENGLISH LANGUAGE LEARNERS

Reinforce Meaning As you read "Anansi: An African Tale," make meaning clear by pointing to specific characters, places, or objects in the illustrations, demonstrating word meanings, paraphrasing text, and asking children questions. For example, on Card 1, point to the desert setting and say: *This is the desert.* Repeat with other habitats from the tale.

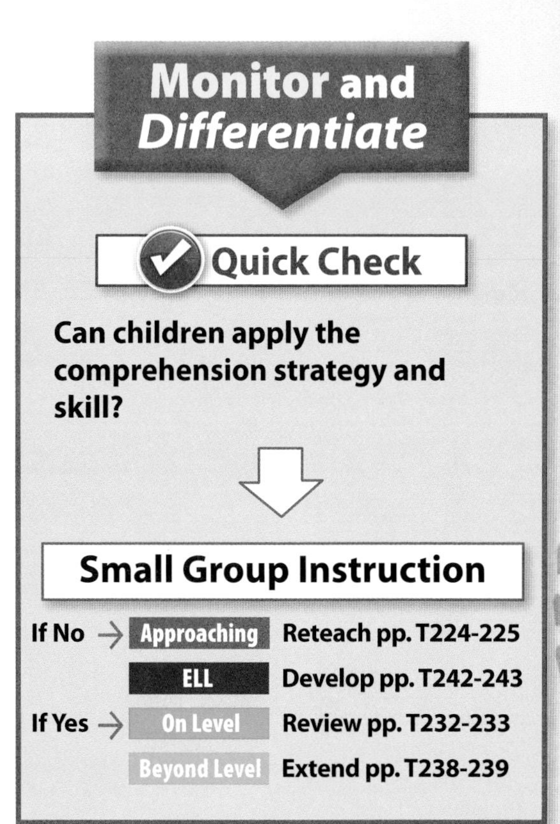

Monitor and Differentiate
Quick Check
Can children apply the comprehension strategy and skill?
Small Group Instruction
If No → Approaching Reteach pp. T224-225
ELL Develop pp. T242-243
If Yes → On Level Review pp. T232-233
Beyond Level Extend pp. T238-239

Word Work

Quick Review

Build Fluency: Sound-Spellings: Display the following **Word-Building Cards:** *a, b, c, d, e, f, g, h, i, k, l, m, n, o, p, r, s, t, u, v, w, x.* Have children chorally say each sound. Repeat and vary the pace.

MINILESSON 5 Mins

Phonemic Awareness

Puppet

OBJECTIVES

CCSS Isolate and pronounce the initial, medial vowel, and final sounds (phonemes) in three-phoneme words. **RF.K.2d**

CCSS Demonstrate basic knowledge of one-to-one letter-sound correspondences by producing the primary or many of the most frequent sound for each consonant. **RF.K.3a**

Read and blend words with *x, v*

Phoneme Blending

1 **Model** *The puppet is going to say sounds in a word /v/ /a/ /n/. It can blend those sounds to make a word: /vvvaaannn/* van. Repeat for /ks/ using the work *ox. Listen as the puppet blends more sounds to make words.* Model phoneme blending with the following:

/v/ /e/ /s/ /t/ vest /v/ /ī/ /n/ vine /a/ /ks/ ax /f/ /o/ /ks/ fox

2 **Guided Practice/Practice** Tell children that the puppet will say the sounds in a word. *Listen to the puppet as it says each sound. Repeat the sounds, then blend them to say the word.* Guide practice with the first word.

/v/ /e/ /s/ /t/ vest /f/ /i/ /ks/ fix /v/ /a/ /t/ vat
/m/ /i/ /ks/ mix /v/ /ō/ /t/ vote

Review /ks/ and /v/. Play and sing "Freddy the Fox Was Carrying a Box." Have children clap when they hear final /ks/. Demonstrate as you sing with them. Repeat with initial /v/ and "It's a Volcano."

Go Digital

Phonemic Awareness

Phonics

Handwriting

Phonics

Word-Building Cards

Review *v* and *x*

1. **Model** Display **Word-Building Card** *v. This is the letter* v. *The letter* v *stands for /v/, the sound you hear at the beginning of* vest. *Say the sound with me: /v/. I will write the letter* v *because* vest *has /v/ at the beginning.* Repeat for /ks/*x* using the word *box*.

2. **Guided Practice/Practice** Tell children that you will say words that have /v/ at the beginning of the word or /ks/ at the end of the word. Have children say /v/ and write the letter *v* on their **Response Boards** when they hear initial /v/. Tell them to say /ks/ and write the letter *x* if they hear final /ks/. Guide practice with the first two words.

van box vet fox ax ox vest vent

Blend Words with Short *i, a, e, o* and *f, x, m, v, n, t*

1. **Model** Display **Word-Building Cards** *f, o, x. This is the letter* f. *It stands for /f/. This is the letter* o. *It stands for /o/. This is the letter* x. *It stands for /ks/. Let's blend the three sounds together: /fffoooks/, /fox/. The word is* fox. Repeat with *fix, mix, van, vet*.

2. **Guided Practice/Practice** Write the following words. Have children read each word, blending the sounds. Guide practice with the first word.

fix van vat fax fox vet

Write these sentences and prompt children to read the connected text, sounding out the decodable words: *I can fix the van. He is a vet. Max can mix it in the vat.*

Corrective Feedback

Sound Error Model the sound that children missed, then have them repeat. For example, say: *My turn.* Tap under the letter *x* in the word *fix* and ask: *Sound?* (/ks/) *What's the sound?* (/ks/) Return to the beginning of the word. *Let's start over.* Blend the word again.

YOUR TURN PRACTICE BOOK p. 208

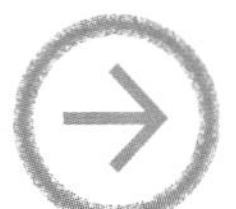

Word Work

Phonics

Word-Building Cards

OBJECTIVES

CCSS Read common high-frequency words by sight. **RF.K.3c**

Sort pictures of objects by initial /v/*v* and final /ks/*x*

ACADEMIC LANGUAGE

sort

Picture Sort

1 Model Remind children that the letter *v* stands for /v/ and the letter *x* stands for /ks/. Place the **Word-Building Card** *v* on the left side of a pocket chart. *What is this letter?* (v) *What sound does this letter stand for?* (/v/) Continue the routine for letter *x*, placing the Word-Building Card *x* on the right side of the pocket chart.

Display the **Photo Card** for *volcano*. *This is a* volcano. Volcano *has the /v/ sound at the beginning. Listen,* volcano. *I will place* volcano *under the letter* v *because the letter* v *stands for the sound /v/.* Repeat the routine for /ks/x and the *box* Photo Card.

2 Guided Practice/Practice Display and name the following Photo Cards: *ax, fox, ox, six, vegetables, vest, vine, violin.* Have children say the word and tell if it has /ks/ at the end of the word or /v/ at the beginning. Have children tell if the Photo Card should be placed under the letter *x* or the letter *v*.

Photo Cards

Go Digital

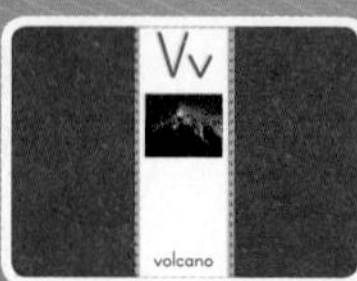

Phonics

High-Frequency Word Routine

High-Frequency Words

said, want

1 Guided Practice Display the **High-Frequency Word Cards** *said* and *want*. Review the words using the **Read/Spell/Write** routine.

2 Practice Point to the High-Frequency Word Card *said* and have children read it. Repeat with *want* and last week's words *they* and *of.*

Build Fluency

Word Automaticity Write the following sentences and have children chorally read aloud as you track the print. Repeat several times.

They *said* they *want* to go.
Max and Val *said* yes.
I *want* the little cat.
I *want* you to fix the van.

Read for Fluency Distribute pp. 209–210 of the **Your Turn Practice Book** and help children assemble their Take-Home Books. Chorally read the Take-Home Books with children. Then have children reread the books to review high-frequency words and build fluency.

YOUR TURN PRACTICE BOOK pp. 209–210

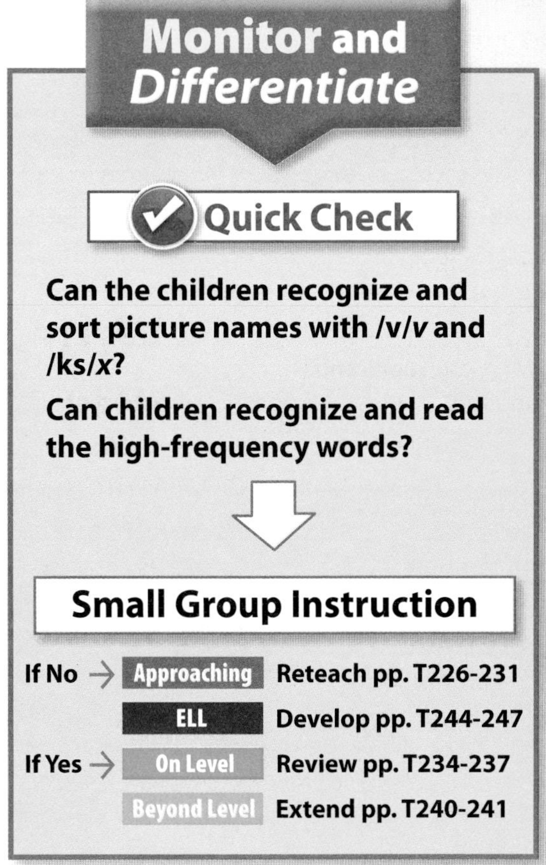
Monitor and *Differentiate*

Quick Check

Can the children recognize and sort picture names with /v/*v* and /ks/*x*?

Can children recognize and read the high-frequency words?

Small Group Instruction

If No →	Approaching	Reteach pp. T226-231
	ELL	Develop pp. T244-247
If Yes →	On Level	Review pp. T234-237
	Beyond Level	Extend pp. T240-241

Language Arts

Reading/Writing Workshop Big Book

OBJECTIVES

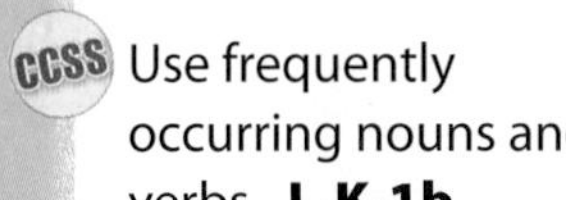

CCSS With guidance and support from adults, recall information from experiences or gather information from provided sources to answer a question. **W.K.8**

CCSS Use frequently occurring nouns and verbs. **L.K.1b**

CCSS Understand and use question words (interrogatives) (e.g., *who, what, where, when, why, how*). **L.K.1d**

- Write questions and answers
- Apply writing trait and grammar to writing

ACADEMIC LANGUAGE

question, answer, action word

MINILESSON 10 Mins

Independent Writing

Writing Trait: Ideas

1. **Practice** Tell children that today they will write questions and answers about animals.

2. **Guided Practice** Share the Readers to Writers page in the **Reading/Writing Workshop**. Read the model sentences aloud.

READING/WRITING WORKSHOP BIG BOOK, pp. 46–47

Write Questions and Answers

Model Display the lists from Day 1. Write and read: *Where does a mouse live?* Ask children to look at the list to answer the question. Write and read: *A mouse lives in a burrow.*

Prewrite

Brainstorm Have children work with a partner to choose an animal to write about. Ask children to think of questions they would like answered about their animal.

Draft

Ask children to draw a picture of their animal showing the home it lives in. Guide them in writing the name of the animal below the picture. Then ask them to write a question and an answer about where the animal lives. Remind children to use the correct end punctuation for each sentence. Help children write their sentences.

Apply Writing Trait As children write and draw, ask them questions about the animal homes.

Apply Grammar Tell children to point to the action words in their questions and answers and to tell who or what does each action.

ENGLISH LANGUAGE LEARNERS

Understand Action Words Use the Photo Card for *kite* for support. Have children dictate a sentence about the kite that includes an action word. For example: "I will fly the kite." Write children's sentences on the board and read them aloud with the class.

Grammar

Action Words (Verbs)

1 Review Write and read aloud: *I will catch the ball.*

Point out that *catch* is an action word that tells what the person will do. Point out that *will* is used before *catch* in the sentence to tell you that the action is going to happen in the future. Remind children that the word *I* is always a capital letter.

2 Guided Practice/Practice Write and read: *Dad will work in the yard.* Ask: *What will Dad do?* (work in the yard) *Which word is the action word in the sentence?* (work) *Is the action happening now, in the past, or in the future? How do you know?* (The action will happen in the future. I know because the word *will* comes before the action word.)

Display and name the **Photo Cards** for *pumpkin* and *quilt*. Have children work with a partner. Write these sentence frames: *I will ______ pumpkin pie. I will ______ a quilt.* Have partners talk about action words that can be used to complete the sentence frames. Write their ideas on the board. Complete the sentence frames with words they suggest, such as *I will eat pumpkin pie. I will make a quilt.*

Talk About It

Have partners work together to create sentences about things they want to do in the future. Encourage children to ask and answer questions about why they want to do certain things.

Daily Wrap Up

- Review the Essential Question and encourage children to discuss it, using the oral vocabulary words *habitat* and *wild. In what kind of habitat do fish live?*
- Prompt children to review and discuss the skills they used today. Guide them to give examples of how they used each skill.

WHOLE GROUP

DAY 4

Materials

Reading/Writing Workshop Big Book
UNIT 7

Literature Big Book
Bear Snores On

Visual Vocabulary Cards
said
want

Interactive Read-Aloud Cards

Word-Building Cards

Puppet

High-Frequency Word Cards
said
want

Photo Cards
bird
mouse
rabbit

Extend the Concept

MINILESSON 10 Mins

Oral Language

OBJECTIVES

CCSS Blend and segment onsets and rimes of single-syllable spoken words. **RF.K.2c**

CCSS Use words and phrases acquired through conversations, reading and being read to, and responding to texts. **L.K.6**

Develop oral vocabulary

ESSENTIAL QUESTION

Tell children that this week they have been talking and reading about animal habitats. Have them recite "The Very Nicest Place" and tell the fish's and the bird's habitats. *Where does Bear live in* Bear Snores On?

Phonological Awareness

Onset/Rime Segmentation

Say: *We can break words into a beginning part and an end part. Listen:* fish, /f/ /ish/. Have children repeat. *Let's do the same with the word* me. *Listen:* me, /m/ /ē/. Have children repeat. Then challenge children to break the following words into beginning and end sounds, saying each word part aloud: *side* (/s/ /īd/); *get* (/g/ /et/); *mad* (/m/ /ad/).

Review Oral Vocabulary

Reread the Interactive Read Aloud Use the **Define/Example/Ask** routine to review the oral vocabulary words *habitat, wild, complain, join,* and *stubborn*. Then have children listen as you reread "Anansi: An African Tale." Then ask:

- *What did Turtle complain about?* (He had to walk all the way back to the river.)
- *What did Anansi do that showed she was stubborn?* (She filled her pockets with rocks so that she could eat at the underwater table.)

Go Digital

Visual Glossary

"Anansi: An African Tale"

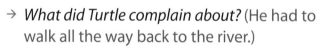

Category Words

Category Words: Animal Homes

1 Explain/Model Chant the following jingle:

A bear lives in lair, a bird lives in a nest.
Home is where they eat and get a bit of rest.
A rabbit lives underground, a squirrel inside a tree.
None of them sounds like a home just right for you or me.

→ Repeat the first line of the chant and ask children which words are animal homes. (lair, nest) Repeat this routine with the remaining lines.

2 Guided Practice Display the **Photo Cards** for *bird, mouse,* and *rabbit*. Read the following sentences and have children identify each animal-home word.

Birds live in nests.
Mice live in holes.
Rabbits live in burrows.

→ Ask children to identify where each animal home is found. Ask what each home is made out of. (a tree; underground; sticks, dirt, mud, leaves)

Vocabulary Strategy: Figurative Language/Shades of Meaning

1 Model Remind children that similar words and phrases can change the meaning of a sentence. Discuss the following sentence on p. 20 from the **Big Book** *Bear Snores On*: "A gopher and a mole tunnel up through the floor." *When I read* tunnel, *I pictured a tunnel being dug by the animals, with the end of the tunnel inside the bear's cave. Another word for tunnel is* dig *but* dig *does not give as clear a picture in my mind as* tunnel. *The words* dig *and* tunnel *are close in meaning but they are slightly different.*

2 Guided Practice/Practice Provide similar word pairs, such as *flutter/float, jumps/stomps,* and *whimper/moan*. Help children create a sentence using the first word and then use the second word in the same sentence. Discuss how using each word changes the meaning of the sentence. Then have children act out the six words to demonstrate understanding of their meanings.

ENGLISH LANGUAGE LEARNERS

Compare and Contrast Look through books or search the Internet to find pictures of animals in their homes to share with children. Review words for animal homes and then discuss how the homes are alike and different. Ask: *Which homes are up high? Which homes are down low? How is a home in a tree different from a home in the ground?*

LET'S MOVE!

Label parts of the classroom as different animal homes. Then give children simple directions: *Hop to the burrow. Fly to the nest. Crawl into the cave.*

YOUR TURN PRACTICE BOOK p. 211

Name

1.

2.

3.

Category Words: Animal Homes
Put a marker on each picture that shows an animal home.
1. Tell about the picture that shows where a bird lives.
2. Tell about the picture that shows where a bee lives.
3. Tell about the picture that shows where a squirrel lives.

Listening Comprehension

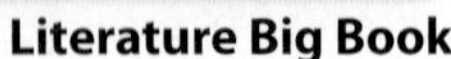

Literature Big Book

OBJECTIVES

CCSS With prompting and support, describe the connection between two individuals, events, ideas, or pieces of information in a text. **RI.K.3**

CCSS With prompting and support, ask and answer questions about unknown words in a text. **RI.K.4**

- Understand the characteristics of informational text
- Use the text feature glossary to gather information
- Apply the comprehension strategy: Make Predictions

ACADEMIC LANGUAGE

- *glossary*
- Cognates: *glosario*

Read "Animal Homes"

Genre: Informational Text

Display "Animal Homes" on pages 35–40 of the **Big Book** and read aloud the title. Remind children that informational text tells about things from real life, but may have things that are not real. In this selection, the information about the animal homes is real, but animals do not talk in real life.

Set a Purpose for Reading

Read aloud page 35. Tell children to listen as you continue reading so they will learn where these wild animals live.

Strategy: Make Predictions

Remind children that they should make, change, and check predictions as they read. Point to the illustrations on page 35. *Where do you think these wild animals live?* Continue reading the selection so children can check to see if their predictions were correct.

Text Feature: Glossary

Explain Point to the glossary on page 40 and read aloud the first entry. *Some stories include glossaries to give the meanings of new or difficult words.*

Apply Have volunteers point to and name the different features of the glossary on page 40. (words, definitions, photographs)

LITERATURE BIG BOOK PAGE 35

KEY DETAILS

Who is speaking in the text? (the animals) *Animals can't speak words to us in real life, but the pictures show what these animals look like in real life.*

Go Digital

Bear Snores On

LITERATURE BIG BOOK PAGES 36–37

CONNECTIONS WITHIN TEXT

How are the prairie dog's home and the snake's home alike? (Both are in the ground.) *How are they different?* (snake's home is rocky)

Ask and Answer Questions
Have children ask a question about an unknown word, such as *predator*. Ask others to figure out the meaning and answer.

LITERATURE BIG BOOK PAGES 38–39

CONNECTIONS WITHIN TEXT

Look at the pictures of the fish's home and the beaver's home. How are they alike? (Both are in water.) *How are they different?* (fish lives in ocean and beaver along river)

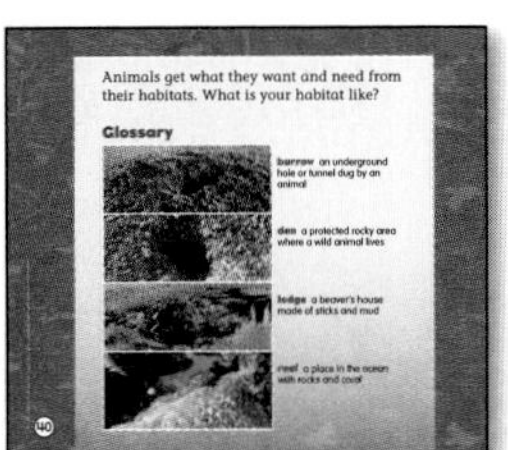

LITERATURE BIG BOOK PAGE 40

CONNECTIONS WITHIN TEXT

Look at the pictures in the glossary. Which animal habitat has soil? (burrow, den, lodge) What animal might you find in each picture? (prairie dog/burrow; snake/den; beaver/lodge; fish/reef)

ENGLISH LANGUAGE LEARNERS

Reinforce Meaning As you read aloud the text, make the meaning clear by pointing to details in the photographs. Asking children questions and elicit language.

Retell and Respond

Have children discuss the selection by asking the following questions:

→ *How does the snake blend into its surroundings?* (Its skin is the same color as the dirt and rocks.)

→ *How are the animal homes alike?* (They protect the animals from harm.) *How are they different?* (Some are in the ground and others are in water.)

Make Connections

COLLABORATE

Have children recall the selections they read this week.

→ *Where did Bear sleep in the winter?* (in a lair)

Write About It Write about where Anasi and Turtle live.

CONNECT TO CONTENT

Animal Habitat Review the different animal homes in the selection (prairie dog town, den, reef, lodge). Have partners discuss another animal's habitat. Ask them to describe the animal's habitat, pretending that they are speaking as that animal. Remind them to use real information to tell about the habitat.

WHOLE GROUP

DAY 4

Word Work

Quick Review

Build Fluency: Sound-Spellings: Show the following **Word-Building Cards:** *a, b, c, d, e, f, g, h, i, k, l, m, n, o, p, r, s, t, u, v, w, x.* Have children chorally say each sound. Repeat and vary the pace.

Phonemic Awareness

Puppet

OBJECTIVES

CCSS Distinguish between similarly spelled words by identifying the sounds of the letters that differ. **RF.K.3d**

CCSS Add or substitute individual sounds (phonemes) in simple, one-syllable words to make new words. **RF.K.2e**

CCSS Read common high-frequency words by sight. **RF.K.3c**

Phoneme Substitution

1 **Model** Use the **puppet** to model phoneme substitution. *The puppet can change the beginning sound in a word to make a new word. Listen to this word:* vet. Vet *has a /v/ sound at the beginning. Say* vet, */v/. Puppet will change /v/ to /g/. Listen:* vet, get. *Puppet made the word* get. Repeat with *van/man.*

2 **Guided Practice/Practice** Have children follow the directions to make new words. Give them ample time to respond. Guide practice with the first word.

Say vine. *Change /v/ to /l/. What word do you have?* (line)
Say vote. *Change /v/ to /n/. What word do you have?* (note)
Say wax. *Change /w/ to /t/. What word do you have?* (tax)
Say fix. *Change /f/ to /s/. What word do you have?* (six)
Say dish. *Change /d/ to /f/. What word do you have?* (fish)
Say sing. *Change /s/ to /r/. What word do you have?* (ring)

MINILESSON 5 Mins

Phonics

Blend Words with Short *a, e, i* and *v, x*

1 **Guided Practice** Display **Word-Building Cards** *v, a, n.* Point to the letter *v. This is the letter* v. *The letter* v *stands for /v/. Say /v/. This is the letter* a. *The letter* a *stands for /a/. Listen as I blend the two sounds together: /vaaa/. This is the letter* n. *The letter* n *stands for /n/. Listen as I blend the three sounds: /vaaannn/,* van. *Now you say it. Let's change the* v *to* t. Use the same routine to blend *tan.*

2 **Practice** Write *vet, bet, get* and *fix, mix.* Have children blend the words. Point to the first set of words. *Which letters are the same?* (e, t) *Which letters are different?* (v, b, g) Discuss the sound each letter stands for and how it changes the word. Repeat with *fix* and *mix.*

Go Digital

Phonemic Awareness

Phonics

Handwriting

Visual Glossary

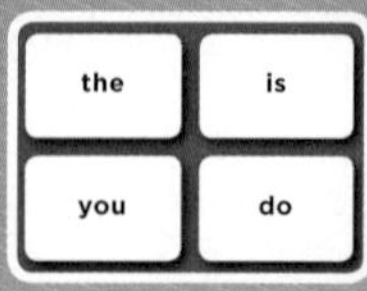

High-Frequency Word Routine

Dictation

Review Dictate these sounds for children to spell. Have them repeat the sound and then write the appropriate letter. Repeat several times.

/v/ /a/ /t/ /e/ /b/ /r/ /i/ /ks/ /f/

Dictate the following words for children to spell: *vat, vet, van, tax, fix, wax.* Model for children how to segment each word to scaffold the spelling. *When I say the word* vat, *I hear three sounds: /v/ /a/ /t/. I know the letter* v *stands for /v/, the letter* a *stands for /a/, and the letter* t *stands for /t/. I will write the letters* v, a, t *to spell the word* vat.

When children finish, write the letters and words for them to self-correct.

High-Frequency Words

Practice Say the word *said* and have children write it. Then display the **Visual Vocabulary Card** *said*. Follow the Teacher Talk routine on the back.

Visual Vocabulary Cards

Repeat for the word *want*.

Build Fluency Build sentences in the pocket chart using the **High-Frequency Word Cards** and **Photo Cards**. Use an index card to create a punctuation card for a period. Have children chorally read the sentences as you track the print. Then have them identify the words *said* and *want*.

They **said** they **want** watermelon.
I **said** I like vegetables.
They **said** they **want** to sing.
They **want** to go.

Have partners create sentences using the words *said* and *want*.

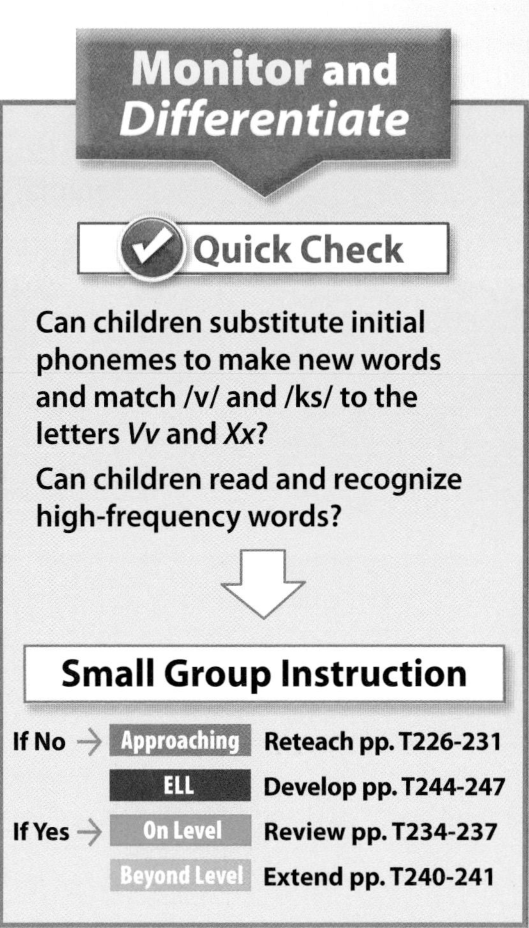

Monitor and *Differentiate*

Quick Check

Can children substitute initial phonemes to make new words and match /v/ and /ks/ to the letters *Vv* and *Xx*?

Can children read and recognize high-frequency words?

Small Group Instruction

If No →	Approaching	Reteach pp. T226-231
	ELL	Develop pp. T244-247
If Yes →	On Level	Review pp. T234-237
	Beyond Level	Extend pp. T240-241

WHOLE GROUP
DAY 4

Shared Read

Reading/Writing Workshop Big Book and Reading/Writing Workshop

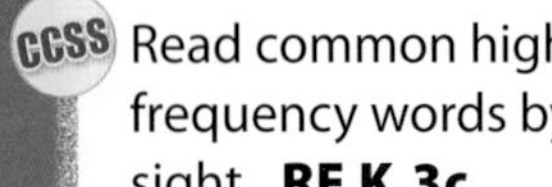

OBJECTIVES

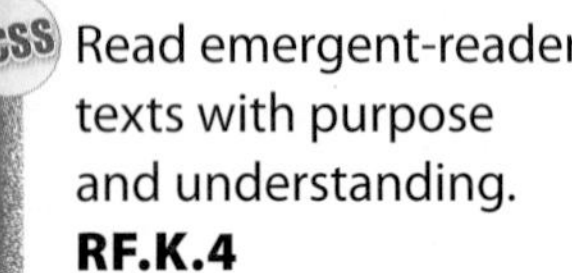

CCSS Read common high-frequency words by sight. **RF.K.3c**

CCSS Read emergent-reader texts with purpose and understanding. **RF.K.4**

MINILESSON 10 Mins

Read "A Vet in a Van"

Model Skills and Strategies

Model Concepts About Print As you read the story, sound out words to reinforce that a sequence of letters in a written word stands for a sequence of sounds in a spoken word. Invite volunteers to read words and sound them out. Then review punctuation marks and have children identify periods and exclamation points in the story.

Reread Invite children to chorally reread the story. Children should sound out the decodable words and say the sight words. Offer support as needed using the student **Reading/Writing Workshop**.

Ask the following:

- → *Look at page 38. What is the fox doing? What did the fox say?* (The fox is sitting in his den. The fox said "I am a red fox.")
- → *Look at page 40. What animal do you see? How would you describe the big cat's fur?* (I see a big cat. Its fur is spotted; the fur is tan and black.)
- → *Look at page 43. What is a vet? What does a vet do?* (A vet is an animal doctor. A vet helps sick or hurt animals get better.)

Go Digital

"A Vet in a Van"

"A Vet in a Van"

READING/WRITING WORKSHOP 7, pp. 36–43

Fluency: Expression

1. **Explain** Tell children that as you read the story, you will read with expression, or feeling. Mention that you will stress different words and change your voice when reading sentences that end with a period or an exclamation point. You will also pause after a word or groups of words for effect.

2. **Model** Model reading "A Vet in a Van" with expression. *When I read the story, I change my tone when I read sentences with different kinds of punctuation. I also pause after sentences, words, or groups of words for effect, like this.* Read each sentence with appropriate emotion or feeling.

3. **Guided Practice** Invite children to choral read the story with feeling. If necessary, have them listen to you first, then echo each sentence. Encourage them to match your intonation and expression.

Language Arts

Independent Writing

OBJECTIVES

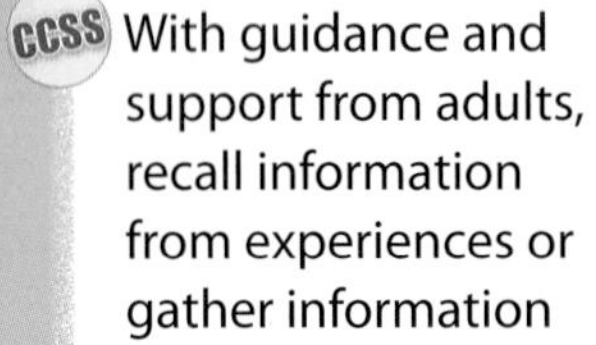

CCSS With guidance and support from adults, recall information from experiences or gather information from provided sources to answer a question. **W.K.8**

CCSS Understand and use question words (interrogatives) (e.g., *who, what, where, when, why, how*). **L.K.1d**

CCSS Use frequently occurring nouns and verbs. **L.K.1b**

CCSS Recognize and name end punctuation. **L.K.2b**

- Revise questions and answers
- Use verbs in sentences

ACADEMIC LANGUAGE

- *revise*
- Cognates: *revisar*

Write Questions and Answers

Revise

Distribute the children's draft questions and answers with drawings from Day 3.

Apply Writing Trait: Ideas Explain that as writers revise, they make sure they have answered the question that was asked. Write and read the following questions and answers: *Where were you born? What is your name? My name is James. I was born in California.* Say: *Which answer goes with each question?* Read each question aloud first, followed by the correct answer.

Write the correct answer next to each question. Read the questions and answers chorally. Then have children reread the questions and answers they wrote on Day 3 and check for the following:

- Did I write a question and an answer about where an animal lives?
- Did I use action words?
- Did I draw a picture of the animal in its home?

Apply Grammar Review with children the end punctuation used for questions and answers. *What mark do we use at the end of questions? What mark do we use at the end of answers?*

Peer Edit Have children work in pairs to do a peer edit, in which they read their partner's draft. Ask partners to check that their pictures show the home their animal lives in. Have children check that they wrote a question and an answer to that question. Provide time for children to make revisions to their sentences.

Final Draft

After children have edited their own papers and finished their peer edits, have them write their final draft. Remind children to use a question mark at the end of the question and a period at the end of the answer. As children work, conference with them to provide guidance.

Go Digital

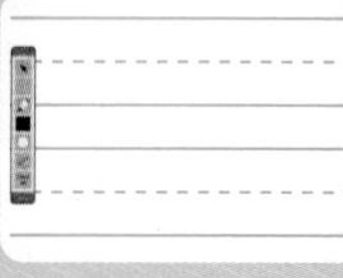

Writing

Grammar

Grammar

Action Words (Verbs)

1 Review Remind children that a verb is an action word. It tells the action in a sentence. Write and read aloud this sentence: *Jamal will read a book.* Ask: *Which word is an action word?* (read) *Is the action happening now, in the past, or in the future?* (in the future) *How do you know?* (because of the word *will*)

2 Guided Practice Write the following sentence and read it aloud: *Maria will write a story.* Ask children to circle the action word in the sentence. Ask volunteers to explain how they know that *write* is an action word.

Say: *We know that* write *is an action word because it tells what the person will do. We know that the action will happen in the future because the word* will *is before the action word.*

3 Practice Write this sentence frame and read it aloud. *Jose will ______ the cookies with his sister.*

Have children work with a partner to choose an action word to complete the sentence. (read, write, eat) Have children work together to tell whether the action happened in the past, is happening now, or will happen in the future.

Talk About It

Have partners work together to ask and answer questions about games they will play in the future. For example: *What game will you play tomorrow? I will play catch.*

ENGLISH LANGUAGE LEARNERS

Photo Cards and Sentences Provide future-tense sentences that go with images on the **Photo Cards**. As you read a sentence aloud, hold up a Photo Card as you say both the action and the person or thing doing the action, such as *The snow will melt.* Have children repeat the sentences with you, modeling correct pronunciation as necessary.

Daily Wrap Up

- Review the Essential Question and encourage children to discuss it, using the oral vocabulary words.
- Prompt children to discuss the skills they practiced and learned today. Guide them to share examples of each skill.

Go Digital
www.connected.mcgraw-hill.com
RESOURCES
Research and Inquiry

Wrap Up the Week
Integrate Ideas

RESEARCH AND INQUIRY

Animal Habitats

OBJECTIVES

Participate in shared research and writing projects (e.g., explore a number of books by a favorite author and express opinions about them). **W.K.7**

With guidance and support from adults, recall information from experiences or gather information from provided sources to answer a question. **W.K.8**

ACADEMIC LANGUAGE

- *research, inquiry, reference, question*
- Cognates: *referencia*

Habitat Diorama

Tell children that today partners will do a research project to make a diorama of an animal habitat. Review the steps in the research process.

STEP 1 Choose a Topic

Guide partners to think about animals and their habitats. Prompt children to think about animals they have seen and have read about. Work with them to identify a habitat (desert, rain forest, ocean, arctic) to research for their diorama.

STEP 2 Find Resources

Review how to locate and use resources. Direct children to use the selections from the week, but discuss the difference between talking animals in fantasy stories and real animals in the wild. Point out that many reference sources about animals' habitats, both in print and online, are available. Have children use the Research Process Checklist online.

STEP 3 Keep Track of Ideas

Have partners collaborate to note the information they find by drawing pictures and writing words. Guide them to print pages from online resources and add the information to their research notes.

Collaborative Conversations

Take Turns Talking As children engage in partner, small-group, and whole-class discussions, encourage them to:

- → take turns talking.
- → speak clearly and loudly enough so others can hear.
- → ask others to share their ideas and opinions.

STEM

STEP 4 Create the Project: Habitat Diorama

This is a rainforest environment.
It is hot and wet.
Leopards live here.

Explain the characteristics of the project:

→ **Information** A diorama presents information in 3D. Help partners plan how to arrange their visual information.

→ **Illustration** Tell children that they can draw pictures of their environment or cut pictures from magazines. They can glue the pictures inside a shoebox or glue them to popsicle sticks and then stick them in a base of Styrofoam or modeling clay.

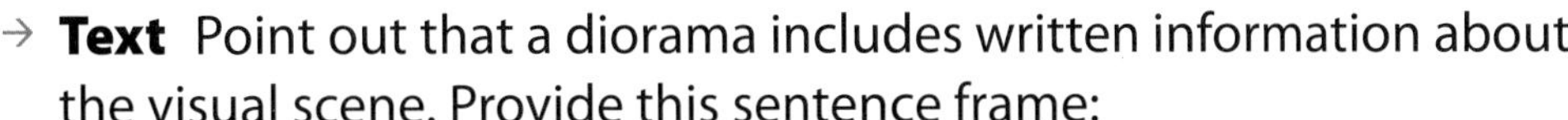

→ **Text** Point out that a diorama includes written information about the visual scene. Provide this sentence frame:

This is a ______ *environment. It is* [hot/cold] *and* [wet/dry]. [Animals] *live here.*

Have partners work together to create their dioramas.

→ Remind children to use words that describe in their captions for the dioramas.

→ Prompt children who can generate more writing to do so.

→ Prompt children to point out the details in their diorama.

ENGLISH LANGUAGE LEARNERS SCAFFOLD

Beginning	Intermediate	Advanced/Advanced High
Use Sentence Frames Pair children with more fluent speakers. While children work and when they share with the class, provide sentence frames that will help children talk about their picture. For example: *This is a* ____. ____ *live here.*	**Expand** Prompt partners to expand their vocabulary by talking about and naming details in their illustrations. Ask prompting questions such as these: *What is this environment called? Where might it be located? What might live here?*	**Describe** Encourage children to give a complete picture of an animal that lives in the environment by telling what the animal does there, what it eats, why it chooses that habitat, and so on.

WHOLE GROUP
DAY 5

Materials

Reading/Writing Workshop Big Book
UNIT 7

Literature Big Book
Bear Snores On

Interactive Read-Aloud Cards

Word-Building Cards

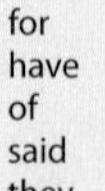

Visual Vocabulary Cards
said
want

High-Frequency Word Cards
for
have
of
said
they
want

Puppet

Response Boards

Integrate Ideas

TEXT CONNECTIONS

Connect to Essential Question

OBJECTIVES

With prompting and support, compare and contrast the adventures and experiences of characters in familiar stories. **RL.K.9**

Participate in collaborative conversations with diverse partners about *kindergarten topics and texts* with peers and adults in small and larger groups. **SL.K.1**

- Make connections among texts
- Make connections to the world

Text to Text

Remind children that all week they have been reading selections about where animals live. Tell them that now they will connect the texts, or think about how the selections are alike. Model comparing *Bear Snores On* with another selection from the week.

COLLABORATE

Think Aloud In *Bear Snores On,* I learned that a bear lives in a place where it's cold in the winter, and he goes to sleep in a cave. In "Anansi: An African Tale," I learned that a turtle lives in a sandy desert area, but the turtle also has a river for food and water. In both stories, the illustrations helped me see the different habitats.

Guide children to compare the habitats of animals they see in *Bear Snores On* and "Animal Habitats."

Text to Self

Have children discuss animal habitats that they have seen near where they live. Do the animals live there during all of the seasons?

Text to World

Talk about the wild animal habitats that children have seen around the community in parks or by the school. *Why is it important to protect animal habitats?*

TALK ABOUT READING

Analyze and Explain

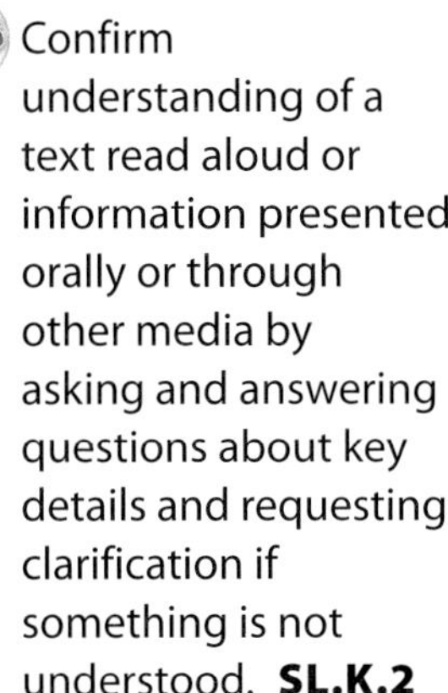

OBJECTIVES

CCSS Confirm understanding of a text read aloud or information presented orally or through other media by asking and answering questions about key details and requesting clarification if something is not understood. **SL.K.2**

Becoming Readers

Talk with children about the genres, strategy, and skill they have learned about this week. Prompt them to discuss how this knowledge helps them to read and understand selections.

- Remind children that one genre they learned about is fantasy. Recall with them some characteristics of fantasy.
- Talk about the strategy of making, confirming, and revising predictions. *Were you right about whether the bear in* Bear Snores On *would wake up or not? How did making predictions help you to understand the story?*
- Discuss how thinking about cause and effect helps readers understand a story. *What causes the bear to wake up in* Bear Snores On*? What happens next? How did looking for causes and effects help you understand events in the story?*

RESEARCH AND INQUIRY

Animal Habitats

OBJECTIVES

CCSS Participate in shared research and writing projects (e.g. explore a number of books by a favorite author and express opinions about them). **W.K.7**

Wrap Up the Project

COLLABORATE

Guide partners to present their habitat dioramas. Prompt them to point out details using words and phrases they learned this week. Have children use the Presenting and Listening checklists online.

WHOLE GROUP
DAY 5

Word Work

Quick Review

Build Fluency: Sound-Spellings: Show the following **Word-Building Cards:** *a, b, c, d, e, f, g, h, i, k, l, m, n, o, p, r, s, t, u, v, w, x*. Have children chorally say the sounds. Repeat and vary the pace.

Phonemic Awareness

OBJECTIVES

CCSS Add or substitute individual sounds (phonemes) in simple, one-syllable words to make new words. **RF.K.2e**

CCSS Spell simple words phonetically, drawing on knowledge of sound-letter relationships. **L.K.2d**

CCSS Read common high-frequency words by sight. **RF.K.3c**

Blend sounds to read words with /v/ and /ks/

Phoneme Substitution

1 **Model** Use the puppet to model phoneme substitution. *The puppet can change the ending sound in words to make new words. Listen to this word:* fin. Fin *has the /n/ sound at the end. Now listen as the puppet changes /n/ in* fin *to /t/:* fit. Repeat with *pan/pat.*

2 **Guided Practice/Practice** Have children follow directions to make new words. Give them ample time to respond. Guide practice with the first word.

Say vat. *Change /t/ to /n/. What word do you have?* (van)
Say man. *Change /n/ to /p/. What word do you have?* (map)
Say bat. *Change /t/ to /k/. What word do you have?* (back)
Say sleeve. *Change /v/ to /p/. What word do you have?* (sleep)

Phonics

Read Words with Short *a, e, i* and *x, v, t*

1 **Guided Practice** Remind children that the letter *x* stands for the sound /ks/. Display **Word-Building Cards** *s, i, x.* Point to the letter *s. The letter* s *stands for the sound /s/. The letter* i *stands for the sound /i/. Say /iii/. The letter* x *stands for /ks/. Say /ks/. Let's blend the sounds to make the word: /sssiiiks/* six. *Now let's change the letter* x *for* t. Blend and read *sit* with children.

2 **Practice** Write these words and sentences for children to read:

Max *vet* *mix* *van* *six* *vat*

I can see the van. Max will go to the vet.
I got a fax. I can mix it in the vat.

Remove words from view before dictation.

Review /ks/*x* and /v/*v*. Have children write *x* on their **Response Boards**. Play and sing "Freddy the Fox Was Carrying a Box." Have children hold up and show the letter *x* when they hear final /ks/. Demonstrate as you sing with children. Repeat with /v/*v* and "It's a Volcano."

Go Digital

Phonemic Awareness

Phonics

Handwriting

High-Frequency Word Cards

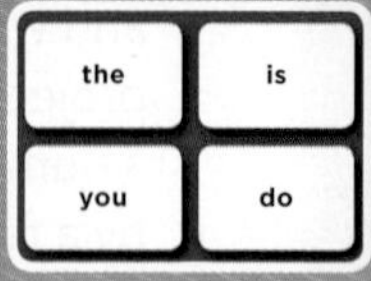

Dictation

1 Review Dictate the following sounds for children to spell. As you say each sound, have children repeat it and then write the letter that stands for the sound.

/s/ /a/ /v/ /e/ /t/ /m/
/i/ /ks/ /n/ /f/ /o/

Dictate the following words for children to spell. Model for children how to use **Sound Boxes** to segment each word to scaffold the spelling. *I will say a word. You will repeat the word, then think about how many sounds are in the word. Use your Sound Boxes to count the sounds. Then write one letter(s) for each sound you hear.*

sax vet mix van Max fox vat

Then write the letters and words for children to self-correct.

MINILESSON 5 Mins

High-Frequency Words

said, want

Visual Vocabulary Cards

1 Review Display the **Visual Vocabulary Card** *said.* Have children **Read/Spell/Write** the word *said.* Then choose a Partner Talk activity.

Repeat the routine for the word *want.*

Distribute one of the following **High-Frequency Word Cards** to children: *said, want, for, have, they, of.* Tell children that you will say some sentences. *When you hear the word that is on your card, stand and hold up the word card.*

I *said* I want to go.
They said to leave the book.
They *want* to go to the beach.
I will wait *for* you.
I have a bag full *of* shells.
We *have* all day to play!

2 Build Fluency: Word Automaticity Display High-Frequency Word Cards *said, want, for, have, they, of.* Point to each card, at random, and have children read the word as quickly as they can.

Monitor and Differentiate
Quick Check
Can children recognize words with /v/ and /ks/?
Can children read and recognize high-frequency words?
Small Group Instruction
If No → Approaching Reteach pp. T226-231
ELL Develop pp. T244-247
If Yes → On Level Review pp. T234-237
Beyond Level Extend pp. T240-241

WHOLE GROUP

DAY 5

Language Arts

MINILESSON 10 Mins

Independent Writing

OBJECTIVES

CCSS Speak audibly and express thoughts, feelings, and ideas clearly. **SL.K.6**

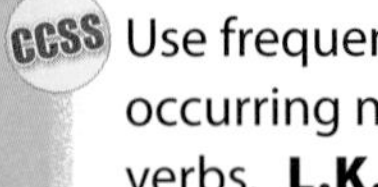

CCSS Use frequently occurring nouns and verbs. **L.K.1b**

CCSS Understand and use question words (interrogatives) (e.g., *who, what, where, when, why, how*). **L.K.1d**

Present questions and answers

ACADEMIC LANGUAGE

- *present, publish*
- Cognates: *presente*

Write Questions and Answers

Prepare

Tell children that they will present their finished questions and answers from Day 4 to the class. Hold up an example from Day 4 and read it aloud, tracking the print. Use words to describe the drawing clearly. Say: *I read the question and answer clearly so that everyone could understand what I was saying. I talked about the drawing clearly and told about the home that the animal lives in.*

Present

Have children take turns standing up, reading aloud their questions and answers, and talking about their drawings. Remind children to speak clearly. Encourage the rest of the class to listen carefully to the person speaking and to wait until the end of the presentation to raise their hands and ask questions.

Evaluate

Have children discuss their own presentations and evaluate their performances, using the presentation rubric. Use the teacher's rubric to evaluate children's writing.

Publish

After children have finished presenting, collect the animal-homes papers. Bind the papers together to create a class book called *Animal Homes.* Read the book to the class and then place it in the reading area so children can read it independently or with a partner.

Go Digital

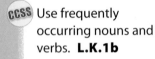

Writing

I see a fish.

Grammar

Grammar

Action Words (Verbs)

1 Review Remind children that a verb is an action word. It tells what happens in a sentence. Write and read aloud these sentences: *Eddie will shop. He will buy new shoes.* Ask: *Which words are action words?* (shop, buy) *What do these action words tell you?* (what Eddie will do in the future)

2 Review Practice Write these sentence frames and words in two columns as shown:

Pat will ______ his mom.	*bake*
Sam will ______ a cake.	*clean*
Joanne will ______ the house.	*help*

Have children work with a partner to choose the correct action word to complete each sentence. Then have volunteers draw a line to match the correct word with each sentence. (Pat will help his mom. Sam will bake a cake. Joanne will clean the house.) Complete the sentences and read them aloud with children.

Have children copy the sentences and circle the verbs. Gather the sentences and store them in a folder for a center or review activity.

Wrap Up the Week

- Review blending words with final /ks/*x* and initial /v/*v*. Remind children that a verb is an action word in a sentence.
- Use the **High-Frequency Word Cards** to review the Words to Know.
- Remind children that when they write questions and answers, they should make sure the answer fits with the question asked.

Approaching Level

Leveled Reader

OBJECTIVES

With prompting and support, identify characters, settings, and major events in a story. **RL.K.3**

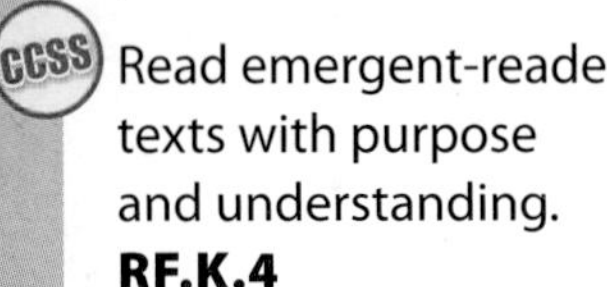

Demonstrate understanding of the organization and basic features of print. **RF.K.1**

Read emergent-reader texts with purpose and understanding. **RF.K.4**

Leveled Reader: *We Want Water*

Leveled Reader

Before Reading

Preview and Predict

Read the title and the names of the author and illustrator. Discuss the cover illustration. Ask: *What animals do you see? Where are they? What do you think this story is about?* Preview each illustration with children.

Review Genre: Fantasy

Remind children that fantasy is a kind of fiction and that events happen that cannot happen in real life. Ask: *What is something that tells you this is fantasy?* (The animals talk.)

Model Concepts of Print

Have children turn to page 2 and point out the quotation marks. Say: *The words inside these quotation marks tell me what Elephant said.*

Review High-Frequency Words

Point out the word *want* on page 2, and read it with children. Have them find the word on page 3.

Essential Question

Remind children of the Essential Question: *Where do animals live?* Set a purpose for reading: *Let's find out where these animals live.*

During Reading

Guided Comprehension

As children whisper-read *We Want Water*, monitor and provide guidance by correcting blending and modeling the strategy and skill.

Strategy: Make, Confirm, and Revise Predictions

Remind children to make predictions as they read by asking themselves what will happen next and then reading to find out. Have them revise their predictions as needed.

Skill: Character, Setting, Plot (Cause and Effect)

Remind children that identifying what is happening in the story and why it is happening will help them understand the plot. Explain that in this story, it is important to look at the illustrations.

Think Aloud After reading pages 2 and 3, I know the setting is a water hole and the characters are the animals that want water. I can also tell from the pictures that after Elephant sprays himself with water, there is less water for hippo. I will keep reading to see what happens to the water hole after each animal drinks.

Ask children to identify the details in the illustrations on pages 4 and 5 that tell about the plot of the story. Guide them to understand that after each animal drinks from the water hole, there is less water left.

After Reading

Respond to Reading

- *Who is the first animal to come to the water hole?* (Elephant)
- *Why do the animals come to the water hole?* (They want water.)
- *What is the effect on the water hole each time an animal drinks?* (There is less water.)

Retell

Have children take turns retelling the story. Help them make a personal connection by asking: *What do you like to drink when you are thirsty?*

Model Fluency

Reread the story aloud. Model emphasizing different words as you read each page, for example: *"I want water," said Giraffe.*

Apply Have children practice reading with expression with partners.

LITERACY ACTIVITIES

Have children complete the activities on the inside back cover of the reader.

Level Up

IF Children read *We Want Water* **Approaching Level** with fluency and correctly answer the Respond to Reading questions,

THEN Tell children that they will read another story about where animals live.

- Have children page through *A New Home* **On Level** as you introduce the setting (a forest) and the characters (the animals that live in a forest).
- Have children read the story, monitoring their comprehension and providing assistance as necessary.

Approaching Level

Phonological Awareness

ONSET/RIME SEGMENTATION

TIER 2

OBJECTIVES

CCSS Blend and segment onsets and rimes of single-syllable spoken words. **RF.K.2c**

Reread "The Very Nicest Place." *The word* brook *can be broken into two parts: /br/ /ůk/. The first part of the word* brook *is /br/. The second part of the word* brook *is* /ůk/. Repeat with *tree*.

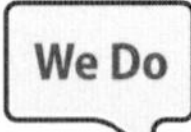

Repeat /br/ /ůk/, *brook*, and have children segment the onset and rime after you. Repeat with /tr/ /ē/, *tree* and /m/ /ē/, *me*.

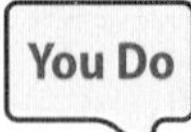

Have children segment the following words into onsets and rimes:

vet /v/ /et/ van /v/ /an/ fox /f/ /oks/ mix /m/ /iks/

PHONEME ISOLATION

TIER 2

OBJECTIVES

Isolate and pronounce the initial, medial vowel, and final sounds (phonemes) in three-phoneme words. **RF.K.2d**

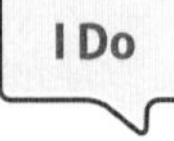

Display the *Vest* **Photo Card**. *This is a vest. The first sound I hear in* vest *is /v/.* Have children repeat the word with you, emphasizing the initial sound. Then have children say the first sound with you: /v/.

Display the *Vine* Photo Card. Name the photo and have children say the name. *What is the first sound in* vine? (/v/) Say the sound together. Repeat with the *Vegetables* Photo Card.

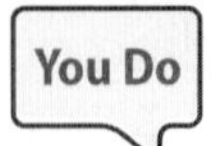

Show the *Violin* Photo Card. Have children name it and say the initial sound of the picture name. Repeat with the *Volcano* Photo Card.

Repeat the routine for /ks/ using the *Fox* Photo Card in *I Do* and the *Ax, Box, Mix,* and *Ox* Photo Cards in the rest of the lesson.

You may wish to review Phonological Awareness and Phonemic Awareness with ELL using this section.

PHONEME BLENDING

OBJECTIVES

CCSS Isolate and pronounce the initial, medial vowel, and final sounds (phonemes) in three-phoneme words. **RF.K.2d**

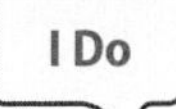

The puppet will say the sounds in a word. Listen: /v/ /e/ /s/ /t/. The puppet will say the sounds and then blend them together: /v/ /e/ /s/ /t/, /vvveeessst/, vest. Repeat with *fix*.

Now the puppet is going to say the sounds in another word. Say the sounds with the puppet: /v/ /ī/ /n/. Let's say the sounds and blend them together: /v/ /ī/ /n/, /vvvīīīnnn/, vine. Repeat with *tax*.

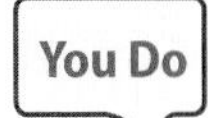

Have children blend sounds to form words. Practice together: /v/ /a/ /n/, /vaaan/, *van*. Then have children blend the following sounds to say the words: /v/ /e/ /t/ vet; /f/ /a/ /n/ fan; /w/ /a/ /ks/ wax; /m/ /i/ /ks/ mix.

PHONEME SUBSTITUTION

OBJECTIVES

CCSS Add or substitute individual sounds (phonemes) in simple, one-syllable words to make new words. **RF.K.2e**

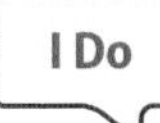

The puppet can change the beginning sound in a word to make a new word. Listen as the puppet says a word: vest. Vest *has the /v/ sound at the beginning. Listen as the puppet changes the /v/ sound to /n/*: nest.

Listen as the puppet says a word: six. *What word does the puppet make when it changes the /ks/ in* six *to /t/?* Together say the word *sit*.

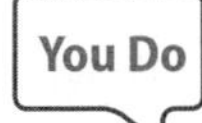

Guide children with phoneme substitution. *Say* vine. *Change /v/ to /f/. What word do you have?* (fine) Repeat the routine substituting initial and final phonemes with the following; /v/ in *van* to /t/ (tan); /v/ in *vase* to /b/ (base); /ks/ in *six* to /ck/ (sick); /g/ in *wag* to /ks/ (wax)

ELL ENGLISH LANGUAGE LEARNERS

For the **ELLs** who need **phonics, decoding,** and **fluency** practice, use scaffolding methods as necessary to ensure children understand the meaning of the words. Refer to the Language Transfer Handbook for phonics elements that may not transfer in students' native languages.

Approaching Level

Phonics

SOUND-SPELLING REVIEW

TIER 2

OBJECTIVES

CCSS Demonstrate basic knowledge of one-to-one letter-sound correspondences by producing the most frequent sounds for each consonant. **RF.K.3a**

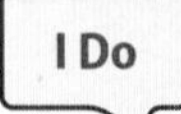

Display the **Word-Building Card** *g*. Say the letter name and the sound it stands for: *g*, /g/. Repeat for *w, u, k, b, l, f,* and *r*.

Display Word-Building Cards one at a time and together say the letter name and the sound that each letter stands for.

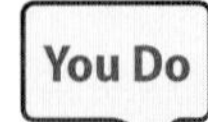

Display Word-Building Cards one at a time and have children say the letter name and the sound that each letter stands for.

CONNECT *v* TO /v/ AND *x* TO /ks/

TIER 2

OBJECTIVES

CCSS Demonstrate basic knowledge of one-to-one letter-sound correspondences by producing the primary or many of the most frequent sounds for each consonant. **RF.K.3a**

Display the *Volcano* **Sound-Spelling Card**. *The letter* v *stands for /v/ as in* volcano. *What is this letter? What sound does it stand for? I will write* v *when I hear /v/* in: *vest, water, vet, bat*. Repeat for /ks/ using the *Box* Sound-Spelling Card and *ax, boat, tent, wax.*

Van *begins with /v/. Let's write v*. Guide children to write *v* when they hear a word that begins with /v/: *vine, look, visit*. Repeat for /ks/*x* in *run, fox, mix*.

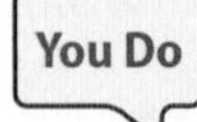

Say these words and have children write *v* if a word begins with /v/: *tree, valentine, vote, jump, very*. Repeat for /ks/*x* in *ax, hold, ox, sing, key, six, fix*.

RETEACH

OBJECTIVES

CCSS Know and apply grade-level phonics and word analysis skills in decoding words. **RF.K.3**

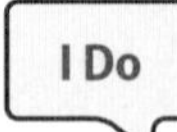

Display **Reading/Writing Workshop**, p. 34. *The letter* v *stands for the /v/ sound you hear at the beginning of* volcano. Say *volcano*, emphasizing the /v/. Repeat with *box* and final /ks/.

Have children name each picture in row 1. Repeat the name, emphasizing /v/. Repeat for row 2, emphasizing /ks/.

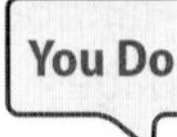

Guide children in reading the words in row 3. Then have them read the words in row 4, offering assistance as needed.

BLEND WORDS WITH /v/*v* AND /ks/*x*

OBJECTIVES

Isolate and pronounce the initial, medial vowel, and final sounds (phonemes) in three-phoneme words. **RF.K.2d**

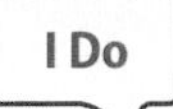

Display **Word-Building Cards** *v, e,* and *t. This is the letter* v. *It stands for /v/. This is the letter* e. *It stands for /e/. This is the letter* t. *It stands for /t/. Listen as I blend all three sounds:* /vvveeet/, vet. *The word is* vet.

Now let's blend more sounds to make words. Make the word *van*. *Let's blend:* /vvvaaannn/, van. Have children blend to read the word.

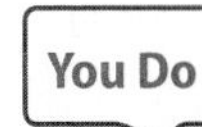

Distribute sets of Word-Building Cards with *v, e, s, t, n, d,* and *a*. Write: *vest, vet, vat, vend*. Have children form the words and then blend and read them.

Repeat the routine for /ks/*x* using the words *ax, fox, fix, wax, box,* and *ox*.

REREAD FOR FLUENCY

OBJECTIVES

CCSS Read emergent-reader texts with purpose and understanding. **RF.K.4**

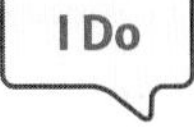

Turn to p. 36 of **Reading/Writing Workshop** and read aloud the title. *Let's read the title together*. Page through the book. Ask children what they see in each picture. Ask children to find the word *said* on pp. 38 and 40 and *want* on p. 37.

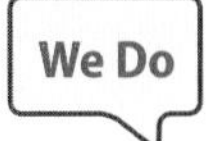

Then have children open their books and chorally read the story. Have children point to each word as they read. Provide corrective feedback as needed. After reading, ask children to tell about some of the animals Pat saw from her van.

Have children reread "A Vet in a Van" with a partner for fluency.

BUILD FLUENCY WITH PHONICS

Sound/Spelling Fluency

Display the following Word-Building Cards: *h, e, f, r, b, l, k, c, u, g, w, v,* and *x*. Have children chorally say each sound. Repeat and vary the pace.

Fluency in Connected Text

Write the following sentences. *They see the vet with the ox and dog. You can mix it. A fox is on my van!* Have children read the sentences and identify the words with /v/ and /ks/.

Approaching Level

High-Frequency Words

TIER 2

RETEACH WORDS

OBJECTIVES

Read common high-frequency words by sight. **RF.K.3c**

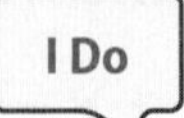
Display the **High-Frequency Word Card** *said* and use the **Read/Spell/Write** routine to reteach the word. Repeat with *want*.

Have children turn to p. 35 of **Reading/Writing Workshop** and discuss the first photo. Then read aloud the first sentence. Reread the sentence with children. Then distribute index cards with the word *said* written on them. Have children match their word cards with the word *said* in the sentence. Use the same routine for *want* and the other sentence on the page.

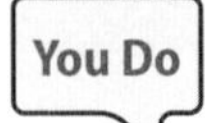
Write the sentence frame *I said, "I want a _____."* Have children copy the sentence frame on their **Response Boards**. Then have partners work together to read and orally complete the frame by talking about something they asked for from a friend. Reteach previously introduced high-frequency words using the **Read/Spell/Write** routine.

CUMULATIVE REVIEW

OBJECTIVES

Read common high-frequency words by sight. **RF.K.3c**

Display the **High-Frequency Word Cards** *I, can, the, we, see, a, like, to, and, go, you, do, my, are, he, with, is, little, she, was, for, have, they, of, said,* and *want*. Use the **Read/Spell/Write** routine to review words. Use the High-Frequency Word Cards and **Word-Building Cards** to create sentences, such as *Do you want to go with me? They said the box is little.*

Use the **Read/Spell/Write** routine with children to review words. Invite a child to write the word on the board. Offer help as needed. Then guide children to create a sentence as a class using the High-Frequency Word Cards and Word-Building Cards.

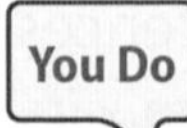
Have partners use the High-Frequency Word Cards and Word-Building Cards to create short sentences. Ask them to read them aloud.

Oral Vocabulary

REVIEW WORDS

OBJECTIVES

CCSS Identify real-life connections between words and their use. **L.K.5c**

Develop oral vocabulary: *habitat, wild, complain, join, stubborn.*

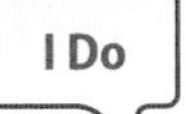

Use the **Define/Example/Ask** routine to review words. Use the following definitions and provide examples:

habitat A **habitat** is the place where an animal lives and grows.

wild A **wild** animal lives in nature and is not cared for by people.

complain When you **complain**, you say that you are upset about something.

join When you **join** someone, you and the other person do something together.

stubborn If you are **stubborn**, you never give up.

Ask questions to build understanding. *What is an animal that lives in a wet habitat? Why is a tiger a wild animal? Why would someone complain about cold weather? When did you join a friend and have a good time? When have you seen someone who was acting stubborn?*

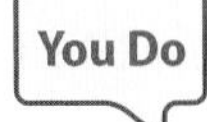

Have children complete these sentence frames: *The habitat of a frog is _____. A wild animal lives _____. I heard someone complain when _____. I sometimes join my classmates to _____. I once acted stubborn when _____.*

Comprehension

SELF-SELECTED READING

OBJECTIVES

CCSS With prompting and support, ask and answer questions about key details in a text. **RL.K.1**

Apply the strategy and skill to reread the text.

Read Independently

Help children select an illustrated story for sustained silent reading. Encourage children to think about what will happen to the people and animals in a book. This will help them better understand what they are reading.

Read Purposefully

Before reading, ask children to identify a person or animal in an illustration. Have them draw a picture or write a sentence to tell what they think will happen to the person or animal. After reading, have children explain if they were right about what they thought would happen. Guide them to revise their predictions as necessary.

On Level

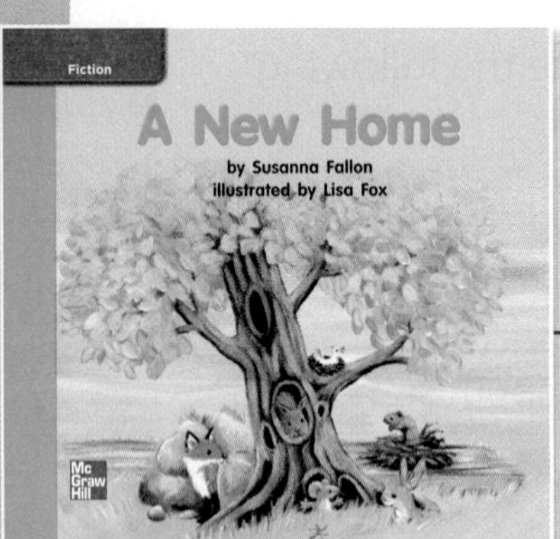

Leveled Reader

OBJECTIVES

CCSS With prompting and support, identify characters, settings, and major events in a story. **RL.K.3**

CCSS Demonstrate understanding of the organization and basic features of print. **RF.K.1**

CCSS Read emergent-reader texts with purpose and understanding. **RF.K.4**

Leveled Reader: *A New Home*

Go Digital

Leveled Reader

Before Reading

Preview and Predict

Read the title and the names of the author and illustrator. Have children describe what they see on the cover. Turn to the title page and have children read the title with you. Preview the illustrations. Explain that the animals are the characters in the story. Ask children what they think the book will be about.

Review Genre: Fantasy

Remind children that fantasy is a kind of fiction in which the events could not happen in real life. Ask: *What tells you that this book is fantasy?* (The animals are talking.)

Model Concepts of Print

Have children follow along in their books as you read the sentence on page 2, modeling an understanding of concepts of print. Point to each word and the spaces between them as you read.

Review High-Frequency Words

Point to the word *said* on page 3, and read it with children. Have them find the word on pages 4 and 5.

Essential Question

Set a purpose for reading: *Let's find out where animals live in a forest.* Remind children to use the illustrations for support as they read.

During Reading

Guided Comprehension

As children whisper-read, model how to use the strategy and skill. Provide support by asking a question after they read each page. For example, ask: *Whose home is this?*

Strategy: Make, Confirm, and Revise Predictions

Remind children to make predictions as they read by asking themselves what will happen next. Encourage them to revise their predictions as needed.

Skill: Character, Setting, Plot (Cause and Effect)

Remind children that knowing the characters, the setting, and the plot, will help them understand the story. Explain that the pictures in this story will provide details about what Squirrel does and why.

Think Aloud After I read pages 2 and 3, I learn that Squirrel wants a new home. On page 3, I look at the picture. I can see the characters, Squirrel and Bird. I can see Bird's home is a nest. It looks too small for Squirrel. I predict that Squirrel will visit other animals' homes.

Have children use the pictures on pages 4, and 5 to find details about the animals' homes. Guide children to see why Squirrel might not want to live in each home and what effect this has on Squirrel.

After Reading

Respond to Reading

- *What is this story about?* (Squirrel wants a new home.)
- *What causes squirrel to visit each animal's home?* (To see if their homes are better than his.)
- *What does Squirrel decide to do at the end of the story?* (live in his original home)

Retell

Invite groups of six children to take turns retelling the story, with each child taking the part of one of the animals from the book.

Model Fluency

Read the sentence "Bird said, 'Can you see my home?'" Then ask: *What did you notice about my voice as I read?* (It goes up at the end.)

Apply Have children take turns practicing reading in small groups and making their voices go up at the end of questions.

LITERACY ACTIVITIES

Have children complete the activities on the inside back cover of the reader.

Level Up

IF Children read *A New Home* **On Level** with fluency and correctly answer the Respond to Reading questions,

THEN Tell children that they will read another story about animals and their homes.

- Have children page through *Bird's New Home* **Beyond Level** as you introduce the characters in the story and unfamiliar words, such as *twigs, cozy, hollow,* and *wax*.
- Have children read the story, monitoring their comprehension and providing assistance as necessary.

On Level

Phonemic Awareness

PHONEME ISOLATION

OBJECTIVES

CCSS Isolate and pronounce the initial, medial vowel, and final sounds (phonemes) in three-phoneme words. **RF.K.2d**

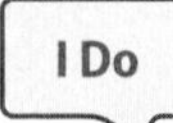

Display the *Volcano* **Photo Card**. *This is a volcano. The first sound is /v/. Say it with me.* Repeat for final /ks/ using the *Mix* Photo Card.

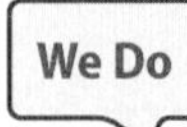

Say *van*. Have children repeat it. *What is the first sound*? Say the sound together. Repeat with *vest, big, vine*. Repeat for final /ks/ using *box, way, wax*.

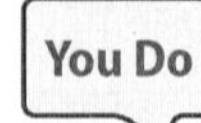

Say these words. Have children isolate initial *v* and final *x* using the words: *very, vet, win, visit, tax, fix, bag, ox*.

PHONEME BLENDING

OBJECTIVES

Isolate and pronounce the initial, medial vowel, and final sounds (phonemes) in three-phoneme words. **RF.K.2d**

Place the *Vest, Vine, Violin, Volcano, Ax, Fox, Mix*, and *Six* Photo Cards facedown. Choose a card. *These are the sounds in the word:* /v/ /e/ /s/ /t/. *I will blend the sounds:* /vvveeessst/, vest. *The word is* vest. Show the picture.

Choose another picture and say the sounds in the word. Together say and blend the sounds to say the word. Then show the picture.

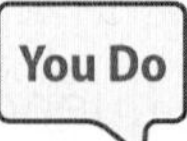

Continue choosing Photo Cards. Say the sounds and have children blend the sounds and say the words.

PHONEME SUBSTITUTION

OBJECTIVES

Add or substitute individual sounds (phonemes) in simple, one-syllable words to make new words. **RF.K.2e**

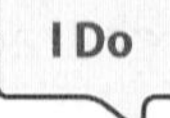

The puppet can say a word and change the first sound to make a new word: van, can. *The puppet changed the /v/ in* van *to /k/ to make the new word* can.

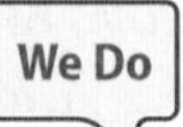

Listen as the puppet says another word: tax. *What word does the puppet make if it changes /ks/ in* tax *to /p/?* (tap) Have children say both words after the puppet. Repeat with *vest/rest* and *fix/fit*.

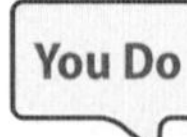

Say vine. *Change /v/ to /l/. What is the new word?* (line) Repeat routine changing: /v/ in *vet* to /p/ (pet); /ks/ in *fox* to /g/ (fog); /s/ in *save* to /g/ (gave).

Phonics

REVIEW PHONICS

OBJECTIVES

CCSS Demonstrate basic knowledge of one-to-one letter-sound correspondences by producing the primary or many of the most frequent sounds for each consonant. **RF.K.3a**

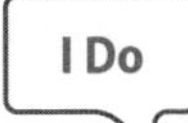

Display **Reading/Writing Workshop**, p. 34. Point to the *Volcano* **Sound-Spelling Card**. *Which letter stands for the /v/ sound you hear at the beginning of* volcano? *The letter is* v. Repeat the routine with the *Box* Sound-Spelling Card.

Have children say the name of each picture in rows 1 and 2. Then ask them to identify the words with /v/ in the beginning. Repeat with identifying words with /ks/ at the end.

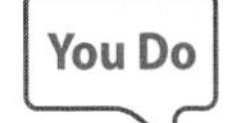

Have children read each word in rows 3 and 4. Repeat, asking them to raise their hands if they hear /v/ at the beginning of the word and keeping their hands lowered if they hear /ks/ at the end of the word.

PICTURE SORT

OBJECTIVES

Demonstrate basic knowledge of one-to-one letter-sound correspondences by producing the primary or many of the most frequent sounds for each consonant. **RF.K.3a**

Display **Word-Building Cards** *v* and *x* in a pocket chart. Then show the *Vine* **Photo Card**. Say /v/ /ī/ /n/, *vine*. Tell children that the sound at the beginning is /v/. *The letter* v *stands for /v/. I will put the vine under the letter* v. Show the *Ox* Photo Card. Say /o/ /ks/, ox. Tell children that the sound at the end is /ks/. *The letter* x *stands for /ks/. I will put the* Ox *Photo Card under the* x.

Show the *Volcano* Photo Card and say *volcano*. Have children repeat. Then have them tell the sound they hear at the beginning of *volcano*. Ask them if they should place the photo under the *v* or the *x*.

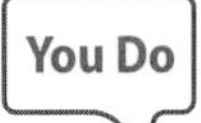

Continue the activity using the *Vest, Violin, Vegetables, Mix, Ax, Box,* and *Six* Photo Cards. Have children say the picture name and the sounds in the name. Then have them place the card under the *v* or *x*.

On Level

Phonics

BLEND WORDS WITH *v* AND *x*

OBJECTIVES

Isolate and pronounce the initial, medial vowel, and final sounds (phonemes) in three-phoneme words. **RF.K.2d**

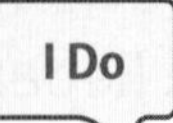

Write *v, e, t. This is the letter* v. *It stands for /v/. Say it with me: /vvv/. This is the letter* e. *It stands for /e/. Say it with me: /eee/. This is the letter* t. *It stands for /t/. Say it with me: /t/. I'll blend the sounds together to read the word:* /vvveeet/, vet. Repeat the routine with final /ks/ and the word *fix*.

Write *visit* and *mix*. Guide children to blend the words sound by sound to read each word.

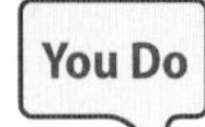

Write the following words and have children blend the words sound by sound to read each word.

vest six van ax

REREAD FOR FLUENCY

OBJECTIVES

Read emergent-reader texts with purpose and understanding. **RF.K.4**

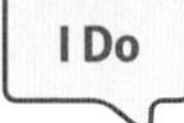

Point to the first sentence on p. 43 of "A Vet in a Van" in **Reading/Writing Workshop**. Tell children that when they see an exclamation point at the end of a sentence, they can read with excitement. Read the sentence aloud and have children repeat after you. Work with children to read for accuracy and expression. Model reading the next sentence: *When I read,* "A vet can fix a sick ox!" *I read with excitement and all the way to the end of the sentence before pausing. This makes my reading sound as if I were talking.*

Reread p. 43. Then have children chorally read the page with you. Remind them to use their voices to show excitement when they read.

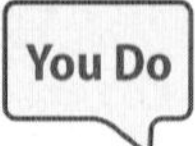

Have children read "A Vet in a Van." Provide time to listen as children read the pages. Comment on their accuracy and expression and provide corrective feedback by modeling proper fluency.

High-Frequency Words

REVIEW WORDS

OBJECTIVES

 Read common high-frequency words by sight. **RF.K.3c**

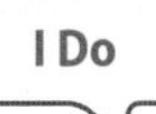

Use the **High-Frequency Word Card** *said* with the **Read/Spell/Write** routine to review the word. Repeat with *want*.

Have children turn to p. 35 of **Reading/Writing Workshop**. Discuss the photographs and read aloud the sentences. Point to the word *said* and have children read it. Then chorally read the sentences. Have children frame the word *said* in the sentences and read the word. Repeat the routine with the word *want*.

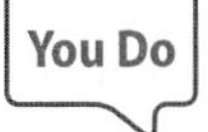

Say the word *said*. Ask children to close their eyes, picture the word, and write it as they see it. Have children self-correct. Repeat the routine with the word *want*.

Reteach previously introduced high-frequency words using the **Read/Spell/Write** routine.

Fluency Point to the High-Frequency Word Cards *I, can, the, we, see, a, like, to, and, go, you, do, my, are, he, with, is, little, she, was, have, for, they, of, said,* and *want* in random order. Have children chorally read. Repeat at a faster pace.

Comprehension

SELF-SELECTED READING

OBJECTIVES

CCSS With prompting and support, ask and answer questions about key details in a text. **RL.K.1**

Apply the strategy and skill to reread the text

Read Independently

Have children select an illustrated story for sustained silent reading. Remind them that they can make predictions about the characters, events, and setting as they read. Tell children they should base their predictions on their own experience, as well as the parts of the book, such as the title and illustrations.

Read Purposefully

Before reading, ask children to note the story title and the cover illustration. Ask them to write one or two sentences predicting who and what the story will be about. Tell them to think about the prediction as they read. After reading, have children explain whether their predictions were right. If their predictions were not right, allow them to revise the predictions.

Beyond Level

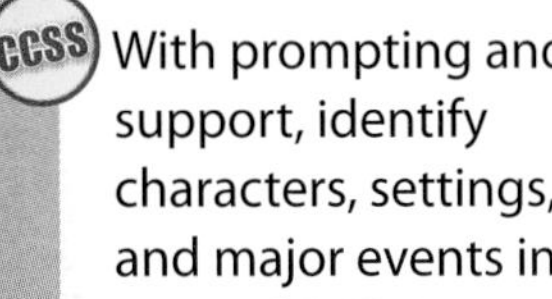

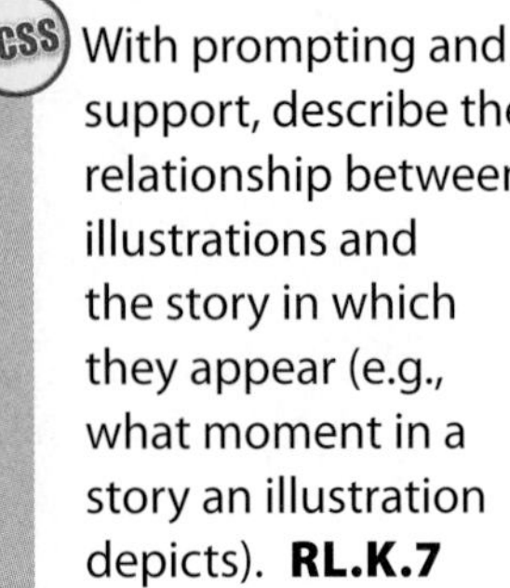

Leveled Reader

OBJECTIVES

CCSS With prompting and support, identify characters, settings, and major events in a story. **RL.K.3**

CCSS With prompting and support, describe the relationship between illustrations and the story in which they appear (e.g., what moment in a story an illustration depicts). **RL.K.7**

CCSS Know and apply grade-level phonics and word analysis skills in decoding words. **RF.K.3**

Leveled Reader: *Bird's New Home*

Go Digital

Leveled Reader

Before Reading

Preview and Predict

Ask children to point to the title on the cover and read it aloud. Read the names of the author and illustrator. Ask children to describe the picture on the front cover. Ask: *What is the setting?* Have children page through the book and look at the illustrations. Ask: *What do you think this book will be about?*

Review Genre: Fantasy

Remind children that fantasy stories are made up and the events cannot happen in real life. The characters and events are not real. Say: *How do you know this is a fantasy?* (There are talking animals.)

Essential Question

Remind children of the Essential Question: *Where do animals live?* Have children set a purpose for reading. Say: *Let's find out what kinds of homes some animals that live in the forest have.*

During Reading

Guided Comprehension

As children whisper-read *Bird's New Home,* monitor and provide guidance by correcting blending and modeling the strategy and skill. Point to the quotation marks and remind children that these show that a character is speaking.

Strategy: Make, Confirm, and Revise Predictions

Remind children that as they read they should continually make predictions about what will happen next, and then confirm or revise their predictions.

Skill: Character, Setting, Plot (Cause and Effect)

Remind children that as they read they should identify the characters, the setting, and the plot. Explain that the pictures and text will provide details about what Bird does and why.

Think Aloud After I read page 3, I learn from the illustration and the text that Vole lives in the ground and that Bird does not want to live in the ground. I will keep reading to see what other animals Bird meets as she looks for twigs to build her home.

Have children read the rest of the book and pay attention to the details in the text and illustrations. Guide children to see that when Bird looks for twigs for her home, other animals try to convince her to build a different home.

After Reading

Respond to Reading

- *What causes Bird to go look for twigs?* (She needs to make her new home.)
- *What happens when Bird meets an animal?* (Each animal tries to convince her to build a home like their home.)
- *Why doesn't Bird want what the other animals have?* (Possible answer: She knew she needed to live in a nest high in a tree.)

Retell

Have pairs of children take turns retelling the story, one acting out the part of Bird and the other acting out all the other animals. Encourage them to make a personal connection by asking: *What makes a good home for you?*

Gifted and Talented

EVALUATING Have children recall the different homes the animals lived in. Challenge children to think about how each home suited the animals that lived there.

HAVE children make a chart of forest animals' homes. Have them include the animal name, where each home is located, and what it's made of.

LITERACY ACTIVITIES

Have children complete the activities on the inside back cover of the reader.

Beyond Level

Phonics

REVIEW

OBJECTIVES

Know and apply grade-level phonics and word analysis skills in decoding words. **RF.K.3**

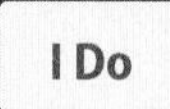

Display **Reading/Writing Workshop**, p. 34. Point to the *Volcano* **Sound-Spelling Card**. *What is the sound at the beginning of* volcano? *What letter can stand for /v/? The letter is* v. Repeat the routine with the *Box* Sound-Spelling Card and final /ks/.

Have children say the name of each picture. Then ask children to share other words they know that begin with /v/ or end with /ks/.

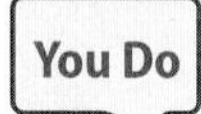

Have partners read each word. Ask them to write the words on their **Response Boards**, underlining the letter in each word that stands for /v/ or /ks/.

Fluency Have children turn to p. 36 in **Reading/Writing Workshop** and reread the story "A Vet in a Van" for fluency.

Innovate Have children create a new page for "A Vet in a Van" by adding another animal Pat sees.

REVIEW

OBJECTIVES

Read common high-frequency words by sight. **RF.K.3c**

Create **High-Frequency Word Cards** for *use* and *green*. Introduce the words using the **Read/Spell/Write** routine.

Display the High-Frequency Word Cards for *they, want, to, a, little,* and *was*. Have children help you complete the following sentence frames using the High-Frequency Word Cards: *They want to use a ____. The little ____ was green.*

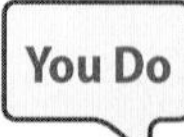

Have partners write sentences using the High-Frequency Words *use* and *green* on their Response Boards. Have them read their sentences.

Vocabulary

ORAL VOCABULARY: SYNONYMS

OBJECTIVES

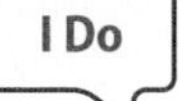

With guidance and support from adults, explore word relationships and nuances in word meanings. **L.K.5**

Develop oral vocabulary: Synonyms

Review the meanings of the oral vocabulary words *habitat* and *complain*. *A synonym is a word that means almost the same thing as another word. A synonym for* habitat *is* environment. *An animal's environment is the place where it lives.* A polar bear lives in a very cold environment. *A synonym for* complain *is* grumble. *When you grumble, you are saying you are unhappy about something.* My brother would always grumble at bathtime.

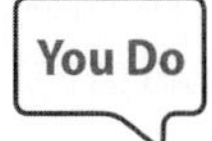

Work with children to create sentences using the new words *environment* and *grumble.*

Have partners create sentences about an animal that lives in the jungle. Tell them to use *environment* and *grumble,* and then share their sentences.

Gifted and Talented

Extend Challenge children to use new words *environment* and *grumble* to interview a partner about animal habitats. Then ask children to share two facts they learned from each other about animal habitats.

Comprehension

SELF-SELECTED READING

OBJECTIVES

With prompting and support, ask and answer questions about key details in a text. **RL.K.1**

Apply the strategy and skill to reread the text

Read Independently

Have children select an illustrated story for sustained silent reading. Remind them that making predictions about characters, setting, and events can help them better understand and enjoy a book as they read.

Read Purposefully

Before reading, have children write two or three sentences predicting who the main character will be and what the plot might be. After reading, have children explain whether their predictions were correct. Then have them suppose that the author will write another book about the same main character. Ask them to predict what the plot of the new book might be and explain why they thought of this idea.

Independent Study Challenge children to create a Prediction Poster. Have them write, "I predicted . . ." in the center of the poster. Then have them illustrate the predictions they made. Have them present their posters to the class.

English Language Learners

Leveled Reader

OBJECTIVES

With prompting and support, ask and answer questions about key details in a text. **RL.K.1**

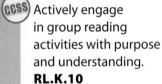

Actively engage in group reading activities with purpose and understanding. **RL.K.10**

Read emergent-reader texts with purpose and understanding. **RF.K.4**

Shared Read: *A New Home*

Leveled Reader

Before Reading

Preview and Predict

Read aloud the title on the cover, pointing to each word. Read aloud the author's and illustrator's names. Have children tell what they see on the cover. Walk children through the book to build vocabulary and familiarize them with the language pattern. Ask: *What animal is this? What do you think Squirrel said here?*

Essential Question

Remind children of the Essential Question: *Where do animals live?* Set a purpose for reading: *Let's find out where these animals live.* Encourage children to seek clarification when they encounter a word or phrase that doesn't make sense to them. Model asking for help: *I'm not sure what Squirrel wants. Can you show me?* Remind children to look at the illustrations and labels as they read and to use them for support.

During Reading

Interactive Question Response

Pages 2–3 Point to the illustration on page 2. Say: *I see Squirrel. Where is Squirrel?* (in his home) *Point to the label that says* squirrel. *Point to the word* squirrel *in the sentence. Let's read this sentence together.* Point to the illustration on page 3. Say: *I see Bird and Squirrel. What is Squirrel doing?* (looking at Bird's home) *Tell your partner what Squirrel wants.* (Squirrel wants Bird's home.)

Pages 4–5 Point to the illustration on page 4. Say: *What animals do you see?* (mouse and squirrel) *What is Squirrel doing?* (looking at Mouse's home) *Point to the words on the page that say* mouse. *Let's read the sentence that tells us what Squirrel wants.* Point to the text on page 5. Ask: *What animal is talking to Squirrel on this page?* (Rabbit) *Point to the words that say* rabbit *on this page. Let's read to find out what Squirrel wants.*

Pages 6–7 Point to the illustration and label on page 6. Ask: *Whose home is this?* (Beaver's home) *What is Squirrel doing?* (looking at Beaver's home) *Point to the text that tells us that.* Read the page with children. Point to the illustration and label on page 7. Ask: *Whose home is this?* (Fox's home) *What does Squirrel say?* (I want Fox's home.)

Page 8 Point to the illustration on page 8. Ask: *Where is Squirrel?* (next to his home) *What does Squirrel want?* (his own home) *Let's reread the sentence that tells us that.* Ask: *What other animals do you see?* (Bird, Mouse, Rabbit, Beaver, Fox)

After Reading

Respond to Reading

- *At first, what does Squirrel want?* (a new home)
- *Whose homes does he look at?* (Bird's, Mouse's, Rabbit's, Beaver's, Fox's)
- *What does Squirrel say in the end?* (I want my home.)
- *Why did Squirrel change his mind?* (He realized his home is best for him.)

Retell

Say: *Let's retell the book together.* Use the pictures in the book as prompts. Ask: *What does Squirrel want?* (a new home) *What does Squirrel say to Bird?* (I want Bird's home.) Repeat with the remainder of the book.

Model Fluency

Read the sentences one at a time as you track the print. Have children chorally repeat. Point out that the words that Squirrel speaks are in quotation marks. Model the idea of a character speaking by inviting children to act out each character in the book.

Apply Have children read with partners. Encourage them to use a different voice than their reading voice for the words that Squirrel says.

LITERACY ACTIVITIES

Have children complete the activities on the inside back cover of the reader.

Level Up

IF Children read *A New Home* **ELL Level** with fluency and correctly answer the Respond to Reading questions,

THEN Tell children that they will read a more detailed version of the story.

- Page through *A New Home* **On Level** with children and ask them to describe each picture in simple language.
- Have children read the story, monitoring their comprehension and providing assistance as necessary.

English Language Learners

Vocabulary

PRETEACH ORAL VOCABULARY

OBJECTIVES

CCSS Speak audibly and express thoughts, feelings, and ideas clearly. **SL.K.6**

LANGUAGE OBJECTIVE

Preview vocabulary

I Do Display the images from the **Visual Vocabulary Cards** and follow the routine to preteach the oral vocabulary words.

We Do Display each image again and explain how it illustrates or demonstrates the word. Model using sentences to describe the image.

You Do Display the word *wild* again. Explain that the word can be used to describe animals that live in nature. Ask children to name wild animals that they know about.

Beginning	Intermediate	Advanced/High
Prompt children to talk about animals in the wild.	Have partners create oral sentences using the words.	Ask children to use the words in their own sentences and say their sentences to a partner.

PRETEACH ELL VOCABULARY

OBJECTIVES

CCSS Speak audibly and express thoughts, feelings, and ideas clearly. **SL.K.6**

LANGUAGE OBJECTIVE

Preview ELL vocabulary

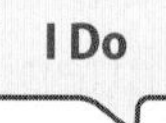

Display the images from the **Visual Vocabulary Cards** one at a time to preteach the ELL vocabulary words *shelter* and *nest*. Follow the routine. Say each word and have children repeat it. Define each word in English.

We Do Display each image again and incorporate the words in a short discussion about the images. Model using sentences to describe the image.

You Do Display the word *nest* again and have children draw a nest with an animal living in it. Ask children to describe their picture using a complete sentence.

Beginning	Intermediate	Advanced/High
Use the words *shelter* and *nest* in the same sentence and have children repeat the sentence chorally after you.	Ask pairs of children to give examples of animals that make a *nest*.	Ask children to use a complete sentence to tell how a *nest* is a kind of *shelter*.

High-Frequency Words

REVIEW WORDS

OBJECTIVES

CCSS Read common high-frequency words by sight (e.g., *the, of, to, you, she, my, is, are, do, does*). **RF.K.3c**

LANGUAGE OBJECTIVE

Review high-frequency words

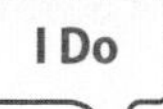

Display the **High-Frequency Word Cards** for *said* and *want*. Read the words. Use the **Read/Spell/Write** routine to teach the words. Have children write the words on their **Response Boards**.

Write a sentence frame that uses the week's high-frequency words: *She said you want* _______. Track the print as children read and complete the sentence. Explain to children that the word *said* shows what someone says.

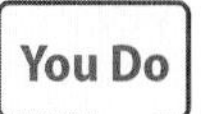

Display a sentence that uses the high-frequency words *said* and *want*. Ask children to point to the words and say them aloud. Then work with children to read and say the entire sentence aloud.

Beginning	Intermediate	Advanced/High
Help children look for the words *said* and *want* in texts in the classroom. Read the sentences and have children repeat.	Ask children to say a sentence to a partner. Have the partner repeat by saying, *She/He said* _____.	Ask children to name things that they *want* and make a list with a partner. Then contrast the idea with the word *need*.

REVIEW CATEGORY WORDS

OBJECTIVES

Identify real-life connections between words and their use (e.g., note places at school that are *colorful*). **L.K.5c**

LANGUAGE OBJECTIVE

Use category words

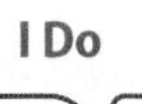

Write and say words that are related to this week's content words about animal homes, such as *cave, den, hive, nest,* and *burrow*. Ask children to repeat the words after you. Define the words in English and then in Spanish, if appropriate, identifying any cognates.

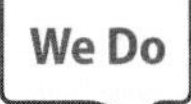

Ask a question and have children identify which category word you used in your sentence.

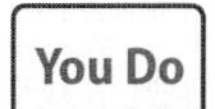

Ask children to talk in pairs about what kind of animal lives in each animal home. Guide partners to match animals to their homes.

Beginning	Intermediate	Advanced/High
Provide children with pictures of animal homes and have them point to and name each one.	Ask children to use one of the category words in a sentence of their own.	Invite pairs to choose one animal home and describe why it is a good shelter for the animal that lives there.

English Language Learners

Writing

SHARED WRITING

OBJECTIVES

CCSS Use a combination of drawing, dictating, and writing to narrate a single event or several loosely linked events, tell about the events in the order in which they occurred, and provide a reaction to what happened. **W.K.3**

LANGUAGE OBJECTIVE

Contribute to a shared writing project

I Do Review the chart from the Whole Group Shared Writing project that lists animals and where they live. Model writing a question and an answer about one animal's habitat: *Where does a bear live? A bear lives in a cave.*

We Do Have children choose an animal from the chart to write about and help you write a shared question and answer about the animal, using the same format as your modeled writing.

You Do Ask partners to use a sentence frame to write a question and an answer: *Where does a* ______ *live? A* ______ *lives in a* ______. Have them draw a picture for their sentence.

Beginning	Intermediate	Advanced/High
Prompt children to discuss what each type of animal home looks like and where each animal lives.	Guide partners to complete the sentence frames and draw a picture to match.	Have children write more than one question and answer about animal homes.

WRITING TRAIT: WORD CHOICE

OBJECTIVES

CCSS With guidance and support from adults, respond to questions and suggestions from peers and add details to strengthen writing as needed. **W.K.5**

LANGUAGE OBJECTIVE

Organize ideas for writing

I Do Explain to children that writers must come up with ideas for their writing before they sit down and begin to write.

We Do Point to the **Big Book** selection *Bear Snores On. The bear sleeps through all the things that go on around him. What could happen during the winter in a bear's cave?* Use the selection to help children get ideas.

You Do Have children write a sentence to describe a bear's home. Have them use a sentence frame to help them: *A bear's den has* ______.

Beginning	Intermediate	Advanced/High
Help children use the selection to describe a bear's den.	Ask children to talk in small groups to complete the sentence frame.	Ask children to use the sentence frame and list things in a bear's den.

Program Information

For Additional Resources

Unit Bibliography

Word Lists

Literature and Informational Text Charts

Web Sites

Resources

www.connected.mcgraw-hill.com

SCOPE & SEQUENCE

	K	1	2	3	4	5	6
READING PROCESS							
Concepts About Print/Print Awareness							
Recognize own name							
Understand directionality (top to bottom; tracking print from left to right; return sweep, page by page)	✔						
Locate printed word on page	✔						
Develop print awareness (concept of letter, word, sentence)	✔						
Identify separate sounds in a spoken sentence	✔						
Understand that written words are represented in written language by a specific sequence of letters	✔						
Distinguish between letters, words, and sentences	✔						
Identify and distinguish paragraphs							
Match print to speech (one-to-one correspondence)	✔						
Name uppercase and lowercase letters	✔						
Understand book handling (holding a book right-side-up, turning its pages)	✔						
Identify parts of a book (front cover, back cover, title page, table of contents); recognize that parts of a book contain information	✔						
Phonological Awareness							
Recognize and understand alliteration							
Segment sentences into correct number of words							
Identify, blend, segment syllables in words		✔					
Recognize and generate rhyming words	✔	✔					
Identify, blend, segment onset and rime	✔	✔					
Phonemic Awareness							
Count phonemes	✔	✔					
Isolate initial, medial, and final sounds	✔	✔					
Blend spoken phonemes to form words	✔	✔					
Segment spoken words into phonemes	✔	✔					
Distinguish between long- and short-vowel sounds	✔	✔					
Manipulate phonemes (addition, deletion, substitution)	✔	✔					
Phonics and Decoding /Word Recognition							
Understand the alphabetic principle	✔	✔					
Sound/letter correspondence	✔	✔	✔	✔			
Blend sounds into words, including VC, CVC, CVCe, CVVC words	✔	✔	✔	✔			
Blend common word families	✔	✔	✔	✔			

KEY	✔ = Assessed Skill Tinted panels show skills, strategies, and other teaching opportunities.

	K	1	2	3	4	5	6
Initial consonant blends		✔	✔	✔			
Final consonant blends		✔	✔	✔			
Initial and medial short vowels	✔	✔	✔	✔	✔	✔	✔
Decode one-syllable words in isolation and in context	✔	✔	✔	✔			
Decode multisyllabic words in isolation and in context using common syllabication patterns		✔	✔	✔	✔	✔	✔
Distinguish between similarly spelled words	✔	✔	✔	✔	✔	✔	✔
Monitor accuracy of decoding							
Identify and read common high-frequency words, irregularly spelled words	✔	✔	✔	✔			
Identify and read compound words, contractions		✔	✔	✔	✔	✔	✔
Use knowledge of spelling patterns to identify syllables		✔	✔	✔	✔	✔	✔
Regular and irregular plurals	✔	✔	✔	✔	✔	✔	✔
Long vowels (silent *e*, vowel teams)	✔	✔	✔	✔	✔	✔	✔
Vowel digraphs (variant vowels)		✔	✔	✔	✔	✔	✔
r-Controlled vowels		✔	✔	✔	✔	✔	✔
Hard/soft consonants		✔	✔	✔	✔	✔	✔
Initial consonant digraphs		✔	✔	✔	✔	✔	
Medial and final consonant digraphs		✔	✔	✔	✔	✔	
Vowel diphthongs		✔	✔	✔	✔	✔	✔
Identify and distinguish letter-sounds (initial, medial, final)	✔	✔	✔				
Silent letters		✔	✔	✔	✔	✔	✔
Schwa words				✔	✔	✔	✔
Inflectional endings		✔	✔	✔	✔	✔	✔
Triple-consonant clusters		✔	✔	✔	✔	✔	
Unfamiliar and complex word families				✔	✔	✔	✔
Structural Analysis/Word Analysis							
Common spelling patterns (word families)		✔	✔	✔	✔	✔	✔
Common syllable patterns		✔	✔	✔	✔	✔	✔
Inflectional endings		✔	✔	✔	✔	✔	✔
Contractions		✔	✔	✔	✔	✔	✔
Compound words		✔	✔	✔	✔	✔	✔
Prefixes and suffixes		✔	✔	✔	✔	✔	✔
Root or base words			✔	✔	✔	✔	✔
Comparatives and superlatives			✔	✔	✔	✔	✔
Greek and Latin roots			✔	✔	✔	✔	✔
Fluency							
Apply letter/sound knowledge to decode phonetically regular words accurately	✔	✔	✔	✔	✔	✔	✔
Recognize high-frequency and familiar words	✔	✔	✔	✔	✔	✔	✔
Read regularly on independent and instructional levels							
Read orally with fluency from familiar texts (choral, echo, partner, Reader's Theater)							
Use appropriate rate, expression, intonation, and phrasing		✔	✔	✔	✔	✔	✔
Read with automaticity (accurately and effortlessly)		✔	✔	✔	✔	✔	✔
Use punctuation cues in reading		✔	✔	✔	✔	✔	✔

	K	1	2	3	4	5	6
Adjust reading rate to purpose, text difficulty, form, and style							
Repeated readings							
Timed readings		✔	✔	✔	✔	✔	✔
Read with purpose and understanding		✔	✔	✔	✔	✔	✔
Read orally with accuracy		✔	✔	✔	✔	✔	✔
Use context to confirm or self-correct word recognition		✔	✔	✔	✔	✔	✔
READING LITERATURE							
Comprehension Strategies and Skills							
Read literature from a broad range of genres, cultures, and periods		✔	✔	✔	✔	✔	✔
Access complex text		✔	✔	✔	✔	✔	✔
Build background							
Preview and predict							
Establish and adjust purpose for reading							
Evaluate citing evidence from the text							
Ask and answer questions	✔	✔	✔	✔	✔	✔	✔
Inferences and conclusions, citing evidence from the text	✔	✔	✔	✔	✔	✔	✔
Monitor/adjust comprehension including reread, reading rate, paraphrase							
Recount/Retell	✔	✔					
Summarize			✔	✔	✔	✔	✔
Story structure (beginning, middle, end)	✔	✔	✔	✔	✔	✔	✔
Visualize							
Make connections between and across texts		✔	✔	✔	✔	✔	✔
Point of view		✔	✔	✔	✔	✔	✔
Author's purpose							
Cause and effect	✔	✔	✔	✔	✔	✔	✔
Compare and contrast (including character, setting, plot, topics)	✔	✔	✔	✔	✔	✔	✔
Classify and categorize		✔	✔				
Literature vs informational text	✔	✔	✔				
Illustrations, using	✔	✔	✔	✔			
Theme, central message, moral, lesson		✔	✔	✔	✔	✔	✔
Predictions, making/confirming	✔	✔	✔				
Problem and solution (problem/resolution)		✔	✔	✔	✔	✔	✔
Sequence of events	✔	✔	✔	✔	✔	✔	✔
Literary Elements							
Character	✔	✔	✔	✔	✔	✔	✔
Plot development/Events	✔	✔	✔	✔	✔	✔	✔
Setting	✔	✔	✔	✔	✔	✔	✔
Stanza				✔	✔	✔	✔
Alliteration						✔	✔
Assonance						✔	✔
Dialogue							
Foreshadowing						✔	✔

KEY	✔ = Assessed Skill Tinted panels show skills, strategies, and other teaching opportunities.

	K	1	2	3	4	5	6
Flashback						✔	✔
Descriptive and figurative language		✔	✔	✔	✔	✔	✔
Imagery					✔	✔	✔
Meter					✔	✔	✔
Onomatopoeia							
Repetition		✔	✔	✔	✔	✔	✔
Rhyme/rhyme schemes		✔	✔	✔	✔	✔	✔
Rhythm		✔	✔				
Sensory language							
Symbolism							
Write About Reading/Literary Response Discussions							
Reflect and respond to text citing text evidence		✔	✔	✔	✔	✔	✔
Connect and compare text characters, events, ideas to self, to other texts, to world							
Connect literary texts to other curriculum areas							
Identify cultural and historical elements of text							
Evaluate author's techniques, craft							
Analytical writing							
Interpret text ideas through writing, discussion, media, research							
Book report or review							
Locate, use, explain information from text features		✔	✔	✔	✔	✔	✔
Organize information to show understanding of main idea through charts, mapping							
Cite text evidence	✔	✔	✔	✔	✔	✔	✔
Author's purpose/ Illustrator's purpose							
READING INFORMATIONAL TEXT							
Comprehension Strategies and Skills							
Read informational text from a broad range of topics and cultures	✔	✔	✔	✔	✔	✔	✔
Access complex text		✔	✔	✔	✔	✔	✔
Build background							
Preview and predict	✔	✔	✔				
Establish and adjust purpose for reading							
Evaluate citing evidence from the text							
Ask and answer questions	✔	✔	✔	✔	✔	✔	✔
Inferences and conclusions, citing evidence from the text	✔	✔	✔	✔	✔	✔	✔
Monitor and adjust comprehension including reread, adjust reading rate, paraphrase							
Recount/Retell	✔	✔					
Summarize			✔	✔	✔	✔	✔
Text structure	✔	✔	✔	✔	✔	✔	✔
Identify text features		✔	✔	✔	✔	✔	✔
Make connections between and across texts	✔	✔	✔	✔	✔	✔	✔
Author's point of view				✔	✔	✔	✔
Author's purpose		✔	✔				

	K	1	2	3	4	5	6
Cause and effect	✔	✔	✔	✔	✔	✔	✔
Compare and contrast	✔	✔	✔	✔	✔	✔	✔
Classify and categorize		✔	✔				
Illustrations and photographs, using	✔	✔	✔	✔			
Instructions/directions (written and oral)		✔	✔	✔	✔	✔	✔
Main idea and key details	✔	✔	✔	✔	✔	✔	✔
Persuasion, reasons and evidence to support points/persuasive techniques						✔	✔
Predictions, making/confirming	✔	✔					
Problem and solution		✔	✔	✔	✔	✔	✔
Sequence, chronological order of events, time order, steps in a process	✔	✔	✔	✔	✔	✔	✔
Writing About Reading/Expository Critique Discussions							
Reflect and respond to text citing text evidence		✔	✔	✔	✔	✔	✔
Connect and compare text characters, events, ideas to self, to other texts, to world							
Connect texts to other curriculum areas							
Identify cultural and historical elements of text							
Evaluate author's techniques, craft							
Analytical writing							
Read to understand and perform tasks and activities							
Interpret text ideas through writing, discussion, media, research							
Locate, use, explain information from text features		✔	✔	✔	✔	✔	✔
Organize information to show understanding of main idea through charts, mapping							
Cite text evidence		✔	✔	✔	✔	✔	✔
Author's purpose/Illustrator's purpose							
Text Features							
Recognize and identify text and organizational features of nonfiction texts		✔	✔	✔	✔	✔	✔
Captions and labels, headings, subheadings, endnotes, key words, bold print	✔	✔	✔	✔	✔	✔	✔
Graphics, including photographs, illustrations, maps, charts, diagrams, graphs, time lines	✔	✔	✔	✔	✔	✔	✔
Self-Selected Reading/Independent Reading							
Use personal criteria to choose own reading including favorite authors, genres, recommendations from others; set up a reading log							
Read a range of literature and informational text for tasks as well as for enjoyment; participate in literature circles							
Produce evidence of reading by retelling, summarizing, or paraphrasing							
Media Literacy							
Summarize the message or content from media message, citing text evidence							
Use graphics, illustrations to analyze and interpret information	✔	✔	✔	✔	✔	✔	✔
Identify structural features of popular media and use the features to obtain information, including digital sources				✔	✔	✔	✔
Identify reasons and evidence in visuals and media message							
Analyze media source: recognize effects of media in one's mood and emotion							

KEY	✔ = Assessed Skill Tinted panels show skills, strategies, and other teaching opportunities.

	K	1	2	3	4	5	6
Make informed judgments about print and digital media							
Critique persuasive techniques							
WRITING							
Writing Process							
Plan/prewrite							
Draft							
Revise							
Edit/proofread							
Publish and present including using technology							
Teacher and peer feedback							
Writing Traits							
Conventions		✔	✔	✔	✔	✔	✔
Ideas		✔	✔	✔	✔	✔	✔
Organization		✔	✔	✔	✔	✔	✔
Sentence fluency		✔	✔	✔	✔	✔	✔
Voice		✔	✔	✔	✔	✔	✔
Word choice		✔	✔	✔	✔	✔	✔
Writer's Craft							
Good topic, focus on and develop topic, topic sentence			✔	✔	✔	✔	✔
Paragraph(s); sentence structure			✔	✔	✔	✔	✔
Main idea and supporting key details			✔	✔	✔	✔	✔
Unimportant details							
Relevant supporting evidence			✔	✔	✔	✔	✔
Strong opening, strong conclusion			✔	✔	✔	✔	✔
Beginning, middle, end; sequence		✔	✔	✔	✔	✔	✔
Precise words, strong words, vary words			✔	✔	✔	✔	✔
Figurative and sensory language, descriptive details							
Informal/formal language							
Mood/style/tone							
Dialogue				✔	✔	✔	✔
Transition words, transitions to multiple paragraphs				✔	✔	✔	✔
Select focus and organization			✔	✔	✔	✔	✔
Points and counterpoints/Opposing claims and counterarguments							
Use reference materials (online and print dictionary, thesaurus, encyclopedia)							
Writing Applications							
Writing about text	✔	✔	✔	✔	✔	✔	✔
Personal and fictional narrative (also biographical and autobiographical)	✔	✔	✔	✔	✔	✔	✔
Variety of expressive forms including poetry	✔	✔	✔	✔	✔	✔	✔
Informative/explanatory texts	✔	✔	✔	✔	✔	✔	✔
Description	✔	✔	✔	✔			
Procedural texts		✔	✔	✔	✔	✔	✔
Opinion pieces or arguments	✔	✔	✔	✔	✔	✔	✔

	K	1	2	3	4	5	6
Communications including technical documents		✔	✔	✔	✔	✔	✔
Research report	✔	✔	✔	✔	✔	✔	✔
Responses to literature/reflection				✔	✔	✔	✔
Analytical writing							
Letters		✔	✔	✔	✔	✔	✔
Write daily and over short and extended time frames; set up writer's notebooks							
Penmanship/Handwriting							
Write legibly in manuscript using correct formation, directionality, and spacing							
Write legibly in cursive using correct formation, directionality, and spacing							
SPEAKING AND LISTENING							
Speaking							
Use repetition, rhyme, and rhythm in oral texts							
Participate in classroom activities and discussions							
Collaborative conversation with peers and adults in small and large groups using formal English when appropriate							
Differentiate between formal and informal English							
Follow agreed upon rules for discussion							
Build on others' talk in conversation, adding new ideas							
Come to discussion prepared							
Describe familiar people, places, and things and add drawings as desired							
Paraphrase portions of text read alone or information presented							
Apply comprehension strategies and skills in speaking activities							
Use literal and nonliteral meanings							
Ask and answer questions about text read aloud and about media							
Stay on topic when speaking							
Use language appropriate to situation, purpose, and audience							
Use nonverbal communications such as eye contact, gestures, and props							
Use verbal communication in effective ways and improve expression in conventional language							
Retell a story, presentation, or spoken message by summarizing							
Oral presentations: focus, organizational structure, audience, purpose							
Give and follow directions							
Consider audience when speaking or preparing a presentation							
Recite poems, rhymes, songs							
Use complete, coherent sentences							
Organize presentations							
Deliver presentations (narrative, summaries, research, persuasive); add visuals							
Speak audibly (accuracy, expression, volume, pitch, rate, phrasing, modulation, enunciation)							
Create audio recordings of poems, stories, presentations							
Listening							
Identify musical elements in language							
Determine the purpose for listening							

KEY	✔ = Assessed Skill Tinted panels show skills, strategies, and other teaching opportunities.

	K	1	2	3	4	5	6
Understand, follow, restate, and give oral directions							
Develop oral language and concepts							
Listen openly, responsively, attentively, and critically							
Listen to identify the points a speaker makes							
Listen responsively to oral presentations (determine main idea and key details)							
Ask and answer relevant questions (for clarification to follow-up on ideas)							
Identify reasons and evidence presented by speaker							
Recall and interpret speakers' verbal/nonverbal messages, purposes, perspectives							
LANGUAGE							
Vocabulary Acquisition and Use							
Develop oral vocabulary and choose words for effect							
Use academic language		✔	✔	✔	✔	✔	✔
Identify persons, places, things, actions		✔	✔	✔			
Classify, sort, and categorize words	✔	✔	✔	✔	✔	✔	✔
Determine or clarify the meaning of unknown words; use word walls		✔	✔	✔	✔	✔	✔
Synonyms, antonyms, and opposites		✔	✔	✔	✔	✔	✔
Use context clues such as word, sentence, paragraph, definition, example, restatement, description, comparison, cause and effect		✔	✔	✔	✔	✔	✔
Use word identification strategies		✔	✔	✔	✔	✔	✔
Unfamiliar words		✔	✔	✔	✔	✔	✔
Multiple-meaning words		✔	✔	✔	✔	✔	✔
Use print and online dictionary to locate meanings, pronunciation, derivatives, parts of speech		✔	✔	✔	✔	✔	✔
Compound words		✔	✔	✔	✔	✔	✔
Words ending in -er and -est		✔	✔	✔	✔	✔	
Root words (base words)		✔	✔	✔	✔	✔	✔
Prefixes and suffixes		✔	✔	✔	✔	✔	✔
Greek and Latin affixes and roots			✔	✔	✔	✔	✔
Denotation and connotation					✔	✔	✔
Word families		✔	✔	✔	✔	✔	✔
Inflectional endings		✔	✔	✔	✔	✔	✔
Use a print and online thesaurus			✔	✔	✔	✔	✔
Use print and online reference sources for word meaning (dictionary, glossaries)		✔	✔	✔	✔	✔	✔
Homographs				✔	✔	✔	✔
Homophones			✔	✔	✔	✔	✔
Contractions		✔	✔	✔			
Figurative language such as metaphors, similes, personification			✔	✔	✔	✔	✔
Idioms, adages, proverbs, literal and nonliteral language			✔	✔	✔	✔	✔
Analogies							
Listen to, read, discuss familiar and unfamiliar challenging text							
Identify real-life connections between words and their use							
Use acquired words and phrases to convey precise ideas							
Use vocabulary to express spatial and temporal relationships							

	K	1	2	3	4	5	6
Identify shades of meaning in related words	✔	✔	✔	✔	✔	✔	✔
Word origins				✔	✔	✔	✔
Morphology				✔	✔	✔	✔
Knowledge of Language							
Choose words, phrases, and sentences for effect							
Choose punctuation effectively							
Formal and informal language for style and tone including dialects							
Conventions of Standard English/Grammar, Mechanics, and Usage							
Sentence concepts: statements, questions, exclamations, commands		✔	✔	✔	✔	✔	✔
Complete and incomplete sentences; sentence fragments; word order		✔	✔	✔	✔	✔	✔
Compound sentences, complex sentences				✔	✔	✔	✔
Combining sentences		✔	✔	✔	✔	✔	✔
Nouns including common, proper, singular, plural, irregular plurals, possessives, abstract, concrete, collective		✔	✔	✔	✔	✔	✔
Verbs including action, helping, linking, irregular		✔	✔	✔	✔	✔	✔
Verb tenses including past, present, future, perfect, and progressive		✔	✔	✔	✔	✔	✔
Pronouns including possessive, subject and object, pronoun-verb agreement, indefinite, intensive, reciprocal; correct unclear pronouns		✔	✔	✔	✔	✔	✔
Adjectives including articles, demonstrative, proper adjectives that compare		✔	✔	✔	✔	✔	✔
Adverbs including telling how, when, where, comparative, superlative, irregular		✔	✔	✔	✔	✔	✔
Subject, predicate; subject-verb agreement		✔	✔	✔	✔	✔	✔
Contractions		✔	✔	✔	✔	✔	✔
Conjunctions				✔	✔	✔	✔
Commas			✔	✔	✔	✔	✔
Colons, semicolons, dashes, hyphens						✔	✔
Question words							
Quotation marks			✔	✔	✔	✔	✔
Prepositions and prepositional phrases, appositives		✔	✔	✔	✔	✔	✔
Independent and dependent clauses						✔	✔
Italics/underlining for emphasis and titles							
Negatives, correcting double negatives					✔	✔	✔
Abbreviations			✔	✔	✔	✔	✔
Use correct capitalization in sentences, proper nouns, titles, abbreviations		✔	✔	✔	✔	✔	✔
Use correct punctuation		✔	✔	✔	✔	✔	✔
Antecedents				✔	✔	✔	✔
Homophones and words often confused			✔	✔	✔	✔	✔
Apostrophes				✔	✔	✔	✔
Spelling							
Write irregular, high-frequency words	✔	✔	✔				
ABC order	✔	✔					
Write letters	✔	✔					
Words with short vowels	✔	✔	✔	✔	✔	✔	✔
Words with long vowels	✔	✔	✔	✔	✔	✔	✔

KEY	✔ = Assessed Skill Tinted panels show skills, strategies, and other teaching opportunities.

	K	1	2	3	4	5	6
Words with digraphs, blends, consonant clusters, double consonants		✔	✔	✔	✔	✔	✔
Words with vowel digraphs and ambiguous vowels		✔	✔	✔	✔	✔	✔
Words with diphthongs		✔	✔	✔	✔	✔	✔
Words with r-controlled vowels		✔	✔	✔	✔	✔	✔
Use conventional spelling		✔	✔	✔	✔	✔	✔
Schwa words				✔	✔	✔	✔
Words with silent letters			✔	✔	✔	✔	✔
Words with hard and soft letters			✔	✔	✔	✔	✔
Inflectional endings including plural, past tense, drop final e and double consonant when adding -ed and -ing, changing y to i		✔	✔	✔	✔	✔	✔
Compound words		✔	✔	✔	✔	✔	✔
Homonyms/homophones			✔	✔	✔	✔	✔
Prefixes and suffixes		✔	✔	✔	✔	✔	✔
Root and base words (also spell derivatives)				✔	✔	✔	✔
Syllables: patterns, rules, accented, stressed, closed, open				✔	✔	✔	✔
Words with Greek and Latin roots						✔	✔
Words from mythology						✔	✔
Words with spelling patterns, word families		✔	✔	✔	✔	✔	✔
RESEARCH AND INQUIRY							
Study Skills							
Directions: read, write, give, follow (includes technical directions)			✔	✔	✔	✔	✔
Evaluate directions for sequence and completeness				✔	✔	✔	✔
Use library/media center							
Use parts of a book to locate information							
Interpret information from graphic aids		✔	✔	✔	✔	✔	✔
Use graphic organizers to organize information and comprehend text		✔	✔	✔	✔	✔	✔
Use functional, everyday documents				✔	✔	✔	✔
Apply study strategies: skimming and scanning, note-taking, outlining							
Research Process							
Generate and revise topics and questions for research				✔	✔	✔	✔
Narrow focus of research, set research goals				✔	✔	✔	✔
Find and locate information using print and digital resources		✔	✔	✔	✔	✔	✔
Record information systematically (note-taking, outlining, using technology)				✔	✔	✔	✔
Develop a systematic research plan				✔	✔	✔	✔
Evaluate reliability, credibility, usefulness of sources and information						✔	✔
Use primary sources to obtain information					✔	✔	✔
Organize, synthesize, evaluate, and draw conclusions from information							
Cite and list sources of information (record basic bibliographic data)					✔	✔	✔
Demonstrate basic keyboarding skills							
Participate in and present shared research							
Technology							
Use computer, Internet, and other technology resources to access information							
Use text and organizational features of electronic resources such as search engines, keywords, e-mail, hyperlinks, URLs, Web pages, databases, graphics							
Use digital tools to present and publish in a variety of media formats							

INDEX

A

Key X = Unit X

B

C

Key X = Unit X

D

INDEX

F

Key X = Unit X

G

H

I

L

M

N

P

Key X = Unit X

S

Key X = Unit X

U

V

Key X = Unit X

W

Key X = Unit X

Common Core State Standards Correlations

English Language Arts

College and Career Readiness Anchor Standards for **READING**

The K–5 standards on the following pages define what students should understand and be able to do by the end of each grade. They correspond to the College and Career Readiness (CCR) anchor standards below by number. The CCR and grade-specific standards are necessary complements—the former providing broad standards, the latter providing additional specificity—that together define the skills and understandings that all students must demonstrate.

Key Ideas and Details
1. Read closely to determine what the text says explicitly and to make logical inferences from it; cite specific textual evidence when writing or speaking to support conclusions drawn from the text.
2. Determine central ideas or themes of a text and analyze their development; summarize the key supporting details and ideas.
3. Analyze how and why individuals, events, and ideas develop and interact over the course of a text.
Craft and Structure
4. Interpret words and phrases as they are used in a text, including determining technical, connotative, and figurative meanings, and analyze how specific word choices shape meaning or tone.
5. Analyze the structure of texts, including how specific sentences, paragraphs, and larger portions of the text (e.g., a section, chapter, scene, or stanza) relate to each other and the whole.
6. Assess how point of view or purpose shapes the content and style of a text.
Integration of Knowledge and Ideas
7. Integrate and evaluate content presented in diverse media and formats, including visually and quantitatively, as well as in words.
8. Delineate and evaluate the argument and specific claims in a text, including the validity of the reasoning as well as the relevance and sufficiency of the evidence.
9. Analyze how two or more texts address similar themes or topics in order to build knowledge or to compare the approaches the authors take.
Range of Reading and Level of Text Complexity
10. Read and comprehend complex literary and informational texts independently and proficiently.

Common Core State Standards
English Language Arts

Grade K

Each standard is coded in the following manner:

Strand	Grade Level	Standard
RL	K	1

CCSS CORRELATIONS

Reading Standards for Literature

Key Ideas and Details		*McGraw-Hill Reading Wonders*
RL.K.1	With prompting and support, ask and answer questions about key details in a text.	**READING WRITING WORKSHOP BIG BOOK:** Unit 1, Week 3: 44-49 **LEVELED READERS: Unit 1, Week 2:** *Hop!* (A), *We Hop!* (O), *We Can Move!* (B) **Unit 2, Week 3:** *We Like Bugs!* (A), *The Bugs Run* (O), *I See a Bug!* (B) **Unit 3, Week 1:** *We Run* (A), *Go, Nat!* (O) **Unit 3, Week 2:** *A Noisy Night* (B) **Unit 4, Week 2:** *My Neighbors* (A), *Neighborhood Party* (O), *Parade Day* (B) **Unit 5, Week 1:** *My Garden* (A), *My Garden Grows* (O) **Unit 6, Week 2:** *The Rain* (A), *Weather Is Fun* (O), *Kate and Tuck* (B) **Unit 7, Week 3:** *We Want Water* (A), *A New Home* (O), *Bird's New Home* (B) **Unit 8, Week 3:** *Going Up* (A), *In the Clouds* (O), *How Sun and Moon Found Home* (B) **Unit 9, Week 1:** *Let Me Help You* (A), *How Can Jane Help?* (O), *I Used to Help Too* (B) **Unit 10, Week 1:** *Animal Band* (A), *We Want Honey* (O), *A Good Idea* (B) **YOUR TURN PRACTICE BOOK:** 29, 37, 45, 234 **READING WORKSTATION ACTIVITY CARDS:** 1, 2 **TEACHER'S EDITION:** Unit 1: T23, T106, T189 **Unit 2:** T177, T186-191 **Unit 3:** T25, T104-109 **Unit 4:** T35, T104-108, T142-143, T150-151, T186-191, T224-225, T232-233, T238-239 **Unit 5:** T61, T69, T238-239 **Unit 6:** T23-26, T61, T69, T75, T105-108, T143, T151, T186-191 **Unit 7:** T45, T107 **Unit 8:** T61, T69, T75, T105-108, T186-191 **Unit 9:** T22-26, T61, T69, T75, T104-109 **Unit 10:** T106-110, T145, T153, T159 **LITERATURE BIG BOOKS:** Unit 1, Week 1: *What About Bear?* **Unit 2 Week 3:** *I Love Bugs!* **Unit 3, Week 1:** *How Do Dinosaurs Go to School?* **Unit 4, Week 2:** *What Can You Do With a Paleta?* **Unit 6, Week 1:** *Mama, Is It Summer Yet?* **Unit 6, Week 2:** *Rain* **Unit 7, Week 2:** *The Birthday Pet* **Unit 7, Week 3:** *Bear Snores On* **Unit 8, Week 1:** *When Daddy's Truck Picks Me Up* **Unit 9, Week 2:** *Hen Hears Gossip* **Unit 10, Week 2:** *All Kinds of Families* **INTERACTIVE READ-ALOUD CARDS:** SS: "The Ugly Duckling", "Tikki Tikki Tembo" **Unit 1, Week 1:** "The Lion and the Mouse" **Unit 1, Week 2:** "The Tortoise and the Hare" **Unit 2, Week 1:** "Timimoto" **Unit 4, Week 1:** "Little Juan and the Cooking Pot" **Unit 4, Week 3:** "A Bundle of Sticks"
RL.K.2	With prompting and support, retell familiar stories, including key details.	**LEVELED READERS: Unit 1, Week 2:** *Hop!* (A), *We Hop!* (O, ELL), *We Can Move!* (B) **Unit 2, Week 3:** *I See a Bug!* (B) **Unit 3, Week 1:** *We Run* (A), *Go, Nat!* (O, ELL), *The Birdhouse* (B) **Unit 3, Week 2:** *City Sounds* (A), *Farm Sounds* (O, ELL), *A Noisy Night* (B) **Unit 4, Week 3:** *We Clean!* (A), *Can You Fix It?* (O, ELL), *Helping Mom* (B) **Unit 5, Week 1:** *The Mystery Seeds* (B) **Unit 6, Week 1:** *It Is Hot!* (A), *Little Bear* (O, ELL), *Ant and Grasshopper* (B) **Unit 6, Week 2:** *The Rain* (A), *Weather Is Fun* (O, ELL), *Kate and Tuck* (B) **Unit 8, Week 1:** *I Go Places* (A), *Run, Quinn!* (O, ELL), *Going to Gran's House* (B) **Unit 10, Week 2:** *My Box* (A), *Let's Make a Band* (O, ELL), *Going Camping* (B) **READING WORKSTATION ACTIVITY CARDS:** 5 **YOUR TURN PRACTICE BOOK:** 157, 167 **TEACHER'S EDITION:** Unit 1: T27, T109, T191 **Unit 2:** T75, T109, T143, T151, T157, T161, T186-191 **Unit 3:** T27, T109, T191 **Unit 4:** T109, T143, T151, T157, T225, T233, T239 **Unit 5:** T61, T69, T75, T79, T109, T143, T151, T157, T191, T225, T233, T239 **Unit 6:** T27, T61, T109, T191, T225 **Unit 7:** T109, T143, T144, T151, T157, T158, T191, T225, T233, T239 **Unit 8:** T61, T69, T75, T143, T151, T157, T191, T225, T233, T239 **Unit 9:** T27, T61, T69, T75, T79, T109, T143, T151, T159, T225, T233, T239 **Unit 10:** T29, T63, T71, T77, T81, T111, T145, T153, T157, T191, T227, T235, T241 **LITERATURE BIG BOOKS:** Unit 1, Week 1: *What About Bear?* **Unit 1, Week 2:** *Pouch!* **Unit 3, Week 1:** *How Do Dinosaurs Go to School?* **Unit 3, Week 2:** *Clang! Clang! Beep! Beep! Listen to the City* **Unit 6, Week 1:** *Mama, Is It Summer Yet?* **Unit 7, Week 2:** *The Birthday Pet*

Reading Standards for Literature

Key Ideas and Details		McGraw-Hill Reading Wonders
RL.K.3	With prompting and support, identify characters, settings, and major events in a story.	**LEVELED READERS: Unit 1, Week 2:** *Hop!* (A), *We Hop!* (O), *We Can Move!* (B) **Unit 2, Week 3:** *The Bugs Run* (O) **Unit 3, Week 2:** *A Noisy Night* (B) **Unit 3, Week 3:** *We Can Go* (A), *Going by Cab* (O), *Cal's Busy Week* (B) **Unit 4, Week 2:** *My Neighbors* (A), *Neighborhood Party* (O) **Unit 5, Week 1:** *My Garden* (A), *My Garden Grows* (O), *The Mystery Seeds* (B) **Unit 7, Week 2:** *My Cats* (A), *Their Pets* (O), *Will's Pet* (B) **Unit 8, Week 1:** *I Go Places* (A), *Run, Quinn!* (O), *Going to Gran's House* (B) **Unit 9, Week 2:** *Mike Helps Out* (A), *Clive and His Friend* (O), *Farmer White's Best Friend* **YOUR TURN PRACTICE BOOK:** 129, 217, 234 **READING WORKSTATION ACTIVITY CARDS:** 3, 4, 6, 7, 10, 11 **TEACHER'S EDITION: Unit 1:** T75, T108 **Unit 3:** T156-157, T186-191, T224-225 **Unit 4:** T104-109, T142-143, T150-151 **Unit 5:** T22-27, T60-61, T68-69, T74-75 **Unit 7:** T104-109, T142-143, T150-151, T156-157, T186-191, T224-225, T232-233, T238-239 **Unit 8:** T22-27, T60-61, T68-69, T75, T186-191 **Unit 9:** T22-29, T60-61, T68-69, T74-75, T104-109, T117, T142-143, T150-151, T156-157 **Unit 10:** T22-29, T62-63, T70-71, T76-77 **LITERATURE BIG BOOKS: Unit 3, Week 3:** *Please Take Me for a Walk* **Unit 4, Week 2:** *What Can You Do with a Paleta?* **Unit 7, Week 3:** *Bear Snores On* **Unit 8, Week 3:** *Bringing Down the Moon* **Unit 9, Week 1:** *Peter's Chair* **Unit 9, Week 2:** *Hen Hears Gossip* **Unit 10, Week 1:** *What's the Big Idea, Molly?* **INTERACTIVE READ-ALOUD CARDS: SS:** "The Ugly Duckling", "Tikki Tikki Tembo" **Unit 1, Week 1:** "The Lion and the Mouse" **Unit 1, Week 2:** "The Tortoise and the Hare" **Unit 3, Week 1:** "The Boy Who Cried Wolf" **Unit 4, Week 1:** "Little Juan and the Cooking Pot" **Unit 7, Week 3:** "Anansi: An African Tale" **Unit 9, Week 2:** "The Little Red Hen"
Craft and Structure		***McGraw-Hill Reading Wonders***
RL.K.4	Ask and answer questions about unknown words in a text.	**READING/WRITING WORKSHOP BIG BOOK: Unit 1, Week 2:** 32-37 **Unit 2, Week 1:** 8-13 **LEVELED READERS: Unit 4, Week 3:** *We Clean!* (A), *Can You Fix It?* (O, ELL), *Helping Mom* (B) **TEACHER'S EDITION: Unit 1:** T74 **Unit 4:** T127, T225, T238 **Unit 6:** T23, T189 **Unit 7:** T45 **Unit 9:** T45 **Unit 10:** T47
RL.K.5	Recognize common types of texts (e.g., storybooks, poems).	**LEVELED READERS: Unit 6, Week 1:** *Ant and Grasshopper* (B) **TEACHER'S EDITION: Unit 1:** T25, T208, T218 **Unit 4:** T126-127 **Unit 5:** T44-45, T54-55 **Unit 6:** T44, T74-75, T186 **Unit 7:** T44-45 **Unit 9:** T44-45, T126 **Unit 10:** T46 **LITERATURE BIG BOOK: Unit 1, Week 3:** *I Smell Springtime* **Unit 5, Week 1:** *Tommy* **Unit 6, Week 1:** *Covers* **Unit 7, Week 1:** *Kitty Caught a Caterpillar* **INTERACTIVE READ-ALOUD CARDS: SS:** "The Ugly Duckling", "Tikki Tikki Tembo" **Unit 1, Week 1:** "The Lion and the Mouse" **Unit 1, Week 2:** "The Tortoise and the Hare" **Unit 2, Week 1:** "Timimoto" **Unit 3, Week 1:** "The Boy Who Cried Wolf" **Unit 4, Week 3:** "A Bundle of Sticks" **Unit 5, Week 2:** "The Pine Tree" **Unit 6, Week 2:** "The Frog and the Locust" **Unit 6, Week 3:** "Rainbow Crow" **Unit 7, Week 3:** "Anansi: An African Tale" **Unit 8, Week 1:** "The King of the Winds" **Unit 9, Week 2:** "The Little Red Hen" **Unit 9, Week 3:** "Spider Woman Teaches the Navajo" **Unit 10, Week 1:** "The Elves and the Shoemakers"
RL.K.6	With prompting and support, name the author and illustrator of a story and define the role of each in telling the story.	**LEVELED READERS: Unit 2, Week 3:** *I See a Bug!* (B) **Unit 4, Week 2:** *Parade Day* (B), *Helping Mom* (B) **Unit 10, Week 1:** *A Good Idea* (B) **TEACHER'S EDITION: Unit 1:** T68, T94, T142 **Unit 2:** T176, T238-239 **Unit 3:** T12, T94, T176 **Unit 4:** T94, T156, T238 **Unit 5:** T12 **Unit 6:** T12, T94, T176 **Unit 7:** T94, T176 **Unit 8:** T12, T176 **Unit 9:** T12, T94-95 **Unit 10:** T12, T76, T96 **LITERATURE BIG BOOKS: Unit 1, Week 1:** *What About Bear?* **Unit 1, Week 2:** *Pouch!* **Unit 2, Week 3:** *I Love Bugs!* **Unit 3, Week 1:** *How Do Dinosaurs Go to School?* **Unit 5, Week 1:** *My Garden* **Unit 6, Week 2:** *Rain* **Unit 7, Week 2:** *The Birthday Pet* **Unit 8, Week 1:** *When Daddy's Truck Picks Me Up* **Unit 9, Week 2:** *Hen Hears Gossip* **Unit 10, Week 1:** *What's the Big Idea, Molly?* **READING WORKSTATION ACTIVITY CARDS:** 6

Reading Standards for Literature

Integration of Knowledge and Ideas		McGraw-Hill Reading Wonders
RL.K.7	With prompting and support, describe the relationship between illustrations and the story in which they appear (e.g., what moment in a story an illustration depicts).	**LEVELED READERS:** Unit 5, Week 1: *My Garden Grows* (O, ELL) **Unit 5, Week 3:** *Farm Fresh Finn* (B) **Unit 6, Week 1:** *It Is Hot!* **Unit 7, Week 3:** *Bird's New Home* (B) **READING WORKSTATION ACTIVITY CARDS:** 1, 4, 11 **TEACHER'S EDITION: Unit 1:** T25, T60-61, T108 **Unit 3:** T24, T60-T61, T68-T69 **Unit 5:** T22-27, T68-69, T238-239 **Unit 6:** T25, T60-61, T105, T188 **Unit 7:** T238-239 **Unit 8:** T25 **Unit 10:** T46-47 **LITERATURE BIG BOOKS: Unit 1, Week 1:** *What About Bear?* **Unit 2, Week 3:** *I Love Bugs!* **Unit 3, Week 1:** *How Do Dinosaurs Go to School?* **Unit 3, Week 2:** *Clang! Clang! Beep! Beep! Listen to the City* **Unit 5, Week 1:** *My Garden* **Unit 6, Week 3:** *Waiting Out the Storm* **Unit 8, Week 1:** *When Daddy's Truck Picks Me Up* **Unit 9, Week 1:** *The Clean Up!* **Unit 10, Week 1:** *The Variety Show* **Unit 10, Week 2:** *All Kinds of Families!* **INTERACTIVE READ-ALOUD CARDS: Unit 5, Week 2:** "The Pine Tree" **Unit 6, Week 2:** "The Frog and the Locust" **Unit 6, Week 3:** "Rainbow Crow"
RL.K.8	(Not applicable to literature.)	
RL.K.9	With prompting and support, compare and contrast the adventures and experiences of characters in familiar stories.	**LEVELED READERS: Unit 3, Week 1:** *Go, Nat!* (O, ELL) **READING WORKSTATION ACTIVITY CARD:** 15 **TEACHER'S EDITION: Unit 1:** S27, S51, S75, T35, T117, T136 **Unit 2:** T218-219 **Unit 3:** T35, T136, T218-219 **Unit 4:** T136-137 **Unit 6:** T54, T117, T136, T199, T218 **Unit 7:** T136-137, T199, T218 **Unit 8:** T35, T54, T218 **Unit 9:** T54, T117, T136 **Unit 10:** T37, T56, T138 **LITERATURE BIG BOOKS: Unit 1, Week 1:** *What About Bear?* **Unit 1, Week 2:** *Pouch!, Baby Animals on the Move* **INTERACTIVE READ-ALOUD CARDS: Unit 1, Week 1:** "The Lion and the Mouse" **Unit 1, Week 2:** "The Tortoise and the Hare" **Unit 2, Week 1:** "Timimoto" **Unit 7, Week 3:** "Anansi: An African Tale" **Unit 8, Week 1:** "The King of the Winds" **Unit 10, Week 1:** "The Elves and the Shoemakers"
Range of Reading and Level of Text Complexity		***McGraw-Hill Reading Wonders***
RL.K.10	Actively engage in group reading activities with purpose and understanding.	**READING/WRITING WORKSHOP BIG BOOKS: SS:** 36-41 **Unit 1:** 34-39, 46-51 **Unit 2:** 10-15, 28-33, 34-39 **Unit 3:** 10-15, 28-33, 46-51 **Unit 4:** 24-31, 38-45 **Unit 5:** 10-17, 38-45 **Unit 6:** 24-31, 38-45 **Unit 7:** 24-31, 38-45 **Unit 8:** 10-17, 24-31 **Unit 9:** 10-17, 24-31 **Unit 10:** 10-17, 24-31 **LEVELED READERS: Unit 5, Week 1:** *My Garden Grows* (ELL) **Unit 7, Week 2:** *Their Pets* (ELL) **Unit 7, Week 3:** *A New Home* (ELL) **TEACHER'S EDITION: Unit 1:** S12, S14, S17, S22, S24, S31, S36, S38, S41, S46, S48, S55, S62, S65, S70, S72, T22-27, T126-127 **Unit 2:** T30-31, T112-113, T130-131 **Unit 3:** T34-35, T94-95, T212-213 **Unit 4:** T112-113, T126-127, T130-131, T194-195, T199 **Unit 5:** T12-13, T48-49, T78-79, T117, T194-195 **Unit 6:** T12-13, T22-26, T94-95, T104-108, T117, T130-131, T176-177, T186-190, T194-195, T199 **Unit 7:** T112-113, T130-131, T160-161, T176-177, T194-195, T199, T212-213, T242-243 **Unit 8:** T12-13, T30-31, T34-35, T48-49, T112-113, T176-177, T212-213 **Unit 9:** T12-13, T30-31, T48-49, T94-95, T112-113, T117, T199, T212-213 **Unit 10:** T12-13, T32-33, T50-51, T96-97, T132-133 **INTERACTIVE READ-ALOUD CARDS: SS:** "The Ugly Duckling", "Tikki Tikki Tembo" **Unit 1, Week 1:** "The Lion and the Mouse" **Unit 1, Week 2:** "The Tortoise and the Hare" **Unit 3, Week 2:** "The Turtle and the Flute" **Unit 4, Week 1:** "Little Juan and the Cooking Pot" **Unit 4, Week 3:** "A Bundle of Sticks" **Unit 5, Week 2:** "The Pine Tree" **Unit 6, Week 2:** "The Frog and the Locust" **Unit 6, Week 3:** "Rainbow Crow" **Unit 7, Week 3:** "Anansi: An African Tale" **Unit 8, Week 1:** "The King of the Winds" **Unit 9, Week 2:** "The Little Red Hen" **Unit 9, Week 3:** "Spider Woman Teaches the Navajo" **Unit 10, Week 1:** "The Elves and the Shoemakers"

Reading Standards for Informational Text

Key Ideas and Details		McGraw-Hill Reading Wonders
RI.K.1	With prompting and support, ask and answer questions about key details in a text.	**READING/WRITING WORKSHOP BIG BOOKS:** Unit 2: 14-19 **LEVELED READERS: Unit 1, Week 3:** *The Beach* (A), *At School* (O), *See It Grow!* (B) **Unit 2, Week 1:** *We Need Tools* (A), *A Trip* (O), *What Can You See?* (B) **Unit 2, Week 2:** *Shapes!* (A), *Play with Shapes!* (O), *Use a Shape!* (B) **Unit 4, Week 1:** *You Cook* (A), *On the Job* (O), *The Neighborhood* (B) **Unit 8, Week 2:** *See This!* (A), *Places to See* (O), *My Trip to Yellowstone* (B) **Unit 9, Week 3:** *Look Where It Is From* (A), *What's for Breakfast?* (O), *Nature at the Craft Fair* (B) **Unit 10, Week 3:** *Help Clean Up* (A), *Let's Save Earth* (O), *Babysitters for Seals* (B) **YOUR TURN PRACTICE BOOK:** 53, 147 **READING WORKSTATION ACTIVITY CARDS:** 1 **TEACHER'S EDITION: Unit 1:** T126-127, T186-191, T225, **Unit 2:** T22-27, T44-45, T107 **Unit 4:** T22-27, T44-45, T61, T69, T75, T186-191, T208-209 **Unit 5:** T104-109, T151, T157, T186-191, T209 **Unit 6:** T23-26, T105-108, T187-188 **Unit 7:** T23, T25 **Unit 8:** T104-109, T126-127, T142-143, T151, T157, T209 **Unit 9:** T35, T127, T186-191 **Unit 10:** T188-193, T227, T241 **LITERATURE BIG BOOKS: Unit 1, Week 2:** *Baby Animals on the Move* **Unit 1, Week 3:** *Senses at the Seashore* **Unit 2, Week 1:** *The Handiest Things in the World, Discover with Tools* **Unit 4, Week 1:** *Whose Shoes?"A Shoe for Every Job"* **Unit 4, Week 3:** *Roadwork* **Unit 5, Week 2:** *A Grand Old Tree* **Unit 5, Week 3:** *An Orange in January* **Unit 7, Week 1:** *ZooBorns!* **Unit 9, Week 3:** *Bread Comes to Life* **Unit 10, Week 3:** *Panda Kindergarten* **INTERACTIVE READ-ALOUD CARDS: SS:** "Kindergarteners Can!" **Unit 1, Week 3:** "A Feast of the Senses" **Unit 2, Week 3:** "From Caterpillar to Butterfly" **Unit 4, Week 2:** "Cultural Festivals" **Unit 9, Week 1:** "Helping Out at Home" **Unit 10, Week 2:** "The Perfect Color"
RI.K.2	With prompting and support, identify the main topic and retell key details of a text.	**LEVELED READERS: Unit 1, Week 3:** *The Beach* (A), *At School* (O, ELL), *See It Grow!* (B) **Unit 2, Week 1:** *We Need Tools* (A), *A Trip* (O, ELL), *What Can You See?* (B) **Unit 5, Week 2:** *The Tree* (A), *Many Trees* (O, ELL), *Our Apple Tree* (B) **Unit 5, Week 3:** *The Farmers' Market* (A), *Let's Make a Salad!* (O, ELL) **Unit 9, Week 3:** *Look Where It Is From* (A) **READING WORKSTATION ACTIVITY CARDS:** 5 **TEACHER'S EDITION: Unit 4:** T191 **Unit 5:** T104-109, T126-127, T142-143, T150-151, T156-157, T186-T190, T208-209, T224-225 **Unit 8:** T104-109, T127, T160-161, T248-249 **Unit 9:** T127, T186-191, T224-225, T232-233, T248-249 **Unit 10:** T188-193, T211, T226-227, T240-241, T250-251 **LITERATURE BIG BOOKS: Unit 1, Week 3:** *Senses on the Seashore* **Unit 5, Week 2:** *A Grand Old Tree,* "From a Seed to a Tree" **Unit 5, Week 3:** *An Orange in January* **Unit 8, Week 2:** *Ana Goes to Washington, D.C.* **Unit 9, Week 3:** *Bread Comes to Life* **Unit 10, Week 3:** *Panda Kindergarten* **INTERACTIVE READ-ALOUD CARDS: Unit 1, Week 3:** "A Feast of the Senses" **Unit 2, Week 3:** "From Caterpillar to Butterfly" **Unit 4, Week 2:** "Cultural Festivals" **Unit 9, Week 1:** "Helping Out at Home" **Unit 10, Week 2:** "The Perfect Color"
RI.K.3	With prompting and support, describe the connection between two individuals, events, ideas, or pieces of information in a text.	**LEVELED READERS: Unit 7:** *Two Cubs* (A), *Animal Bodies* (O, ELL), *Two Kinds of Bears* (B); **Unit 9:** *Look Where It is From* (A), *What's for Breakfast?* (O, ELL) **READING WORKSTATION ACTIVITY CARDS:** 8, 9 **TEACHER'S EDITION: Unit 6:** T24, T25, T106 **Unit 7:** T22-26, T60-61, T68-69, T74-75, T208-209 **Unit 8:** T44-45, T95 **LITERATURE BIG BOOKS: Unit 2, Week 2:** *Shapes All Around* **Unit 7, Week 1:** *ZooBorns!* **Unit 7, Week 3:** "Animal Homes" **Unit 8, Week 1:** *Getting from Here to There* **Unit 8, Week 2:** *Ana Goes to Washington, D.C.* **Unit 9, Week 3:** *Bread Comes to Life* **INTERACTIVE READ-ALOUD CARDS: Unit 2, Week 3:** "From Caterpillar to Butterfly" **Unit 6, Week 1:** "A Tour of the Seasons" **Unit 8, Week 2:** "The Best of the West" **Unit 9, Week 1:** "Helping Out at Home" **Unit 10, Week 3:** "Protect the Environment"
Craft and Structure		**McGraw-Hill Reading Wonders**
RI.K.4	With prompting and support, ask and answer questions about unknown words in a text.	**LEVELED READERS: Unit 1, Week 3:** *At School* (O, ELL), *See It Grow!* (B) **Unit 2, Week 1:** *A Trip* (O, ELL) **Unit 4, Week 1:** *You Cook* (A), *On the Job* (O, ELL) **Unit 5, Week 2:** *The Tree* (A) **Unit 5, Week 3:** *The Farmers' Market* (A) **Unit 7, Week 1:** *Animal Bodies* (O, ELL) **Unit 9, Week 3:** *Nature at the Craft Fair* (B) **Unit 10, Week 3:** *Let's Save Earth* (O, ELL), *Babysitters for Seals* (B) **TEACHER'S EDITION: Unit 4:** T127 **Unit 5:** T107 **Unit 7:** T209 **Unit 8:** T127, T209 **Unit 10:** T234
RI.K.5	Identify the front cover, back cover, and title page of a book.	**READING/WRITING WORKSHOP: Unit 1:** 8-13, 26-31, 44-49 **Unit 2:** 8-13, 26-31, 44-49 **Unit 3:** 8-13, 26-31, 44-49 **Unit 4:** 8-15, 22-29, 36-43 **LEVELED READERS: Unit 10, Week 3:** *Help Clean Up* (A) **TEACHER'S EDITION: Unit 1:** T30-31, T176 **Unit 4:** T12 **Unit 5:** T94, T176, T232 **Unit 7:** T12, T60, T68, T74, T94 **Unit 8:** T87, T94 **Unit 9:** T176 **Unit 10:** T178, T226 **LITERATURE BIG BOOKS: Unit 1, Week 3:** *Senses at the Seashore* **Unit 2, Week 1:** *The Handiest Things in the World* **Unit 4, Week 1:** *Whose Shoes? A Shoe for Every Job*

Reading Standards for Informational Text

Craft and Structure		McGraw-Hill Reading Wonders
RI.K.6	Name the author and illustrator of a text and define the role of each in presenting the ideas or information in a text.	**LEVELED READERS:** **Unit 5, Week 3:** *Let's Make a Salad!* (O, ELL), **Unit 7, Week 1:** *Two Cubs* (A), *Animal Bodies* (O, ELL), *Two Kinds of Bears* (B) **READING WORKSTATION ACTIVITY CARDS:** 12 **TEACHER'S EDITION:** **Unit 1:** T176 **Unit 2:** T12 **Unit 4:** T12 **Unit 5:** T94, T176, T232 **Unit 6:** T12, T94, T176 **Unit 7:** T12, T60, T68, T74, T94 **Unit 8:** T94 **Unit 9:** T176 **Unit 10:** T178 **LITERATURE BIG BOOKS:** **Unit 1, Week 3:** *Senses at the Seashore* **Unit 2, Week 1:** *The Handiest Things in the World* **Unit 2, Week 2:** *Shapes All Around* **Unit 8, Week 2:** *Ana Goes to Washington, D.C.* **Unit 9, Week 3:** *Bread Comes to Life*
Integration of Knowledge and Ideas		***McGraw-Hill Reading Wonders***
RI.K.7	With prompting and support, describe the relationship between illustrations and the text in which they appear (e.g., what person, place, thing, or idea in the text an illustration depicts).	**READING/WRITING WORKSHOP BIG BOOK:** **Unit 2, Week 1:** 14-19 **LEVELED READERS:** **Unit 1, Week 3:** *The Beach* (A) **Unit 2, Week 1:** *We Need Tools* (A) **Unit 2, Week 2:** *Shapes!* (A), *Play with Shapes!* (O, ELL), *Use a Shape!* (B) **Unit 9, Week 3:** *What's for Breakfast?* (O, ELL) **READING WORKSTATION ACTIVITY CARDS:** 1 **TEACHER'S EDITION:** **Unit 1:** T126-T127, T186-191, T224-225 **Unit 2:** T24, T60-61, T124-T127, 143 **Unit 3:** T45, 127, T208-209 **Unit 4:** T22-27 **Unit 6:** T126-127, T209 **Unit 9:** T208-209, T232-233 **Unit 10:** T190, T244-245 **LITERATURE BIG BOOKS:** **Unit 1, Week 3:** *Senses at the Seashore*, pp. 4-34 **Unit 2, Week 1:** *The Handiest Things in the World* **Unit 2, Week 2:** *Shapes All Around* **Unit 3, Week 2:** *Sounds Are Everywhere* **Unit 3, Week 3:** *A Neighborhood* **Unit 4, Week 1:** *Whose Shoes? A Shoe for Every Job* **Unit 6, Week 2:** *Cloud Watch* **Unit 9, Week 3:** *Nature's Artists* **INTERACTIVE READ-ALOUD CARDS:** **Unit 3, Week 3:** "Field Trips" **Unit 6, Week 1:** "A Tour of the Seasons" **Unit 9, Week 1:** "Helping Out at Home"
RI.K.8	With prompting and support, identify the reasons an author gives to support points in a text.	**READING WORKSTATION ACTIVITY CARDS:** 12 **TEACHER'S EDITION:** **Unit 2:** T26, T108 **Unit 4:** T26, T190 **Unit 5:** T108, T190 **Unit 8:** T108 **Unit 9:** T190 **Unit 10:** T210-211 **LITERATURE BIG BOOKS:** **Unit 1, Week 3:** *Senses at the Seashore* **Unit 2, Week 1:** *The Handiest Things in the World* **Unit 2, Week 2:** *Shapes All Around* **Unit 4, Week 1:** *Whose Shoes? A Shoe for Every Job* **Unit 4, Week 3:** *Roadwork* **Unit 5, Week 2:** *A Grand Old Tree* **Unit 5, Week 3:** *An Orange in January* **Unit 8, Week 2:** *Ana Goes to Washington, D.C.* **Unit 9, Week 3:** *Bread Comes to Life* **Unit 10, Week 3:** *Save Big Blue!*
RI.K.9	With prompting and support, identify basic similarities in and differences between two texts on the same topic (e.g., in illustrations, descriptions, or procedures).	**READING/WRITING WORKSHOP BIG BOOK:** **Unit 1, Week 3:** A Feast of the Senses **READING WORKSTATION ACTIVITY CARDS:** 16 **TEACHERS EDITION:** **Unit 1:** T199 **Unit 2:** T54-55, T117, T126-127 **Unit 4:** T116-117, T218-219 **Unit 5:** T136-137, T198-199, T208-209, T218-219 **Unit 7:** T35, T54, T117 **Unit 8:** T136 **Unit 9:** T218 **Unit 10:** T128-129, T201, T220 **LITERATURE BIG BOOKS:** **Unit 1, Week 3:** *Senses at the Seashore* **Unit 2, Week 1:** *The Handiest Things in the World* **Unit 2, Week 2:** *Shapes All Around,* "Find the Shapes" **Unit 5, Week 3:** *An Orange in January,* "Farmers' Market" **Unit 10, Week 2:** *Good For You* **INTERACTIVE READ-ALOUD CARDS:** **Unit 1, Week 3:** "A Feast of the Senses" **Unit 2, Week 2:** "Kites in Flight" **Unit 5, Week 3:** "Farms Around the World" **Unit 7, Week 1:** "Baby Farm Animals" **Unit 7, Week 2:** "The Family Pet" **Unit 10, Week 3:** "Protect the Environment!"
Range of Reading and Level of Text Complexity		***McGraw-Hill Reading Wonders***
RI.K.10	Actively engage in group reading activities with purpose and understanding.	**READING/WRITING WORKSHOP BIG BOOKS:** **Start Smart:** 18-23, 53-58 **Unit 1:** 10-15, 28-33, 52-57 **Unit 2:** 16-21, 52-57 **Unit 3:** 34-39, 52-57 **Unit 4:** 10-17 **Unit 5:** 24-31 **Unit 6:** 10-17 **Unit 7:** 10-17 **Unit 8:** 38-45 **Unit 9:** 38-45 **Unit 10:** 38-45 **LEVELED READERS:** **Unit 5, Week 2:** *Many Trees* (ELL) **TEACHER'S EDITION:** **Unit 1:** S60, T112-113, T126-127, T199 **Unit 2:** T22-27, T44-45, T74-75, T186-191 **Unit 3:** T126-127, T198-199, T212-213 **Unit 4:** T12-13, T30-31, T116-117, T176-177 **Unit 5:** T34-35, T92-95, T160-161, T174-177, T198-199 **Unit 6:** T35, T126-127, T208-209 **Unit 7:** T12-13, T22-27, T30-31, T34-35, T48-49, T116-117 **Unit 8:** T94-95, T116-117 **Unit 9:** T34-35, T176-177, T194-195, T208-209 **Unit 10:** T118-119, T178-179, T201 **INTERACTIVE READ-ALOUD CARDS:** **SS:** "Kindergarteners Can!" **Unit 1, Week 3:** "A Feast of the Senses" **Unit 2, Week 3:** "From Caterpillar to Butterfly" **Unit 3, Week 3:** "Field Trips" **Unit 4, Week 2:** "Cultural Festivals" **Unit 5, Week 1:** "Growing Plants" **Unit 5, Week 3:** "Farms Around the World" **Unit 6, Week 1:** "A Tour of the Seasons" **Unit 7, Week 1:** "Baby Farm Animals" **Unit 7, Week 2:** "The Family Pet" **Unit 8, Week 2:** "The Best of the West" **Unit 8, Week 3:** "A View from the Moon" **Unit 9, Week 1:** "Helping Out at Home" **Unit 10, Week 2:** "The Perfect Color" **Unit 10, Week 3:** "Protect the Environment"

Reading Standards for Foundational Skills

These standards are directed toward fostering students' understanding and working knowledge of concepts of print, the alphabetic principle, and other basic conventions of the English writing system. These foundational skills are not an end in and of themselves; rather, they are necessary and important components of an effective, comprehensive reading program designed to develop proficient readers with the capacity to comprehend texts across a range of types and disciplines. Instruction should be differentiated: good readers will need much less practice with these concepts than struggling readers will. The point is to teach students what they need to learn and not what they already know—to discern when particular children or activities warrant more or less attention.
Note: In Kidergarten, children are expected to demonstrate increasing awareness and competence in the areas that follow.

Print Concepts		***McGraw-Hill Reading Wonders***
RF.K.1	Demonstrate understanding of the organization and basic features of print.	**TEACHER'S EDITION: Unit 1:** S10, S18, S23, S28, S29, S32, S37, S39, S42, S43, S47, S52, S53, S56, S61, S62, S63, S66, S71, S77, T12, T15, T16, T60, T97, T98, T180, T189, T192 **Unit 2:** T12, T15, T30, T97, T112, T179, T180, T212, T224 **Unit 3:** T15, T26, T94, T97, T106,T112, T130, T142, T176, T179, T211, T232 **Unit 4:** T12, T15, T23, T30, T47, T48, T60, T68, T94, T97, T105, T108, T112, T129, T130, T142, T150, T179, T187, T194, T211, T212, T224 **Unit 5:** T12, T15, T30, T47, T48, T60, T68, T94, T97, T112, T129, T130, T142, T150, T176, T179, T211, T212, T224, T232 **Unit 6:** T12, T15, T29, T37, T47, T97, T129, T179, T211 **Unit 7:** T15, T16, T47, T94, T97, T98, T129, T150, T176, T179, T180, T211, T212, T232 **Unit 8:** T12, T15, T47, T48, T68, T94, T97, T129, T142, T179 **Unit 9:** T12, T15, T25, T47, T60, T94, T97, T129, T142, T176, T179, T211 **Unit 10:** T12, T15, T49, T62, T96, T97, T13, T144, T178, T179, T213
RF.K.1a	Follow words from left to right, top to bottom, and page by page.	**READING/WRITING WORKSHOP:** Start Smart: 4-5, 22-23, 40-41 **LITERATURE BIG BOOK:** Start Smart, Week 3: *ABC Big Book* **Unit 4, Week 2:** *What Can You Do With a Paleta?* **TEACHER'S EDITION: Unit 1:** S10, S62, T12, T60, T189 **Unit 2:** T30, T112, T224 **Unit 3:** T26, T94, T176 **Unit 4:** T12, T23, T30, T48, T60, T68, T94, T105, T108, T112, T130, T142, T150, T187, T194, T212, T224 **Unit 5:** T68, T94, T112, T130, T142, T150, T176, T212, T224, T232 **Unit 6:** T12 **Unit 7:** T94, T150 **Unit 8:** T12, T68, T94, T142 **Unit 9:** T12, T25, T60, T94, T142 **Unit 10:** T12, T62, T96, T144, T178
RF.K.1b	Recognize that spoken words are represented in written language by specific sequences of letters.	**TEACHER'S EDITION: Unit 1:** S39, S63 **Unit 2:** T212 **Unit 3:** T47-129, T211 **Unit 4:** T47, T129, T211 **Unit 5:** T47, T129, T211 **Unit 6:** T29, T37, T47, T129, T211 **Unit 7:** T47, T129, T176, T211, T212 **Unit 8:** T47, T48, T129, T211 **Unit 9:** T47, T129, T176, T211 **Unit 10:** T49, T131, T213
RF.K.1c	Understand that words are separated by spaces in print.	**TEACHER'S EDITION: Unit 1:** S29, S39, S43, S53, S63, S77 **Unit 2:** T12, T180 **Unit 3:** T94, T106, T112, T130, T142, T232 **Unit 5:** T12, T30, T48, T60, T94 **Unit 7:** T232
RF.K.1d	Recognize and name all upper- and lowercase letters of the alphabet.	**YOUR TURN PRACTICE BOOK:** 3, 7, 8, 11, 15, 16, 20, 24, 34, 42, 50, 58, 66, 84, 92, 100, 108, 116, 134, 142, 143-144, 162, 172, 192, 202, 212, 222, 232 **TEACHER'S EDITION: Unit 1:** S23, S18, S23, S28, S32, S37, S42, S47, S52, S56, S61, S66, S71, T15, T16, T97, T98, T180, T192 **Unit 2:** T15, T97, T179 **Unit 3:** T15, T97, T179 **Unit 4:** T15, T97, T179 **Unit 5:** T15, T97, T179 **Unit 6:** T15, T97, T179 **Unit 7:** T15, T16, T97, T98, T179, T180 **Unit 8:** T15, T97, T179 **Unit 9:** T15, T97, T179 **Unit 10:** T15, T97, T179
Phonological Awareness		***McGraw-Hill Reading Wonders***
RF.K.2	Demonstrate understanding of spoken words, syllables, and sounds (phonemes).	**TEACHER'S EDITION: Unit 1:** S13, S18, S23, S42, S47, S52, S56, S61, S66, S71, T14, T36, T102, T118, T124, T184, T206 **Unit 2:** T14, T20, T42, T70, T96, T102, T124, T144, T178, T184, T206, T210, T226 **Unit 3:** T20, T36, T42, T62, T96, T102, T118, T124, T144, T184, T206, T226 **Unit 4:** T20, T28, T42, T56, T62, T70, T102, T118, T128, T138, T145, T152, T184,T192, T200, T206, T210, T220, T226 **Unit 5:** T14, T20, T28, T36, T42, T62, T63, T72, T102, T110, T118, T124, T138, T144, T145, T152, T184, T192, T206, T210, T226, T227, T234 **Unit 6:** T20, T28, T36, T42, T46, T56, T62,T63, T70, T102, T124, T138, T144, T152, T154, T184, T192, T206, T210, T220, T227, T234 **Unit 7:** T20, T28, T36, T42, T46, T62, T102, T110, T118, T124, T128, T138, T144, T145, T178, T184, T206, T210, T220,T226, T234 **Unit 8:** T20, T28, T42,T46, T56, T62, T63, T102, T110, T118, T124, T128, T138, T144, T145, T152, T184, T200, T206, T226, T227, T234 **Unit 9:** T14, T20, T42, T62, T102, T124, T144, T184, T206, T210, T220, T226, T227, T234 **Unit 10:** T20, T44, T48, T58, T64, T72, T104, T126, T130, T140, T146, T147, T154, T212, T222, T229, T236
RF.K.2a	Recognize and produce rhyming words.	**LITERATURE BIG BOOKS:** Start Smart, Weeks 1-3: *Big Book of Rhymes* **TEACHER'S EDITION: Unit 1:** S23, S42, S47, S52, T102, T124 **Unit 2:** T210 **Unit 3:** T20, T42, T62 **Unit 4:** T184, T206, T226 **Unit 5:** T184, T206, T226 **Unit 6:** T102, T124, T144 **Unit 7:** T102, T124, T144 **Unit 8:** T102, T124, T144 **Unit 9:** T102, T124, T144
RF.K.2b	Count, pronounce, blend, and segment syllables in spoken words.	**LITERATURE BIG BOOK:** Smart Start, Week 3: *Big Book of Rhymes* **TEACHER'S EDITION: Unit 1:** S56, S61, S66, S71 **Unit 2:** T184, T206, T226 **Unit 3:** T184, T206, T226 **Unit 5:** T20, T42, T62 **Unit 9:** T20, T42, T62, T184, T206, T226 **Unit 10:** T20, T44, T64

Reading Standards for Foundational Skills

Phonological Awareness		*McGraw-Hill Reading Wonders*
RF.K.2c	Blend and segment onsets and rimes of single-syllable spoken words.	**YOUR TURN PRACTICE BOOK:** 88, 96, 104, 112, 124, 130, 138, 148, 158, 168, 182, 183, 188, 198, 208, 228, 242, 243, 248, 256, 264, 272, 280, 293 **TEACHER'S EDITION:** **Unit 1:** T184, T206 **Unit 2:** T102, T124, T144 **Unit 3:** T102, T124, T144 **Unit 4:** T20, T42, T62 **Unit 5:** T102, T124, T144 **Unit 6:** T20, T42, T62 **Unit 7:** T20, T42, T62, T184, T206, T226 **Unit 8:** T20, T42, T62, T184, T206, T226 **Unit 10:** T104, T126, T146
RF.K.2d	Isolate and pronounce the initial, medial vowel, and final sounds (phonemes) in in three-phoneme (consonant-vowel-consonant, or CVC) words. (This does not include CVCs ending with /l/, /r/, or /x/.)	**YOUR TURN PRACTICE BOOK:** 80, 193 **TEACHER'S EDITION:** **Unit 1:** T14, T36, T118 **Unit 2:** T14, T70, T96, T178 **Unit 3:** T36, T96, T118 **Unit 4:** T28, T70, T110, T118, T128, T138, T145, T152, T192, T200, T210, T220 **Unit 5:** T14, T28, T36, T63, T72, T110, T118, T138, T145, T152, T192 **Unit 6:** T28, T36, T46, T56, T62, T63, T70, T138, T152, T154, T184, T192, T206 **Unit 7:** T28, T36, T110, T118, T178 **Unit 8:** T28, T46, T56, T63, T110, T118, T145, T152
RF.K.2e	Add or substitute individual sounds (phonemes) in simple, one-syllable words to make new words.	**TEACHER'S EDITION:** **Unit 5:** T210, T220, T227, T234 **Unit 6:** T210, T220, T227, T234 **Unit 7:** T128, T138, T145, T152, T210, T220, T227, T234 **Unit 8:** T128, T138, T145, T152, T200, T227, T234 **Unit 9:** T210, T220, T227, T234 **Unit 10:** T48, T58, T72, T130, T140, T147, T154, T212, T222, T229, T236
Phonics and Word Recognition		***McGraw-Hill Reading Wonders***
RF.K.3	Know and apply grade-level phonics and word analysis skills in decoding words.	**TEACHER'S EDITION:** **Unit 1:** S19, S43, S67, T28, T29, T97, T105, T121, T179, T181, T210, T211, T220, T245 **Unit 2:** T15, T39, T46, T97, T128-129, T179, T203, T221 **Unit 3:** T15, T38, T39, T46, T56, T97, T110, T111, T128, T179, T181, T210 **Unit 4:** T15, T17, T28-29, T30-31, T37 , T39, T46, T47, T48-49, T57, T66, T73, T76, T81, T97, T99, T110, T111, T112-113, T121, T128, T129, T130-131, T139, T148, T155, T158, T163, T179, T181, T193, T194-195, T203, T210, T211, T212-213, T221, T230, T237, T240, T245 **Unit 5:** T14, T17, T28, T29, T30-31, T36, T39, T47, T48-49,T56, T57, T66, T73, T76, T81, T99, T110-111, T112-113, T118, T119, T121, T128, T129, T130-131, T138, T139, T146, T148, T153,T155, T158, T163, T181, T192, T193, T194-195, T200, T203, T210, T211, T212-213, T220, T221, T228, T230, T237, T240, T245 **Unit 6:** T15, T17, T29, T30-31, T39, T46, T47, T48-49, T57, T66, T73, T81, T97, T99, T111, T112-113, T121, T128, T129, T130-131, T139, T148, T155, T158, T163, T178, T179, T181, T193, T194-195, T201, T203, T210, T212-213, T221, T230, T237, T240, T245 **Unit 7:** T15, T17, T28-29, T30-31, T37, T46, T47, T48-49, T56, T57, T64, T65, T66, T73, T76, T81, T96, T97, T99, T110, T112-113, T119, T121, T128, T129, T130-131, T139, T146, T148, T155, T158, T163, T178, T179, T181, T192, T193, T194-195, T201, T203, T210, T211, T212-213, T220, T221, T230, T237, T240, T245 **Unit 8:** T15, T17, T29, T30-31, T39, T46, T47, T48-49, T57, T66, T73, T76, T81, T97, T99, T111, T112-113, T121, T128, T129, T130-131, T139, T148, T155, T158, T163, T179, T181, T193, T194-195, T201, T203, T210, T211, T212-213, T220, T221, T230, T237, T240, T245 **Unit 9:** T15, T17, T29, T30-31, T37, T39, T46, T47, T48-49, T56, T57, T64, T65, T66, T71, 72, T73, T76, T81, T97, T99, T110-111, T112-113, T119, T120, T121, T128, T129, T130-131, T138, T139, T146, T147,T148, T153, T154, T155, T158, T163, T179, T181, T192-193, T194-195, T201, T202, T203, T210, T211, T212-213, T220, T221, T228, T229, T230, T235, T236, T237, T240, T245 **Unit 10:** T15, T17, T30-31, T32-33, T39, T40, T41, T48, T49, T50-51, T58, T59, T66, T67, T68, T74, T75,T83, T97, T99, T101, T110, T112-113, T114-115, T121, T123, T130, T131, T140, T141, T148, T149, T150, T156, T157, T160, T165, T179, T181, T182, T183, T191, T194-195, T196-197, T203, T204, T205, T212-213, T222, T223, T230, T231, T232, T238, T239, T242, T247
RF.K.3a	Demonstrate basic knowledge of one-to-one letter-sound correspondences by producing the primary or many of the most frequent sounds for each consonant.	**PHONICS/WORD STUDY WORKSTATION ACTIVITY CARDS:** 1, 2, 3, 4, 5, 6, 7, 8, 9, 10, 11, 12, 13, 14, 15, 16, 17, 18, 19, 20, 21, 22, 23, 24 **TEACHER'S EDITION:** **Unit 1:** T28, T179, T210, T220 **Unit 2:** T15, T97, T179 **Unit 3:** T97, T110, T179 **Unit 4:** T97, T110, T179 **Unit 5:** T14, T28, T36, T56, T118, T138, T192, T200, T220, T228 **Unit 6:** T15, T97, T179 **Unit 7:** T56, T96, T97, T110, T146, T178, T179, T192, T220 **Unit 8:** T15, T97, T179 **Unit 10:** T97, T110, T179

Reading Standards for Foundational Skills

Phonics and Word Recognition		*McGraw-Hill Reading Wonders*
RF.K.3b	Associate the long and short sounds with the common spellings (graphemes) for the five major vowels.	**YOUR TURN PRACTICE BOOK:** 36, 62, 101-102, 135-136, 138, 246, 248, 254, 256, 262, 264, 270, 278 **PHONICS/WORD STUDY WORKSTATION ACTIVITY CARDS:** 2, 7, 10, 14, 19, 25, 26, 27, 28, 29, 30 **TEACHER'S EDITION: Unit 1:** T97, T105 **Unit 2:** T46, T128–T129, T221 **Unit 3:** T15, T38, T56 **Unit 4:** T15, T28-29, T37 **Unit 5:** T110-111, T119, T146, T153 **Unit 6:** T193, T201, T211 **Unit 7:** T15, T28-29, T37, T46, T64, T65, T119, T201 **Unit 8:** T201, T220 **Unit 9:** T15, T29, T37, T56, T64, T65, T71, 72, T76, T97, T110-111, T119, T120, T138, T146, T147, T153, T154, T179, T192-193, T201, T202, T220, T228, T229, T235, T236 **Unit 10:** T15, T30-31, T39, T40, T58, T66, T67, T74, T99, T112-113, T121, T140, T148, T149, T156, T181, T182, T191, T194-195, T203, T204, T222, T230, T231, T238
Phonological Awareness		***McGraw-Hill Reading Wonders***
RF.K.3c	Read common high-frequency words by sight (e.g., *the, of, to, you, she, my, is, are, do, does*).	**READING/WRITING WORKSHOP:** Start Smart: 9, 16-22, 27 **Unit 1:** 7-13, 14-19, 25-31 **Unit 2:** 7-13, 14-19, 25-31 **Unit 3:** 7-13, 25-31, 32-37 **Unit 4:** 7-15, 21-29, 35-43 **Unit 5:** 7-15, 21-29, 35-43 **Unit 6:** 7-15, 21-29, 35-43 **Unit 7:** 7-15, 21-29, 35-43 **Unit 8:** 7-15, 21-29, 35-43 **Unit 9:** 7-15, 21-29, 35-43 **Unit 10:** 7-15, 21-29, 35-43 **YOUR TURN PRACTICE BOOK:** 4, 9-10, 12, 17-18, 21, 25-26], 31-32, 39-40, 47-48, 55-56, 63-64, 71-72, 89-90, 97-98, 105-106, 113-114,121-122, 131-132, 139-140, 149-150, 159-160, 169-170, 179-180, 189-190, 199-200, 209-210, 219-220, 229-230, 239-240, 249-250, 257-258, 265-266, 273-274, 281-282, 291-292 **TEACHER'S EDITION: Unit 1:** S19, S43, S67, T29, T121, T181, T211, T245 **Unit 2:** T39, T129, T203 **Unit 3:** T39, T111, T181 **Unit 4:** T17, T29, T30-31, T39, T47, T48-49, T57, T66, T73, T76, T81, T99, T111, T112-113, T121, T129, T130-131, T139, T148, T155, T158, T163, T181, T193, T194-195, T203, T211, T212-213, T221, T230, T237, T240, T245 **Unit 5:** T17, T29, T30-31, T39, T47, T48-49, T57, T66, T73, T76, T81, T99, T111, T112-113, T121, T129, T130-131, T139, T148, T155, T158, T163, T181, T193, T194-195, T203, T211, T212-213, T221, T230, T237, T240, T245 **Unit 6:** T17, T29, T30-31, T39, T47, T48-49, T57, T66, T73, T81, T99, T111, T112-113, T121, T129, T130-131, T139, T148, T155, T158, T163, T181, T193, T194-195, T203, T211, T212-213, T221, T230, T237, T240, T245 **Unit 7:** T17, T29, T30-31, T39, T47, T48-49, T57, T66, T73, T76, T81, T99, T111, T112-113, T121, T129, T130-131, T139, T148, T155, T158, T163, T181, T193, T194-195, T203, T211, T212-213, T221, T230, T237, T240, T245 **Unit 8:** T17, T29, T30-31, T39, T47, T48-49, T57, T66, T73, T76, T81, T99, T111, T112-113, T121, T129, T130-131, T139, T148, T155, T158, T163, T181, T193, T194-195, T203, T211, T212-213, T221, T230, T237, T240, T245 **Unit 9:** T17, T29, T30-31, T39, T47, T48-49, T57, T66, T73, T76, T81, T99, T111, T112-113, T121, T129, T130-131, T139, T148, T155, T158, T163, T181, T193, T194-195, T203, T211, T212-213, T221, T230, T237, T240, T245 **Unit 10:** T17, T31, T32-33, T41, T49, T50-51, T59, T68, T75, T78, T83, T101, T113, T114-115, T123, T131, T141, T150, T157, T160, T165, T183, T195, T196-197, T205, T212-213, T223, T232, T239, T242, T247
RF.K.3d	Distinguish between similarly spelled words by identifying the sounds of the letters that differ.	**TEACHER'S EDITION: Unit 2:** T46, T128 **Unit 3:** T46, T128, T210 **Unit 4:** T46, T128, T210 **Unit 5:** T128, T210 **Unit 6:** T46, T128, T210 **Unit 7:** T46, T128, T210 **Unit 8:** T46, T128, T210 **Unit 9:** T46, T128, T210 **Unit 10:** T48, T130, T212

Reading Standards for Foundational Skills		
Fluency		***McGraw-Hill Reading Wonders***
RF.K.4	Read emergent-reader texts with purpose and understanding.	**READING/WRITING WORKSHOP:** **Unit 1:** 32-37, 44-49, 50-55 **Unit 2:** 32-37, 44-49, 50-55 **Unit 3:** 8-13, 32-37, 50-55 **Unit 4:** 8-15, 22-29, 36-43 **Unit 5:** 8-15, 22-29, 36-43 **Unit 6:** 8-15, 22-29, 36-43 **Unit 7:** 8-15, 22-29, 36-43 **Unit 8:** 8-15, 22-29, 36-43 **Unit 9:** 8-15, 22-29, 36-43 **Unit 10:** 8-15, 22-29, 36-43 **LEVELED READERS:** **Unit 1, Week 1:** *Soup!* (A), *Mouse and Monkey* (O, ELL), *Come and Play!* (B) **Unit 1 Week 2:** *Hop!* (A), *We Hop!* (O, ELL) *We Can Move!* (B) **Unit 1, Week 3:** *The Beach* (A), *At School* (O, ELL), *See It Grow!* (B) **Unit 2, Week 1:** *We Need Tools* (A), *A Trip* (O, ELL), *What Can You See?* (B) **Unit 2, Week 2:** *Shapes!* (A), *Play with Shapes!* (O, ELL), *Use a Shape!* (B) **Unit 2, Week 3:** *We Like Bugs!* (A), *The Bugs Run* (O, ELL), *I See a Bug!* (B) **Unit 3, Week 1:** *We Run* (A), *Go, Nat!* (O, ELL), *The Birdhouse* (B) **Unit 3, Week 2:** *City Sounds* (A), *Farm Sounds* (O, ELL), *A Noisy Night* (B) **Unit 3, Week 3:** *We Can Go* (A), *Going by Cab* (O, ELL), *Cal's Busy Week* (B) **Unit 4, Week 1:** *You Cook* (A), *On the Job* (O, ELL), *The Neighborhood* (B) **Unit 4, Week 2:** *My Neighbors* (A), *Neighborhood Party* (O, ELL), *Parade Day* (B) **Unit 4, Week 3:** *We Clean!* (A) *Can You Fix It?* (O, ELL), *Helping Mom* (B) **Unit 5, Week 1:** *My Garden* (A), *My Garden Grows* (O, ELL), *The Mystery Seeds* (B) **Unit 5, Week 2:** *The Tree* (A), *Many Trees* (O, ELL), *Our Apple Tree* (B) **Unit 5, Week 3:** *The Farmer* (A), *Let's Make a Salad!* (O, ELL), *Farm Fresh Finn* (B) **Unit 6, Week 1:** *It Is Hot!* (A), *Little Bear* (O, ELL), *Ant and Grasshopper* (B) **Unit 6, Week 2:** *The Rain* (A), *Weather Is Fun* (O, ELL), *Kate and Tuck* (B) **Unit 6 Week 3:** *Bad Weather* (A), *Getting Ready* (O, ELL), *The Storm* (B) **Unit 7, Week 1:** *Two Cubs* (A), *Animal Bodies* (O, ELL), *Two Kinds of Bears* (B) **Unit 7, Week 2:** *My Cats* (A), *Their Pets* (O, ELL), *Will's Pet* (B) **Unit 7, Week 3:** *We Want Water* (A) *A New Home* (O, ELL), *Bird's New Home* (B) **Unit 8, Week 1:** *I Go Places* (A), *Run, Quinn!* (O, ELL), *Going to Gran's House* (B) **Unit 8, Week 2:** *See This!* (A), *Places to See* (O, ELL), *My Trip to Yellowstone* (B) **Unit 8, Week 3:** *Going Up* (A), *In the Clouds* (O, ELL), *How Sun and Moon Found Home* (B) **Unit 9, Week 1:** *Let Me Help You* (A), *How Can Jane Help?* (O, ELL), *I Used to Help, Too* (B) **Unit 9, Week 2:** *Mike Helps Out* (A), *Clive and His Friend* (O, ELL), *Farmer White's Best Friend* (B) **Unit 9, Week 3:** *Look Where It Is From* (A), *What's for Breakfast?* (O, ELL), *Nature at the Craft Fair* (B) **Unit 10, Week 1:** *Animal Band* (A), *We Want Honey* (O, ELL), *A Good Idea* (B) **Unit 10, Week 2:** *My Box* (A), *Let's Make a Band* (O, ELL), *Going Camping* (B) **Unit 10, Week 3:** *Help Clean Up* (A), *Let's Save Earth* (O, ELL), *Babysitters for Seals* (B) **TEACHER'S EDITION:** **Unit 1:** S14, S48, T48-49, T112-113, T150-151, T232-233 **Unit 2:** T48-49, T130-131, T224-225 **Unit 3:** T60-61, T130-131, T212-213 **Unit 4:** T30-31, T48-49, T60-61, T65, T68-69, T72, T74-75, T78-79, T112-113, T130-131, T142-143, T147, T150-151, T156-157, T160-161, T194-195, T212-213, T224-225, T229, T232-233, T236, T238-239, T242-243 **Unit 5:** T30-31, T48-49, T60-61, T65, T68-69, T72, T74-75, T78-79, T112-113, T130-131, T142-143, T147, T150-151, T156-157, T160-161, T194-195, T212-213, T224-225, T229, T232-233, T236, T238-239, T242-243 **Unit 6:** T30-31, T48-49, T60-61, T65, T68-69, T72, T74-75, T78-79, T112-113, T130-131, T142-143, T147, T150-151, T194-195, T212-213, T224-225, T229, T232-233, T236 **Unit 7:** T30-31, T48-49, T60-61, T65, T68-69, T72, T74-75, T78-79, T112-113, T130-131, T142-143, T147, T150-151, T156-157, T160-161, T194-195, T212-213, T224-225, T229, T232-233, T236, T238-239, T242-243 **Unit 8:** T30-31, T48-49, T60-61, T65, T68-69, T72, T74-75, T78-79, T112-113, T10-131, T142-143, T147, T150-151, T156-157, T160-161, T194-195, T212-213, T224-225, T229, T232-233, T236, T238-239, T242-243 **Unit 9:** T30-31, T48-49, T60-61, T65, T68-69, T72, T74-75, T78-79, T112-113, T130-131, T142-143, T147, T150-151, T156-157, T160-161, T194-195, T212-213, T224-225, T229, T232-233, T236, T238-239, T242-243 **Unit 10:** T32-33, T50-51, T62-63, T67, T70-71, T74, T76-77, T80-81, T114-115, T132-133, T144-145, T149, T152-153, T156, T158-159, T162-163, T196-197, T214-215, T226-227, T231, T234-235, T238, T240-241, T244-245

College and Career Readiness Anchor Standards for WRITING

The K–5 standards on the following pages define what students should understand and be able to do by the end of each grade. They correspond to the College and Career Readiness (CCR) anchor standards below by number. The CCR and grade-specific standards are necessary complements—the former providing broad standards, the latter providing additional specificity—that together define the skills and understandings that all students must demonstrate.

Text Types and Purposes
1. Write arguments to support claims in an analysis of substantive topics or texts, using valid reasoning and relevant and sufficient evidence.
2. Write informative/explanatory texts to examine and convey complex ideas and information clearly and accurately through the effective selection, organization, and analysis of content.
3. Write narratives to develop real or imagined experiences or events using effective technique, well-chosen details, and well-structured event sequences.
Production and Distribution of Writing
4. Produce clear and coherent writing in which the development, organization, and style are appropriate to task, purpose, and audience.
5. Develop and strengthen writing as needed by planning, revising, editing, rewriting, or trying a new approach.
6. Use technology, including the Internet, to produce and publish writing and to interact and collaborate with others.
Research to Build and Present Knowledge
7. Conduct short as well as more sustained research projects based on focused questions, demonstrating understanding of the subject under investigation.
8. Gather relevant information from multiple print and digital sources, assess the credibility and accuracy of each source, and integrate the information while avoiding plagiarism.
9. Draw evidence from literary or informational texts to support analysis, reflection, and research.
Range of Writing
10. Write routinely over extended time frames (time for research, reflection, and revision) and shorter time frames (a single sitting or a day or two) for a range of tasks, purposes, and audiences.

CCSS

Common Core State Standards
English Language Arts
Grade K

Writing Standards

Text Types and Purposes		*McGraw-Hill Reading Wonders*
W.K.1	Use a combination of drawing, dictating, and writing to compose opinion pieces in which they tell a reader the topic or the name of the book they are writing about and state an opinion or preference about the topic or book (e.g., My favorite book is…).	**READING/WRITING WORKSHOP:** Unit 1: 38-39 **Unit 3:** 58 **Unit 5:** 32-33 **Unit 6:** 18-19 **Unit 9:** 18-19 **Unit 10:** 46-47 **TEACHER'S EDITION:** Unit 1: T87, T100, T114, T122 **Unit 3:** T196, T204, T214 **Unit 5:** T100, T114, T122-123, T132, T144 **Unit 6:** T32, T40, T41 **Unit 9:** T5, T18, T32, T40-41, T50 **Unit 10:** T17, T184, T198, T206, T216 **WRITING WORKSTATION ACTIVITY CARDS:** 5, 20
W.K.2	Use a combination of drawing, dictating, and writing to compose informative/explanatory texts in which they name what they are writing about and supply some information about the topic.	**READING/WRITING WORKSHOP:** Unit 2: 20-21 **Unit 4:** 44 **Unit 5:** 44-45 **Unit 6:** 44 **Unit 7:** 16-17, 44 **Unit 8:** 30-31 **Unit 9:** 44 **TEACHER'S EDITION:** Unit 1: S15, S33, S53, S67, S77, T182, T196, T204 **Unit 2:** T100, T122, T164 **Unit 3:** T18, T32, T40 **Unit 4:** T18, T32, T40, T114, T122, T196, T204 **Unit 5:** T182, T196, T204 **Unit 6:** T52-53, T135 **Unit 7:** T18, T32, T40, T100, T114, T122 **Unit 8:** T53, T100, T114, T122, T135 **Unit 9:** T182, T196, T204, T214 **Unit 10:** T18, T34, T42-43, T52 **WRITING WORKSTATION ACTIVITY CARDS:** 18, 23
W.K.3	Use a combination of drawing, dictating and writing to narrate a single event or several loosely linked events, tell about the events in the order in which they occurred, and provide a reaction to what happened.	**READING/WRITING WORKSHOP:** Unit 3: 38-39, 56 **Unit 5:** 44 **Unit 6:** 30 **Unit 8:** 16, 46-47 **Unit 9:** 30 **Unit 10:** 16 **TEACHER'S EDITION:** Unit 2: T196, T204, T246 **Unit 3:** T114, T122, T164 **Unit 5:** T32, T40, T82, T164, T246 **Unit 6:** T114, T123, T164, T246 **Unit 8:** T32, T40, T82, T196, T204 **Unit 9:** T82, T100, T114, T122-123, T132 **Unit 10:** T18, T34, T42, T43, T52, T84, T116, T166, T248 **WRITING WORKSTATION ACTIVITY CARDS:** 1, 4, 5, 7, 15

Writing Standards

Production and Distribution of Writing		McGraw-Hill Reading Wonders
W.K.4	(Begins in grade 3.)	
W.K.5	With guidance and support from adults, respond to questions and suggestions from peers and add details to strengthen writing as needed.	**TEACHER'S EDITION:** **Unit 1:** T32, T40 (Go Digital: Writing), T50, T58 (Go Digital: Writing), T122 (Go Digital: Writing), T132, T140 (Go Digital: Writing), T204 (Go Digital: Writing), T214, T222 (Go Digital: Writing) **Unit 2:** T40 (Go Digital: Writing), T50, T58 (Go Digital: Writing), T122 (Go Digital: Writing), T132, T140 (Go Digital: Writing), T204 (Go Digital: Writing), T214, T222 (Go Digital: Writing) **Unit 3:** T40 (Go Digital: Writing), T50, T58 (Go Digital: Writing), T122 (Go Digital: Writing), T132, T140 (Go Digital: Writing), T204 (Go Digital: Writing), T222 (Go Digital: Writing) **Unit 4:** T40 (Go Digital: Writing), T50, T58 (Go Digital: Writing), T122 (Go Digital: Writing), T132, T140 (Go Digital: Writing), T204 (Go Digital: Writing), T214, T222 (Go Digital: Writing) **Unit 5:** T40 (Go Digital: Writing), T50, T58 (Go Digital: Writing), T122 (Go Digital: Writing), T132, T140 (Go Digital: Writing), T204 (Go Digital: Writing), T214, T222 (Go Digital: Writing) **Unit 6:** T40 (Go Digital: Writing), T50, T58 (Go Digital: Writing), T122 (Go Digital: Writing), T132, T140 (Go Digital: Writing), T204 (Go Digital: Writing), T214, T222 (Go Digital: Writing) **Unit 7:** T40 (Go Digital: Writing), T58 (Go Digital: Writing), T122 (Go Digital: Writing), T140 (Go Digital: Writing), T164, T204 (Go Digital: Writing), T222 (Go Digital: Writing) T246 **Unit 8:** T40 (Go Digital: Writing), T50, T58 (Go Digital: Writing), T122 (Go Digital: Writing), T132, T140 (Go Digital: Writing), T164, T204 (Go Digital: Writing), T214, T222 (Go Digital: Writing), T246 **Unit 9:** T40 (Go Digital: Writing), T50, T58 (Go Digital: Writing), T122 (Go Digital: Writing), T132, T140 (Go Digital: Writing), T204 (Go Digital: Writing), T214, T222 (Go Digital: Writing) **Unit 10:** T42 (Go Digital: Writing), T52, T60 (Go Digital: Writing), T124 (Go Digital: Writing), T134, T142 (Go Digital: Writing), T166, T206 (Go Digital: Writing), T224 (Go Digital: Writing), T248 **WRITING WORKSTATION ACTIVITY CARDS:** 10, 11, 12, 13, 14, 16
W.K.6	With guidance and support from adults, explore a variety of digital tools to produce and publish writing, including in collaboration with peers.	**TEACHER'S EDITION:** **Unit 1:** T134 **Unit 2:** T216 **Unit 6:** T248-249 **Unit 7:** T52, T134, T216, T248-249 **Unit 8:** T52, T134, T216, T248-249 **Unit 9:** T216, T248-249 **Unit 10:** T218, T250-251 **ConnectED Digital Resources:** My Binder (My Work)
Research to Build and Present Knowledge		**McGraw-Hill Reading Wonders**
W.K.7	Participate in shared research and writing projects (e.g., explore a number of books by a favorite author and express opinions about them).	**TEACHER'S EDITION:** **Unit 1:** T52, T134, T216 **Unit 2:** T52, T134, T216 **Unit 3:** T52, T134, T216 **Unit 4:** T52, T134, T216 **Unit 5:** T52, T100, T114, T122-123 **Unit 6:** T52, T134, T216 **Unit 7:** T52, T134, T216, T248-249 **Unit 8:** T52, T134, T216 **Unit 9:** T52, T134, T216 **Unit 10:** T54, T136, T218 **WRITING WORKSTATION ACTIVITY CARDS:** 20, 23 **ConnectED Digital Resources:** Collaborate (Projects)
W.K.8	With guidance and support from adults, recall information from experiences or gather information from provided sources to answer a question.	**READING/WRITING WORKSHOP:** Unit 7: 44 **TEACHER'S EDITION:** **Unit 1:** T32, T40, T100 **Unit 2:** T52, T134, T216 **Unit 3:** T100, T214 **Unit 4:** T18, T52, T100, T134, T182, T216 **Unit 5:** T18, T52, T134, T216 **Unit 6:** T52, T100, T134, T216 **Unit 7:** T50, T52, T132, T134, T196, T204, T214, T216 **Unit 8:** T52, T134, T216 **Unit 9:** T52, T134, T216 **Unit 10:** T54, T102, T136, T218
W.K.9	(Begins in grade 4.)	
Range of Writing		**McGraw-Hill Reading Wonders**
W.K.10	(Begins in grade 3.)	

College and Career Readiness Anchor Standards for SPEAKING AND LISTENING

The K–5 standards on the following pages define what students should understand and be able to do by the end of each grade. They correspond to the College and Career Readiness (CCR) anchor standards below by number. The CCR and grade-specific standards are necessary complements—the former providing broad standards, the latter providing additional specificity—that together define the skills and understandings that all students must demonstrate.

Comprehension and Collaboration
1. Prepare for and participate effectively in a range of conversations and collaborations with diverse partners, building on others' ideas and expressing their own clearly and persuasively.
2. Integrate and evaluate information presented in diverse media and formats, including visually, quantitatively, and orally.
3. Evaluate a speaker's point of view, reasoning, and use of evidence and rhetoric.
Presentation of Knowledge and Ideas
4. Present information, findings, and supporting evidence such that listeners can follow the line of reasoning and the organization, development, and style are appropriate to task, purpose, and audience.
5. Make strategic use of digital media and visual displays of data to express information and enhance understanding of presentations.
6. Adapt speech to a variety of contexts and communicative tasks, demonstrating command of formal English when indicated or appropriate.

Common Core State Standards
English Language Arts

Grade K

Speaking and Listening Standards

Comprehension and Collaboration		McGraw-Hill Reading Wonders
SL.K.1	Participate in collaborative conversations with diverse partners about kindergarten topics and texts with peers and adults in small and larger groups.	**TEACHER'S EDITION:** **Unit 1:** S10-11, S44, S58, T11, T54-55, T117, T134, T136-137, T216 **Unit 2:** T34, T51, T52, T134, T222 **Unit 3:** T20, T33, T45, T175, T216 **Unit 4:** T11, T20, T52, T54, T58, T93, T134, T136, T140, T175, T216, T218 **Unit 5:** T11, T20, T52, T93, T120, T136, T174, T175, T216, T222 **Unit 6:** T11, T52, T54, T93, T136, T140, T216, T218 **Unit 7:** T10-11, T52, T54, T55, T93, T134, T136, T137, T175, T218, T219 **Unit 8:** T11, T54, T58, T80, T92, T93, T134, T136, T140, T175, T218, T222 **Unit 9:** T10-11, T52, T54, T93, T136, T140, T175, T218, T222 **Unit 10:** T11, T20, T56, T60, T95, T104, T136, T138, T142, T177, T186, T220, T224
SL.K.1a	Follow agreed-upon rules for discussions (e.g., listening to others and taking turns speaking about the topics and texts under discussion).	**READING/WRITING WORKSHOP:** **Unit 1:** 6-7, 24-25 **Unit 2:** 24-25 **Unit 3:** 6-7, 24-25, 42-43 **Unit 4:** 6-7, 20-21, 34-35 **Unit 5:** 6-7, 20-21, 34-35 **Unit 6:** 6-7, 20-21, 36-43 **Unit 7:** 6-7, 20-21, 34-35 **Unit 8:** 6-7, 20-21 **Unit 9:** 6-7, 8-15, 20-21, 34-35 **Unit 10:** 6-7, 20-21 **YOUR TURN PRACTICE BOOK:** 31-32, 45, 68, 70-71, 81-82, 93 **READING WORKSTATION ACTIVITY CARDS:** 1, 6, 18, 19 **WRITING WORKSTATION ACTIVITY CARDS:** 1, 11, 13, 21+D89 **TEACHER'S EDITION:** **Unit 1:** T11, T134, T216 **Unit 2:** T52, T134, T222 **Unit 3:** T175, T216 **Unit 4:** T11, T52, T58, T93, T134, T140, T216 **Unit 5:** T11, T52, T93, T175, T216 **Unit 6:** T11, T52, T93, T140, T216 **Unit 7:** T11, T52, T55, T93, T134, T137, T219 **Unit 8:** T11, T58, T93, T134, T140, T222 **Unit 9:** T11, T52, T93, T140, T175, T222 **Unit 10:** T11, T60, T95, T142, T224
SL.K.1b	Continue a conversation through multiple exchanges.	**READING/WRITING WORKSHOP:** **Unit 1:** SS4-SS5, SS22-SS23, SS40-SS41, 6-7, 24-25, 42-43 **Unit 2:** 6-7, 8, 14-19, 24, 25, 42-43, 46, 47, 48, 51, 54, 55, 58 **Unit 3:** 6-7, 14-19, 24-35, 42-43 **Unit 4:** 6-7, 20-21, 34-35 **Unit 5:** 6-7, 20-21, 34-35 **Unit 6:** 8-15 **Unit 7:** 6-7, 8-15, 20-21, 22-29, 34-35, 36-43 **Unit 8:** 6-7, 8-15, 20-21, 22-29, 34-35, 36-43 **Unit 9:** 6-7, 8-15, 20-21, 22-29, 34-35 **Unit 10:** 6-7, 8-15, 20-21, 22-29, 34-35, 36-43 **YOUR TURN PRACTICE BOOK:** 29, 45, 53, 61, 68 **READING WORKSTATION ACTIVITY CARDS:** 1, 6, 17, 18 **WRITING WORKSTATION ACTIVITY CARDS:** 1, 9, 11 **PHONICS/WORD STUDY WORKSTATION ACTIVITY CARDS:** W11, W12, R2, R3 **SCIENCE/SOCIAL STUDIES WORKSTATION ACTIVITY CARDS:** W4, W26, R10 **LITERATURE BIG BOOKS:** **Smart Start:** *Animals in the Park* **Unit 2, Week 1:** *The Handiest Things in the World* **Unit 2, Week 2:** *Shapes All Around* **Unit 3, Week 2:** *Clang! Clang! Beep! Beep! Listen to the City* **Unit 4, Week 1:** *Whose Shoes? A Shoe for Every Job* **Unit 4, Week 2:** *What Can You Do with a Paleta?* **Unit 4, Week 3:** *Roadwork* **Unit 5, Week 3:** *An Orange in January* **Unit 6, Week 1:** *Mama, Is It Summer Yet?* **Unit 6, Week 2:** *Rain* **Unit 7, Week 1:** *ZooBorns!* **Unit 7, Week 2:** *The Birthday Pet* **Unit 8, Week 1:** *When Daddy's Truck Picks Me Up* **Unit 8, Week 2:** *Ana Goes to Washington, D.C.* **Unit 9, Week 3:** *Bread Comes to Life* **Unit 10, Week 3:** *Panda Kindergarten* **TEACHER'S EDITION:** **Unit 1:** S10-S11, S21, S26-S27, S34-S35, S44-S45, S54, S58-S59, S64, S68-S69, S74-S75, T11, T34, T35, T52, T53, T54-55, T81, T84, T93, T101, T117, T123, T133, T134, T135, T136-137, T162, T175, T183, T197, T199, T215, T216, T217, T218 **Unit 2:** T11, T19, T33, T41, T51, T52, T64, T93, T134, T136, T137, T175, T204, T215, T216, T217, T218 **Unit 3:** T11, T19, T54-55, T58, T93, T117, T134, T135, T136-137, T175, T216, T217, T218 **Unit 4:** T11, T54, T93, T134, T136, T175, T216, T218 **Unit 5:** T11, T52, T54, T93, T136, T175, T216, T218 **Unit 6:** T11, T52, T54, T136, T218 **Unit 7:** T10-11, T52, T54, T93, T134, T136, T175, T218 **Unit 8:** T11, T54, T58, T80, T92, T93, T136, T140, T175, T218, T222 **Unit 9:** T10-11, T54, T93, T136, T140, T175, T218 **Unit 10:** T11, T56, T95, T136, T138, T177, T220 **INTERACTIVE READ-ALOUD CARDS:** **Smart Start, Week 1:** "The Ugly Duckling" **Smart Start, Week 2:** "Tikki Tikki Tembo" **Smart Start, Week 3:** "Kindergarteners Can!" **Unit 1, Week 1:** "The Lion and the Mouse" **Unit 1, Week 2:** "The Tortoise and the Hare" **Unit 1, Week 3:** "A Feast of the Senses" **Unit 2, Week 1:** "Timimoto" **Unit 2, Week 2:** "Kites in Flight" **Unit 2, Week 3:** "From Caterpillar to Butterfly" **Unit 3, Week 1:** "The Boy Who Cried Wolf" **Unit 3, Week 2:** "The Turtle and the Flute" **Unit 3, Week 3:** "Field Trips" **Unit 4, Week 1:** "Little Juan and the Cooking Pot" **Unit 4, Week 2:** "Cultural Festivals" **Unit 4, Week 3:** "The Bundle of Sticks" **Unit 5, Week 1:** "Growing Plants" **Unit 5, Week 2:** "The Pine Tree" **Unit 5, Week 3:** "Farmers Around the World" **Unit 6, Week 1:** "A Tour of the Seasons" **Unit 6, Week 1:** "The Frog and the Locust" **Unit 6, Week 3:** "Rainbow Crow" **Unit 7, Week 1:** "Baby Farm Animals" **Unit 7, Week 2:** "The Family Pet" **Unit 7, Week 3:** "Anansi, An African Tale" **Unit 8, Week 1:** "The King of the Winds" **Unit 8, Week 2:** "The Best of the West" **Unit 8, Week 3:** "A View From the Moon" **Unit 9, Week 1:** "Helping Out at Home" **Unit 9, Week 2:** "The Little Red Hen" **Unit 9, Week 3:** "Spider Woman Teaches the Navajo" **Unit 10, Week 1:** "The Elves and the Shoemakers" **Unit 10, Week 1:** "Good for You!" **Unit 10, Week 1:** "Help Save Big Blue!"

CCSS CORRELATIONS

Speaking and Listening Standards

Comprehension and Collaboration		*McGraw-Hill Reading Wonders*
SL.K.2	Confirm understanding of a text read aloud or information presented orally or through other media by asking and answering questions about key details and requesting clarification if something is not understood.	**READING/WRITING WORKSHOP:** **Unit 1:** 6-7, 26-31, 33, 35, 37, 42-43, 45, 47, 49, 51, 53, 55 **Unit 2:** 6-7, 8, 9, 10, 13, 14-19, 24-25, 27, 28, 30, 33, 34, 35, 46, 47, 48, 51, 54, 55, 58 **Unit 3:** 6-7, 9, 12, 13, 16, 17, 19, 33, 34, 37, 42-43, 46, 47, 49, 51, 53, 55 **Unit 4:** 6-7, 9-15, 20-21, 23-25, 28-29, 34-43 **Unit 5:** 8-15, 23-28 **Unit 6:** 8-15, 22-29 **Unit 7:** 8-15, 18-19, 20-21, 22-29, 34-35, 36-43 **Unit 8:** 6-7, 8-15, 20-21, 22-29, 34-35, 36-43 **Unit 9:** 6-7, 8-15, 20-21, 22-29, 34-35, 36-43 **Unit 10:** 6-7, 8-15, 20-21, 22-29, 34-35, 36-43 **LEVELED READERS:** **Unit 1, Week 3:** *The Beach* (A), *See It Grow!* (O, ELL), *At School* (B) **Unit 2, Week 1:** *We Need Tools* (A), *A Trip* (O, ELL), *What Can You See?* (B) **Unit 3, Week 1:** *We Run* (A), *Go, Nat!* (O, ELL), *The Birdhouse* (B) **Unit 4, Week 2:** *My Neighbors* (A), *Neighborhood Party* (O, ELL), *Parade Day* (B) **Unit 5, Week 1:** *My Garden* (A), *My Garden Grows* (O, ELL), *The Mystery Seeds* (B) **Unit 5, Week 3:** *The Farmer* (A), *Let's Make a Salad!* (O, ELL), *Farm Fresh Finn* (B) **Unit 6, Week 1:** *It Is Hot!* (A), *Little Bear* (O, ELL), *Ant and Grasshopper* (B) **Unit 7, Week 2:** *My Cats* (A), *Their Pets* (O, ELL), *Will's Pet* (B) **Unit 7, Week 3:** *We Want Water* (A), *A New Home* (O, ELL), *Bird's New Home* (B) **Unit 8, Week 2:** *See This!* (A), *Places to See* (O, ELL), *My Trip to Yellowstone* (B) **Unit 8, Week 3:** *Going Up* (A), *In the Clouds* (O, ELL) *How Sun and Moon Found Home* (B) **Unit 9, Week 2:** *Mike Helps Out* (A), *Clive and His Friend* (O, ELL), *Farmer White's Best Friend* (B) **Unit 9, Week 3:** *Look Where It Is From* (A), *What's for Breakfast?* (O, ELL), *Nature at the Craft Fair* (B) **Unit 10, Week 2:** *My Box* (A), *Let's Make a Band* (O, ELL), *Going Camping* (B) **Unit 10, Week 3:** *Help Clean Up* (A), *Let's Save Earth* (O, ELL) *Babysitters for Seals* (B) **YOUR TURN PRACTICE BOOK:** 29-30, 35-38, 45-46, 53, 59-61, 68, 79-80, 85-86, 93-94, 99, 101-103, 107, 109-111, 115, 118, 123, 127-128, 129, 137, 141, 143-144, 147, 153-154, 164-165, 174, 187, 207, 217, 221, 227, 231, 234 **READING WORKSTATION ACTIVITY CARDS:** 7, 8, 16, 20 **WRITING WORKSTATION ACTIVITY CARDS:** 4, 6, 9 **TEACHER'S EDITION:** **Unit 1:** T11, T22-26, T186-191 **Unit 2:** T35, T186-191, T244 **Unit 3:** T104-108, T137, T175 **Unit 4:** T11, T55, T92, T137, T175, T219, T244 **Unit 5:** T11, T52, T93, T175, T186 **Unit 6:** T11, T20, T26, T93, T175 **Unit 7:** T11, T52, T55, T93, T137, T175, T219, T242 **Unit 8:** T11, T55, T78, T92-93 **Unit 9:** T11, T52, T55, T80, T93, T137, T162, T175, T219, T242 **Unit 10:** T11, T57, T80, T95, T139, T221, T244 **LITERATURE BIG BOOKS:** **Unit 1, Week 1:** *What About Bear?* **Unit 1, Week 2:** *Pouch!* **Unit 1, Week 3:** *Senses at the Seashore* **Unit 2, Week 1:** *The Handiest Things in the World* **Unit 2, Week 2:** *Shapes All Around* **Unit 3, Week 1:** *How Do Dinosaurs Go to School?* **Unit 3, Week 2:** *Clang! Clang! Beep! Beep! Listen to the City* **Unit 3, Week 3:** *Please Take Me for a Walk* **Unit 4, Week 1:** *Whose Shoes? A Shoe for Every Job* **Unit 4, Week 2:** *What Can You Do with a Paleta?* **Unit 4, Week 3:** *Roadwork* **Unit 5, Week 1:** *My Garden* **Unit 5, Week 2:** *A Grand Old Tree* **Unit 6, Week 3:** *Waiting Out the Storm* **Unit 7, Week 3:** *Bear Snores On* **Unit 8, Week 3:** *Bringing Down the Moon* **Unit 9, Week 1:** *Peter's Chair* **Unit 9, Week 2:** *Hen Hears Gossip* **Unit 10, Week 1:** *What's the Big Idea, Molly?* **Unit 10, Week 2:** *All Kinds of Families* **INTERACTIVE READ-ALOUD CARDS:** **Smart Start, Week 1:** "The Ugly Duckling" **Smart Start, Week 2:** "Tikki Tikki Tembo" **Smart Start, Week 3:** "Kindergarteners Can!" **Unit 1, Week 1:** "The Lion and the Mouse" **Unit 1, Week 2:** "The Tortoise and the Hare" **Unit 1, Week 3:** "A Feast of the Senses" **Unit 2, Week 1:** "Timimoto" **Unit 2, Week 2:** "Kites in Flight" **Unit 2, Week 3:** "From Caterpillar to Butterfly" **Unit 4, Week 1:** "Little Juan and the Cooking Pot" **Unit 4, Week 2:** "Cultural Festivals" **Unit 4, Week 3:** "The Bundle of Sticks" **Unit 5, Week 1:** "Growing Plants" **Unit 5, Week 2:** "The Pine Tree" **Unit 6, Week 1:** "A Tour of the Seasons" **Unit 6, Week 2:** "The Frog and the Locust" **Unit 6, Week 3:** "Rainbow Crow" **Unit 8, Week 1:** "The King of the Winds" **Unit 8, Week 2:** "The Best of the West" **Unit 8, Week 3:** "A View From the Moon" **Unit 9, Week 1:** "Helping Out at Home" **Unit 9, Week 2:** "The Little Red Hen" **Unit 9, Week 3:** "Spider Woman Teaches the Navajo" **Unit 10, Week 1:** "Help Save Big Blue!"

Speaking and Listening Standards

Comprehension and Collaboration		McGraw-Hill Reading Wonders
SL.K.3	Ask and answer questions in order to seek help, get information, or clarify something that is not understood.	**READING/WRITING WORKSHOP:** Unit 1: 6-7, 26-31, 33, 36, 37, 42-43, 45, 47, 49, 51, 53, 55 **Unit 2:** 6, 7, 14-19 **Unit 3:** 8-13, 14-19, 42-43 **Unit 4:** 6-7, 9, 11, 14, 20-29, 34-43 **Unit 5:** 6-7, 9, 11, 14, 20-29, 34-43 **Unit 6:** 6-7, 9, 11, 14, 20-29, 34-43 **Unit 7:** 6-7, 20-21 **Unit 8:** 6-7, 20-21 **Unit 9:** 6-7, 20-21 **Unit 10:** 6-7 **LEVELED READERS:** Unit 2, Week 1: *We Need Tools* (A), *What Can You See?* (O, ELL), *A Trip* (B) **Unit 4, Week 1:** *You Cook* (A), *On the Job* (O, ELL), *The Neighborhood* (B) **Unit 4, Week 3:** *We Clean!* (A), *Can You Fix It?* (O, ELL), *Helping Mom* (B) **Unit 5, Week 1:** *My Garden* (A), *My Garden Grows* (O, ELL), *The Mystery Seeds* (B) **Unit 5, Week 3:** *The Farmer* (A), *Let's Make a Salad!* (O, ELL), *Farm Fresh Finn* (B) **Unit 6, Week 1:** *It Is Hot!* (A), *Little Bear* (O, ELL), *Ant and Grasshopper* (B) **Unit 6, Week 3:** *Bad Weather* (A), *Getting Ready* (O, ELL), *The Storm* (B) **Unit 7, Week 1:** *Two Cubs* (A), *Animal Bodies* (O, ELL), *Two Kinds of Bears* (B) **Unit 8, Week 2:** *See This!* (A), *Places to See* (O, ELL), *My Trip to Yellowstone* (B) **Unit 9, Week 1:** *Let Me Help You* (A) *How Can Jane Help?* (O, ELL), *I Used to Help Too* (B) **Unit 10, Week 1:** *Animal Band* (A), *We Want Honey* (O, ELL), *A Good Idea* (B) **Unit 10, Week 3:** *Help Clean Up* (A), *Let's Save Earth* (O, ELL) *Babysitters for Seals* (B) **READING WORKSTATION ACTIVITY CARDS:** 7, 16, 20 **WRITING WORKSTATION ACTIVITY CARDS:** 4, 6, 9 **TEACHER'S EDITION:** Unit 1: T13, T216, T233 **Unit 2:** T95, T131, T137 **Unit 3:** T31, T49 **Unit 4:** T11, T55, T93, T137, T216, T219 **Unit 5:** T11, T52, T134, T216 **Unit 6:** T11, T93 **Unit 7:** T52, T93, T134, T182, T196, T205 **Unit 8:** T11, T93, T175 **Unit 9:** T13, T22, T52, T55 **Unit 10:** T11, T95, T97 **LITERATURE BIG BOOKS:** Unit 1, Week 1: *What About Bear?* **Unit 1, Week 2:** *Pouch!* **Unit 1, Week 3:** *Senses at the Seashore* **Unit 2, Week 1:** *The Handiest Things in the World* **Unit 2, Week 2:** *Shapes All Around* **Unit 3, Week 1:** *How Do Dinosaurs Go to School?* **Unit 3, Week 2:** *Clang! Clang! Beep! Beep! Listen to the City* **Unit 3, Week 3:** *Please Take Me for a Walk* **Unit 4, Week 1:** *Whose Shoes? A Shoe for Every Job* **Unit 4, Week 2:** *What Can You Do with a Paleta?* **Unit 4, Week 3:** *Roadwork* **Unit 9, Week 1:** *Peter's Chair* **Unit 9, Week 2:** *Hen Hears Gossip* **Unit 10, Week 2:** *All Kinds of Families!* **Unit 10, Week 3:** *Panda Kindergarten* **INTERACTIVE READ-ALOUD CARDS:** Unit 1, Week 1: "The Lion and the Mouse" **Unit 1, Week 2:** "The Tortoise and the Hare" **Unit 1, Week 3:** "A Feast of the Senses" **Unit 2, Week 1:** "Timimoto" **Unit 2, Week 2:** "Kites in Flight" **Unit 2, Week 3:** "From Caterpillar to Butterfly" **Unit 3, Week 1:** "The Boy Who Cried Wolf" **Unit 3, Week 2:** "The Turtle and the Flute" **Unit 4, Week 1:** "Little Juan and the Cooking Pot" **Unit 4, Week 2:** "Cultural Festivals" **Unit 9, Week 2:** "The Little Red Hen"
Presentation of Knowledge and Ideas		**McGraw-Hill Reading Wonders**
SL.K.4	Describe familiar people, places, things, and events and, with prompting and support, provide additional detail.	**READING/WRITING WORKSHOP BIG BOOK:** Unit 1: 6-7, 42-43 **Unit 2:** 6-7, 24-25, 42-43 **Unit 3:** 6-7, 24-25, 42-43 **Unit 4:** 6-7, 20-21, 34-35 **Unit 5:** 6-7, 20-21, 34-35 **Unit 6:** 6-7, 20-21, 34-35 **Unit 7:** 6-7, 20-21, 34-35 **Unit 8:** 6-7, 20-21, 34-35 **Unit 9:** 6-7, 20-21, 34-35 **Unit 10:** 6-7, 20-21, 34-35 **YOUR TURN PRACTICE BOOK:** 27-28, 35-38, 51-52, 61, 67, 68, 83, 85-86, 93-94, 103, 107, 109-110, 115, 117, 118, 141, 157, 167, 174, 193, 221, 231 **READING WORKSTATION ACTIVITY CARDS:** 10, 12, 14, 16 **WRITING WORKSTATION ACTIVITY CARDS:** 1, 2, 8, 16, 19, 22 **TEACHER'S EDITION:** Unit 1: S58, S74-75, T19, T33, T134, T183, T197, T205 **Unit 2:** T175, T182 **Unit 3:** T11, T93, T175, T177 **Unit 4:** T10-11, T18-19, T92, T114-115, T132-133, T135, T175, T182-183, T197, T214-215 **Unit 5:** T54, T136, T175, T218 **Unit 6:** T11, T13, T52, T54, T136, T175, T218 **Unit 7:** T54, T136, T163, T175, T218 **Unit 8:** T54, T175, T216 **Unit 9:** T11, T93, T136, T175, T183 **Unit 10:** T102, T116, T136, T177 **LITERATURE BIG BOOKS:** Smart Start: *Animals in the Park* **Unit 1, Week 1:** *What About Bear?* **Unit 1, Week 2:** *Pouch!* **Unit 1, Week 3:** *Senses at the Seashore* **Unit 2, Week 3:** *I Love Bugs!* **Unit 4, Week 1:** *Whose Shoes? A Shoe for Every Job* **Unit 4, Week 2:** *What Can You Do with a Paleta?* **Unit 4, Week 3:** *Roadwork* **Unit 5, Week 1:** *My Garden* **Unit 5, Week 2:** *A Grand Old Tree* **Unit 5, Week 3:** *An Orange in January* **Unit 6, Week 1:** *Mama, Is It Summer Yet?* **Unit 6, Week 2:** *Rain* **Unit 7, Week 1:** *ZooBorns!* **Unit 7, Week 2:** *The Family Pet* **Unit 7, Week 3:** *Bear Snores On* **Unit 8, Week 1:** *When Daddy's Truck Picks Me Up* **Unit 8, Week 2:** *Ana Goes to Washington, D.C.* **Unit 9, Week 1:** *Peter's Chair* **Unit 9, Week 2:** *Hen Hears Gossip* **Unit 9, Week 3:** *Bread Comes to Life* **Unit 10, Week 1:** *What's the Big Idea, Molly?* **Unit 10, Week 2:** *All Kinds of Families!* **INTERACTIVE READ-ALOUD CARDS:** Smart Start, Week 2: "Tikki Tikki Tembo" **Smart Start, Week 3:** "Kindergarteners Can!" **Unit 1, Week 1:** "The Lion and the Mouse" **Unit 1, Week 2:** "The Tortoise and the Hare" **Unit 1, Week 3:** "A Feast of the Senses" **Unit 2, Week 1:** "Timimoto" **Unit 2, Week 2:** "Kites in Flight" **Unit 2, Week 3:** "From Caterpillar to Butterfly" **Unit 3, Week 1:** "The Boy Who Cried Wolf" **Unit 3, Week 2:** "The Turtle and the Flute" **Unit 4, Week 3:** "The Bundle of Sticks" **Unit 5, Week 3:** "Farms Around the World" **Unit 6, Week 3:** "Rainbow Crow" **Unit 7, Week 3:** "Anansi: An African Tale" **Unit 8, Week 3:** "A View From the Moon" **Unit 9, Week 3:** "Spider Woman Teaches the Navajo" **Unit 10, Week 1:** "The Elves and the Shoemakers" **Unit 10, Week 1:** "Good for You!"

Speaking and Listening Standards

Presentation of Knowledge and Ideas		McGraw-Hill Reading Wonders
SL.K.5	Add drawings or other visual displays to descriptions as desired to provide additional detail.	**YOUR TURN PRACTICE BOOK:** 27-28, 30-32, 35-38, 43-46, 51-53, 59-60, 61, 62, 67-70, 77-80, 83, 85-86, 88, 93-94, 99, 101-102, 103-104, 107, 109-112, 115, 117-118, 123, 127-128, 129, 130, 133, 135-136, 137, 138, 141, 143-144, 147, 148, 151, 153-154, 157, 158, 164-165, 167, 168, 174, 187, 193, 207, 217, 221, 227, 231, 234 **READINGWORK STATION ACTIVITY CARDS:** 1, 6, 12, 15, 16, 20 **WRITING WORKSTATION ACTIVITY CARDS:** 1, 2, 4, 9, 17, 20, 23 **TEACHER'S EDITION:** **Unit 1:** T32, T41, T123, T214 **Unit 2:** T40-41, T123, T132 **Unit 3:** T41, T134, T217 **Unit 4:** T32, T41, T52, T123, T134, T205 **Unit 5:** T53, T134, T217 **Unit 6:** T53, T122-123, T135, T140, T163, T197, T205, T222 **Unit 7:** T33, T41, T114, T123 **Unit 8:** T53, T132, T134, T216 **Unit 9:** T41, T53, T123, T205, T214, T241 **Unit 10:** T43, T137, T216
SL.K.6	Speak audibly and express thoughts, feelings, and ideas clearly.	**READING/WRITING WORKSHOP:** **Unit 1:** 6-7, 8-13, 14-19, 24-25, 26-31, 42-43 **Unit 2:** 6-7, 8, 9, 10, 13, 14-19, 24-25, 33, 34, 35, 42-43, 46, 47, 48, 51, 54, 55, 58 **Unit 3:** 6-7, 13, 26, 27, 30, 31, 42-43, 44-49 **Unit 4:** 6-8, 22-29, 34-35 **Unit 5:** 6-7 **Unit 6:** 6-7 8-15, 22-29 **Unit 7:** 6-7 **Unit 8:** 20-21, 34-35 **LEVELED READERS:** **Unit 1, Week 2:** *Hop!* (A), *We Hop!* (O, ELL), *We Can Move!* (B) **Unit 2, Week 3:** *We Like Bugs!* (A), *The Bugs Run* (O, ELL), *I See a Bug* (B) **Unit 3, Week 1:** *We Run* (A), *Go, Nat!* (O, ELL), *The Birdhouse* (B) **Unit 5, Week 3:** *The Farmer* (A), *Let's Make a Salad!* (O, ELL), *Farm Fresh Finn* (B) **Unit 6, Week 1:** *It Is Hot!* (A), *Little Bear* (O, ELL), *Ant and Grasshopper* (B) **Unit 6, Week 2:** *The Rain* (A), *Weather Is Fun* (O, ELL), *Kate and Tuck* (B) **YOUR TURN PRACTICE BOOK:** 29, 37, 39-40, 43-44, 45, 47-48, 53, 61, 68, 71-72, 81-82, 83, 89-90, 97-98, 103, 105-106, 107, 113-114, 115, 121-122, 129, 131-132, 137, 141, 147, 149-150, 151, 187, 221, 227, 231 **READING WORKSTATION ACTIVITY CARDS:** 1, 3, 12, 17 **WRITING WORKSTATION ACTIVITY CARDS:** 1, 2, 6, 20, 25 **TEACHER'S EDITION:** **Unit 1:** T134, T175, T222 **Unit 2:** T58, T175, T222 **Unit 3:** T58, T140, T222 **Unit 4:** T58, T140, T175, T222 **Unit 5:** T11, T58, T140, T222 **Unit 6:** T11, T58, T140, T175, T222 **Unit 7:** T52, T58, T140, T175, T222 **Unit 8:** T11, T58, T93, T40, T175, T222 **Unit 9:** T11, T52, T58, T140, T222, T245 **Unit 10:** T11, T95, T142, T177, T224 **LITERATURE BIG BOOKS:** **Unit 1, Week 1:** *What About Bear?* **Unit 1, Week 2:** *Pouch!* **Unit 1, Week 3:** *Senses at the Seashore* **Unit 2, Week 1:** *The Handiest Things in the World* **Unit 2, Week 2:** *Shapes All Around* **Unit 2, Week 3:** *I Love Bugs!* **Unit 3, Week 2:** *A Grand Old Tree* **Unit 3, Week 3:** *An Orange in January* **Unit 5, Week 1:** *My Garden* **Unit 6, Week 1:** *Mama, Is It Summer Yet?* **Unit 8, Week 2:** *Ana Goes to Washington, D.C.* **INTERACTIVE READ-ALOUD CARDS:** **Unit 1, Week 1:** "The Lion and the Mouse" **Unit 1, Week 2:** "The Tortoise and the Hare" **Unit 1, Week 3:** "A Feast of the Senses" **Unit 2, Week 1:** "Timimoto" **Unit 2, Week 2:** "Kites in Flight" **Unit 2, Week 3:** "From Caterpillar to Butterfly" **Unit 3, Week 1:** "The Boy Who Cried Wolf" **Unit 3, Week 2:** "The Turtle and the Flute" **Unit 3, Week 3:** "Field Trips" **Unit 4, Week 1:** "Little Juan and the Cooking Pot" **Unit 4, Week 2:** "Cultural Festivals" **Unit 4, Week 3:** "The Bundle of Sticks" **Unit 5, Week 1:** "Growing Plants" **Unit 7, Week 2:** "The Family Pet"

College and Career Readiness Anchor Standards for LANGUAGE

The K–5 standards on the following pages define what students should understand and be able to do by the end of each grade. They correspond to the College and Career Readiness (CCR) anchor standards below by number. The CCR and grade-specific standards are necessary complements—the former providing broad standards, the latter providing additional specificity—that together define the skills and understandings that all students must demonstrate.

Conventions of Standard English
1. Demonstrate command of the conventions of standard English grammar and usage when writing or speaking.
2. Demonstrate command of the conventions of standard English capitalization, punctuation, and spelling when writing.
Knowledge of Language
3. Apply knowledge of language to understand how language functions in different contexts, to make effective choices for meaning or style, and to comprehend more fully when reading or listening.
Vocabulary Acquisition and Use
4. Determine or clarify the meaning of unknown and multiple-meaning words and phrases by using context clues, analyzing meaningful word parts, and consulting general and specialized reference materials, as appropriate.
5. Demonstrate understanding of figurative language, word relationships, and nuances in word meanings.
6. Acquire and use accurately a range of general academic and domain-specific words and phrases sufficient for reading, writing, speaking, and listening at the college and career readiness level; demonstrate independence in gathering vocabulary knowledge when encountering an unknown term important to comprehension or expression.

Common Core State Standards English Language Arts

Grade K

Language Standards

Conventions of Standard English		*McGraw-Hill Reading Wonders*
L.K.1	Demonstrate command of the conventions of standard English grammar and usage when writing or speaking.	**TEACHER'S EDITION: Unit 1:** T16, T19, T32-33, T41, T36, T98, T101, T114-115, T122-123, T125, T133, T141, T165, T180, T183, T197, T205, T214-215, T223, T247 **Unit 2:** T16, T18-19, T32-33, T40-41, T50-51, T59, T83, T98, T101, T115, T123, T133, T141, T165, T180, T183, T185, T197, T205, T215, T223 **Unit 3:** T16, T98, T180, T183, T197, T215 **Unit 4:** T16, T18-19, T32-33, T40-41, T47, T51, T59, T98, T101, T114-115, T122-123, T129,T133, T139, T141, T180, T182-183, T196-197, T204-205, T211, T215, T221, T223 **Unit 5:** T16, T21, T43, T83, T98, T103, T180, T196, T247 **Unit 6:** T16, T19, T33, T41, T44, T47, T51, T53, T59, T83, T98, T101, T114, T115, T123, T129, T133, T141, T180, T183, T185, T197, T205, T207, T211, T215, T223, T247 **Unit 7:** T16, T19, T33, T41, T47, T51, T83, T98, T114-115, T123, T129,T133, T139, T141, T165, T180, T182, T183, T196, T197, T204-205, T211, T215, T223, T247 **Unit 8:** T16, T19, T21, T33, T41, T47, T50-51, T83, T98, T101, T115, T123, T129,T133, T141, T180, T182-183, T196-197, T205, T211, T215, T223 **Unit 9:** T16, T19, T21, T32-33, T41, T47, T51, T59, T83, T98,T101, T103, T114-115, T123, T133, T141, T165, T129, T180, T183, T185, T197, T205, T211, T215, T223, T247 **Unit 10:** T16, T21, T34, T42, T49, T85, T100, T131, T182, T187, T198, T213, T249
L.K.1a	Print many upper- and lowercase letters.	**TEACHER'S EDITION: Unit 1:** T16, T98, T180 **Unit 2:** T16, T98, T180 **Unit 3:** T16, T98, T180 **Unit 4:** T16, T47, T98, T129, T139, T180, T211, T221 **Unit 5:** T16, T98, T180 **Unit 6:** T16, T47, T98, T129, T180, T211 **Unit 7:** T16, T47, T98, T129, T139, T180, T211 **Unit 8:** T16, T47, T98, T129, T180, T211 **Unit 9:** T16, T47, T98, T129, T180, T211 **Unit 10:** T16, T49, T100, T131, T182, T213 **YOUR TURN PRACTICE BOOK:** 34, 42, 50, 58, 66, 76, 84, 92, 100, 108, 116, 126, 134, 142, 152, 162, 172, 184, 192, 202, 212, 222, 232, 244, 252, 260, 268, 276, 284
L.K.1b	Use frequently occurring nouns and verbs.	**TEACHER'S EDITION: Unit 1:** T19, T32-33, T41, T36, T101, T114-115, T122-123, T125, T133, T141, T165, T183, T197, T205, T214-215, T223, T247 **Unit 2:** T18-19, T32-33, T40-41, T50-51, T59, T83, T101, T115, T123, T133, T141, T165, T183, T185, T197, T205, T215, T223 **Unit 5:** T103 **Unit 6:** T19, T33, T44, T51, T53, T83, T114, T223, T247 **Unit 7:** T19, T33, T41, T51, T83, T114-115, T123, T133, T141, T165, T183, T197, T205, T215, T223, T247 **Unit 8:** T10, T18, T114, T115 **Unit 9:** T21, T103, T185 **Unit 10:** T187 **YOUR TURN PRACTICE BOOK:** 23, 41, 65, 73, 83, 107, 115, 141, 151, 161, 191, 201, 211, 221, 241, 251, 259, 267, 295
L.K.1c	Form regular plural nouns orally by adding /s/ or /es/ (e.g., *dog, dogs; wish, wishes*).	**TEACHER'S EDITION: Unit 5:** T21, T43 **Unit 6:** T33, T41, T51, T59, T101, T115, T123, T133, T141, T183, T197, T205, T215
L.K.1d	Understand and use question words (interrogatives) (e.g., *who, what, where, when, why, how*).	**TEACHER'S EDITION: Unit 3:** T183, T197, T215 **Unit 6:** T185, T207 **Unit 7:** T182, T196, T204-205 **Unit 9:** T103, T125 **Unit 10:** T21
L.K.1e	Use the most frequently occurring prepositions (e.g., *to, from, in, out, on, off, for, of, by, with*).	**TEACHER'S EDITION: Unit 3:** T29, T47 **Unit 5:** T193, T211 **Unit 7:** T29, T47 **Unit 8:** T19, T33, T41, T50-51, T83, T101, T115, T123, T133, T141, T183, T197, T205, T223
L.K.1f	Produce and expand complete sentences in shared language activities.	**TEACHER'S EDITION: Unit 4:** T18-19, T32-33, T40-41, T51, T59, T101, T114-115, T122-123, T133, T141, T182-183, T196-197, T204-205, T215, T223 **Unit 5:** T83, T196, T247 **Unit 8:** T182-183, T196-197, T215, T223; **Unit 9:** T19, T32-33, T41, T51, T59, T83, T101, T114-115, T123, T133, T141, T165, T183, T197, T205, T215, T223, T247 **Unit 10:** T34, T42, T85, T198, T249

Language Standards

Conventions of Standard English		*McGraw-Hill Reading Wonders*
L.K.2	Demonstrate command of the conventions of standard English capitalization, punctuation, and spelling when writing.	**TEACHER'S EDITION:** **Unit 1:** T16, T72, T129, T211, T221 **Unit 2:** T47, T57, T129, T139, T211, T221 **Unit 3:** T19, T47, T50-51, T53, T57, T59, T83, T101, T115, T120, T123, T132-133, T139, T141, T183, T196-197, T205, T211, T214-215, T221, T223, T247 **Unit 4:** T16, T47, T57, T98, T129, T139, T211, T221 **Unit 5:** T16, T47, T57, T98, T101, T115, T123, T139, T180, T211, T221 **Unit 6:** T12, T16, T47, T57, T98, T129, T139, T176, T211, T221 **Unit 7:** T16, T47, T57, T98, T129, T139, T180, T211, T214, T221 **Unit 8:** T16, T32, T47, T98, T101, T114, T129, T132, T164, T211, T221 **Unit 9:** T47, T129, T211 **Unit 10:** T49, T53, T103, T116, T131, T213, T216
L.K.2a	Capitalize the first word in a sentence and the pronoun *I*.	**TEACHER'S EDITION:** **Unit 3:** T19, T50-51, T53, T59, T83, T115, T123, T132-133, T197, T223 **Unit 5:** T101, T115, T123 **Unit 8:** T32, T101, T114, T132 **Unit 10:** T53, T103, T116, T216
L.K.2b	Recognize and name end punctuation.	**TEACHER'S EDITION:** **Unit 3:** T101, T115, T123, T132-133, T141, T183, T196-197, T205, T214-215, T223, T247 **Unit 6:** T12, T176 **Unit 7:** T214 **Unit 8:** T32, T101, T114, T132, T164
L.K.2c	Write a letter or letters for most consonant and short-vowel sounds (phonemes).	**TEACHER'S EDITION:** **Unit 1:** T16, T72, T129, T211 **Unit 2:** T47, T129, T211 **Unit 3:** T47, T120, T211 **Unit 4:** T16, T47, T98, T129, T139, T211, T221 **Unit 5:** T16, T47, T98, T180, T211 **Unit 6:** T16, T47, T98, T129, T211 **Unit 7:** T16, T47, T57, T98, T129, T139, T180, T211 **Unit 8:** T16, T47, T98, T129, T211 **Unit 9:** T47, T129, T211 **Unit 10:** T49, T131, T213 **YOUR TURN PRACTICE BOOK:** 34, 42, 50, 58, 51-52, 62, 66, 76, 84, 85, 86, 88, 92, 100, 104, 108, 116, 126, 130, 134, 138, 142, 148, 158, 162, 164-165, 168, 172, 192, 202, 212, 222, 232 **PHONICS AND WORD STUDY WORKSTATION ACTIVITY CARDS:** 1, 2, 3, 4, 5, 6, 7, 8, 9, 10, 11, 12, 13, 14, 15, 16, 17, 18, 19, 20, 21, 22, 23, 24
L.K.2d	Spell simple words phonetically, drawing on knowledge of sound-letter relationships.	**TEACHER'S EDITION:** **Unit 1:** T221 **Unit 2:** T57, T139, T221 **Unit 3:** T57, T139, T221 **Unit 4:** T47, T57, T129, T139, T211, T221 **Unit 5:** T57, T139, T221 **Unit 6:** T57, T139, T221 **Unit 7:** T47, T57, T129, T139, T211, T221 **Unit 8:** T47, T129, T139, T211, T221 **YOUR TURN PRACTICE BOOK:** 30, 38, 46, 54, 62, 74, 75, 80, 88, 96, 104, 112, 124, 125, 130, 138, 148, 158, 168, 182, 183, 188, 198, 208, 228, 242, 243, 256, 264, 272, 280, 293, 294
Knowledge of Language		***McGraw-Hill Reading Wonders***
L.K.3	(Begins in grade 2.)	
Vocabulary Acquisition and Use		***McGraw-Hill Reading Wonders***
L.K.4	Determine or clarify the meaning of unknown and multiple-meaning words and phrases based on *kindergarten reading and content*.	**TEACHER'S EDITION:** **Unit 4:** T127 **Unit 5:** T45, T46, T108, T187 **Unit 6:** T21, T23, T33, T41 **Unit 7:** T24, T45, T189, T209 **Unit 9:** T21, T24, T25, T43, T185, T189, T207 **Unit 10:** T25, T187, T209
L.K.4a	Identify new meanings for familiar words and apply them accurately (e.g., knowing *duck* is a bird and learning the verb to *duck*).	**TEACHER'S EDITION:** **Unit 5:** T108, T185, T187 T207 **Unit 6:** T21, T189 **Unit 7:** T24, T45, T189 **Unit 8:** T21 **Unit 9:** T25, T45, T185, T207 **Unit 10:** T25, T47
L.K.4b	Use the most frequently occurring inflections and affixes (e.g., *-ed, -s, re-, un-, pre-, -ful, -less*) as a clue to the meaning of an unknown word.	**TEACHER'S EDITION:** **Unit 5:** T45, T46, T187 **Unit 6:** T23, T33, T41 **Unit 9:** T21, T24, T43, T189 **Unit 10:** T187, T209

Language Standards

Vocabulary Acquisition and Use		McGraw-Hill Reading Wonders
L.K.5	With guidance and support from adults, explore word relationships and nuances in word meanings.	**TEACHER'S EDITION: Unit 1:** T10-11, T34, T43 **Unit 2:** T10, T43, T103, T116, T125, T135, T175, T185, T207, T245 **Unit 3:** T10, T116, T175 **Unit 4:** T10-11, T12-13, T21, T34, T43, T44-45, T54, T67, T80, T81, T83, T92-93, T94-95, T103, T116, T125, T126-127, T133, T136, T141, T149, T165, T174-175, T176-177, T183, T185, T188, T198, T207, T208-209, T218, T231, T245, T247 **Unit 5:** T10-11, T12-13, T21, T34, T43, T54, T67, T80, T81, T92-93, T94-95, T116, T149, T174-175, T185, T195, T207, T218, T245 **Unit 6:** T10-11, T20, T34, T35, T42, T43, T44, T67, T81, T92-93, T103, T108, T116, T125, T126-127, T136, T149, T163, T174-175, T176-177, T185, T198, T208-209, T218, T231, T245 **Unit 7:** T10-11, T12-13, T21, T25, T34, T43, T54, T67, T81, T92-93, T94-95, T103, T116, T126-127, T136, T149, T163, T174-175, T185, T190, T207, T208-209, T218, T231, T245 **Unit 8:** T10-11, T12-13, T21, T23, T34, T43, T44-45, T54, T67, T81, T92-93, T94-95, T103, T116, T125, T126-127, T136, T149, T163, T174-175, T185, T198, T207, T208-209, T218, T231, T245 **Unit 9:** T10-11, T12-13, T34, T44-45, T54, T67, T81, T92-93, T103, T116, T126-127, T136, T149, T163, T174-175, T176-177, T185, T198, T207, T208-209, T218, T231, T245 **Unit 10:** T10-11, T25, T36, T46-47, T56, T69, T83, T94-95, T96-97, T105, T106-111, T118, T127, T128-129, T136-137, T138, T151, T165, T176-177, T178-179, T187, T189, T190, T200, T209, T210-211, T220, T233, T247
L.K.5a	Sort common objects into categories (e.g., shapes, foods) to gain a sense of the concepts the categories represent.	**TEACHER'S EDITION: Unit 2:** T43, T103, T125, T135 **Unit 4:** T103, T183 **Unit 5:** T21, T185, T207 **Unit 6:** T43 **Unit 8:** T43 **Unit 10:** T127, T129, T136-137
L.K.5b	Demonstrate understanding of frequently occurring verbs and adjectives by relating them to their opposites (antonyms).	**YOUR TURN PRACTICE BOOK:** 241, 283 **TEACHER'S EDITION: Unit 6:** T44 **Unit 7:** T25 **Unit 8:** T23, T185, T207 **Unit 9:** T189 **Unit 10:** T25, T105, T127, T189, T190
L.K.5c	Identify real-life connections between words and their use (e.g., note places at school that are colorful).	**READING/WRITING WORKSHOP: Unit 1: Smart Start:** 4-5, 22-23, 40-41; 6-7, 24-25, 42-43 **Unit 2:** 6-7, 24-25, 42-43 **Unit 3:** 6-7, 24-25, 42-43 **Unit 4:** 6-7, 20-21, 34-35 **Unit 5:** 6-7, 20-21, 34-35 **Unit 6:** 6-7, 20-21, 34-35 **Unit 7:** 6-7, 20-21, 34-35 **Unit 8:** 6-7, 20-21, 34-35 **Unit 9:** 6-7, 20-21, 34-35 **Unit 10:** 6-7, 20-21, 34-35 **YOUR TURN PRACTICE BOOK:** 23, 33, 41, 49, 57, 65, 73, 83, 107, 115, 133, 141, 151, 161, 171, 191, 201, 211, 221, 241, 251, 259, 267, 275, 283, 295 **TEACHER'S EDITION: Unit 1:** T10-11, T34, T43 **Unit 2:** T10, T116, T175 **Unit 3:** T10, T116, T175 **Unit 4:** T10-11, T12-13, T21, T34, T43, T44-45, T54, T67, T80, T81, T83, T92-93, T94-95, T103, T116, T125, T126-127, T133, T136, T141, T149, T165, T174-175, T176-177, T183, T185, T198, T207, T208-209, T218, T231, T245, T247 **Unit 5:** T10-11, T12-13, T21, T34, T43, T54, T67, T80, T81, T92-93, T94-95, T116, T149, T174-175, T185, T198, T218, T245 **Unit 6:** T10-11, T20, T34, T35, T42, T67, T81, T92-93, T103, T116, T125, T126-127, T136, T149, T163, T174-175, T176-177, T185, T198, T208-209, T218, T231, T245 **Unit 7:** T10-11, T12-13, T21, T25, T34, T43, T54, T67, T81, T92-93, T94-95, T103, T116, T126-127, T136, T149, T163, T174-175, T185, T207, T208-209, T218, T231, T245 **Unit 8:** T10-11, T34, T81, T92-93, T102, T116, T124, T136, T149, T163, T174-175, T185, T198, T207, T208-209, T218, T231, T245 **Unit 9:** T10-11, T12-13, T20, T34, T42-43, T54, T67, T92-93, T103, T116-117, T124-125, T136, T149, T174-175, T176-177, T185, T198, T206-207, T218, T231 **Unit 10:** T10-11, T25, T36, T46-47, T56, T69, T83, T94-95, T96-97, T106-111, T118, T128-129, T138, T151, T165, T176-177, T178-179, T187, T190, T200, T209, T210-211, T220, T233, T247 **INTERACTIVE READ-ALOUD CARDS: SS:** "The Ugly Duckling", "Kindergarteners Can!", "Tikki Tikki Tembo" **Unit 1, Week 1:** "The Lion and the Mouse" **Unit 1, Week 2:** "The Tortoise and the Hare" **Unit 2, Week 3:** "From Caterpillar to Butterfly" **Unit 3, Week 2:** "The Turtle and the Flute" **Unit 4, Week 1:** "Little Juan and the Cooking Pot" **Unit 4, Week 2:** "Cultural Festivals" **Unit 4, Week 3:** "A Bundle of Sticks" **Unit 6, Week 3:** "Rainbow Crow" **Unit 7, Week 3:** "Anansi: An African Tale" **Unit 9, Week 2:** "The Little Red Hen" **Unit 9, Week 3:** "Spider Woman Teaches the Navajo" **Unit 10, Week 1:** "The Elves and the Shoemakers" **ConnectED Digital Resources:** Visual Glossary

Language Standards

Vocabulary Acquisition and Use		*McGraw-Hill Reading Wonders*
L.K.5d	Distinguish shades of meaning among verbs describing the same general action (e.g., *walk, march, strut, prance*) by acting out the meanings.	**TEACHER'S EDITION:** **Unit 2:** T185, T207, T245 **Unit 4:** T188 **Unit 6:** T35, T108 **Unit 7:** T185, T190, T207
L.K.6	Use words and phrases acquired through conversations, reading and being read to, and responding to texts.	**READING/WRITING WORKSHOP:** **Smart Start:** 4-5, 22-23, 40-41 **Unit 1:** 6-7, 24-25, 42-43 **Unit 2:** 6-7, 24-25, 42-43 **Unit 3:** 6-7, 24-25, 42-43 **Unit 4:** 6-7, 20-21, 34-35 **Unit 5:** 6-7, 20-21, 34-35 **Unit 6:** 6-7, 20-21, 34-35 **Unit 7:** 6-7, 20-21, 34-35 **Unit 8:** 6-7, 20-21, 34-35 **Unit 9:** 6-7, 20-21, 34-35 **Unit 10:** 6-7, 20-21, 34-35 **TEACHER'S EDITION:** **Unit 1:** S26, S34, S44 **Unit 2:** T20-21, T93, T198 **Unit 3:** T20, T93, T198 **Unit 4:** T10-11, T12-13, T20-21, T22-27, T34, T42-43, T44-45, T54-55, T67, T80, T81, T92-93, T94-95, T176-177, T184-185, T186-191, T198, T205, T206-207, T208-209, T215, T218-219, T223, T218-219, T231, T244, T245 **Unit 5:** T10-11, T12-13, T20-21, T22-27, T34, T42-43, T44-45, T54-55 , T117, T162-163, T174-175, T176-177, T184-185, T186-191, T198, T199, T206-207, T208-209, T218-219, T231, T244-245 **Unit 6:** T10-11, T20-21, T34-35, T42-43, T44-45, T54-55, T67, T80, T81, T92-93, T94-95, T102-103, T104-109, T116, T124-125, T126-127, T136-137, T149, T231, T244 **Unit 7:** T10-11, T12-13, T20-21, T22-27, T34-35, T42-43, T44-45, T54-55, T67, T80, T81, T92-93, T94-95, T102-103, T104-109, T116, T124-125, T126-127, T136-137, T149, T231, T244, T245 **Unit 8:** T10-11, T12-13, T20-21, T22-27, T34-35, T42-43, T44-45, T54-55, T67, T80, T81, T92-93, T94-95, T102-103, T104-109, T116, T124-125, T126-127, T136-137, T149, T231, T244, T245 **Unit 9:** T10-11, T12-13, T20-21, T22-27, T34-35, T42-43, T44-45, T54-55, T162, T163, T174-175, T176-177, T184-185, T186-191, T198, T199, T206-207, T208-209, T218-219, T231, T244, T245 **Unit 10:** T10-11, T12-13, T20-21, T22-29, T36, T44-45, T46-47, T56-57, T69, T82, T83, T94-95, T96-97, T104-105, T106-111, T118, T126-127, T128-129, T138-139, T151, T179, T233, T246, T247 **LITERATURE BIG BOOKS:** **Unit 1, Week 2:** *Pouch!* **Unit 2, Week 2:** *Shapes All Around* **Unit 2, Week 3:** *I Love Bugs!* **Unit 3, Week 1:** *How Do Dinosaurs Go to School?* **Unit 4, Week 1:** *Whose Shoes? A Shoe for Every Job* **Unit 4, Week 2:** *What Can You Do with a Paleta?* **Unit 5, Week 2:** *A Grand Old Tree* **Unit 5, Week 3:** *An Orange in January* **Unit 6, Week 1:** *Mama, Is It Summer Yet?* **Unit 7, Week 1:** *ZooBorns!* **Unit 7, Week 2:** *The Birthday Pet* **Unit 8, Week 2:** *Ana Goes to Washington, D.C.* **Unit 8, Week 3:** *Bringing Down the Moon* **Unit 9, Week 3:** *Bread Comes to Life* **Unit 10, Week 1:** *What's the Big Idea, Molly?* **Unit 10, Week 2:** *All Kinds of Families!* **INTERACTIVE READ-ALOUD CARDS:** **SS:** "The Ugly Duckling", "Kindergarteners Can!", "Tikki Tikki Tembo" **Unit 1, Week 1:** "The Lion and the Mouse" **Unit 1, Week 2:** "The Tortoise and the Hare" **Unit 2, Week 3:** "From Caterpillar to Butterfly" **Unit 3, Week 2:** "The Turtle and the Flute" **Unit 4, Week 1:** "Little Juan and the Cooking Pot" **Unit 4, Week 2:** "Cultural Festivals" **Unit 4, Week 3:** "A Bundle of Sticks" **Unit 6, Week 3:** "Rainbow Crow" **Unit 7, Week 3:** "Anansi: An African Tale" **Unit 9, Week 2:** "The Little Red Hen" **Unit 9, Week 3:** "Spider Woman Teaches the Navajo" **Unit 10, Week 1:** "The Elves and the Shoemakers"